RACE, CLASS, & GENDER

Gender & Society Readers

Sponsored by Sociologists for Women in Society

Gender & Society Readers address key issues in contemporary gender studies informed by feminist writing, theory, and research. Readers are based on articles appearing in, and special theme issues of, the scholarly journal *Gender & Society*, sponsored by Sociologists for Women in Society.

Titles in this series:

Judith Lorber and Susan A. Farrell (eds.)
   THE SOCIAL CONSTRUCTION OF GENDER (1991)
Pauline B. Bart and Eileen Geil Moran (eds.)
   VIOLENCE AGAINST WOMEN: The Bloody Footprints (1993)
Esther Ngan-ling Chow, Doris Wilkinson, Maxine Baca Zinn (eds.)
   RACE, CLASS, AND GENDER: Common Bonds,
   Different Voices (1996)

RACE, CLASS, & GENDER

Common Bonds, Different Voices

EDITORS

ESTHER NGAN-LING CHOW
DORIS WILKINSON
MAXINE BACA ZINN

A *Gender & Society* Reader
Published in cooperation with
Sociologists for Women in Society

SAGE Publications
International Educational and Professional Publisher
Thousand Oaks   London   New Delhi

For information address:

 SAGE Publications, Inc.
2455 Teller Road
Thousand Oaks, California 91320
E-mail: order@sagepub.com

SAGE Publications Ltd.
6 Bonhill Street
London EC2A 4PU
United Kingdom

SAGE Publications India Pvt. Ltd.
M-32 Market
Greater Kailash I
New Delhi 110 048 India

Printed in the United States of America

Library of Congress Cataloging-in-Publication Data

Race, class, and gender: Common bonds, different voices / editors,
   Esther Ngan-ling Chow, Doris Wilkinson, Maxine Baca Zinn.
      p. cm. — (Gender and society readers)
   Includes bibliographical references.
   ISBN 0-8039-7056-0 (cloth: acid-free paper). —
ISBN 0-8039-7057-9 (pbk.: acid-free paper)
   1. Women—Social conditions.   2. Women—Economic conditions.
3. Sex role.   4. Ethnicity.   5. Feminist theory.   I. Chow, Esther
Ngan-ling, 1943-   II. Wilkinson, Doris Y.   III. Zinn, Maxine Baca,
1942-   .   IV. Series: Gender & society readers.
HQ1206.R33   1996
305.42—dc20   96-4428

This book is printed on acid-free paper.

   97 98 99 10 9 8 7 6 5 4 3 2

Sage Production Editor: Gillian Dickens

Contents .

Foreword

"Race matters," writes the African American philosopher Cornel West (1993). Actually, class, gender, *and* race matter, and they matter because they structure interactions, opportunities, consciousness, ideology, and the forms of resistance that characterize American life. This new volume shows just how much race, class, and gender matter. They matter in shaping the social location of different groups in contemporary society. They matter in shaping concepts of leadership and the attitudes of diverse groups. They matter by influencing the process of social mobility and by configuring the opportunity structures different groups experience. They matter in structuring family experience. They matter because they situate public policy and people's ideas about what must be done. They matter because they bring a more progressive and inclusive vision for change that is sorely lacking in most public discussions of the current political scene.

Cornel West says that race matters because it is a "constitutive element of life" in America. Race is not just something that is a trait or characteristic of individuals. Race is a social structure, constructed through social interaction and manifested in the institutions of society, interpersonal interactions, and the minds and identities of those living in racially based social orders. Similarly, class is a social structure that, like race, organizes material, ideological, and interpersonal relations; and, as feminist scholars have shown, gender is more than a matter of interpersonal relations. Gender is institutionalized in the fabric of society and shapes, like race and class, material well-being, social identities, and group relationships.

Studying race, class, and gender is thus not just about studying people of color, just as gender is not just about studying women. Nor is the analysis of race, class, and gender simply about the social problems of American society (although studying race, class, and gender goes a long way toward developing a better understanding of those problems). When West calls race a constitutive element of life, he is pointing to the fact that race, along with gender and class, is a fundamental structure in society—one that, like class and gender, is socially constructed, but that nonetheless shapes all social institutions and, therefore, the experiences of all people (although in different ways, depending on their social location). The articles included in this new anthology reflect the commitment of feminist scholars to understanding the complex intersections and workings of race, class, and gender. Each article was published earlier in *Gender & Society*—the journal of Sociologists for Women in Society (SWS). SWS is committed to social policy and social action that produces equity for all women in society. As a caucus within sociology, much of its activity is directed toward transforming sociology although, from the start, SWS has understood that sociology does not exist in isolation from society. *Gender & Society* is an academic journal dedicated to producing the knowledge that will both transform sociology and other social sciences and that will provide the basis for transformation of society. During my term as editor of *Gender & Society,* I tried to bring race, class, and gender to a central place in the journal; thus, it has been a special pleasure to see this volume develop and to see the journal become more inclusive of work in this area.

Race, class, and, to some extent, gender, have long been studied by sociologists. One could argue that recognizing the importance of these social structures is one of the major contributions of the sociological perspective. Traditionally, most of that insight has been found in the areas of stratification and race and ethnic relations. New studies of race, class, and gender build on that work but also are developing in new directions. I have argued, in earlier works, that the new scholarship on race, class, and gender differs from traditional studies of stratification by being grounded in feminist analysis and by understanding race, class, and gender as simultaneous social processes that shape all societal relations (Andersen 1993).

Studies of social stratification have historically studied access to material resources, class consciousness, and patterns of social mobility. All of these processes are influenced by race, class, and gender stratification, but new studies of race, class, and gender go beyond studying patterns of inequality. As the articles in this volume show, work on race, class, and gender might reveal how political activism is shaped by women's social location as poor mothers (Naples), how eating disorders are influenced by race, class, gender, and lesbian oppression (Thompson), how work environments are shaped by race and class (Segura), or how leadership in social movements is understood (Barnett), to give just a few examples. The point is that new race, class, and gender studies are affecting the whole of sociology, not just studies of stratification or race relations.

This collection furthers this work by showing the significance of analyses grounded in a race, class, and gender perspective for understanding various dimensions of women's and men's lives. New scholarship on race, class, and gender is currently transforming work in most disciplines. This collection will further that transformation by grounding race, class, and gender studies in specific empirical contributions, by developing new, more inclusive theoretical analyses that further this discussion, by documenting the experiences of diverse groups in society, and by suggesting new directions for social policy that can account for the effects of race, class, and gender on the difficulties different groups experience.

That we develop such analyses is especially urgent. The current political climate challenges scholars not only to protect the academic freedom to ask new questions and develop potentially controversial analyses of race, class, and gender, but also makes it imperative that we develop an understanding of the forces shaping our current history. There is little doubt that race, class, and gender lie at the heart of many current issues, as a quick perusal of any newspaper headlines on a given day will show. Dominant forces, however, are hostile to such thinking, wishing instead to repress it under the rubric of "returning to the basics" or eliminating "political correctness."

At the same time, developing a sociological perspective on current issues is essential to and often missed by new multicultural studies. The multicultural movement in education has brought new life to the study of diverse groups and has been an important impetus for change, but much within multicultural studies is void of a sociological perspective —instead relegating analyses of diversity to "cultural studies," "valuing differences," and interpersonal awareness. While these may be valuable dimensions of understanding diversity, such approaches fail to capture the underlying social structures that produce oppression—oppression that is more than cultural differences or transient cultural images.

Oppression is embodied in social structures; however one conceptualizes it, social structure shapes and directs people's lives and their very ability to survive. Absent a sociological perspective, studies of diversity deteriorate into mere good will, but are not grounded in sound empirical and theoretical analyses.

Common Bonds, Different Voices provides this much-needed perspective and thus adds to the process of reconstructing knowledge to be inclusive of all groups. This collection does so with sound sociology in mind and with a vision and commitment to a better society. As the editors in this volume say, new studies of race, class, and gender embrace a feminist vision, integrating theory and research with social practices intended to better the experiences of women, men, and children in society. Rooting one's understanding in the framework provided by this book moves us closer to this goal.

MARGARET L. ANDERSEN
University of Delaware

REFERENCES

Andersen, Margaret. 1993. From the editor. *Gender & Society* 2 (June): 157-161.

West, Cornel. 1993. *Race matters*. Boston: Beacon Press.

Preface

Feminist scholarship has illuminated the significance of gender as a basic principle of social organization and as a central category in theoretical analysis. Since the 1980s, critiques of feminist scholarship have provided intellectual challenges to reassess the salience and influence of race and class, as well as gender, in all spheres of social life. Recognizing that the study of gender is incomplete without examining the varied social locations and experiences of women, the editorial board of *Gender & Society* has consistently encouraged study of the structural linkages among race, class, and gender to build inclusive feminist scholarship.

In 1990, when we began our work as *Gender & Society* guest coeditors for the special issue on "Race, Class, and Gender," there were fewer analyses of the subject. This major project culminated in a special issue published in September 1992. Since then, the issue has expanded intellectual discourse on the prominence of race, ethnicity, class, and gender. Relevant critiques and analyses have centered around the interlocking nature of these dynamic social forces. Many significant writings on race, class, and gender published in *Gender & Society* since the journal's inception in 1987 are synthesized in this anthology. This collection is the third Sage reader sponsored by Sociologists for Women in Society (SWS).

Because of its broad scope and interdisciplinary emphasis, this volume has wide usefulness as a required or supplementary textbook for introductory or advanced, undergraduate or graduate courses in a variety of disciplines and fields. We hope that colleagues in associations of the social and behavioral sciences, political interest groups, and policy-making agencies in both the private and public sectors will find the anthology informative, interesting, and useful. This anthology is designed to document needs pertinent to the development of policies and programs that would have a constructive impact on the lives of women and men. Finally, we hope that it will appeal to the general public, which may find the information meaningful and valuable for enhancing its personal learning.

We, as three women of color coauthors and coeditors, are connected through our common bonds, united in our shared identities and intellectual zeal to transform existing knowledge. We hope to build a better world for people today and generations to come. Through this joint effort, we have experienced "unity in diversity" as well as "diversity in unity." As we have personally and intellectually evolved through our being, living, and thinking on the topic, we hope that this experience will influence those around us and touch the lives of those we try to understand.

ESTHER NGAN-LING CHOW
DORIS WILKINSON
MAXINE BACA ZINN

Acknowledgments

The following chapters were originally published as articles in *Gender & Society* and are reprinted with the permission of the authors: Adler, K. S., " 'Always Leading Our Men in Service and Sacrifice': Amy Jacques Garvey, Feminist Black Nationalist," 6:346-375; Baca Zinn, M., "Family, Feminism, and Race in America,' " 4:68-82; Barnett, B. M., "Invisible Southern Black Women Leaders in the Civil Rights Movement: The Triple Constraints of Gender, Race, and Class," 7:162-182; Blankenship, K. M., "Bringing Gender and Race In: U.S. Employment Discrimination Policy," 7:204-226; Brenner, J. and Laslett, B., "Gender, Social Reproduction, and Women's Self-Organization: Considering the U.S. Welfare State," 1:447-465; Chow, E. N., "The Development of Feminist Consciousness Among Asian American Women," 1:284-299; Deitch, C., "Gender, Race, and Class Politics and the Inclusion of Women in Title VII of the 1964 Civil Rights Act," 7:183-203; Dugger, K., "Social Location and Gender-Role Attitudes: A Comparison of Black and White Women," 4:425-448; Gorelick, S., "Contradictions of Feminist Methodology," 5:459-477; Higginbotham, E. and Weber, L., "Moving Up With Kin and Community: Upward Social Mobility for Black and White Women," 6:416-440; Hondagneu-Sotelo, P., "Overcoming Patriarchal Constraints: The Reconstruction of Gender Relations Among Mexican Immigrant Women and Men," 6:393-415; Kibria, N., "Power, Patriarchy, and Gender Conflict in the Vietnamese Immigrant Community," 4:464-479; Messner, M. A., "Masculinities and Athletic Careers," 7:121-137; Naples, N. A., "Activist Mothering: Cross-Generational Continuity in the Community Work of Women From Low-Income Urban Neighborhoods," 6:441-463; Segura, D. A.,

"Chicana and Mexican Immigrant Women at Work: The Impact of Class, Race, and Gender on Occupational Mobility," 3:37-52; Thompson, B. W., " 'A Way Outa No Way': Eating Problems Among African American, Latina, and White Women," 6:546-561; West, C. and Fenstermaker, S., "Doing Difference," 9:8-37; Xu, W. and Leffler, A., "Gender and Race Effects on Occupational Prestige, Segregation, and Earnings," 6:376-392; Zsembik, B. A. and Peek, C. W., "The Effect of Economic Restructuring on Puerto Rican Women's Labor Force Participation in the Formal Sector," 8:525-540.

This unique anthology is clearly a collaborative work that has depended on the efforts, encouragement, and support of many people. We want to thank our colleagues within Sociologists for Women in Society (SWS), who entrusted us with the major responsibility of coediting the special issue of *Gender & Society* on "Race, Class, and Gender" in 1992, as well as this anthology, the third Sage SWS reader. Former editors of other SWS readers, Judith Lorber, Pauline Bart, and Christine Bose, have unselfishly shared their wisdom, experience, and advice. Marcia Segal and members of the SWS Publications Committee that she chairs gave us strong support. Her efficiency and consulting style ensured the smooth operation of this project. She, along with Cynthia Deitch, read our introduction chapter critically and offered many valuable suggestions.

We owe a tremendous debt to our colleague and friend, Margaret Andersen, who has given us concrete assistance, editorial advice, and intellectual impetus for the earlier special issue and this anthology. Her feminist vision and ability to translate her ideals into actual practice have served as models for us. We also thank her staff, Kim Logio, Catherine Simile, Heather Smith, and Lara Zeises, who responded expeditiously to facilitate the book project.

Many others contributed to the development of the present work. Johanna Foster, Dave Ramsaran, and Heidi Thackeray provided much-needed research assistance. Johanna Foster's dedication and efficiency helped get the project off the ground. Elaine Stahl Leo and Heidi Thackeray performed their editorial and clerical services competently and conscientiously.

We are also grateful for the generosity of Sage Publications, which awarded us a small grant to cover needed expenses. Mitch Allen and Peter Labella, editors at Sage, offered essential resources, support, and patience throughout the project. Frances Borghi facilitated our collective efforts promptly whenever needed.

Esther would like to thank her spouse Norman, her children, Paul and Jennifer, and her friends, Fu Liu and Lucianti Li, for bearing with her as she engaged in intellectual labor, forfeiting time and effort much needed inside and outside of the home.

Introduction:
Transforming Knowledgment:
Race, Class, and Gender

ESTHER NGAN-LING CHOW

The social sciences and humanities increasingly recognize the need for a broader, more inclusive paradigm to illuminate the multiple facets of gender understanding. Basic to a feminist transformation of knowledge is not only the discovery of the significance of gender but also the incorporation of race and class as central foci of analysis.[1] Race, class, and gender are basic principles of social organization and of the human interaction process. These principles also constitute systems of meaning that influence social institutions and affect individual identity, consciousness, and behavior. An inclusive feminist vantage point sees gender not through one lens but through a multiplicity of lenses that form a prism for analyzing the social construction of race, class, and gender.

Just as feminist scholarship is broadening its perspective on gender, traditional scholarship in race and ethnic relations and class analysis is now beginning to revise theoretical formulations to incorporate a gender focus. A shared view is emerging across disciplines that race, class, and gender are inseparable determinants of inequalities. Functioning interdependently, these determinants form interlocking patterns that serve as bases for developing multiple systems of domination that affect access to power and privileges, influence social relationships, construct meanings, and shape people's everyday experience.

The thesis of this book is that *race and class are as significant as gender, each contributing bases for common bonds as well as generating divergent patterns of structural relationships and life experiences that shape the social construction of diverse kinds of women and men in different historical and sociocultural contexts.*[2] This thesis emphasizes the existence and challenges of the common bonds of identity and social locations of women and men and their collective understanding and actions based on the meanings of these identities and locations. Race, class, and gender are manifested differently, depending on the particular ways in which their various configurations with each other affect social institutions, intergroup relationships, and personal lives. The experiences and outlooks that various groups of women and men bring to their social relationships further produce and reinforce significant differences from which a matrix of domination is derived. Focusing on alliances and diversity thus reveals the underlying interdependence of what at first appear to be sets of fixed binary oppositions.

Feminist scholarship is becoming increasingly inclusive and comprehensive, bringing the standpoints and experiences of diverse kinds of women and men, different racial-ethnic groups, and different classes into the core of analysis. As marginalized women, people of color, and other disempowered groups gain attention at the center of gender analysis, the basic assumptions in "mainstream" social sciences that use White, middle-class, and male perspectives as standards by which to measure all social action are being challenged. New research reveals that this group's domination and resources depend on the subordination of other groups, and these privileges can be retained only so long as they are validated by groups from the margin or below.

Addressing this thesis is timely because it reflects realistically the demographic shift in the U.S. from a predominantly White population rooted in western culture to a multiracial and multiethnic society characterized by social pluralism and cultural diversity.[3] The subject matters covered by the chapters in this book reflect social diversity.

BASIC QUESTIONS AND
MAJOR EMERGENT THEMES

In this volume, we bring together a collection of research studies, interpretive essays, and theoretical works addressing the main thesis from varying viewpoints. Several major questions guide the inquiry:

1. How do race, class, and gender interrelate?
2. How does the interlocking of race, class, and gender form patterns of social relations and develop into hierarchical orders? How are these relations institutionalized into stratified structures resulting in different forms of social inequality in different historical and societal contexts?
3. How are these patterns manifested in the daily lives of women and men in their social relationships throughout society?
4. What are the dilemmas and contradictions created by the simultaneity of race, class, and gender?
5. How can feminist scholarship based on the complex understanding of the interlocking nature of race, class, and gender transform our knowledge and social life?

Central to the underlying thesis is the first theme that *the interlocking of race, class, and gender simultaneously forms multiple systems of domination and meaning that have interactive, reciprocal, and cumulative effects on structural conditions and social processes that shape the life experiences of women and men.* Race, class, and gender are all *relational* in that gender dynamics are bound up in broader systems of race and class inequality. These relations form the structural and symbolic bases for both the objective conditions and the subjective meanings of women's and men's lives. Race, class, and gender are conceptualized as "interlocking categories," as "intersecting systems," as "interdependent dimensions" of inequality, and as "multiple bases" for oppression rather than separate types of identity as they normally are treated. This conceptualization requires us to focus our analysis on their *interactive, reciprocal,* and *cumulative effects.*

Theoretical formulations move us away from a simple additive model to multiplicative, geometric, and ethnomethodological models (Brewer 1993; see also West and Fenstermaker in this volume). As Deborah King (1988) has observed, the relationships among race, class, and gender are not simply additive, as implied by such terms as "double" and "triple" jeopardy." Instead, these relationships are interactive and produce dissimilar results for women and men in particular circumstances. Criticizing the additive model as missing the structural connections, Andersen and Collins (1995) view race, class, and gender as different but interrelated axes of social structure that in their simultaneity form a matrix of domination and meaning. Recent theoretical insights reveal that the intersection of these axes and their simultaneous configuration are highly fluid. Several authors (e.g., Gorelick, Hondagneu-Sotelo, and West and Fenstermaker) in this book address race, class, and gender as dynamic *processes* in both social change and human interaction. The second major theme of this book is that *race and class are as important as gender in describing and interpreting the intricacies of social structure and self and the relationships between macrostructural forces and microprocesses of human interaction.* The interlocking of race, class, and gender produces distinct social conditions and experiences for women and men in different historical times and places. This interlocking creates a set of stratifying forces embedded in social institutions that legitimize social practices, reinforce power relationships, and create conditions that shape human interaction and everyday life experience. Contextualizing these interlocking forces requires us to study the social locations of women and men in the multifaceted stratification system and in relationship to social institutions. These institutions are highly gendered, race-specific, and class-relevant and serve as systems of control to maintain existing hierarchical orders and to determine differential opportunities, privileges, and resources for diverse groups of women and men.

When linking women's objective conditions and subjective experience to larger social forces, many authors in this volume take on the intellectual challenge of reconceptualizing macro and micro connections. Social phenomena addressed encompass women's consciousness, leadership, labor force participation, occupational mobility, social movements, political activism, and self-organizations. The examinations of these phenomena are situated in various historical processes (e.g., in the chapters by Adler, Dugger, Hondagneu-Sotelo, Kibria, and Brenner and Laslett) and in different institutional settings such as the family, the economy, the community, and the polity (as in the chapters by Adler, Baca Zinn, Barnett, Blankenship, Chow, Deitch, Higginbotham and Weber, Messner, Naples, Segura, Thompson, and Zsembik and Peek).

The third theme of this book centers on *the ways in which the private and public spheres are closely interconnected and production and social reproduction are intricately linked.* The "doctrine of separate spheres" is the traditional belief that husbands and fathers are the sole breadwinners, employed in the public domain to earn a family wage to support the family, whereas wives and mothers are homemakers, primarily responsible for unpaid household labor in the private sphere and for providing emotional support, love, and care to the family. The ideology of woman's place is based on and reinforced by "the cult of true womanhood" (Andersen 1993). Although this doctrine may reflect a partial reality primarily for White, middle-class women, it does not apply universally. For women of color, immigrant women, and female heads of single-parent families, paid employment outside the home has historically been an integral, normative component of their roles as daughters, wives, and mothers. At the same time, such women have engaged in unpaid domestic labor, child care, and maintenance in the home, creating double or even triple shifts for many of them. These women are overburdened but undervalued both as producers in the public sphere and as social reproducers in the private sphere.

The increase in the number of women participating in the labor force, a rising divorce rate that disadvantages women and children, the growing number of single-parent households headed by women, and the demand to combine work and family have made the "separate spheres" model increasingly inapplicable even to White women. The interpenetration of the two spheres in most women's lives has rendered obsolete the functional description of a gendered division of labor for the two spheres.

The fourth theme of this book is that *race, class, and gender create dialectical realities in women's and men's lives.* The dialectics between these multiple yet interlocking forces of oppression generate tension, contradictions, and constraints for women and men. In addition, they enhance and restrict features of culture and society, structure and process, and institutions and individuals. Contrary to the functionalist formulation, these dialectics are not always dysfunctional but may create opportunities for women to negotiate, cope with, and even resist various forms of structural domination and inequality. For example, Dill (1979) observes that Black women have historically taken on contradictory roles in response to multiple oppressions. She notes that they have enacted their role as the moral backbone of the family and thus the community that has encouraged them to develop cultures of resistance and strategies for community survival and institutional change.

Race, class, and gender are structural sources of the dialectics of oppression. A number of authors, including Brenner and Laslett, Dugger, Hondagneu-Sotelo, Kibria, and Naples characterize homeplace and community as sites of contradiction and contested terrains where opposing forces are intricately interwoven into women's everyday lives.

The last theme of the book is *the need to study the interlocking of race, class, and gender to transform sociological knowledge through theory, research, and praxis.* As part of a larger feminist theoretical emphasis and research agenda, this work seeks not only to understand the relationships between women's and men's positions in society and their life experiences but also to raise their consciousness and to improve their social conditions. The authors, whose work is included here, recognize the need to approach the subject of the interconnections among race, class, and gender theoretically, empirically, and through practical application if we are to bring new insight and understanding through feminist knowledge and praxis. New feminist scholarship has changed the intellectual discourse in gender analysis, widening its contours and deepening its perspective. This has created an enhanced vision and conviction that can inspire collective empowerment and generate action to uplift diverse kinds of women and men.

The articles selected for this book, although varying in focus and scope, explore a range of probing questions, assumptions, paradigms, and methods. Realizing that generalizations about sexism are race-specific and class-relevant prompts us to re-evaluate key concepts and theoretical frameworks and urges us to think about how current explanatory frameworks might be illuminated and changed when the perspectives and experiential bases of women of color and other disempowered groups are taken into consideration (Wilkinson 1995). Many of the chapters emphasize the importance of the agency of women and vividly illustrate their "feminist" practices in everyday coping; their strategies of struggle and resistance; their political activism to uplift their race, family, and community; and their advocacy for social reform.

Therefore, we seek in this volume to celebrate a diversity of voices, yet voices unified for racial and ethnic, sexual and gender, and class equality. However, thinking about diversity as only giving voice to and listening to previously silenced groups is not enough. We must decipher the lived experiences of these voices and place them in concrete historical and social contexts in our analyses as well as social action.

ORGANIZATION OF THE BOOK

Articles were selected for inclusion on the basis of their originality, unique perspective, insightful analysis, and thoughtful formulation contributing toward building an inclusive feminist scholarship. Although by no means comprehensive, the collection reflects the views of women and men of various racial, ethnic, and class backgrounds, of different sexual orientations, and across generations. All chapters offer thoughtful, systematic discussions of how race, ethnicity, class, and gender are structurally interconnected in major social institutions and in daily interaction by describing, explaining, and interpreting various intricacies of social structure and personal life.

The book consists of five major parts. Each one addresses all or many of the main themes as identified. Part I introduces inclusive feminist scholarship by illustrating how sociological work has broadened to incorporate race, ethnicity, class, and, to some extent, sexual orientation into gender analysis. Part II examines how the interlocking of race, class, and gender as structurally embedded in the economy, the wage labor market, the occupational structure, and work organizations affects women's employment, mobility, and labor experience. In Part III, we highlight through our contributors the historical and contemporary linkages between the interlocking forces and social relations in the family and community contexts, including intergenerational relations. Feminist thinking about the importance of women as human agents and the politics of their empowerment through community activism, social movements, and policy change is the emphasis of the studies included in Part IV. Finally, Part V explores the potential for theory construction and methodological strategizing in the study of interrelations among race, class, and gender. Critical and insightful views concerning theoretical and methodological issues are presented that lay a foundation for future theorizing.

The book offers a contextualized understanding of the complexities of commonalities and differences, domination and subordination, marginality and centrality in diverse women's and men's respective locations as related to the interlocking of race, class, and gender in the larger societal context. Our shared conviction is that the volume embraces the feminist vision of inclusive, balanced knowledge, blending theory and research with social practice to transform society for the betterment of women, men, and children.

NOTES

1. *Sex* and *gender* are analytically distinct in our conceptualization, the first term referring to a biological descriptor and the second to a social construction. Because most of the chapters in this volume essentially address gender rather than sex, gender is used herein to encompass the sexual dimension as well. Similarly, we use the term *race* here to include *ethnicity*. For those who are interested in sex and sexuality, see *Gender & Society*, which published two special issues—one on "Violence Against Women" in December 1989 and another on "Sexual Identities/Sexual Communities" in September 1994—that more thoroughly consider sexual stratification and oppression.

2. As reflected in the articles selected, this book focuses on race, class, and gender as prime interlocking categories for analysis. We also recognize the importance of sexual orientation, age, nationality, religion, and physical ability in shaping systems of relationship, meaning, and privileges and these are dealt with in some of the chapters.

3. The term *racial-ethnic* refers to groups that are socially and legally subordinated and remain culturally distinct within U.S. society. The term is meant to refer to both systematic discrimination against socially constructed racial groups and their distinctive cultural arrangements. Historically, the categories of African American, Latino, Asian American, and Native American were constructed to be both racially and culturally distinct (Baca Zinn and Dill 1994, 11-12).

REFERENCES

Andersen, Margaret. 1993. *Thinking about women: Sociological perspectives on sex and gender.* Third edition. New York: Macmillan.

Andersen, Margaret, and Patricia Hill Collins. 1995. *Race, class, and gender: An anthology.* Belmont, CA: Wadsworth.

Baca Zinn, Maxine, and Bonnie Thornton Dill, eds. 1994. *Women of Color in U.S. Society.* Philadelphia, PA: Temple University Press.

Brewer, Rose M. 1993. Theorizing race, class, and gender: The new scholarship of Black feminist intellectuals and Black women's labor. In *Theorizing Black feminism: The visionary pragmatism of Black women,* edited by A. P. A. Busia and S. M. James. New York: Routledge.

Dill, Bonnie Thornton. 1979. The dialectics of Black womanhood. *Signs: Journal of Women in Culture and Society* 4: 543-55.

King, Deborah. 1988. Multiple jeopardy, multiple consciousness: The context of a Black feminist ideology. *Signs: Journal of Women in Culture and Society* 14: 42-72.

Wilkinson, Doris. 1995. Gender and social inequality: The prevailing significance of race. *Daedalus* 124: 167-178.

Part I

Bringing Race and Class
Into Gender Analysis

This section introduces the ways that race and class interlock with gender analysis. To develop an inclusive scholarship, this section includes empirical studies to illustrate how social locations of women and men are related to the ways they experience the complexity and simultaneity of race, class, and gender. Each of the selections in this part concentrates on the impact of two or more of these important social dimensions on the lives of women and men.

In the first chapter, " 'Always Leading Our Men in Service and Sacrifice,' " Karen S. Adler's biographical analysis of Amy Jacques Garvey is an interesting profile of the co-creator and key architect of Garveyism. Adler shows how race, class, and gender oppression converged to shape the life, social thought, and activism of a woman long regarded as the "helpmate" of Marcus Garvey. Amy Jacques Garvey's remarkable perspective on the Black nationalism, sexism, and class politics of her time served as a foundation for the evolving ideology of Garveyism. Her conflicted commitment to Marcus Garvey himself vividly illustrates the contradictions between her conservative personal politics and her radical politics in the Black nationalist liberation movement. Her life reflects the paradox of Black women activists living conventional private lives while simultaneously leading radical public lives. The analysis contributes to the understanding of the intricate interplay between structure and individual, social history and personal life.

Karen Dugger challenges the additive model in Chapter 2, "Social Location and Gender-Role Attitudes," using an interactive model of the effects of racism and classism to study the commonalities and differences in gender-role attitudes of Black and White women from distinct social locations. She assesses the applicability to Black women of the

1

hypothesis that investment in reproductive relations exerts a conservative influence on gender-role attitudes, whereas investment in productive relations has a radical impact. Her data partly support the hypothesis but more so for White than for Black women. She found that Black women were more likely to reject the dominant culture's value of gender roles than were White women. This study criticizes feminist theory by illuminating the fallacy of treating race and gender as separable or discrete phenomena. Recognizing that gender is constitutively related to race directs readers to consider the historical and sociocultural contexts of women's lives when theorizing about the forces that shape their gender identity and attitudes.

Focusing on everyday behavior, Becky Wangsgaard Thompson in Chapter 3, " 'A Way Outa No Way,' " demonstrates how incomplete and exclusive knowledge about eating problems has produced partial and biased understanding of them. Normative epidemiological research has described eating problems largely as a White, middle- and upper-class, heterosexual phenomenon. Thompson's insightful analysis reveals that eating problems also originate in the traumas created by the structural inequalities of poverty, sexual abuse, racism, and heterosexism. Eating problems, in fact, are gendered survival strategies adopted by African American, Latina, and lesbian women as they struggle against a "simultaneity of oppression" relating to life traumas. Challenging theoretical reliance on the "culture of thinness" model, Thompson has advanced theoretical thinking about the structural etiology of eating behavior. She specifically suggests using the term *eating problems* to replace *eating disorders* and the term *body consciousness* instead of *body image* as more useful ways to understand the range of bodily responses to trauma.

In Chapter 4, "Masculinities and Athletic Careers," Michael A. Messner investigates the construction of masculinities within sport, viewing sport as an institution that serves to construct gender, class, and race inequalities. He argues that organized sports provide a context in which men's separation from and power over women is embodied and naturalized. Based on in-depth interviews with former male athletes from different race and class backgrounds, Messner examines how these men socially construct a variety of masculinities and argues that their choice to pursue an athletic career derives from each man's rational assessment of the available means for constructing a public masculinity. Masculinities are clearly differentiated, creating bonding and hegemonic masculinity for high-status White male athletes and limiting choices and constructing marginalized masculinity for the lower-status, non-White athletes. The social construction of masculinity among male athletes is also a dialectical process. Men's domination over women, as Messner points out, may tie all men together but it creates contradictions among men who, because of their race and class, share very unequally in the fruits of this domination.

What follows are some creative ways of bringing race and class into gender analysis to more accurately interpret the structural linkages between these stratifying forces. Independently and jointly, these forces create categories of people who occupy unique social spaces and whose collective historical experiences powerfully shape their gender identities and attitudes, creating race-specific and class-relevant gender effects in various aspects of their lives.

1 "Always Leading Our Men in Service and Sacrifice": Amy Jacques Garvey, Feminist Black Nationalist

KAREN S. ADLER

Marcus Garvey is the universally acknowledged founder and leader of the Garvey movement, the most powerful Black nationalist movement ever established in the United States. Many works have been written about Marcus Garvey as a Black "genius" and "hero." Very little has been written, however, about the most important woman in Garveyism —Marcus's second wife, Amy Jacques Garvey. While she never held an official title in the Universal Negro Improvement Association (UNIA), Amy was a daunting intellectual, orator, writer, social activist, and leader. Her value, nonetheless, has never been fully recognized and the references to her are meager. Although Theodore G. Vincent, author of *Black Power and the Garvey Movement,* wrote that "the life and works of Amy Jacques Garvey . . . deserve attention from students of both women's liberation and Black nationalism" (1972, 131), few scholars have heeded this claim.

In this chapter, I explore the life and works of Amy Jacques Garvey.[1] Through analyzing her participation in the Garvey movement, her life with and without Marcus, her thought, her writings, and her activities

AUTHOR'S NOTE: I thank Shulamit Reinharz and anonymous editors from *Gender & Society* for their incisive editorial suggestions and revisions. I am especially grateful to Professor Reinharz for recommending publication of this work and for her vital support throughout the editorial process.

after Marcus's death, I highlight her roles as a key architect of Garvey-ism and as an outspoken social activist whose lifelong commitment to social change transcended her relationship with Marcus. I examine how the interacting forces of race, class, and gender shaped Amy Jacques Garvey's life and informed her philosophy of social change. The ostensible contradiction between Amy's conventional private life and her radical public agenda is also analyzed.

GARVEYISM AND THE GARVEY MOVEMENT

At its peak in the early 1920s, the Garvey movement and its political arm, the Universal Negro Improvement Association (UNIA), represented the most powerful organization of Black people in the world. Founded in 1914, the UNIA had, by the early 1920s, over 800 chapters in 40 countries on four continents. It contained nearly one million official members, and an estimated two to three times as many people participated in its activities. To this day, the UNIA remains the largest Black organization ever developed in the United States (Vincent 1972).

Highly complex, Garveyism is a comprehensive philosophical and political program espousing the worldwide liberation of all descendants of Black Africa. This freedom is supposed to be achieved through self-help and self-sufficiency in all spheres of life: "The Universal Negro Improvement Association teaches our race self-help and self-reliance, not only in one essential, but in all those things which contribute to human happiness and well-being" (Garvey 1963, 22). By teaching Blacks to embrace their African heritage and to establish their own separate society (in Africa ultimately), the movement's ideology laid the basis for every Black power movement in the United States in this century (Vincent 1972). Unlike most Black movements, Garveyism derived its strength primarily from the Black urban working class and thus had revolutionary potential. By undermining the pervasive acceptance of Black dependence on White society and exposing the true depth of Black rage, the movement posed a severe threat to White bourgeois society (Matthews 1979).

AMY JACQUES GARVEY IN LITERATURE

The few references to Amy Jacques Garvey in the literature on Garveyism describe her as the nurturing spouse and companion of Marcus Garvey. For example, in *Marcus Garvey: Hero,* Tony Martin

(1983), one of the foremost scholars on Garvey and Garveyism, describes Amy as the "perfect spouse" for someone in Marcus's position. While Martin offhandedly claims that Amy—in reality a prolific writer —"tried her hand" at writing essays and short stories (p. 67), he also mentions casually that she was the second woman and tenth person to be awarded the Jamaica Institute's Musgrave Gold Medal in December 1971. Amy was awarded this medal for her "dedicated and distinguished contribution to the history of the people of African descent, and particularly her *erudite dissertations on the philosophy of Garveyism. . . .*" (Martin 1983, 156; emphasis added). Clearly, one who writes "erudite dissertations" is hardly the literary dilettante that Martin describes.

One of the few articles ever written that specifically addresses Amy Jacques Garvey and *her* work appeared more than 15 years ago in the journal *Black Scholar* (Matthews 1979). Matthews claims that Amy Jacques Garvey is one of the most remarkable women in history, and he laments the fact that she has never been mentioned in articles on Black women (or any other subject for that matter). Matthews censures the minimalization of Black women like Amy Jacques Garvey in the Garvey movement and argues that the movement had a profound impact on Black women. What he does not say is that women like Amy Jacques Garvey also had a prodigious effect on the Garvey movement and played an integral part in its shaping.

GROWING UP IN JAMAICA

Amy Jacques Garvey was born in Jamaica in 1896. Her brief accounts of her life prior to meeting Marcus reveal the makings of a strong-willed, self-possessed, and gifted woman. The social circumstances in which Amy lived influenced her views toward Black nationalism, feminism, and class politics. She was apparently raised in a middle-class home with bourgeois Victorian values; she was taught to play the piano because music and music appreciation were considered the "cultural finishing to a girl's education" (Garvey 1963, 106).

Amy attended high school during a time when less than 2 percent of Jamaican youths received a high school education (Hurwitz and Hurwitz 1971). As the eldest child in her family, Amy was obliged to read foreign newspapers and periodicals with her father in order to enhance her knowledge of the world. In this way she absorbed her father's deep interest in political issues, including racial progress (Vincent 1972). Like many middle-class women of her generation (White and Black),

Amy Jacques Garvey was reared to be well-educated and socially conscious during an era of constricted career opportunities for women —particularly Black women. For Amy, as for her middle-class, educated peers interested in social change, social reform work was among the few viable means for advancing her social and political agenda. Her middle-class status allowed her to develop the verbal and intellectual skills necessary for becoming an effective movement leader.

Amy's childhood (at the turn of the century) coincided with a period of intensified bigotry and discrimination against Black Americans. Entrenched segregation, political disenfranchisement, and mob violence against Black Americans characterized this era, described as the "nadir in U.S. race relations" (Barkley Brown 1989, 190). Recognizing that dependence on White society was tantamount to race suicide, Black Americans (still concentrated in the South) developed their own social, political, and economic infrastructure in an effort to secure racial progress. This philosophy of self-help, race pride, and economic autonomy that pervaded the Black community during the early twentieth century undoubtedly influenced Amy's development as a Black nationalist and advocate of Black self-sufficiency.

Amy was exposed to race consciousness in Jamaica. During the late nineteenth century, Europe's colonization of Africa led many African-born Jamaicans to develop a sense of African consciousness. Some Jamaicans returned to Africa, while many others spoke out in Africa's defense. This nationalistic fervor spread throughout the West Indies and contributed to the development of the first Pan-African Conference in London in 1900 (Martin 1983).[2] In 1914, Marcus Garvey founded the Universal Negro Improvement and Conservation Association and African Communities League in Jamaica, the precursor to the UNIA. This nascent nationalism in Jamaica must have affected Amy Jacques Garvey's burgeoning race consciousness as a young woman.

Amy was influenced by other factors as well. As a girl, she received mixed messages from her father about her place in life. While he encouraged her intellectual development, he also constrained her career options. In high school, Amy won a prize for her outstanding performance in typewriting and shorthand and was offered an entry-level position in the legal firm to which her teacher was connected. Her father, however, barred her from taking the job, claiming that he did not want "any daughter of mine to be exposed to the wiles of men in an office" (Garvey 1963, 106). Her father apparently believed that such work was inappropriate for a "proper lady."

As fate would have it, Amy's father died suddenly of a stroke at this time. In response, the family's lawyer suggested to her mother that Amy work in his office as a clerk, to oversee her father's estate. Her mother agreed, and Amy worked in the law office for four years, becoming knowledgeable about law to the point that she could "attend to every legal phase of the work" (Garvey 1963, 106). Out of the tragedy of her father's death, Amy gained the opportunity to pursue avenues that he had closed to her. Significantly, her relationship with her domineering father was reenacted in her marriage to Marcus. Her experiences of sexism within the family, in the workplace, and later in the Garvey movement contributed to her development as a feminist.

This feminist consciousness was likely already blossoming when, after four years at the law office, Amy decided to go to the United States against the will of her mother and her employer. Amy left for the United States in 1918, promising to return in three months if conditions proved to be "unbearable." She claimed her primary reasons for going were to further her education and to see the "land of opportunity and limitations, according to my father's description" (Garvey 1963, 107).[3] Amy did not return to Jamaica in three months, and her life was to take a major turn shortly after her arrival in the United States. By defying her family's wishes and going to a foreign country alone when this was an anomaly for most women, Amy demonstrated independence of mind, courage, and thirst for knowledge—all of which characterized her for the rest of her life.

AMY JACQUES MEETS MARCUS GARVEY

Not long after arriving in New York, Amy heard a great deal about the UNIA, then headquartered in New York City. Given conflicting reports about the organization, she decided to attend a meeting at Liberty Hall one summer evening in 1919. Marcus gave a speech that night and Amy allegedly went up to him afterward to congratulate him on his fine oratory and to ask him questions. Because there were many points that she believed he did not address, Amy claimed that she did this to be convinced of Marcus's righteousness and to test her ability "to argue on my conviction" (Garvey 1963, 37). Marcus's answers evoked more questions from Amy, and they agreed to meet again at his office to talk more about Garveyism. Amy's self-initiated introduction to Marcus, already a famous man, reveals her to have been an assertive, self-confident woman. Her eagerness to engage Marcus in dialogue suggests that she had already developed ideas regarding the "race issue."[4]

The details surrounding Amy Jacques's courtship and marriage to Marcus are ambiguous and full of contradictions. It is unclear whether or not Amy Jacques and Marcus began their romance during Marcus's marriage to Amy Ashwood. Ashwood claimed she left Marcus in the summer of 1921 after a period of separation, when she discovered that Marcus and Amy Jacques, at that point his private secretary, were living together (Cronon 1955). Amy Jacques claimed, however, that her romance with Marcus began only after he decided to divorce Amy Ashwood (Garvey 1963).

Either way, while Amy Ashwood was away in England in June 1922, Marcus received a divorce from her in Kansas City, without her knowledge. He then married Amy Jacques one month later on July 27, 1922, in Baltimore. While the facts are muddled, one can surmise that Marcus behaved less than sincerely in his dealings with Amy Ashwood and Amy Jacques. These two women had been best friends as teens in Jamaica, and Amy Jacques had been Amy Ashwood's chief bridesmaid at her wedding to Marcus. Unfortunately, this long-term friendship was greatly damaged, if not severed, by the struggle over Marcus.

EARLY LIFE WITH MARCUS

Amy Jacques's relationship with Marcus, at least in the beginning, was founded on mutual respect and admiration; she respected his "creative genius," he, her "intellectual prowess" (Vincent 1972, 131). Early in their relationship, Amy was one of Marcus's staunchest supporters and portrayed herself publicly as his companion and helpmate. In March 1923, shortly before Amy published her first volume of the *Philosophy and Opinions of Marcus Garvey,* a compilation of Marcus's writings and speeches, Amy was interviewed by the *Negro World* regarding her forthcoming book. When asked what occupied her thoughts most, Amy responded, "my husband." She went on to say that Marcus's work was "his whole life. . . . Knowing this, I endeavor to be conversant with subjects that would help in his career, and try to make home a haven of rest and comfort for him" (G. 1923, 8).

Amy edited volume 1 of the *Philosophy and Opinions of Marcus Garvey* only seven months after she married Marcus. Her initial purpose was not to publish but, rather, to keep a personal record of Marcus's "opinions and sayings" (Garvey [1923] 1967, xxxiii). She eventually decided to produce the book so that the public could cultivate opinions about Marcus based on *his* words versus the misleading, biased material propagated by the media. By the time Amy decided to publish, Marcus had already been indicted for mail fraud and had countless enemies determined to undermine him.[5] Convinced of her husband's righteousness, Amy was determined to exonerate him through her book. Moreover, she believed that by dissemination of the truth, "Negroes the world over may be informed and inspired, for truth, brought to light, forces conviction, and a state of conviction inspires action" (Garvey [1923] 1967, xxxiii).

A VITAL PLAYER IN THE GARVEY MOVEMENT

While Amy may genuinely have believed at first that her primary role was as Marcus's "comforter," she did not remain in that role for very long and quickly became a central force in the Garvey movement. Amy's place in the movement became, according to one author (Matthews 1979, 4), "second only to Marcus" in the UNIA. Perhaps instead she should be considered "first," alongside Marcus. In *Garvey and Garveyism*, Amy claimed that a significant portion of the speeches, writings, and even thought of "Marcus" was the result of her efforts. She described how Marcus asked her to read through magazines and newspapers for important articles and then explain their content and significance to him. He would in turn use this material as the basis for "his" speeches and front-page articles and would seek Amy's opinions before going to press. He also incorporated information from Amy's own articles in the *Negro World* into his speeches. Amy clearly had a profound impact on Marcus's thought and was undoubtedly a cocreator, if not *the* creator, of aspects of Garveyite philosophy.

Amy toured extensively with and without Marcus (when he was in jail) and was considered to be an "excellent speaker" (Martin 1983, 126). Marcus seemed extremely ambivalent about Amy's (and even women's) role in the movement. While he overtly advocated women's participation in Garveyism and strongly relied on Amy for intellectual and emotional support, he clearly viewed her as an aide in *his* work. This is evident in a message he sent to his supporters in the *Negro World* while he was in Tombs Prison in 1923:

> I commend to your care and attention my wife, who has been *my helpmate* and inspiration for years. . . . Her tale of woe has not been told, but . . . I

feel sure that a day will come when the whole world will know the story of her noble sacrifice for the cause *I* love so much. (Garvey 1963, 117; emphasis added)

Despite this public plea on behalf of his wife, Marcus failed to show Amy his appreciation for her efforts. He expected self-sacrificing behavior from his wife and was perhaps threatened by her rival status, rendering him unable to acknowledge her capabilities and accomplishments. In the end, Amy never posed a threat to Marcus's leadership and Marcus played an active part in ensuring this fact.

UNOFFICIAL LEADER OF THE UNIA

Because of unexpected circumstances, Amy eventually moved to center stage within the UNIA. On June 21, 1923, less than a year after Amy married Marcus, Marcus was convicted of mail fraud and sentenced to five years in prison. When he failed to win any of his appeals, he was sent to the Atlanta Federal Penitentiary on February 8, 1925, to serve a five-year sentence. While authors claim that Amy became Marcus's "personal representative" and "principal lieutenant" during his imprisonment (e.g., Hill 1987, 397), one can easily argue that she became the UNIA leader during this time. It is virtually impossible to measure the amount of work that Amy accomplished during this period. In addition to speaking all over the country to raise money for Marcus's defense fund, Amy met constantly with officials and UNIA officers, organized UNIA conferences and affairs, was associate editor of the *Negro World* and editor of its "Woman's Page," worked tirelessly with lawyers to get Marcus released from jail, compiled and published volume 2 of the *Philosophy and Opinions of Marcus Garvey* as well as two volumes of Marcus's poetry, and visited Marcus almost every three weeks in Atlanta.

Despite her Herculean efforts, Amy apparently never received from Marcus the appreciation she thought she deserved. That she never became the official leader of the UNIA during Marcus's imprisonment is due largely to the fact that Marcus prohibited it. At one point during Amy's unofficial tenure, some UNIA officers and branch members asked Marcus if they could call an emergency convention to vote Amy in as the assistant president-general, in an effort to save the organization's dwindling assets. Marcus refused, fearing that if Amy were ensnared by their enemies, he would then "be left to rot" in jail (Garvey 1963, 162). Marcus relied on Amy's emotional support and tactical ingenuity for his well-being. His decision to inhibit her growth in the UNIA was based primarily on selfish reasons; as far as he was concerned, Amy's main role in life was to save *him*.

A TROUBLED MARRIAGE

In *Garvey and Garveyism,* Amy's initially laudatory tone toward Marcus is transformed into outright vituperation as the book progresses. At points she is unabashed in her feelings about Marcus's flagrant disregard for her well-being. Marcus was released from prison and deported to Jamaica in November 1927. Shortly after Amy and Marcus settled in Jamaica, Marcus decided to go on a tour to England. Still reeling from previous events, Amy reluctantly joined him—as did his secretary. This appeared to be more than Amy could take and in *Garvey and Garveyism,* she expressed hurt and rage over feeling abused and manipulated by her selfish and callous husband:

> His attitude toward his eleven years of struggle in America, particularly his imprisonments, and all the suffering they caused us, were brushed aside as past history. . . . He turned the pages of his past life as an avid reader turns the pages of an adventure story, and loses interest in the early chapters after reading them. Those who get hurt in the tense moments of the adventure are only regarded as necessary props to the build-up of the hero. He was quite as impersonal in this regard as any reader. (Garvey 1963, 180)

In the pages of *Garvey and Garveyism,* Amy shows that her emotional needs were far from fulfilled in her relationship with Marcus.

Amy had extreme difficulty in reconciling her relationship with Marcus. At times she resorted to rationalizations of his behavior, as in the beginning of *Garvey and Garveyism,* where she depicted Marcus as someone with a divine calling and with virtually no control over his behaviors or actions:

> Heredity and environment seem to influence them, and used [sic] by them to carry out a spiritual urge in a given line. . . . They seem to have a Supreme Purpose in life, and once started, even against personal interests will not give up. They are, as it were, impelled to go on, even to death. (Garvey 1963, 3)

While this may be true of Marcus, it also reveals Amy's need to explain Marcus's behavior to herself. Beyond placating the emotional turmoil of living with a sexist and narcissistic husband, Amy may have needed to assuage her own disappointment or shame over having "settled" for such an unfulfilling relationship. Her feminist consciousness was likely fueled by, and became more fully articulated through, her relationship with Marcus. Amy's feminist thought was further honed through her writings in the *Negro World,* the major Garveyite newspaper and most sophisticated Black paper during the Harlem Renaissance (Matthews 1979).

BLACK WOMEN AND REFORM

Amy Jacques Garvey's social activism and writings in the *Negro World* reflect a long-standing tradition among Black women in this country to advance racial, gender, and class equality. Although Black women, like Amy, historically worked within movements for racial progress, this hardly meant that they were unconscious of gender and class oppression. On the contrary, Black women were highly attuned to the overlapping effects of racism, sexism, and classism on their lives—what Deborah King (1988) calls "multiple jeopardy."[6] Black women addressed issues of race, gender, and class within the context of uniracial organizations largely because of racial discrimination in White women's movements, special problems that Black women faced (including widespread charges of depravity), and the ascendancy of the race consciousness and self-help among Black Americans during the late nineteenth century (hooks 1981; Terborg-Penn 1978).

Because racism, sexism, and classism have always operated as "interdependent control systems" in the lives of Black women (King 1988, 270), Black women reformers have historically treated these issues as inextricably linked in their work. Like her counterparts in the club movement, Amy Jacques Garvey believed that poverty, poor health conditions, child welfare, mob violence, and racial segregation were women's issues as much as women's suffrage and women's higher education were strategies for racial advancement (Barkley Brown 1989). Consistently, the legacy of economic deprivation among Black Americans meant that most movements for racial progress, including Garveyism, incorporated programs for economic equality (King 1988).

As a Garveyite, Amy Jacques Garvey's racial and class politics were more radical than those of other contemporary Black reformers, men and women alike. The racial uplift movement of the early twentieth century was led primarily by middle-class Blacks who advocated equality and upward mobility for Black Americans within the existing social order. Many movement leaders, including Black clubwomen, strove to instill a sense of middle-class gentility in their poor brethren. The Garvey movement, however, catered primarily to urban working-class Blacks and repudiated the bourgeois values of White society. In the belief that White racism was inevitable, Garveyites strove to establish an independent Black society.

Significantly, Garveyism burgeoned during a period of "northern fever" (1916-1921) when an estimated one-half million Blacks migrated from southern plantations to northern urban industrial centers (Jones 1985). By 1920, a total of 31 percent of Black workers were employed in industry. Their experiences of racism, classism, and sexism (in the case of Black women) in the industrial sector rendered them the most exploited and alienated workers (Matthews 1979). Amy Jacques Garvey addressed the plight of Black industrial workers in her writings. She revered Lenin (to whom she devoted her first editorial in the "Woman's Page") for attempting to establish an egalitarian society based on nonexploitive social relations.

Nevertheless, Amy's writings at times belied her middle-class origins. Presenting herself as an enlightened role model for the Black community, Amy sometimes foisted her middle-class values onto her readers. For example, she unrealistically urged an overworked and underfed Black populace to read daily in order to become "interesting conversationalists, and be able to intelligently discuss other subjects besides the weather and football or prize fighting" (Garvey 1926i, 7). Amy's condescension, however, was tempered by her profound recognition that as a Black woman living in an intensely racist society, her fate was bound up with the Black masses. Racial self-preservation, rather than a sense of noblesse oblige,[7] motivated middle-class Black women like Amy Jacques Garvey to embark on racial reform (Giddings 1984; hooks 1981). In the effort to combat the multiple effects of racism and classism on the Black community, Amy was more interested in addressing the fundamental needs of Black Americans than in "bestowing culture" upon them.

"OUR WOMEN AND WHAT THEY THINK"

Amy Jacques Garvey edited "Our Women and What They Think" in the *Negro World* from 1924 to 1927. It is important to remember that during that time she was also unofficially leading the UNIA (given Marcus's imprisonment). While there were other Black periodicals with a women's page or column at the time (such as the *Half Century Magazine*), most of them differed greatly from "Our Women." As Amy herself put it:

> Usually a Woman's Page is any journal devoted solely to dress, home hints and love topics but our Page is unique in that it seeks to give out the thoughts of our women on all subjects affecting them. . . . This pleases the modern Negro woman, who believes that God Almighty has not limited her intellect because of her sex. . . .
>
> By your contributions you will be showing the world the worth and ability of Negro Women, and gain the appreciation of our own men whose lives are guided by our influence and who get inspiration from us. (Matthews 1979, 5)

Extending far beyond women's domestic matters, "Our Women" covered a formidable spectrum of issues. Common themes included national liberation struggles worldwide, feminist movements and the changing status of women at home and abroad, the fight for Black liberation in the United States, and the sweep of technological change (Matthews 1979).

In her editorials Amy demonstrated a remarkable breadth and sophistication of knowledge regarding world events. She believed that it was imperative for Blacks to be well informed about international affairs so that they could be prepared for the "war of tomorrow" and make appropriate countermoves for their own safety (Garvey 1926m, 8). It was also important to be cognizant of world affairs because anticolonial liberation movements were taking place worldwide (e.g., China and India) and Blacks had much to learn from these struggles in their own battles for liberation. Amy seemed to have a special reverence for Jewish Zionists. In many of her editorials, she upheld Zionism as the embodiment of "racial love and ambition" (Garvey 1926g, 5). She argued that Zionists' persevering efforts to establish a Jewish homeland in Palestine should be emulated by Blacks, who sought to reclaim Africa as their home.

Amy wrote about the economic exploitation of people of color in the United States and around the world. She understood that White imperialists decimated the indigenous economies of Third World peoples just as White capitalists and industrialists at home exploited Black American workers:

> The Negro's place in the economic life of America has been that of the underdog. His job is any class of work white men refuse to do. With so many poor Europeans pouring into the country, willing to do anything to get a start in the land of opportunity, the question that now rudely confronts the Negro is, where is his job? . . . Not only has the white immigrant deprived the Negro of jobs, but labor-saving devices have added to the dearth of employment. (Garvey 1926c, 6)

The Garvey movement identified strongly with foreign national liberation movements (i.e., in India) in part because many of these movements were led by working-class people, particularly after World War I (Matthews 1979). Amy Jacques Garvey urged Black Americans to join the international struggle for self-determination by investing their resources in "a factory or some avenue of employment for poor Negroes who are being turned away from the white man's factory door" (Garvey 1926h, 7).

Amy's economic (as well as social and political) analysis corresponded with her husband's in many respects. Unlike Marcus, however, Amy systematically applied her analyses to Black *women,* acknowledging that their experience of oppression was often distinguishable from that of Black men. For example, Amy noted that the interaction of racism, classism, *and* sexism took on special meaning for Black women in the burgeoning American industrial economy:

> Negro women, who have always had to bear the responsibility of providing for the home co-equal with their mates, are experiencing the same difficulty in securing jobs as domestics, which formerly was the Negro woman's only source of employment. Electricity is now the servant in the house. (Garvey 1926c, 6)

Amy devoted many editorials to women's struggles for emancipation in the United States and elsewhere, particularly in colonial and semi-colonial countries. She believed that the women's movement was one of the most remarkable movements in history and lauded women's efforts toward liberation. The Garvey movement's identification with national liberation struggles abroad encouraged such an international perspective on women's issues. A consistent motif in Amy's editorials was her belief that the patriarchal family was becoming archaic the world over, given that modern technology made it possible and even necessary for women to participate in and contribute to all spheres of life (Matthews 1979).

Most striking about Amy's ideological stance in "Our Women" is the fundamental connection she makes between nationalist and women's liberation movements. While Amy claimed that her primary dedication was to Black liberation, she believed that Black and Third World *women* represented the backbone of all Black and Third World nationalist struggles. Women of color's struggles against imperialist domination, combined with their own ongoing battles for liberation, ultimately would humanize and transform the world, according to Amy. This recognition of the rudimentary links between racial, gender, class, and imperialistic oppression and of the central role that women played in human liberation movements, represents in my view Amy Jacques Garvey's most noteworthy contribution to Garveyism.

Amy wrote approvingly of the modernization taking place in colonial and semicolonial countries and of women's corresponding rejection of sexist traditions that inhibited their growth. While Amy wrote about the changing status of women in the Philippines, Turkey, Japan, and Syria, she focused much attention on women in Egypt, India, and China— countries in the midst of national liberation struggles (Matthews 1979). In an editorial focused on India's decision to elect its first woman president to the Fortieth National Congress, Amy highlighted the synergetic relationship between national liberation and women's emancipation. She noted that women's changing status in society was both fueling and being fueled by movements for national independence (Garvey, 1926l, 7).

Beyond securing national liberation and women's emancipation, Amy believed that women's particular sensibilities and attributes could be harnessed as redeeming forces in the world. In the same editorial on India, Amy wrote that

> women have a purifying effect on politics, and it is felt that India will be greatly benefited by the activities of the gentle sex in its swaraj program. Men play politics sometimes for personal gain, financially or just to be in the limelight, but women enter politics, mainly for the good they feel they can

accomplish. They are self-sacrificing—a quality borne of motherhood—
. . . And so in emerging from the home into the larger field, they go forth
well trained to serve others, and to subordinate their own feelings, for the
common good. (Garvey 1926l, 7)

By arguing that women had special powers that could be employed
toward the betterment of humanity, Amy aligned herself with other
contemporary White and Black social feminists (e.g., Jane Addams and
Anna Julia Cooper) who purported to believe in women's humanizing
potential. Consistent with the separate spheres ideology, these social
feminists believed that women cultivated certain qualities—such as
tenderness, compassion, and "intuition"—because of their role as domestic caregivers.[8] During the Progressive Era, middle-class, educated
White women confronted by limited career options began to espouse
"social housekeeping": the notion that women's private virtues should
be extended to the public realm in order to combat entrenched social
problems (Giddings 1984; Hewitt 1985). These ideas had a clear impact
on Amy, who wrote many editorials espousing women's entrance into
all spheres of life in order to wield their "purifying" influence on the
world. Amy's determination to prove women's civic and political capabilities was likely bolstered by the passage of women's suffrage in this
country in 1920.

It is important to note that Black women had recognized the link
between the public and private realms long before the concept of "social
housekeeping" came into being. According to Bonnie Thornton Dill
(1979), Black women have historically been forced to adopt the roles
of wife, mother, and worker simultaneously in response to their experiences of racism, sexism, and classism. Amy Jacques Garvey understood that "competing demands [were] a primary influence on the Black
woman's definition of her womanhood" (King 1988, 274) and viewed
Black women's ability to appropriate diverse social roles as an indication of their fortitude.

In her editorials, Amy underscored the fluidity between the public
and private domains in the lives of women—particularly Black women.
Amy openly refuted the false dichotomy between motherhood and
professional life for women, claiming that women could choose any and
every path they saw fit. She did, however, recognize the key role that
women played as child rearers and geared many of her editorials toward
this subject. Amy viewed "scientific," "educated" child rearing as
integral to racial progress (Garvey 1924b, 10) and believed that

women's intellectual development would lead to "expert" mothering (Garvey 1925a, 7). Amy had tremendous respect for Black women, whom she believed were *the* leaders in the development of the race, and even humanity, through their roles as mothers and community builders:

> The editor of the Woman's Page is proud of the splendid work our women have done in the home and school and church, . . . and she has faith that they will do better work in the coming days. . . . [W]e should keep constantly in mind the fact that "the hand that rocks the cradle rules the world." (Garvey 1924a, 12)

Amy Jacques Garvey impugned the fact that Black women were rarely acknowledged as primary contributors to Black history and progress, even though they were "measuring up to the highest standards of service, of accomplishment, and always leading our men in service and sacrifice" (Garvey 1924b, 10). She belonged to a legacy of Black women activists (i.e., Mary Church Terrell and Maggie Lena Walker) who believed that Black women's unique experience of "multiple jeopardy" compelled them to cultivate inner strengths that rendered them natural leaders in the fight for equality (Barkley Brown 1989).

> The Negro woman is the backbone of the race. . . . Take the days of slavery when she toiled on the plantations alongside of her men [sic], at the same time having to bear him children, and be subjected to the vicious propensities of her white slave-master. Follow her after emancipation and you will find her washing and ironing, doing odd jobs besides her own house work so as to support her children through school, giving them what she never had—an education. Look at her today, educated, independent and well-equipped . . . to compete with her men and in many instances outclass them. . . . Ethiopian queens once ruled great empires, and they are riding back into power on their own merits and achievements. (Garvey 1926a, 3)

Contrary to her attitudes toward Black women, Amy was often vitriolic in her criticisms of Black men and believed that they were primarily responsible for the demise of racial progress. Amy continually described Black men as "slothful," "lethargic," and "parasitic" beings who were failing to provide for their women, children, and future, and moreover, the posterity of the race. According to Amy, Black men were "all talk and no action" and required women's constant cajolery:

The doom of the race lies in the lethargy of its men. . . . Black men you are failing on your jobs! . . . Be honest enough to admit your laziness. Now shake yourselves, lift your head high, expand your chests, put right foot forward, then left, don't be afraid, now step right off and tackle your jobs. The world expects you to play a man's part, and is fed up on [sic] your whinings and "can't be done" moans. (Garvey 1926f, 5)

Amy was equally intolerant of Black men within the UNIA who prevented women members from acquiring leadership positions. Amy believed that Black women were the primary force behind the UNIA and she continually applauded their efforts in the "Woman's Page." She took an uncompromising stance against sexism within the UNIA and was wholly determined to secure for Black women the leadership roles they deserved:

If the United States Senate and Congress can open their doors to white women, we serve notice to our men that Negro women will demand equal opportunity to fill any position in the Universal Negro Improvement Association or anywhere else without discrimination because of sex. . . . We not only make the demand, but we intend to enforce it. (Garvey 1926a, 3)

Amy's cynicism toward Black men posed a great dilemma for her. While her foremost purpose in life was to achieve Black liberation, this goal was jeopardized by her flagging faith in Black men. At first Amy believed that it was Black women's job to get behind their men and urge them forward. This view changed over time, as her disdain for Black men escalated. Amy eventually came to believe that Black women were destined to remain the "burden bearers of the race"; therefore it was incumbent upon them to "keep pace with daily events" and "train [their] minds to cope with situations and problems" (Garvey 1927b, 7), given that Black men were not going to.[9] Amy was ultimately disgusted with all men and believed that women would (and should) replace men as the leaders of the world in order to secure its salvation:

As to the statement . . . that some day women may rule men, we agree with the prediction, and feel sure that the world will then be a better place in which to live, for women have a conscience, while men have not, and even-handed justice will more likely be meted out. . . . You [men] had your day at the helm of the world, and a pretty mess you have made of it . . . and perhaps women's rule will usher in the era of real brotherhood [sic], when national and racial lines will disappear, leaving mankind [sic] in peace and harmony one with another. Who knows? (Garvey 1926j, 5)

In her derision of Black men, Amy revealed her own ambivalence toward Whites. While Amy, like Marcus, roundly denounced miscegenation and lambasted "want-to-be-white" Blacks who were still striving to be like "Massa" (Garvey 1926b, 5), she also upheld Whites as role models for Blacks and criticized Black men for not being more like White men. According to Amy, the White race dominated the Black race in part because White men, unlike Black men, admired, respected, and protected their women. This fact, combined with White men's pioneering spirit, compelled them to go to the ends of the earth to establish civilizations and exploit material wealth for their women's benefit. Amy described this scenario repeatedly in her editorials and besides being uncharacteristically sexist, it further reflected her own love/hate relationship with the White race and capitalism. For while Amy claimed that each person must live by the dictates of his or her spiritual conscience and contribute to humanity "not with the hope of worldly reward, but with the inner satisfaction of having done right by himself [sic] and his fellow man [sic]" (Garvey 1925b, 7), she also clearly admired Whites for their capitalist spirit and material goods.[10]

Amy was ambivalent about materialism and spiritualism. While she clearly was a religious believer and made many references to God in her editorials, she also claimed that "the race that is silly enough to think that it can fight materialism with spiritualism, is doomed to extermination" (Garvey 1927a, 7). According to Amy, "Power is the keynote of the age" (Garvey 1927a, 7), and Blacks' survival hinged upon their ability to match might with might:

Prayerful petitions and tearful appeals are a waste of time and energy; when you make your demands in the white man's language—FORCE—he will readily yield. (Garvey 1926d, 7)

Amy had no illusions about the fact that the worldwide hegemony of the White race was maintained through military power. She urged Blacks to "acquire . . . weapons of warfare" to "rout the robbers in their houses" (Garvey 1927c, 7).

One can only imagine that Amy had mixed feelings about her support of Black violence. This belief clearly contradicted her feminism, which sought to spread women's humanizing, compassionate influence throughout the world. Perhaps she justified her stance as an imperative self-defense measure for Black *men*. Just as likely, this ostensible contradiction, along with her others, reflected her complexity and even flexibility. As a Black woman confronting multiple hardships, Amy Jacques Garvey was compelled to evince tremendous adaptability in her approach to social change. Her ability to devise multiple strategies for combating diverse social problems demonstrated her keen intelligence and tenacity. Amy's holistic approach to social change was characteristic of many Black women activists; Black women's inclusive activist orientation meant that their struggles for racial advancement embodied conservative and radical elements (Dodson and Townsend Gilkes 1987).

Through her editorials, Amy had tried to inform and educate her readers and thus inspire them to action. According to Amy, "Thought rules the world" (Garvey 1926k, 5), and she recognized that enlightened, free thought was feared by oppressors because it was the cornerstone for social change. Amy not only continually urged Blacks to "read twenty minutes daily" (Garvey 1926i, 7) but gave her readers "pep talks" of every kind to enlist them in the fight for emancipation. Amy was fully aware of the profound difficulties inherent in the struggle for liberation and constantly advised Blacks to just keep going, for "movement suggests advancement and advancement means progress. Life depends on motion" (Garvey 1926e, 5). Amy's role as "othermother" to the larger Black community was historically commonplace among Black women activists. In the effort to ensure racial survival, Black "othermothers" like Amy developed a "culture of resistance" that offered Blacks an alternative to prevailing ideologies and customs that were racist, classist, and sexist (Collins 1991, 147).

Like many Blacks who led the fight for racial advancement, Amy Jacques Garvey's roles as educator and racial activist were intertwined. Historically, Black women viewed education as a vehicle for improving the economic, social, and political well-being of Black Americans. Their central role as educators in the Black community underscored their status as "everyday political activists" (Collins 1991, 148). Amy Jacques Garvey's educational efforts paralleled those of other Black women activists, representing

a form of Afrocentric feminist political activism essential to the struggle for group survival. By placing family, children, education, and community at the center of [their] political activism, African-American women [drew] on Afrocentric conceptualizations of mothering, family, community, and empowerment. (Collins 1991, 151)

THE END OF A MARRIAGE

The anger and frustration that Amy expressed toward Black men in her "Woman's Page" may have reflected and further foreshadowed her growing discontent with Marcus. In *Garvey and Garveyism,* Amy depicted a relationship that deteriorated with time, particularly after she and Marcus started a family. Amy gave birth to two sons, Marcus Garvey, Jr. in 1930 and Julius Winston Garvey in 1933. According to Amy, Marcus was a neglectful father, who, like the men she excoriated in her "Woman's Page," failed to provide for his family and children. Marcus continually sacrificed his family for the movement, causing Amy and the children to "suffer great deprivations" (Garvey 1963, 185).

In 1935 Marcus decided to move to London, leaving Amy to raise their two small children alone in Jamaica. Amy and the children eventually joined Marcus in England in 1937. While Marcus was away in Canada at the UNIA's Eighth Convention, Amy, at her doctor's urgings, moved the children back to Jamaica. Junior's leg had become severely contracted by rheumatic fever and only warm weather could cure it. Amy made the move very quickly, without informing Marcus. She seemed to justify this decision by the urgency of the situation and argued that "if Junior fretted and died in an orthopaedic home away from us, [Marcus] would blame me to the world, for not using good judgement in his absence" (Garvey 1963, 235).

While this may be partially correct, it is more likely that Amy had become thoroughly alienated from Marcus and viewed her son's condition as an opportunity to extricate herself from the relationship. Her decision to leave England without telling Marcus was clearly a statement of anger. This move signified the formal end of her relationship with Marcus, for while she wrote him two letters from Jamaica, he was apparently too angry to respond and they ceased direct contact thereafter. Marcus died in England of a paralytic stroke on June 10, 1940.

Given her tumultuous relationship with Marcus, one is compelled to question why Amy Jacques Garvey, a powerful woman and feminist, stayed with a psychologically abusive man for almost 20 years. Bonnie Dill's (1979) hypothesis that Black women have historically taken on contradictory roles in response to racial, gender, and class oppression helps to demystify Amy's "baffling" behavior. According to Dill, Black women's "attitudes, behaviors and interpersonal relationships . . . were adaptations to a variety of factors, including the harsh realities of their environment, Afro-American cultural images of black womanhood, and the sometimes conflicting values and norms of the wider society" (p. 69). Perhaps, facing a highly discriminatory job market in which most Black women were low-paid domestics,[11] Amy was afraid that she would not be able to support her family on her own. Furthermore, because Amy viewed Black women as the moral backbone of the family and even of the community, she may have believed that it was her duty to "keep the family together" at whatever cost. As a "race woman," Amy upheld family unity as integral to racial progress and wanted to project herself as a role model for other Black Americans. In light of her multiple burdens and responsibilities, Amy's decision to stay with her husband must be seen as an intelligent coping strategy, rather than as a character flaw.

LIFE AFTER MARCUS:
A DEVOTED SOCIAL ACTIVIST

While one can only speculate as to the reasons Amy Jacques Garvey stayed with her husband, there is no question that her commitment to Garveyism outdistanced her relationship with Marcus. In addition to raising her sons, Amy Jacques Garvey remained a devoted participant in the movement for Black nationalism. She worked for the radical People's National Party of Jamaica in the 1940s and edited their party paper. Amy continued to write about Black nationalism as well. Besides editing the People's National Party's newspaper, she was a contributing editor between 1945 and 1947 to the *African,* a short-lived Black nationalist journal based in Harlem during the 1940s. Furthermore, Amy established the African Study Circle of the World in Jamaica in the late 1940s. Interestingly, only one work (Hill 1987) mentions this fact and it says nothing more about it. Amy maintained close connections with the Black nationalist community worldwide, evidenced by the fact that her one-time nemesis, W.E.B. Du Bois, solicited her help in recruiting delegates for the Fifth Pan-African Congress in 1949.

Amy Jacques Garvey's most important work was *Garvey and Garveyism,* written in 1958. Amy claimed that she decided to write this book in response to the constant questionnaires she received from "Students, Teachers [sic] and political aspirants" (Garvey 1963, 1), as well as in response to the rising tide of African independence movements. Amy was very excited about the events taking place in Africa and believed that the need to disseminate Garveyite philosophy was greater than ever. Although she was unable to secure a publisher for *Garvey and Garveyism,* she was relentless in her efforts to get it published. At the end of 1962, four years after writing the book, Amy managed to get two one-time UNIA members in the United States to loan her more than half of the printing costs. Amy, however, still had to sell the books herself and had to repay the loans with interest. In addition to selling the books, Amy sent free copies at her own expense to libraries all over the world.

A LEGACY IS CREATED

Amy Jacques Garvey's *Garvey and Garveyism* is a highly significant work for various reasons. In his book *Marcus Garvey and the Vision of Africa,* John Henrik Clarke (1974) claims that the world distribution of *Garvey and Garveyism* "brought about *the renaissance* of Garveyism" (p. 373; emphasis added). Numerous works have been written on Marcus Garvey in the past twenty years, many of which quote liberally from *Garvey and Garveyism.* In addition to elucidating Garveyism in an incisive fashion, *Garvey and Garveyism* is a comprehensive source of biographical information about Marcus Garvey. While the book also provides extensive information on Amy Jacques Garvey and her relationship with Marcus, few have ever paid any attention to this aspect of the book.

In addition to participating in many interviews for books on Marcus Garvey, Amy Jacques Garvey collaborated on works about Marcus and "his" ideals.[12] It is noteworthy that after *Garvey and Garveyism,* Amy appeared to revert to giving Marcus full credit for creating Garveyism and the Garvey movement. Perhaps she tired of fighting her invisibility to no avail, or maybe the passing of time led Amy to romanticize Marcus and her relationship with him. Whatever the case may be, the fact remains that Amy Jacques Garvey functioned as *the* central interpreter, disseminator, and guardian of the Garvey legacy. If it were not for Amy Jacques Garvey, Marcus Garvey and Garveyism might have receded into historical oblivion. That Marcus Garvey was posthumously awarded Jamaica's Order of the National Hero—the country's highest honor—is undoubtedly the result of Amy Jacques Garvey's indefatigable efforts to keep Marcus and "his" thought alive.

CONCLUSION

Amy Jacques Garvey died in Jamaica in 1973. It is unclear whether or not her death was publicly recognized. Only one work (Hill 1987) even mentions the year that she died. While Marcus's passing was received with international fanfare, Amy's death was barely noticed in comparison.

Amy seemed to blame Marcus most for having been relegated to the shadows of the Garvey movement—a fact that she made quite clear in *Garvey and Garveyism*. It is as much for this reason as any other that *Garvey and Garveyism* is an invaluable work. In addition to providing a rare window into Amy's stormy relationship with Marcus, the book establishes Amy Jacques Garvey as a highly influential person in her own right. Amy manifested the intellectual acuity and analytic sophistication of a scholar. She also embodied the personal dedication, political savvy, emotional wherewithal, and creative vision of an effective movement leader. Underlying Amy's Black nationalism and feminism was a profound commitment to social justice. Toward the end of her life, Amy still maintained that Garveyism was not only a "theoretical philosophy" but also a "working idealism" (Essien-Udom and Garvey 1977, 247). This meshing of theory with practice was integral to her social activism.

Amy's feminism represented more than a gender-conscious approach to Black nationalism. Rather, her feminism and Black nationalism were inextricably linked. Amy's ultimate goal was the liberation of all Black and Third World peoples. Nevertheless, she believed that Black and Third World women's experience of multiple oppression prepared them to lead worldwide movements for national and even human liberation. Women of color would pave the way for creating a more humane, just, and cooperative world society. According to Amy, racial uplift went beyond the desire for middle-class respectability to demand the development of a new economic order that defied the racial, class, and sexual exploitation inherent in a capitalist economy. Her comprehensive analysis of race, class, and gender, written more than 70 years ago, remains trenchant today.

The contradictions between Amy's Black nationalism and feminism and her public and private personas reflect dilemmas that many Black feminists have faced. How does one uphold racial solidarity and oppose intraracial sexism at the same time? What does it mean to be an uncompromising social activist in public and a self-sacrificing spouse in private? Such paradoxes, which have long pervaded the lives of Black women, enhance our understanding of the complex relationships among race, class, and gender.

Amy Jacques Garvey's political activism has wider implications for Black women's social change work. Like many Black women historically, Amy's activism embodied the overlapping battles for community survival and institutional change. Black women activists like Amy developed Black female "cultures of resistance" that refuted dominant ideologies about, and expectations of, Black women—both in the larger society and in Black social change movements. These Black female cultures were salient because they were often "all that [stood] between many Black women and the internalized oppression fostered by [their] status as the Other" (Collins 1991, 144). In the "Woman's Page," Amy Jacques Garvey strove to reclaim Black women's dignity and subjectivity by celebrating their lives and thought and, moreover, by placing them at the center of discourse.

The history of Black women's political activism challenges conventional definitions of power. Amy Jacques Garvey's social change work supports the claim that, historically, Black women activists rebuked traditional authority founded on lopsided power relationships. Rather, their activism was characterized by collaboration and reciprocity between "leaders" and "followers," a style reflected in the motto of the Black women's club movement: "Lifting as we climb" (Collins 1991, 158). Amy was among many Black women leaders who believed that their mission was to empower the masses to advocate on their own behalf rather than to cultivate dependence on movement leaders. Although many Black women, like Amy, never held formal titles in their respective organizations, their formidable power emanated from their Afrocentric and feminist conceptions of social change. The power that Black women garnered as community othermothers and as creators and guardians of Black feminist culture informed the platforms of many Black social change organizations, including Garveyism (Collins 1991).

Finally, one should not underestimate the role that anger played in Amy Jacques Garvey's life. Although Amy lived during a time when a woman's anger was social anathema (which it still is), she was not afraid to express her ire pointedly. Some of Amy's most radical and memorable statements were characterized by scathing anger. Perhaps because Amy Jacques Garvey was Black and female, her indignation was not seen as dangerous, certainly not as dangerous as her husband's. It is important, however, to note that Amy did not become consumed by her anger. Rather, she used it to fuel her efforts toward social change. In this way and countless others, Amy Jacques Garvey was an extraordinary woman. One can only assume that she had a profound impact on the lives of many women and men during her lifetime. Because we still have much to learn from Amy Jacques Garvey today, it is incumbent upon us to bring her life and works back into public circulation. We must create for Amy Jacques Garvey the same legacy that she so vigorously built for her husband.

NOTES

1. I credit Paula Giddings's book *When and Where I Enter: The Impact of Black Women on Race and Sex in America* (1984) for inspiring me to do research on Amy Jacques Garvey.

2. The Pan-African Conference was an outgrowth of the Pan-African Congress founded by W. E. B. DuBois.

3. Amy was among thousands of Jamaicans to emigrate in search of expanded work or educational opportunities during the early twentieth century.

4. There is an alternative explanation of how Amy Jacques was introduced to Marcus Garvey. According to one-time UNIA member George A. Weston, Amy was introduced to Marcus by Amy Ashwood after having been evicted from her apartment. Marcus then hired Amy Jacques as Amy Ashwood's assistant secretary in the UNIA (see Fax 1972). I am inclined to believe Amy Jacques's version of the introduction, which is consistent with her assertive and inquisitive nature.

5. In 1923, Marcus Garvey was convicted of using the mail to defraud individuals who held stock in his Black Star Line corporation, a Black-run shipping company he founded. Many scholars question the fairness of the trial and believe that the conviction was intended to undermine Garvey's power in the United States.

6. Most turn-of-the-century Black female reformers, such as Mary Church Terrell and Anna Julia Cooper, explicitly addressed the effects of racism and sexism on Black women's lives. Nevertheless, they clearly understood the economic implications of this "double jeopardy" for Black women.

7. The reform work of White middle-class women during the late nineteenth and early twentieth centuries (i.e., the White women's club movement) was often characterized by elitism and condescension toward the "unfortunate."

8. It is possible that many so-called "social feminists" espoused these views in the public realm only, using them primarily as ruses for advancing their public agendas.

9. Amy's criticisms of Black men presaged some of the problems addressed by Black women writers in the late 1960s and 1970s, including Toni Cade (*The Black Woman: An Anthology*) and Michele Wallace (*Black Macho and the Myth of the Superwoman*).

10. It is important to note, however, that Amy encouraged Blacks to adopt middle-class values *not* in order to become more like Whites but, rather, as a strategy for advancing racial progress.

11. In 1930, a total of 76.5 percent of employed Black women in the United States worked in personal and domestic service (see Barkley Brown 1989).

12. Amy collaborated on *More Philosophy and Opinions of Marcus Garvey* (1977) with Essien-Udom and *Marcus Garvey and the Vision of Africa* (1974) with Clarke; she authored *Black Power in America: Marcus Garvey's Impact on Jamaica and Africa* (1968) and "The Political Activities of Marcus Garvey in Jamaica" (1972).

REFERENCES

Barkley Brown, Elsa. 1989. "Womanist consciousness: Maggie Lena Walker and the Independent Order of Saint Luke." In *Black women in America: Social science perspectives,* edited by Micheline R. Malson, Elisabeth Mudimbe-Boyi, Jean F. O'Barr, and Mary Wyer. Chicago: University of Chicago Press.

Cade, Toni. 1970. *The Black woman: An anthology.* New York: New American Library.

Clarke, John Henrik. 1974. Commentary. In *Marcus Garvey and the vision of Africa,* edited by John Henrik Clarke. New York: Random House.

Collins, Patricia Hill. 1991. *Black feminist thought: Knowledge, consciousness, and the politics of empowerment.* New York: Routledge.

Cronon, Edmund David. 1955. *Black Moses.* Madison: University of Wisconsin Press.

Dill, Bonnie Thornton. 1979. The dialectics of Black womanhood. In *Black women in America: Social science perspectives,* edited by Micheline R. Malson, Elisabeth Mudimbe-Boyi, Jean F. O'Barr, and Mary Wyer. Chicago: University of Chicago Press.

Dodson, Jualyne E., and Cheryl Townsend Gilkes. 1987. Something within: Social change and collective endurance in the sacred world of Black Christian women. In *Women and religion in America.* Vol. 3, *1900-1968,* edited by Rosemary Reuther and R. Keller. New York: Harper & Row.

Essien-Udom, E. U., and Amy Jacques Garvey, eds. 1977. *More philosophy and opinions of Marcus Garvey.* London: Cass.

Fax, Elton C. 1972. *Garvey: The story of a pioneer Black nationalist.* New York: Dodd, Mead.

G., J. A. 1923. 10 minutes with Mrs. Garvey. *Negro World,* 17 March.

Garvey, Amy Jacques. 1924a. The hand that rocks the cradle. *Negro World,* 5 July.

———. 1924b. More attention given to our child life. *Negro World,* 31 May.

———. 1925a. The duty of parents to children. *Negro World,* 2 May.

———. 1925b. Is life worth living? *Negro World,* 17 October.

———. 1926a. Black women's resolve for 1926. *Negro World,* 9 January.

———. 1926b. I am a Negro—and beautiful. *Negro World,* 10 July.

———. 1926c. Labor-saving devices create unemployment among Negroes. *Negro World,* 16 October.

———. 1926d. Minerals and raw products attract white exploitation. *Negro World,* 11 September.

———. 1926e. Movement is life, stagnation death. *Negro World,* 26 June.

———. 1926f. The Negro race needs trained men. *Negro World,* 3 July.

———. 1926g. New York Jews raise over six million dollars—what of Negroes? *Negro World,* 5 June.

———. 1926h. Northern whites want Negroes sent back south. *Negro World,* 16 January.

————. 1926i. Read, think, then talk. *Negro World,* 17 July.

————. 1926j. Scanty clothes make hardy women. *Negro World,* 27 November.

————. 1926k. Why men fear thought. *Negro World,* 29 May.

————. 1926l. A woman's hands guide Indian National Congress. *Negro World,* 28 August.

————. 1926m. The world today. *Negro World,* 6 March.

————. 1927a. Acquit yourselves like men! *Negro World,* 30 April.

————. 1927b. Listen women! *Negro World,* 9 April.

————. 1927c. Populations and world areas. *Negro World,* 12 March.

————. 1963. *Garvey and Garveyism.* Kingston, Jamaica: United Printers.

————. [1923] 1967. Preface. In *Philosophy and opinions of Marcus Garvey.* Vols 1 and 2, edited by Amy Jacques Garvey. London: Cass.

————. 1968. *Black power in America: Marcus Garvey's impact on Jamaica and Africa.* Kingston, Jamaica: Author.

————. 1972. The political activities of Marcus Garvey in Jamaica. *Jamaica Journal.*

Giddings, Paula. 1984. *When and where I enter: The impact of Black women on race and sex in America.* New York: William Morrow.

Hewitt, Nancy A. 1985. Beyond the search for sisterhood: American women's history in the 1980s. *Social History* 10:299-321.

Hill, Robert A. 1987. *Marcus Garvey: Life and lessons.* Berkeley: University of California Press.

hooks, bell. 1981. *Ain't I a woman: Black women and feminism.* Boston: South End.

Hurwitz, Samuel J., and Edith F. Hurwitz. 1971. *Jamaica: A historical portrait.* New York: Praeger.

Jones, Jacqueline. 1985. *Labor of love, labor of sorrow: Black women, work and the family, from slavery to the present.* New York: Vintage.

King, Deborah K. 1988. Multiple jeopardy, multiple consciousness: The context of a Black feminist ideology. In *Black women in America: Social science perspectives,* edited by Micheline R. Malson, Elisabeth Mudimbe-Boyi, Jean F. O'Barr, and Mary Wyer. Chicago: University of Chicago Press.

Martin, Tony. 1983. *Marcus Garvey: Hero.* Dover, DE: Majority Press.

Matthews, Mark D. 1979. "Our women and what they think": Amy Jacques Garvey and the *Negro World. Black Scholar: Journal of Black Studies and Research* 10(8, 9): 2-18.

Terborg-Penn, Roslyn. 1978. Discrimination against Afro-American women in the woman's movement, 1830-1920. In *The Afro-American woman: Struggles and images,* edited by Sharon Harley and Roslyn Terborg-Penn. Port Washington, NY: Kennikat.

Vincent, Theodore G. 1972. *Black power and the Garvey movement.* Berkeley: Ramparts.

Wallace, Michele. 1979. *Black macho and the myth of the superwoman.* New York: Dial.

2 Social Location and Gender-Role Attitudes: A Comparison of Black and White Women

KAREN DUGGER

An interactive analysis of the joint effects of racism and sexism sees them as "processes standing in dynamic relation to each other" and not as "independent parallel processes" that are cumulative in their effect (Smith and Stewart 1983, 1, 6). For Black women, racism and sexism should be viewed as combining in such a way that they create a distinct social location rather than an additive form of "double disadvantage." The idea that the intersection of race and gender creates categories of people who occupy unique social spaces whose collective historical experience powerfully shapes their gender identity and attitudes is articulated in Ransford and Miller's (1983) concept of "ethgender," which they derive from Gordon's (1964) concept of "ethclass." By conceptualizing race and gender interactively, researchers are forced to recognize that racism and sexism combine to produce race-specific gender effects that generate important experiential cleavages among women. These cleavages may in turn result in ideological differences or differences in women's identity and gender-role attitudes (Dill 1983; Smith and Stewart 1983; White 1984).

AUTHOR'S NOTE: My experience at the Race and Gender Summer Institute at Memphis State University was particularly invaluable in providing me with the conceptual framework necessary for an adequate expression of my ideas. This work has also benefited from comments and suggestions by Myra Marx Ferree, the editor, and anonymous reviewers, of *Gender & Society,* and Daniel Quinlan's advice on data analysis.

If the forms and effects of sexism as well as responses to it vary according to race, more race-gender groups must be included in research designs (Smith and Stewart 1983). Identification of differences and commonalities among race-gender groups will dispel false universalization, which has portrayed the experience of White,[1] often middle-class, women as the experience of womankind and has distorted analyses of the operation and consequences of sexism. False universalization also sets up White women as the norm against which Black women may appear to be deviant cases (Gilkes 1979; Gump 1980). Realizing that generalizations about sexism are race specific promotes a reevaluation of feminist theories by forcing us to ask to what gender-race group our knowledge applies and how current explanatory frameworks might be changed if the perspective and experiential base of Black women's lives were considered (Dill 1983; hooks 1984; Smith and Stewart 1983).

Several theorists have maintained that women's position within two systems of social relations, that of production and that of reproduction, is primary in the formation of their gender-role attitudes and identity (Eisenstein 1981; Hartmann 1983; Petchesky 1983). At the crux of these theoretical formulations is the assertion that women's increased independence in both spheres makes them more likely to challenge the dominant culture's[2] views of gender. Concerning production, Eisenstein asserts that women's combined work as wage laborers and wives and mothers heightens the contradiction between the ideology of equal employment opportunity found in the marketplace and the patriarchal structuring of women's location in this marketplace and in the home. She further argues that women's labor-force participation encourages questioning the low valuation and justice of women's primary responsibility for domestic labor. In support of Eisenstein's thesis, research on White women has consistently demonstrated that employed women are more likely than women not in the labor force to hold nontraditional attitudes toward gender roles (Mason, Czajka, and Arber 1986; Spitze 1978; Thorton and Freedman 1979; Thorton, Alwin, and Camburn 1983). However, in the few studies that have included Black women, the results were mixed (Macke, Hudis, and Larrick 1977; Ransford and Miller 1983).

Concerning reproduction, Petchesky contends that women's reproductive relationships determine whether they will possess a "pro-life" or "pro-choice" orientation. For her, women highly invested in production, as evidenced by high labor-force participation and low fertility, are more likely to reject culturally dominant views of gender, whereas those highly invested in reproduction, as evidenced by low labor-force participation and high fertility, are likely to "adhere to traditional family forms and ideologies that certify woman's primary function as a homemaker and childrearer" (1983, 236).

The interactive approach just outlined informs the aims and analytical strategy of this study. These aims are twofold: to explore the commonalities and differences in the gender-role attitudes of Black and White women and to assess the applicability to Black women of the hypothesis that investment in reproductive relations exerts a conservative influence on gender-role attitudes, whereas investment in productive relations has a radical impact.

SOURCES OF GENDER-ROLE ATTITUDES

The argument that the differential location of women in the systems of production and reproduction creates distinct life experiences and, hence, distinct forms of attitudes toward gender roles suggests a wide gap between Black and White women. From slavery to the present, it is precisely with regard to productive and reproductive activities that racial oppression has most dramatically differentiated them. While nineteenth-century culture in the United States stereotyped White women as too frail and dainty to undertake physical labor, Black women were viewed as beasts of burden and subjected to the same demeaning labor and hardships as Black men (hooks 1981; King 1975; Ladner 1971; Welter 1978). Angela Davis asserts that slavery constructed for Black women an alternative definition of womanhood, one that included a tradition of "hard work, perseverance and self-reliance, a legacy of tenacity, resistance and an insistence on sexual equality" (1981, 29).

The continued exploitation of Black labor into the twentieth century has meant the continued coercion of Black women into the paid labor force. Racial discrimination has produced high rates of unemployment among Black men and segregated them into low-paying jobs, and thus the Black family needs the labor of more than one wage earner. While Black women do not work only out of economic necessity (Gump 1980), the reality of racism continues to shape the context within which they develop and construct their definitions of womanhood. Thus a primary cleavage in the life experiences of Black and White women is their past and present relationship to the labor process. In consequence, Black women's conceptions of womanhood emphasize self-reliance, strength, resourcefulness, autonomy, and the responsibility of providing for the material as well as emotional needs of family members (Ladner 1971). Black women do not see labor-force participation and being a wife and mother as mutually exclusive; rather, within Black culture, employment is an integral, normative, and traditional component of the roles of wife and mother (Gump 1980; Malson 1983).

Thus it could be hypothesized that Black women will be more likely than White women to challenge the dominant culture's definitions of women and their socially prescribed roles. However, recent demographic trends show a growing similarity in the productive and reproductive profiles of Black and White women. An increasing number of White women are having children outside marriage, living without husbands, and heading households, coming more to resemble Black women (Hartmann 1983). Almquist (1979) argues that the objective status of Black and White women is converging as their labor force participation rates, earnings, and occupational distribution have become virtually indistinguishable. On the basis of these trends and the premise that productive and reproductive relationships are primary in constructing women's gender-role attitudes, we could expect White women to also reject a view of gender roles that makes market work and family work incompatible, and evidence exists that more and more they do (Cherlin and Walters 1981; Macke et al. 1977; Mason et al. 1986; Thorton et al. 1983; Thorton and Freedman 1979). But, in the instances in which Black women formed a comparison group, they were *more* likely than White women to reject this view of appropriate roles for women (Cherlin and Walters 1981; Fulenwider 1980). Other confounding data showed that Black women were at least as *accepting* as White women, if not more accepting, of views of women that emphasized femininity, self-sacrifice, and motherhood (Gump 1975; Hermons 1980; Hershey 1978).

In an attempt to reconcile these findings, Ransford and Miller (1983) took a multidimensional approach to measuring gender-role traditionalism and found no difference between Black and White women. They concluded that the Black female autonomy and independence described by Ladner does not appear to translate into a critique of women's traditional roles. Weitzman (1984) has argued that the inconsistencies may be due to social class differences in the populations studied. Though class variation in research samples may to some degree account for the discrepancies, nationally representative samples that controlled for class are also inconsistent (Cherlin and Walters 1981; Fulenwider

1980; Ransford and Miller 1983). Another source of the diverse results is the dimensions of gender roles used. Cherlin and Walters (1981) and Ransford and Miller (1983), for example, examined attitudes about the suitability and appropriateness of women's presence in the public worlds of work and politics, while Gump (1975), Hershey (1978), and Hermons (1980) measured women's identification with the values of "femininity" and the private roles of wife and mother.

Lastly, an important source of these diverse findings may simply be the contradictory nature of Black women's lives. Dill (1979) cautions that any analysis of Black women must consider the contradictions imposed on them by White norms and expectations. Black women have had to reconcile being strong, independent economic providers with simultaneously investing a substantial part of their identity in being wives and mothers and feminine women. The constant cultural assaults on their identity, being labeled "jezebels," "matriarchs," and "sapphires" (Gilkes 1979; White 1985) may have generated an idealization of certain components of the dominant culture's views of womanhood.

RESEARCH DESIGN

Hypotheses

This study investigates two competing hypotheses concerning the gender-role attitudes of Black and White women. One is that Black women will be more rejecting of the dominant culture's views than White women because their productive and reproductive experiences have stood in greater contradiction to these views. Alternatively, it could be expected that there will be little difference in Black and White women's gender-role attitudes because White women's productive and reproductive profiles have increasingly come to resemble those of Black women, and because the dominant culture's assaults on Black women may lead them to embrace the views of gender embodied in these assaults.

The structures of racial privilege and racial oppression that have determined the historical experiences of Black and White women created distinct cultural legacies. As discussed, the legacy available to Black women has been more at odds with culturally dominant definitions of gender than that of White women. The socialization of Black women into this cultural legacy, as well as the continued precarious condition of Black women as a collectivity, may be more important in shaping their gender-role attitudes than their own individual productive and reproductive experiences. White women's history of race privilege, on the other hand, has served to affirm rather than undermine the dominant culture's definition of appropriate roles for women. Individual productive and reproductive experiences at variance with White women's cultural heritage may, therefore, play a more important part in shaping their gender-role attitudes. Given these considerations, it is expected that the hypothesis regarding investment in production and reproduction will be more applicable to White than Black women.

Sample

The data for this study come from the Roper Organization's 1980 Virginia Slims American Women's Opinion Poll. Roper employed a multistage stratified probability sample of the noninstitutionalized adult female population of the continental United States. There were 296 Black women and 2,607 White women in the sample.

Measures

Scales representing eight dimensions of gender-role attitudes were constructed from questionnaire items (available upon request from the author). The scales spanned a variety of gender-role attitudes. All were coded such that higher scores indicated greater rejection of culturally dominant views. Face validity of these scales implied congruence with challenges to culturally dominant definitions of gender roles found in recent feminist writings and articulated in a variety of women's movement activities. Perceptions of sex discrimination (*discrimination*), of women's ability to perform competently in public-sphere positions dominated by men (*public sphere*), admiration for women who are independent, intelligent, and outspoken (*female gender stereotyping*), and a rejection of stereotypical roles for boys and girls (*stereotyping of children's gender roles*) are core components of such challenges. Values concerning sexual freedom (*new morality*), the acceptance of nontraditional family structures (*traditional family*), rejection of marital roles that define the husband as provider and wife as nurturer (*traditional marriage*), and support for the efforts and goals of the women's movement (*women's movement*), are likewise integral components of contemporary challenges to culturally dominant views of appropriate gender roles.

Investment in production was measured by combining the scores on two variables, employment status (employed full- or part-time, not employed) and preference for working versus staying at home and taking care of a house and family. A 4-point continuum was constructed on which 1 = not working and prefer not to, 2 = working but prefer not to, 3 = not working but prefer to, and 4 = working and prefer to. Marital status and having children were combined to create live dummy variables as indicators of *investment in reproduction:* married, no children; separated or divorced, no children; never married, no children; separated or divorced with children; and never-married with children. Married women with children served as the reference category.

Three other sociodemographic variables were included in the analysis: the respondent's education (measured on a 7-point scale ranging from 1 = no school to 7 = postgraduate), family income (measured on an 8-point scale ranging from 1 = under $3,000 to 8 = over $25,000), and age (measured on an 8-point scale ranging from 1 = 18-20 to 8 = 65 and over). Age was taken as an indicator of the cultural milieu in which the respondent was living and was socialized (Mason et al., 1976).

RESULTS

Effects of Race on Gender-Role Attitudes

The bivariate regressions showed Black women to be more rejecting of the dominant culture's views of gender than White women on all but two of the eight indices (see Table 2.1). The gender-role attitudes that evidenced the largest differences were *women's movement* (b = .322), *new morality* (b = .234), and *female gender stereotyping* (b = . 332). Black women were also somewhat more likely than White women to reject the dominant culture's definitions of *traditional family* (b = .155) and *traditional marriage* (b = .137) and to believe that women are victims of *discrimination* (b = .084). No significant difference was found between Black and White women's attitudes toward women in the *public sphere* (b = −.042). In contrast to their greater rejection of *female gender stereotyping,* Black women were more likely than White women to support the *stereotyping of children's gender roles* (b = −.089). When other sociodemographic variables were controlled, the effects of *race* remained virtually unchanged or only slightly reduced on five of the six variables for which the bivariate regressions indicated

TABLE 2.1 Regression of Gender-Role Attitudes on Race Alone, and Controlling for Socioeconomic Status, Age, and Investment in Production and Reproduction

	Women's Movement		New Morality		Traditional Family		Traditional Marriage		Public Sphere		Discrimination		Stereotyping of Children's Gender Roles		Female Gender Stereotyping	
	b	β	b	β	b	β	b	β	b	β	b	β	b	β	b	β
Bivariate regression																
Race	.322	.15**	.234	.11*	.155	.06**	.137	.07**	−.042	.04	.084	.05*	−.089	−.10**	.332	.11**
R^2		.021		.011		.004		.055		.001		.002		.010		.011
Multivariate regression																
Race	.296	.14**	.187	.09**	.112	.05*	.034	.02	−.020	−.02	.079	.04*	−.058	−.06**	.331	.11**
Education	.049	.09**	.012	.02	.040	.07**	.027	.06**	.041	.14**	.027	.06**	.034	.15**	.058	.07**
Income	.015	.05*	.022	.07**	.019	.05*	−.002	−.01	.010	.06*	.019	.07**	.013	.10**	.003	.01
Age	−.034	−.11**	−.068	−.23**	−.076	−.22	−.032	−.12**	−.042	−.25**	−.020	−.08**	−.004	−.03	−.046	−.10**
Investment in production	.115	.22**	.061	.12*	.080	.13**	.174	.38**	.029	.10**	.044	.10**	.021	.10**	.037	.05*
Never-married, with children	.149	.03	.401	.07**	.461	.07**	.10	.02	−.051	−.02	.228	.05*	.023	.01	.076	.01
Never-married, no children	−.005	.00	.142	.06**	−.014	−.01	.020	.01	−.015	−.01	.012	.01	−.008	−.01	−.007	.00
Separated or divorced, with children	.124	.05**	.120	.05**	.207	.08**	.210	.10**	.057	.04*	.181	.09**	.064	.06**	.094	.03
Separated or divorced, no children	.112	.02	.312	.06**	.185	.03	.249	.06**	.003	.00	.141	.03	.012	.01	.295	.04*
Married, no children	.005	.00	.051	.03	−.022	−.01	.00	.00	−.011	−.01	−.023	−.01	−.056	−.07**	−.049	−.02
R^2		.13		.14		.13		.22		.14		.06		.08		.04
Intercept		1.94		1.63		1.80		1.24		1.60		1.58		1.56		1.56

*$p < .05$; **$p < .01$.

significant racial differences (see Table 2.1). The original effect of *race* on *traditional marriage* (b = .137) was substantially reduced (b = .034).

Correlates of Gender-Role
Attitudes and Interaction Effects

The hypothesis that the impact of investment in production and reproduction on gender-role attitudes would be race specific required a method for determining the presence of interaction effects. One such method would be to add product terms representing these interactions to the regression equations. However, to avoid problems of multicollinearity and to obtain more detailed data on the forms of the interactions, an alternative method was employed (Ransford and Miller 1983). Separate regressions for Black and White women were performed and differences in their slopes tested for significance.

The unstandardized regression coefficients for *investment in production* supported the hypothesis that its effects on gender-role attitudes would be race specific and more radicalizing of White than Black women (see Tables 2.2 and 2.3). For White women, *investment in production* consistently predicted gender-role attitudes across all eight dimensions. For Black women, it significantly predicted only two dimensions: *women's movement* and *traditional marriage*. One-tailed *t* tests indicated that race interacted significantly with *new morality* ($p < .05$), *traditional family* ($p < .05$), and *traditional marriage* ($p < .01$). Thus *investment in production* did predict White women's attitudes toward sexuality and family issues but failed to do so for Black women. While *investment in production* was an important predictor of both Black (b = 105, β = .19) and White (b = .180, β = .40) women's attitudes toward *traditional marriage,* its effect for Whites was significantly and substantially stronger.

Analysis of the unstandardized regression coefficients for *investment in reproduction* also demonstrated race-specific effects. According to Petchesky's hypothesis, we would expect never-married women and divorced or separated women without children to be the most rejecting of culturally dominant views. The results for White women (see Table 2.2) showed, however, that except on the issue of *new morality* (b = .127), never-married women without children did not differ significantly from married women with children in their gender-role attitudes. Rather, it was separated or divorced women *with* children who were most likely to challenge the dominant culture's views of gender roles,

TABLE 2.2 Regression of Gender-Role Attitudes on Socioeconomic Status, Age, and Investment in Production and Reproduction for White Women

	Women's Movement		New Morality		Traditional Family		Traditional Marriage		Public Sphere		Discrimination		Stereotyping of Children's Gender Roles		Female Gender Stereotyping	
	b	β	b	β	b	β	b	β	b	β	b	β	b	β	b	β
Socioeconomic status																
Education	.051	.09**	.008	.02	.041	.07**	.029	.06**	.047	.16**	.028	.06**	.037	.16**	.061	.08**
Family income	.020	.06**	.016	.05*	.015	.04	-.002	-.01	.009	.05*	.018	.07**	.014	.10**	.00	.00
Age	-.035	-.11**	-.068	-.23**	-.079	-.23**	-.035	-.13**	-.046	-.28**	-.021	-.09**	-.005	-.04	-.047	-.11**
Social location																
Investment in production	.113	.21**	.063	.12**	.087	.15**	.180	.40**	.031	.11**	.044	.11**	.022	.10**	.034	.05*
Never-married, with children	.319	.04	.418	.05*	.588	.06**	.303	.05*	-.061	-.01	.287	.04*	-.015	.00	.064	.01
Never-married, no children	.020	.01	.127	.06**	-.080	-.03	-.032	-.02	-.047	-.04	-.030	-.02	-.012	-.01	.025	-.01
Separated or divorced, with children	.155	.06**	.158	.07**	.235	.08**	.200	.09**	.027	.02	.186	.10**	.077	.08**	.106	.03
Separated or divorced, no children	.169	.03	.332	.06**	.205	.03	.216	.05*	-.024	-.01	.108	.02	.015	.01	.332	.04*
Married, no children	.007	.00	.049	.02	-.049	-.02	-.014	-.01	-.026	-.02	-.015	-.01	-.050	-.06**	-.052	-.02
R²	.12		.12		.12		.24		.16		.05		.08		.03	
Intercept	1.90		1.67		1.82		1.24		1.60		1.59		1.54		1.58	

*$p < .05$; **$p < .01$.

41

TABLE 2.3 Regression of Gender-Role Attitudes on Socioeconomic Status, Age, and Investment in Production and Reproduction for Black Women

	Women's Movement		New Morality		Traditional Family		Traditional Marriage		Public Sphere		Discrimination		Stereotyping of Children's Gender Roles		Female Gender Stereotyping	
	b	β	b	β	b	β	b	β	b	β	b	β	b	β	b	β
Socioeconomic status																
Education	.029	.07	.023	.04	.025	.04	.029	.06	.000	.00	.016	.03	.008	.03	.014	.02
Family income	-.013	-.06	.061	.21**	.059	.18*	.006	.02	.019	.12	.023	.08	.008	.06	.029	.07
Age	-.024	-.11	-.069	-.24**	-.055	-.16*	-.006	-.02	-.003	-.02	.007	.03	.007	.05	-.031	-.07
Social location																
Investment in production	.134	.31**	.011	.02	.017	.03	.105	.19**	.017	.05	.051	.09	.023	.08	.085	.10
Never-married, with children	-.043	-.02	.391	.16**	.526	.18**	.096	.04	.151	.11	.255	.11	.067	.06	.159	.04
Never-married, no children	-.200	-.12	.224	.11	.477	.20**	.427	.20**	.276	.23**	.346	.17*	.031	.03	.150	.05
Separated or divorced, with children	-.078	-.05	-.068	-.04	.149	.07	.355	.19**	.257	.24**	.181	.10	-.006	-.01	.015	.01
Separated or divorced, no children	-.143	-.06	.239	.07	.167	.04	.410	.12*	.107	.06	.250	.08	-.021	-.01	.179	.04
Married, no children	-.082	-.06	.062	.04	.131	.06	.065	.04	.053	.05	-.075	-.04	-.13	-.15*	-.029	-.01
R^2	.13		.24		.18		.15		.11		.10		.05		.05	
Intercept	2.40		1.71		1.81		1.23		1.43		1.56		1.57		1.73	

*$p < .05$; **$p < .01$.

differing positively from married women with children on six of the eight dimensions. Children were also a radicalizing force for White never-married women who, compared to their married counterparts with children, were more rejecting of the dominant culture's views on four dimensions. Among White women, the most conservative reproductive category was married women without children. They were similar to married women with children except that they were *more* likely to hold gender-stereotyped views of children's roles (b = −.050). The only unequivocal support for the hypothesis that lack of *investment in reproduction* is radicalizing was the finding that on three of the dimensions of gender-role attitudes, separated or divorced women with no children were more liberal than married women with children.

Among Black women it was never-married women without children who most rejected the dominant culture's views of gender roles. They differed significantly from their married counterparts with children on four of the eight dimensions: *traditional family* (b = .477), *traditional marriage* (b = .427), *public sphere* (b = .276), and *discrimination* (b = .346). One-tailed *t* tests comparing these coefficients with those for White women of the same reproductive category showed all four were significantly different ($p < .001$). Thus the data demonstrated a significant gap in the gender-role attitudes of Black never-married women without children and Black married women with children. However, there was no such gap between these same categories of White women. This finding is contrary to the prediction that *investment in reproduction* would have a more conservative influence on the gender-role attitudes of White than Black women.

Similar to the results for Whites, children were also a radicalizing force for Black never-married and separated or divorced women. Never-married mothers were more likely than married mothers to reject the belief that sexual freedom (b = .391) causes the disintegration of family and society and to view family forms other than the nuclear one as legitimate (b = .526). While not significant, most probably due to the small N for Black women, never-married mothers were also more likely to believe women to be competent in the *public sphere* (b = .151) and to be discriminated against in this sphere (b = .255). One-tailed *t* tests found no significant differences in the slopes of Black and White women in this reproductive category. Hence having children without being married appears to affect the gender-role attitudes of Black and White women in similar ways.

The results for separated and divorced Black women with children showed that on two dimensions, *public sphere* (b = .257) and *traditional marriage* (b = .355), they were more likely than their married counterparts to reject the dominant culture's views of gender roles. The gap in gender-role attitudes between separated and divorced mothers and married mothers was, however, greater for White than Black women. One-tailed t tests showed that on two variables, *women's movement* ($p < .05$) and *new morality* ($p < .05$), the unstandardized regression coefficients of Black separated and divorced women with children and those of White women in the same reproductive category were significantly different. Hence being separated or divorced and having children appears to be more radicalizing for White than for Black women.

Other sociodemographic variables also evidenced race-specific effects. In general, among both Blacks and Whites, older women were more accepting of culturally dominant views of gender-roles. However, for White women, age predicted acceptance of *traditional marriage* (b = −.035) and rejection of women in the *public sphere* (b = −.046), while for Black women, it did not (b = −.006 and b = −.003, respectively). The differences in these coefficients were significant at $p < .01$ and $p < .001$, respectively.

On indicators of SES, *education* and *income* were important predictors of White women's gender-role altitudes, while for Black women, *income* exerted a stronger influence. That is, White women with more education and higher income rejected culturally dominant views of women; Black women with greater income did so. On the variables *public sphere* (b = .047) and *stereotyping of children's gender roles* (b = .037), *education* substantially influenced the attitudes of White women and had virtually no effect on those of Black women (b = .000 and b = .008, respectively). Differences in the unstandardized regression coefficients of Black and White women on these variables were significant at $p < .01$ and $p < .05$, respectively. On the other hand, one-tailed t tests showed *income* had a more liberalizing impact on Black women's attitudes toward *new morality* ($p < .01$) and *traditional family* ($p < .05$) than it did on White women's.

SUMMARY AND DISCUSSION

This chapter has examined the commonalities and differences in the gender-role attitudes of Black and White women. It has done so from a perspective that views the intersection of race and gender as creating distinct collective historical experiences for Black and White women that have differentially shaped their definitions of womanhood and gender-role expectations. The pattern of similarities and differences found in the data are consistent with, and offer some insights into, the contradictory results of past research.

To summarize, when sociodemographic variables other than race were controlled, as in five of the eight dimensions of gender-role attitudes, Black women were more rejecting of culturally dominant views than White women. This set of findings supports the contention of Ladner (1971), Dill (1979), Davis (1981), and others that Black women's long history of economic participation has given rise to definitions of womanhood at odds with those of the dominant culture. On the other hand, the findings of no difference between Black and White women on the variables *traditional marriage* and *public sphere* are consistent with the research of Ransford and Miller (1983) and suggest that as the objective statuses of Black and White women become similar, we can expect greater similarity in their gender-role attitudes. The fact that *age* was more strongly correlated with these gender-role attitudes for White than Black women strengthens this interpretation. Thus Black and White women's views of gender roles appear to be most similar on issues related to preference for wage labor and the ability and right of women to achieve in the public-sphere worlds of work and politics, which makes sense given that the greatest demographic shift for White women has been the dramatic increase in their labor-force participation (Hartmann 1983; Smith 1979).

The finding that Black women were more likely than White women to hold stereotypical views of girls' and boys' domestic roles accords with the results of Gump (1975), Hermons (1980), and Hershey (1978), and indicates that on issues of "femininity" and "masculinity," Black women's longer history of economic activity does not translate into a greater propensity to challenge the dominant culture's views. Their attitudes may be due to the labeling of Black women as "matriarchs" and "sapphires" who rob their sons and men in general of their manhood. This accusation, thrown at Black women by both the White and Black communities (Bond and Peery 1970; Moynihan 1965; Staples 1971), may generate a defensive acceptance of the normative structure that produced the cultural assault in the first place (Terrelonge 1984).

Taken as a whole, the preceding data are compatible with the conclusion that the commonalities and differences in Black and White women's gender-role attitudes are partly explicable in terms of the extent of historical overlap and divergence in their collective productive and reproductive experiences. However, the finding that Black women are more accepting than White women of stereotypical gender roles for children suggests the importance of the dominant culture in creating different experiences for Black and White women and, therefore, different responses to gender-role prescriptions.

In addition to examining the gender-role attitudes of Black and White women, this study also assessed the applicability to Black women of the hypothesis that investment in reproduction exerts a conservative influence on women's gender-role attitudes whereas investment in production has a radical impact. This hypothesis was expected to be less valid for Black than White women, and in part the data supported this contention. While investment in market work did influence the gender-role altitudes of both racial groups, it had a more extensive and pronounced effect on those of White women. Particularly important in this regard was the lack of correlation between Black women's commitment to labor-force participation and their attitudes toward family structure and sexual freedom. These issues are hallmarks of the "pro-life" platform and the dimensions of gender-role attitudes that, according to Petchesky (1983), investment in production should best predict.

The cultural legacies bequeathed to Black and White women by virtue of their distinct productive and reproductive histories may account for these results. Since the majority of White women have only recently entered the paid labor force, the experience has meant a greater break with the dominant culture's views of gender roles than for Black women and may, therefore, provoke a wider and stronger questioning of these views. Conversely, within Black culture wage labor has been a normative and integral component of womanhood. Moreover, Black women's experience of family has been fundamentally structured by racial oppression. The investment-in-production hypothesis ignores this reality. Yet it is reasonable to posit that the dynamics of racial subordination are as important, if not more so, in shaping Black women's gender-role attitudes, particularly those concerning issues of family, as are the dynamics of gender subordination. Several writers have contended that White feminist analysis has portrayed the family as the major site of women's oppression, ignoring the reality of Black women, who view the family as a refuge from the racism of the larger society and who find family work, in contrast to market work, affirming of their humanity (Davis 1981; Dill 1983; hooks 1984; White, 1984). Moreover, racial discrimination in the labor market has produced low-wage jobs and high levels of unemployment among Black men, creating a higher incidence of woman-headed families in the Black than in the White community. Black women's long experience with family forms at odds with those of the dominant culture may partially explain the failure of investment in production to predict their attitudes toward family structure. The finding that investment in production did not predict Black women's attitudes toward sexual freedom may have similar roots. Because racial subordination has made Black family life highly problematic, Black women are likely to view the disintegration of their family and community life as more a product of racism than of sexual freedom for women.

The thesis that investment in reproduction commits women to conservative views of gender roles received limited support. To the contrary, both Black and White married women without children were no more rejecting of culturally dominant views of gender roles than married women with children. The finding that White never-married women without children were basically as accepting of the dominant culture's definition of gender roles as married women with children also contradicts the investment-in-reproduction argument. Finally, the data clearly demonstrated that single parenting could be a radicalizing experience. Among both Blacks and Whites, separated, divorced, and never-married women with children were more likely to challenge culturally dominant views of women's roles than were married women without children.

The contention that investment in reproduction would have a more conservative impact on the gender-role attitudes of White than Black women received mixed support. It was contradicted by the finding that, among Blacks, never-married women without children were those most likely to challenge culturally dominant views, whereas among Whites, never-married women without children were as accepting of these views as married women with children. It was supported, however, by the results that showed that the gender-role attitudes of White separated or divorced mothers diverged more dramatically from those of White married mothers than was the case for Blacks.

The cultural traditions into which Black and White women are socialized may account for these race-specific effects. Joseph (1981) found that the messages White daughters received from their mothers conveyed a more positive view of men and a more romanticized notion of marriage than those received by Black women. Other researchers have pointed out that Black women hold negative attitudes toward the reliability of men and are skeptical of the desirability and security of marriage (Hershey 1978; Ladner 1971). Thus being a separated or divorced woman with children is more likely to contradict the cultural expectations of White than Black women and consequently can be expected to have a greater impact on their gender-role attitudes. Conversely, White never-married women without children and White married women with and without children are less likely to have experienced circumstances dramatically at odds with their cultural heritage, and this may explain the similarity in their gender-role attitudes. Finally, the results also suggest that Black women's greater rejection of the dominant culture's views of gender roles is weakened by being married and, to a lesser extent, by having been married.

Implications for Feminist Theory

The results previously summarized have several implications for constructing feminist theory. The data showing that single parenting could have a radicalizing impact on the gender-role attitudes of both Black and White women underscore the theoretical insights to be gained by theorizing from the perspective of women of color. For example, underlying the contention that high fertility makes women more likely to adopt conservative views of gender is the assumption that having children creates dependency on a male breadwinner and, therefore, commits women to a system of values that protects and promotes this dependency. Had the reality of Black women's lives informed this analysis, a more nuanced understanding of the role of reproduction in structuring women's views of gender would have emerged. To begin with, both Ladner (1971) and Stack (1974) have documented that to ensure the survival of themselves and their children, Black women have developed kin networks centered on the close domestic cooperation of adult women, leaving them less reliant on husband, father, or the traditional family structure. Further, several writers have pointed out that it is often Black women's high investment in reproduction, that is, their commitment to family and children, that has been the force behind their political activism (Gilkes 1979, 1986; Jones 1982; White 1985).

The results of this study also illuminate the fallacy of treating race and gender as separable or discrete phenomena structured by dynamics unique to each. The race-specific effects found in the data become comprehensible only by considering how the dynamics of race have differentially structured Black and White women's experience of gender. Moreover, by recognizing that gender is constitutively related to race, we are forced to consider the historical and sociocultural context of women's lives when theorizing about the forces that shape their gender identity and attitudes. In so doing, we avoid the tendency to treat gender in abstract and universalistic ways. We also avoid treating such phenomena as production and reproduction as though the meaning and impact they have on women's lives is independent of their race (and class) location. In conclusion, the findings of this study make clear that as long as women of color are excluded form our analyses, the result will be a partial and distorted understanding of the forces structuring women's experience of and attitudes toward gender.

NOTES

1. I capitalize *White* and *Black* to emphasize the point that race structures the experiences of both groups, albeit in different ways. Both racial privilege and racial oppression create categories of people with unique historical experiences that significantly shape their gender identity and attitudes.
2. I use the concept *dominant culture* with regard to views of gender instead of *traditional* for two reasons. First, several authors have pointed out that what has been the traditional role of women in the dominant White culture has differed from the traditional role of women in Black culture (Dill 1979; Gump 1980; hooks 1984). Thus using the term dominant culture as opposed to traditional avoids false universalization. Second, the term dominant culture acknowledges the cultural hegemony of Whites in defining the traditional role of womankind.

REFERENCES

Almquist, Elizabeth. 1979. Black women and the pursuit of equality. In *Women: A feminist perspective,* edited by Jo Freeman. Palo Alto, CA: Mayfield.
Bond, Jean Carey, and Pat Peery. 1970. Is the black male castrated? In *The black woman: An anthology,* edited by Toni Cade. New York: New American Library.
Cherlin, Andrew, and Pamela Walters. 1981. Trends in United States men's and women's sex-role attitudes: 1972-1978. *American Sociological Review* 46:453-60.
Davis, Angela. 1981. *Women, race and class.* New York: Random House.
Dill, Bonnie Thornton. 1979. The dialectics of black womanhood. *Signs: Journal of Women in Culture and Society* 4:535-55.
———. 1983. Race, class, and gender: Prospects for an all-inclusive sisterhood. *Feminist Studies* 9:131-49.
Eisenstein, Zillah. 1981. *The radical future of liberal feminism.* New York: Longman.
Fulenwider, Claire Knoche. 1980. *Feminism in American politics.* New York: Praeger.
Gilkes, Cheryl Townsend. 1979. Black women's work as deviance: Social sources of racial antagonism within contemporary feminism. Working Paper No. 66. Center for Research on Women, Wellesley College, Wellesley, MA.

————. 1986. Approaches to social change: Racial-ethnic women's community work. Paper presented at the Summer Research Institute on Race and Gender. Memphis State University, Memphis, TN.

Gordon, Milton. 1964. *Assimilation in American life.* New York: Oxford University Press.

Gump, Janice Porter. 1975. Comparative analysis of black women's and white women's sex-role attitudes. *Journal of Consulting and Clinical Psychology* 43:858-63.

————. 1980. Reality and myth: Employment and sex-role ideology in black women. In *The psychology of women: Directions in research,* edited by Julia Sherman and Florence L. Denmark. New York: Psychological Dimensions.

Hartmann, Heidi. 1983. Changes in women's economic and family roles in post World War II United States. Paper presented at the Conference on Women and Structural Transformation: The Crises of Work and Family Life, Rutgers University, New Brunswick, NJ.

Hermons, Willa Mae. 1980. The women's liberation movement: Understanding black women's attitudes. Pp. 285-99 in *The black woman,* edited by La Frances Rogers-Rose. Beverly Hills, CA: Sage.

Hershey, Marjorie Randon. 1978. Racial differences in sex-role identities and sex stereotyping: Evidence against a common assumption. *Social Science Quarterly* 58:583-96.

hooks, bell. 1981. *Ain't I a woman?* Boston: South End Press.

————. 1984. *Feminist theory: From margin to center.* Boston: South End Press.

Jones, Jacqueline. 1982. My mother was much of a woman: Black women, work, and the family under slavery. *Feminist Studies* 8:235-69.

Joseph, Gloria. 1981. Black mothers and daughters: Their roles and functions in American society. In *Common differences,* by Gloria Joseph and Jill Lewis. New York: Doubleday Anchor.

King, Mae C. 1975. Oppression and power: The unique status of the black woman in the American political system. *Social Science Quarterly* 56:116-28.

Ladner, Joyce. 1971. *Tomorrow's tomorrow.* Garden City, NY: Doubleday.

Macke, Anne Statham, Paula Hudis, and Don Larrick. 1977. Sex-role attitudes and employment among women: A dynamic model of change and continuity. Paper prepared for the Secretary of Labor's Invitational Conference on the National Longitudinal Surveys of Mature Women, Washington, DC.

Malson, Michelene Ridley. 1983. Black women's sex roles: The social context for a new ideology. *Journal of Social Issues* 39:101-13.

Mason, Karen Oppenheim, John L. Czajka, and Sara Arber. 1986. Change in U.S. women's sex-role attitudes, 1964-1974. *American Sociological Review* 81:573-96.

Moynihan, Daniel. 1965. *The Negro family: The case for national action.* Office of Policy Planning and Research, Department of Labor. Washington, DC: Government Printing Office.

Petchesky, Rosalind Pollack. 1983. Reproduction and class divisions among women. In *Class, race, and sex: The dynamics of control,* edited by Amy Swerdlow and Hanna Lessinger. Boston: G. K. Hall.

Ransford, Edward H., and John Miller. 1983. Race, sex and feminist outlooks. *American Journal of Sociology* 48:46-59.

Smith, Althea, and Abigail J. Stewart. 1983. Approaches to studying racism and sexism in black women's lives. *Journal of Social Issues* 39:1-15.

Smith, Ralph E. 1979. The movement of women into the labor force. In *The subtle revolution,* edited by Ralph E. Smith. Washington, DC: Urban Institute.

Spitze, Glenna D. 1978. Labor force and work attitudes: A longitudinal test of the role hiatus hypothesis. *Journal of Marriage and the Family* 40:471-79.

Stack, Carol B. 1974. *All our kin.* New York: Harper & Row.

Staples, Robert. 1971. The myth of black matriarchy. In *The black family: Essays and studies,* edited by Robert Staples. Belmont, CA: Wadsworth.

Terrelonge, Pauline. 1984. Feminist consciousness and black women. In *Women: A feminist perspective,* edited by Jo Freeman. Palo Alto, CA: Mayfield.

Thorton, Arland, Duane F. Alwin, and Donald Camburn. 1983. Causes and consequences of sex-role attitudes and attitude change. *American Sociological Review* 48:211-27.

Thorton, Arland, and Deborah Freedman. 1979. Changes in the sex-role attitudes of women, 1962-1977: Evidence from a panel study. *American Sociological Review* 44:831-42.

Weitzman, Lenore J. 1984. Sex-role socialization: A focus on women. In *Women: A feminist perspective,* edited by Jo Freeman. Palo Alto, CA: Mayfield.

Welter, Barbara. 1978. The cult of true womanhood: 1820-1860. In *The American family in social-historical perspective,* edited by Michael Gordon. New York: St. Martin's.

White, Debra Gray. 1985. *Ain't I a woman?* New York: Norton.

White, E. Frances. 1984. Listening to the voices of black feminism. *Radical America* 18:7-25.

3 "A Way Outa No Way": Eating Problems Among African American, Latina, and White Women

BECKY W. THOMPSON

Bulimia, anorexia nervosa, binging, and extensive dieting are among the many health issues women have been confronting in the last twenty years. Until recently, however, there has been almost no research about eating problems among African American, Latina, Asian American, or Native American women, working-class women, or lesbians.[1] In fact, according to the normative epidemiological portrait, eating problems are largely a white, middle-, and upper-class heterosexual phenomenon. Further, while feminist research has documented how eating problems are fueled by sexism, there has been almost no attention paid to how other systems of oppression may also be implicated in the development of eating problems.

In this chapter, I reevaluate the portrayal of eating problems as issues of appearance based on the "culture of thinness." I propose that eating problems begin as ways women cope with various traumas including sexual abuse, racism, classism, sexism, heterosexism, and poverty. Showing the interface between these traumas and the onset of eating problems explains why women may use eating to numb pain and cope with violations to their bodies. This theoretical shift also permits an

AUTHOR'S NOTE: I am grateful to Margaret Andersen, Liz Bennett, Esther Ngan-ling Chow, Lynn Davidman, Mary Gilfus, Evalynn Hammonds, Doris Wilkinson, and Maxine Baca Zinn for their support of this work.

understanding of the economic, political, social, educational, and cultural resources that women need to change their relationship to food and their bodies.

EXISTING RESEARCH ON EATING PROBLEMS

There are three theoretical models used to explain the epidemiology, etiology, and treatment of eating problems. The biomedical model offers important scientific research about possible physiological causes of eating problems and the physiological dangers of purging and starvation (Copeland 1985; Spack 1985). However, this model adopts medical treatment strategies that may disempower and traumatize women (Garner 1985; Orbach 1985). In addition, this model ignores many social, historical, and cultural factors that influence women's eating patterns. The psychological model identifies eating problems as "multidimensional disorders" that are influenced by biological, psychological, and cultural factors (Garfinkel and Garner 1982). While useful in its exploration of effective therapeutic treatments, this model, like the biomedical one, tends to neglect women of color, lesbians, and working-class women.

The third model, offered by feminists, asserts that eating problems are gendered. This model explains why the vast majority of people with eating problems are women, how gender socialization and sexism may relate to eating problems, and how masculine models of psychological development have shaped theoretical interpretations. Feminists offer the *culture of thinness model* as a key reason why eating problems predominate among women. According to this model, thinness is a culturally, socially, and economically enforced requirement for female beauty. This imperative makes women vulnerable to cycles of dieting, weight loss, and subsequent weight gain, which may lead to anorexia nervosa and bulimia (Chernin 1981; Orbach 1978, 1985; Smead 1984).

Feminists have rescued eating problems from the realm of individual psychopathology by showing how the difficulties are rooted in systematic and pervasive attempts to control women's body sizes and appetites. However, researchers have yet to give significant attention to how race, class, and sexuality influence women's understanding of their bodies and appetites. The handful of epidemiological studies that include African American women and Latinas casts doubt on the accuracy of the normative epidemiological portrait. The studies suggest that this portrait reflects which particular populations of women have been studied rather than actual prevalence (Andersen and Hay 1985; Gray, Ford, and Kelly 1987; Hsu 1987; Nevo 1985; Silber 1986). More important, this research shows that bias in research has consequences for women of color. Tomas Silber (1986) asserts that many well-trained professionals have either misdiagnosed or delayed their diagnoses of eating problems among African American and Latina women due to stereotypical thinking that these problems are restricted to white women. As a consequence, when African American women or Latinas are diagnosed, their eating problems tend to be more severe due to extended processes of starvation prior to intervention. In her autobiographical account of her eating problems, Retha Powers (1989), an African American woman, describes being told not to worry about her eating problems since "fat is more acceptable in the Black community" (p. 78). Stereotypical perceptions held by her peers and teachers of the "maternal Black woman" and the "persistent mammy-brickhouse Black woman image" (p. 134) made it difficult for Powers to find people who took her problems with food seriously.

Recent work by African American women reveals that eating problems often relate to women's struggles against a "simultaneity of oppressions" (Clarke 1982; Naylor 1985; White 1991). Byllye Avery (1990), the founder of the National Black Women's Health Project, links the origins of eating problems among African American women to the daily stress of being undervalued and overburdened at home and at work. In Evelyn C. White's (1990) anthology, *The Black Woman's Health Book: Speaking for Ourselves,* Georgiana Arnold (1990) links her eating problems partly to racism and racial isolation during childhood.

Recent feminist research also identifies factors that are related to eating problems among lesbians (Brown 1987; Dworkin 1989; Iazzetto 1989; Schoenfielder and Wieser 1983). In her clinical work, Brown (1987) found that lesbians who have internalized a high degree of homophobia are more likely to accept negative attitudes about fat than are lesbians who have examined their internalized homophobia. Autobiographical accounts by lesbians have also indicated that secrecy about eating problems among lesbians partly reflects their fear of being associated with a stigmatized illness ("What's Important" 1988).

Attention to African American women, Latinas, and lesbians paves the way for further research that explores the possible interface between facing multiple oppressions and the development of eating problems. In this way, this study is part of a larger feminist and sociological research agenda that seeks to understand how race, class, gender, nationality, and sexuality inform women's experiences and influence theory production.

METHODOLOGY

I conducted eighteen life history interviews and administered lengthy questionnaires to explore eating problems among African American, Latina, and white women. I employed a snowball sample, a method in which potential respondents often first learn about the study from people who have already participated. This method was well suited for the study since it enabled women to get information about me and the interview process from people they already knew. Typically, I had much contact with the respondents prior to the interview. This was particularly important given the secrecy associated with this topic (Russell 1986; Silberstein, Striegel-Moore, and Rodin 1987), the necessity of women of color and lesbians to be discriminating about how their lives are studied, and the fact that I was conducting across-race research.

To create analytical notes and conceptual categories from the data, I adopted Glaser and Strauss's (1967) technique of theoretical sampling, which directs the researcher to collect, analyze, and test hypotheses during the sampling process (rather than imposing theoretical categories onto the data). After completing each interview transcription, I gave a copy to each woman who wanted one. After reading their interviews, some of the women clarified or made additions to the interview text.

Demographics of the Women in the Study

The 18 women I interviewed included 5 African American women, 5 Latinas, and 8 white women. Of these women, 12 are lesbian and 6 are heterosexual. Five women are Jewish, 8 are Catholic, and 5 are Protestant. Three women grew up outside of the United States. The women represented a range of class backgrounds (both in terms of origin and current class status) and ranged in age from 19 to 46 years old (with a median age of 33.5 years).

The majority of the women reported having had a combination of eating problems (at least two of the following: bulimia, compulsive eating, anorexia nervosa, and/or extensive dieting). In addition, the particular types of eating problems often changed during a woman's life span. (For example, a woman might have been bulimic during adolescence and anorexic as an adult.) Among the women, 28 percent had been bulimic, 17 percent had been bulimic and anorexic, and 5 percent had been anorexic. All of the women who had been anorexic or bulimic also had a history of compulsive eating and extensive dieting. Of the women, 50 percent were either compulsive eaters and dieters (39 percent) or compulsive eaters (11 percent) but had not been bulimic or anorexic. Two-thirds of the women have had eating problems for more than half of their lives, a finding that contradicts the stereotype of eating problems as transitory. The weight fluctuation among the women varied from 16 to 160 pounds, with an average fluctuation of 74 pounds. This drastic weight change illustrates the degree to which the women adjusted to major changes in body size at least once during their lives as they lost, gained, and lost weight again. The average age of onset was 11 years old, meaning that most of the women developed eating problems prior to puberty. Almost all of the women (88 percent) considered themselves as still having a problem with eating, although the majority believed they were well on the way to recovery.

THE INTERFACE OF TRAUMA
AND EATING PROBLEMS

One of the most striking findings in this study was the range of traumas the women associated with the origins of their eating problems, including racism, sexual abuse, poverty, sexism, emotional or physical abuse, heterosexism, class injuries, and acculturation.[2] The particular constellation of eating problems among the women did not vary with race, class, sexuality, or nationality. Women from various race and class backgrounds attributed the origins of their eating problems to sexual abuse, sexism, and emotional and/or physical abuse. Among some of the African American and Latina women, eating problems were also associated with poverty, racism, and class injuries. Heterosexism was a key factor in the onset of bulimia, compulsive eating, and extensive dieting among some of the lesbians. These oppressions are not the same nor are the injuries caused by them. And certainly, there are a variety of potentially harmful ways that women respond to oppression (such as using drugs, becoming a workaholic, or committing suicide). However, for all these women, eating was a way of coping with trauma.

Sexual Abuse

Sexual abuse was the most common trauma that the women related to the origins of their eating problems. Until recently, there has been virtually no research exploring the possible relationship between these two phenomena. Since the mid-1980s, however, researchers have begun identifying connections between the two, a task that is part of a larger feminist critique of traditional psychoanalytic symptomatology (DeSalvo 1989; Herman 1981; Masson 1984). Results of a number of incidence studies indicate that between one-third and two-thirds of women who have eating problems have been abused (Oppenheimer et al. 1985; Root and Fallon 1988). In addition, a growing number of therapists and researchers have offered interpretations of the meaning and impact of eating problems for survivors of sexual abuse (Bass and Davis 1988; Goldfarb 1987; Iazzetto 1989; Swink and Leveille 1986). Kearney-Cooke (1988) identifies dieting and binging as common ways in which women cope with frequent psychological consequences of sexual abuse (such as body image disturbances, distrust of people and one's own experiences, and confusion about one's feelings). Root and Fallon (1989) specify ways that victimized women cope with assaults by binging and purging: bulimia serves many functions, including anesthetizing the negative feelings associated with victimization. Iazzetto's innovative study (1989), based on in-depth interviews and art therapy sessions, examines how a woman's relationship to her body changes as a consequence of sexual abuse. Iazzetto discovered that the process of leaving the body (through progressive phases of numbing, dissociating and denying) that often occurs during sexual abuse parallels the process of leaving the body made possible through binging.

Among the women I interviewed, 61 percent were survivors of sexual abuse (11 of the 18 women), most of whom made connections between sexual abuse and the beginning of their eating problems. Binging was the most common method of coping identified by the survivors. Binging helped women "numb out" or anesthetize their feelings. Eating sedated, alleviated anxiety, and combated loneliness. Food was something that they could trust and was accessible whenever they needed it. Antonia (a pseudonym) is an Italian American woman who was first sexually abused by a male relative when she was four years old. Retrospectively, she knows that binging was a way she coped with the abuse. When the abuse began, and for many years subsequently, Antonia often woke up during the middle of the night with anxiety attacks or nightmares and would go straight to the kitchen cupboards to get food. Binging helped her block painful feelings because it put her back to sleep.

Like other women in the study who began binging when they were very young, Antonia was not always fully conscious as she binged. She described eating during the night as "sleep walking. It was mostly desperate—like I had to have it." Describing why she ate after waking up with nightmares, Antonia said, "What else do you do? If you don't have any coping mechanisms, you eat." She said that binging made her "disappear," which made her feel protected. Like Antonia, most of the women were sexually abused before puberty; four of them before they were five years old. Given their youth, food was the most accessible and socially acceptable drug available to them. Because all of the women endured the psychological consequences alone, it is logical that they coped with tactics they could use alone as well.

One reason Antonia binged (rather than dieted) to cope with sexual abuse is that she saw little reason to try to be the small size girls were supposed to be. Growing up as one of the only Italian Americans in what she described as a "very WASP town," Antonia felt that everything from her weight and size to having dark hair on her upper lip were physical characteristics she was supposed to hide. From a young age she knew she "never embodied the essence of the good girl. I don't like her. I have never acted like her. I can't be her. I sort of gave up." For Antonia, her body was the physical entity that signified her outsider status. When the sexual abuse occurred, Antonia felt she had lost her body. In her mind, the body she lived in after the abuse was not really hers. By the time Antonia was 11, her mother put her on diet pills. Antonia began to eat behind closed doors as she continued to cope with the psychological consequences of sexual abuse and feeling like a cultural outsider.

Extensive dieting and bulimia were also ways in which women responded to sexual abuse. Some women thought that the men had abused them because of their weight. They believed that if they were smaller, they might not have been abused. For example, when Elsa, an Argentine woman, was sexually abused at the age of 11, she thought her chubby size was the reason the man was abusing her. Elsa said, "I had this notion that these old perverts liked these plump girls. You heard adults say this too. Sex and flesh being associated." Looking back on her childhood, Elsa believes she made fat the enemy partly due to the shame and guilt she felt about the incest. Her belief that fat was the source of her problems was also supported by her socialization. Raised by strict German governesses in an upper-class family, Elsa was taught that a woman's weight was a primary criterion for judging her worth. Her mother "was socially conscious of walking into places with a fat daughter and maybe people staring at her." Her father often referred to Elsa's body as "shot to hell." When asked to describe how she felt about

her body when growing up, Elsa described being completely alienated
from her body. She explained,

> Remember in school when they talk about the difference between body and
> soul? I always felt like my soul was skinny. My soul was free. My soul sort
> of flew. I was tied down by this big bag of rocks that was my body. I had
> to drag it around. It did pretty much what it wanted and I had a lot of trouble
> controlling it. It kept me from doing all the things that I dreamed of.

As is true for many women who have been abused, the split that Elsa
described between her body and soul was an attempt to protect herself
from the pain she believed her body caused her. In her mind, her fat
body was what had "bashed in her dreams." Dieting became her solution
but, as is true for many women in the study, this strategy soon led to
cycles of binging and weight fluctuation.

Ruthie, a Puerto Rican woman who was sexually abused from 12 until
16 years of age, described bulimia as a way she responded to sexual
abuse. As a child, Ruthie liked her body. Like many Puerto Rican
women of her mother's generation, Ruthie's mother did not want skinny
children, interpreting that as a sign that they were sick or being fed
improperly. Despite her mother's attempts to make her gain weight,
Ruthie remained thin through puberty. When a male relative began
sexually abusing her, Ruthie's sense of her body changed dramatically.
Although she weighed only 100 pounds, she began to feel fat and
thought her size was causing the abuse. She had seen a movie on
television about Romans who made themselves throw up and so she
began doing it, in hopes that she could look like the "little kid" she was
before the abuse began. Her symbolic attempt to protect herself by
purging stands in stark contrast to the psychoanalytic explanation of
eating problems as an "abnormal" repudiation of sexuality. In fact, her
actions and those of many other survivors indicate a girl's logical
attempt to protect herself (including her sexuality) by being a size and
shape that does not seem as vulnerable to sexual assault.

These women's experiences suggest many reasons why women develop eating problems as a consequence of sexual abuse. Most of the
survivors "forgot" the sexual abuse after its onset and were unable to
retrieve the abuse memories until many years later. With these gaps in
memory, frequently they did not know why they felt ashamed, fearful,
or depressed. When sexual abuse memories resurfaced in dreams, they
often woke feeling upset but could not remember what they had

dreamed. These free floating, unexplained feelings left the women feeling out of control and confused. Binging or focusing on maintaining a new diet were ways women distracted or appeased themselves, in turn, helping them regain a sense of control. As they grew older, they became more conscious of the consequences of these actions. Becoming angry at themselves for binging or promising themselves they would not purge again was a way to direct feelings of shame and self-hate that often accompanied the trauma.

Integral to this occurrence was a transference process in which the women displaced onto their bodies painful feelings and memories that actually derived from or were directed toward the persons who caused the abuse. Dieting became a method of trying to change the parts of their bodies they hated, a strategy that at least initially brought success as they lost weight. Purging was a way women tried to reject the body size they thought was responsible for the abuse. Throwing up in order to lose the weight they thought was making them vulnerable to the abuse was a way to try to find the body they had lost when the abuse began.

Poverty

Like sexual abuse, poverty is another injury that may make women vulnerable to eating problems. One woman I interviewed attributed her eating problems directly to the stress caused by poverty. Yolanda is a Black Cape Verdean mother who began eating compulsively when she was twenty-seven years old. After leaving an abusive husband in her early twenties, Yolanda was forced to go on welfare. As a single mother with small children and few financial resources, she tried to support herself and her children on $539 a month. Yolanda began binging in the evenings after putting her children to bed. Eating was something she could do alone. It would calm her, help her deal with loneliness, and make her feel safe. Food was an accessible commodity that was cheap. She ate three boxes of macaroni and cheese when nothing else was available. As a single mother with little money, Yolanda felt as if her body was the only thing she had left. As she described it,

> I am here, [in my body] 'cause there is no where else for me to go. Where am I going to go? This is all I got . . . that probably contributes to putting on so much weight cause staying in your body, in your home, in yourself, you don't go out. You aren't around other people. . . . You hide and as long as you hide you don't have to face . . . nobody can see you eat. You are safe.

When she was eating, Yolanda felt a momentary reprieve from her worries. Binging not only became a logical solution because it was cheap and easy but also because she had grown up amid positive messages about eating. In her family, eating was a celebrated and joyful act. However, in adulthood, eating became a double-edged sword. While comforting her, binging also led to weight gain. During the three years Yolanda was on welfare, she gained seventy pounds.

Yolanda's story captures how poverty can be a precipitating factor in eating problems and highlights the value of understanding how class inequalities may shape women's eating problems. As a single mother, her financial constraints mirrored those of most female heads of households. The dual hazards of a race- and sex-stratified labor market further limited her options (Higginbotham 1986). In an article about Black women's health, Byllye Avery (1990) quotes a Black woman's explanation about why she eats compulsively. The woman told Avery,

> I work for General Electric making batteries, and, I know it's killing me. My old man is an alcoholic. My kids got babies. Things are not well with me. And one thing I know I can do when I come home is cook me a pot of food and sit down in front of the TV and eat it. And you can't take that away from me until you're ready to give me something in its place. (p. 7)

Like Yolanda, this woman identifies eating compulsively as a quick, accessible, and immediately satisfying way of coping with the daily stress caused by conditions she could not control. Connections between poverty and eating problems also show the limits of portraying eating problems as maladies of upper-class adolescent women.

The fact that many women use food to anesthetize themselves, rather than other drugs (even when they gained access to alcohol, marijuana, and other illegal drugs), is partly a function of gender socialization and the competing demands that women face. One of the physiological consequences of binge eating is a numbed state similar to that experienced by drinking. Troubles and tensions are covered over as a consequence of the body's defensive response to massive food intake. When food is eaten in that way, it effectively works like a drug with immediate and predictable effects. Yolanda said she binged late at night rather than getting drunk because she could still get up in the morning, get her children ready for school, and be clearheaded for the college classes she attended. By binging, she avoided the hangover or sickness that results from alcohol or illegal drugs. In this way, food was her drug of choice since it was possible for her to eat while she continued to care for her children, drive, cook, and study. Binging is also less expensive than drinking, a factor that is especially significant for poor women. Another woman I interviewed said that when her compulsive eating was at its height, she ate breakfast after rising in the morning, stopped for a snack on her way to work, ate lunch at three different cafeterias, and snacked at her desk throughout the afternoon. Yet even when her eating had become constant, she was still able to remain employed. While her patterns of eating no doubt slowed her productivity, being drunk may have slowed her to a dead stop.

Heterosexism

The life history interviews also uncovered new connections between heterosexism and eating problems. One of the most important recent feminist contributions has been identifying compulsory heterosexuality as an institution which truncates opportunities for heterosexual and lesbian women (Rich 1986). All of the women interviewed for this study, both lesbian and heterosexual, were taught that heterosexuality was compulsory, although the versions of this enforcement were shaped by race and class. Expectations about heterosexuality were partly taught through messages that girls learned about eating and their bodies. In some homes, boys were given more food than girls, especially as teenagers, based on the rationale that girls need to be thin to attract boys. As the girls approached puberty, many were told to stop being athletic, begin wearing dresses, and watch their weight. For the women who weighed more than was considered acceptable, threats about their need to diet were laced with admonitions that being fat would ensure becoming an "old maid."

While compulsory heterosexuality influenced all of the women's emerging sense of their bodies and eating patterns, the women who linked heterosexism directly to the beginning of their eating problems were those who knew they were lesbians when very young and actively resisted heterosexual norms. One working-class Jewish woman, Martha, began compulsively eating when she was 11 years old, the same year she started getting clues of her lesbian identity. In junior high school, as many of her female peers began dating boys, Martha began fantasizing about girls, which made her feel utterly alone. Confused and ashamed about her fantasies, Martha came home every day from school and binged. Binging was a way she drugged herself so that being alone was tolerable. Describing binging, she said, "It was the only thing I knew. I was looking for a comfort." Like many women, Martha binged because it softened painful feelings. Binging sedated her, lessened her anxiety, and induced sleep.

Martha's story also reveals ways that trauma can influence women's experience of their bodies. Like many other women, Martha had no sense of herself as connected to her body. When I asked Martha whether she saw herself as fat when she was growing up she said, "I didn't see myself as fat. I didn't see myself. I wasn't there. I get so sad about that because I missed so much." In the literature on eating problems, *body image* is the term that is typically used to describe a woman's experience of her body. This term connotes the act of imagining one's physical appearance. Typically, women with eating problems are assumed to have difficulties with their body image. However, the term body image does not adequately capture the complexity and range of bodily responses to trauma experienced by the women. Exposure to trauma did much more than distort the women's visual image of themselves. These traumas often jeopardized their capacity to consider themselves as having bodies at all.

Given the limited connotations of the term body image, I use the term *body consciousness* as a more useful way to understand the range of bodily responses to trauma.[3] By body consciousness I mean the ability to reside comfortably in one's body (to see oneself as embodied) and to consider one's body as connected to oneself. The disruptions to their body consciousness that the women described included leaving their bodies, making a split between their body and mind, experiencing being "in" their bodies as painful, feeling unable to control what went in and out of their bodies, hiding in one part of their bodies, or simply not seeing themselves as having bodies. Binging, dieting, or purging were common ways women responded to disruptions to their body consciousness.

Racism and Class Injuries

For some of the Latinas and African American women, racism coupled with the stress resulting from class mobility related to the onset of their eating problems. Joselyn, an African American woman, remembered her white grandmother telling her she would never be as pretty as her cousins because they were lighter skinned. Her grandmother often humiliated Joselyn in front of others, as she made fun of Joselyn's body while she was naked and told her she was fat. As a young child, Joselyn began to think that although she could not change her skin color, she could at least try to be thin. When Joselyn was young, her grandmother was the only family member who objected to Joselyn's weight. However, her father also began encouraging his wife and daughter to be thin as the family's class standing began to change. When the family was working class, serving big meals, having chubby children, and keeping plenty of food in the house was a sign the family was doing well. But, as the family became mobile, Joselyn's father began insisting that Joselyn be thin. She remembered, "When my father's business began to bloom and my father was interacting more with white businessmen and seeing how they did business, suddenly thin became important. If you were a truly well-to-do family, then your family was slim and elegant."

As Joselyn's grandmother used Joselyn's body as territory for enforcing her own racism and prejudice about size, Joselyn's father used her body as the territory through which he channeled the demands he faced in the white-dominated business world. However, as Joselyn was pressured to diet, her father still served her large portions and bought treats for her and the neighborhood children. These contradictory messages made her feel confused about her body. As was true for many women in this study, Joselyn was told she was fat beginning when she was very young even though she was not overweight. And, like most of the women, Joselyn was put on diet pills and diets before even reaching puberty, beginning the cycles of dieting, compulsive eating, and bulimia.

The confusion about body size expectations that Joselyn associated with changes in class paralleled one Puerto Rican woman's association between her eating problems and the stress of assimilation as her family's class standing moved from poverty to working class. When Vera was very young, she was so thin that her mother took her to a doctor who prescribed appetite stimulants. However, by the time Vera was eight years old, her mother began trying to shame Vera into dieting. Looking back on it, Vera attributed her mother's change of heart to competition among extended family members that centered on "being white, being successful, being middle class, . . . and it was always, 'Ay Bendito. She is so fat. What happened?' "

The fact that some of the African American and Latina women associated the ambivalent messages about food and eating to their family's class mobility and/or the demands of assimilation while none of the eight white women expressed this (including those whose class was stable and changing) suggests that the added dimension of racism was connected to the imperative to be thin. In fact, the class expectations that their parents experienced exacerbated standards about weight that they inflicted on their daughters.

EATING PROBLEMS AS SURVIVAL STRATEGIES

Feminist Theoretical Shifts

My research permits a reevaluation of many assumptions about eating problems. First, this work challenges the theoretical reliance on the culture-of-thinness model. Although all of the women I interviewed were manipulated and hurt by this imperative at some point in their lives, it is not the primary source of their problems. Even in the instances in which a culture of thinness was a precipitating factor in anorexia, bulimia, or binging, this influence occurred in concert with other oppressions.

Attributing the etiology of eating problems primarily to a woman's striving to attain a certain beauty ideal is also problematic because it labels a common way that women cope with pain as essentially appearance-based disorders. One blatant example of sexism is the notion that women's foremost worry is about their appearance. By focusing on the emphasis on slenderness, the eating problems literature falls into the same trap of assuming that the problems reflect women's "obsession" with appearance. Some women were raised in families and communities in which thinness was not considered a criterion for beauty. Yet they still developed eating problems. Other women were taught that women should be thin but their eating problems were not primarily in reaction to this imperative. Their eating strategies began as logical solutions to problems rather than problems themselves as they tried to cope with a variety of traumas.

Establishing links between eating problems and a range of oppressions invites a rethinking of both the groups of women who have been excluded from research and those whose lives have been the basis of theory formation. The construction of bulimia and anorexia nervosa as appearance-based disorders is rooted in a notion of femininity in which white middle- and upper-class women are portrayed as frivolous, obsessed with their bodies, and overly accepting of narrow gender roles. This portrayal fuels women's tremendous shame and guilt about eating problems—as signs of self-centered vanity. This construction of white middle- and upper-class women is intimately linked to the portrayal of working-class white women and women of color as their opposite: as somehow exempt from accepting the dominant standards of beauty or as one step away from being hungry and therefore not susceptible to eating problems. Identifying that women may binge to cope with poverty contrasts the notion that eating problems are class bound. Attending to the intricacies of race, class, sexuality, and gender pushes us to rethink the demeaning construction of middle-class femininity and establishes bulimia and anorexia nervosa as serious responses to injustices.

Understanding the link between eating problems and trauma also suggests much about treatment and prevention. Ultimately, their prevention depends not simply on individual healing but also on changing the social conditions that underlie their etiology. As Bernice Johnson Reagon sings in Sweet Honey in the Rock's song "Oughta Be a Woman," "A way outa no way is too much to ask/too much of a task for any one woman" (Reagon 1980).[4] Making it possible for women to have healthy relationships with their bodies and eating is a comprehensive task. Beginning steps in this direction include insuring that (1) girls can grow up without being sexually abused, (2) parents have adequate resources to raise their children, (3) children of color grow up free of racism, and (4) young lesbians have the chance to see their reflection in their teachers and community leaders. Ultimately, the prevention of eating problems depends on women's access to economic, cultural, racial, political, social, and sexual justice.

NOTES

1. I use the term *eating problems* as an umbrella term for one or more of the following: anorexia nervosa, bulimia, extensive dieting, or binging. I avoid using the term *eating disorder* because it categorizes the problems as individual pathologies, which deflects attention away from the social inequalities underlying them (Brown 1985). However, by using the term *problem* I do not wish to imply blame. In fact, throughout, I argue that the eating strategies that women develop begin as logical solutions to problems, not problems themselves.

2. By trauma I mean a violating experience that has long-term emotional, physical, and/or spiritual consequences that may have immediate or delayed effects. One reason the term *trauma* is useful conceptually is its association with the diagnostic label Post Traumatic Stress Disorder (PTSD) (American Psychological Association 1987). PTSD is one of the few clinical diagnostic categories that recognizes social problems (such as war or the Holocaust) as responsible for the symptoms identified (Trimble 1985). This concept adapts well to the feminist assertion that a woman's symptoms cannot be understood as

solely individual, considered outside of her social context, or prevented without significant changes in social conditions.

3. One reason the term *consciousness* is applicable is its intellectual history as an entity that is shaped by social context and social structures (Delphy 1984; Marx 1964). This link aptly applies to how the women described their bodies because their perceptions of themselves as embodied (or not embodied) directly relate to their material conditions (living situations, financial resources, and access to social and political power).

4. Copyright © 1980. Used by permission of Songtalk Publishing.

REFERENCES

American Psychological Association. 1987. *Diagnostic and statistical manual of mental disorders.* 3rd ed. rev. Washington, DC: American Psychological Association.

Andersen, Arnold, and Andy Hay. 1985. Racial and socioeconomic influences in anorexia nervosa and bulimia. *International Journal of Eating Disorders* 4:479-87.

Arnold, Georgiana. 1990. Coming home: One Black woman's journey to health and fitness. In *The Black women's health book: Speaking for ourselves,* edited by Evelyn C. White. Seattle, WA: Seal.

Avery, Byllye Y. 1990. Breathing life into ourselves: The evolution of the National Black Women's Health Project. In *The Black women's health book: Speaking for ourselves,* edited by Evelyn C. White. Seattle, WA: Seal.

Bass, Ellen, and Laura Davis. 1988. *The courage to heal: A guide for women survivors of child sexual abuse.* New York: Harper & Row.

Brown, Laura S. 1985. Women, weight and power: Feminist theoretical and therapeutic issues. *Women and Therapy* 4:61-71.

———. 1987. Lesbians, weight and eating: New analyses and perspectives. In *Lesbian psychologies,* edited by the Boston Lesbian Psychologies Collective. Champaign: University of Illinois Press.

Chernin, Kim. 1981. *The obsession: Reflections on the tyranny of slenderness.* New York: Harper & Row.

Clarke, Cheryl. 1982. *Narratives.* New Brunswick, NJ: Sister Books.

Copeland, Paul M. 1985. Neuroendocrine aspects of eating disorders. In *Theory and treatment of anorexia nervosa and bulimia: Biomedical sociocultural and psychological perspectives,* edited by Steven Wiley Emmett. New York: Brunner/Mazel.

Delphy, Christine. 1984. *Close to home: A materialist analysis of women's oppression.* Amherst: University of Massachusetts Press.

DeSalvo, Louise. 1989. *Virginia Woolf: The impact of childhood sexual abuse on her life and work.* Boston: Beacon.

Dworkin, Sari H. 1989. Not in man's image: Lesbians and the cultural oppression of body image. In *Loving boldly: Issues facing lesbians,* edited by Ester D. Rothblum and Ellen Cole. New York: Harrington Park.

Garfinkel, Paul E., and David M. Garner. 1982. *Anorexia nervosa: A multidimensional perspective.* New York: Brunner/Mazel.

Garner, David. 1985. Iatrogenesis in anorexia nervosa and bulimia nervosa. *International Journal of Eating Disorders* 4:701-26.

Glaser, Barney G., and Anselm L. Strauss. 1967. *The discovery of grounded theory: Strategies for qualitative research.* New York: Aldine DeGruyter.

Goldfarb, Lori. 1987. Sexual abuse antecedent to anorexia nervosa, bulimia and compulsive overeating: Three case reports. *International Journal of Eating Disorders* 6:675-80.

Gray, James, Kathryn Ford, and Lily M. Kelly. 1987. The prevalence of bulimia in a Black college population. *International Journal of Eating Disorders* 6:733-40.

Herman, Judith. 1981. *Father-daughter incest*. Cambridge, MA: Harvard University Press.

Higginbotham, Elizabeth. 1986. We were never on a pedestal: Women of color continue to struggle with poverty, racism and sexism. In *For crying out loud*, edited by Rochelle Lefkowitz and Ann Withorn. Boston: Pilgrim.

Hsu, George. 1987. Are eating disorders becoming more common in Blacks? *International Journal of Eating Disorders* 6:113-24.

Iazzetto, Demetria. 1989. When the body is not an easy place to be: Women's sexual abuse and eating problems. Ph.D. diss., Union for Experimenting Colleges and Universities, Cincinnati, OH.

Kearney-Cooke, Ann. 1988. Group treatment of sexual abuse among women with eating disorders. *Women and Therapy* 7:5-21.

Marx, Karl. 1964. *The economic and philosophic manuscripts of 1844*. New York: International.

Masson, Jeffrey. 1984. *The assault on the truth: Freud's suppression of the seduction theory*. New York: Farrar, Strauss & Giroux.

Naylor, Gloria. 1985. *Linden Hills*. New York: Ticknor & Fields.

Nevo, Shoshana. 1985. Bulimic symptoms: Prevalence and ethnic differences among college women. *International Journal of Eating Disorders* 4:151-68.

Oppenheimer, R., K. Howells, R. L. Palmer, and D. A. Chaloner. 1985. Adverse sexual experience in childhood and clinical eating disorders: A preliminary description. *Journal of Psychiatric Research* 19:357-61.

Orbach, Susie. 1978. *Fat is a feminist issue*. New York: Paddington.

———. 1985. Accepting the symptom: A feminist psychoanalytic treatment of anorexia nervosa. In *Handbook of psychotherapy for anorexia nervosa and bulimia*, edited by David M. Garner and Paul E. Garfinkel. New York: Guilford.

Powers, Retha. 1989. Fat is a Black women's issue. *Essence*, Oct., 75, 78, 134, 136.

Reagon, Bernice Johnson. 1980. Oughta be a woman. On Sweet Honey in the Rock's album, *Good News*. Music by Bernice Johnson Reagon; lyrics by June Jordan. Washington, DC: Songtalk.

Rich, Adrienne. 1986. Compulsory heterosexuality and lesbian existence. In *Blood, bread and poetry*. New York: Norton.

Root, Maria P. P., and Patricia Fallon. 1988. The incidence of victimization experiences in a bulimic sample. *Journal of Interpersonal Violence* 3:161-73.

———. 1989. Treating the victimized bulimic: The functions of binge-purge behavior. *Journal of Interpersonal Violence* 4:90-100.

Russell, Diana E. 1986. *The secret trauma: Incest in the lives of girls and women*. New York: Basic Books.

Schoenfielder, Lisa, and Barbara Wieser, eds. 1983. *Shadow on a tightrope: Writings by women about fat liberation*. Iowa City, IA: Aunt Lute Book Co.

Silber, Tomas. 1986. Anorexia nervosa in Blacks and Hispanics. *International Journal of Eating Disorders* 5:121-28.

Silberstein, Lisa, Ruth Striegel-Moore, and Judith Rodin. 1987. Feeling fat: A woman's shame. In *The role of shame in symptom formation,* edited by Helen Block Lewis. Hillsdale, NJ: Lawrence Erlbaum.

Smead, Valerie. 1984. Eating behaviors which may lead to and perpetuate anorexia nervosa, bulimarexia, and bulimia. *Women and Therapy* 3:37-49.

Spack, Norman. 1985. Medical complications of anorexia nervosa and bulimia. In *Theory and treatment of anorexia nervosa and bulimia: Biomedical sociocultural and psychological perspectives,* edited by Steven Wiley Emmett. New York: Brunner/ Mazel.

Swink, Kathy, and Antoinette E. Leveille. 1986. From victim to survivor: A new look at the issues and recovery process for adult incest survivors. *Women and Therapy* 5:119-43.

Trimble, Michael. 1985. Post-traumatic stress disorder: History of a concept. In *Trauma and its wake: The study and treatment of post-traumatic stress disorder,* edited by C. R. Figley. New York: Brunner/Mazel.

What's important is what you look like. 1988. *Gay Community News,* July, 24-30.

White, Evelyn C., ed. 1990. *The Black women's health book: Speaking for ourselves.* Seattle, WA: Seal Press.

———. 1991. Unhealthy appetites. *Essence,* Sept., 28, 30.

4 Masculinities and Athletic Careers

MICHAEL A. MESSNER

The growth of women's studies and feminist gender studies has in recent years led to the emergence of a new men's studies (Brod 1987; Kimmel 1987). But just as feminist perspectives on women have been justifiably criticized for falsely universalizing the lives and issues of white, middle-class, U.S. women (Baca Zinn, Cannon, Higginbotham, and Dill 1986; hooks 1984), so, too, men's studies has tended to focus on the lives of relatively privileged men. As Brod (1983-1984) points out in an insightful critique of the middle-class basis and bias of the men's movement, if men's studies is to be relevant to minority and working-class men, less emphasis must be placed on personal lifestyle transformations and more emphasis must be placed on developing a structural critique of social institutions. Although some institutional analysis has begun in men's studies, very little critical scrutiny has been focused on that very masculine institution, organized sports (Messner 1985; Sabo 1985; Sabo and Runfola 1980). Not only is the institution of sports an ideal place to study men and masculinity, careful analysis would make it impossible to ignore the realities of race and class differences.

In the early 1970s, Edwards (1971, 1973) debunked the myth that the predominance of blacks in sports to which they have access signaled an

AUTHOR'S NOTE: Parts of this work were presented as papers at the American Sociological Association Annual Meeting in Chicago, in August 1987, and at the North American Society for the Sociology of Sport Annual Meeting in Edmonton, Alberta, in November 1987. I thank Maxine Baca Zinn, Bob Blauner, Bob Dunn, Pierrette Hondagneu-Sotelo, Carol Jacklin, Michael Kimmel, Judith Lorber, Don Sabo, Barrie Thorne, and Carol Warren for constructive comments on earlier versions of this work.

end to institutionalized racism. It is now widely accepted in sport sociology that social institutions such as the media, education, the economy, and (a more recent and controversial addition to the list) the black family itself all serve to systematically channel disproportionately large numbers of young black men into football, basketball, boxing, and baseball, where they are subsequently "stacked" into low-prestige and high-risk positions, exploited for their skills, and, finally, when their bodies are used up, excreted from organized athletics at a young age with no transferable skills with which to compete in the labor market (Edwards 1984; Eitzen and Purdy 1986; Eitzen and Yetman 1977).

While there are racial differences in involvement in sports, class, age, and educational differences seem more significant. Rudman's (1986) initial analysis revealed profound differences between whites' and blacks' orientations to sports. Blacks were found to be more likely than whites to view sports favorably, to incorporate sports into their daily lives, and to be affected by the outcome of sporting events. However, when age, education, and social class were factored into the analysis, Rudman found that race did not explain whites' and blacks' different orientations. Blacks' affinity for sports is best explained by their tendency to be clustered disproportionately in lower-income groups.

The 1980s ushered in what Wellman (1986, 43) calls "new political linguistics of race," which emphasize cultural rather than structural causes (and solutions) to the problems faced by black communities. The advocates of the cultural perspective believe that the high value placed on sports by black communities has led to the development of unrealistic hopes in millions of black youths. They appeal to family and community to bolster other choices based upon a more rational assessment of "reality." Visible black role models in many other professions now exist, they say, and there is ample evidence which proves that sports careers are, at best, a bad gamble.

Critics of the cultural perspective have condemned it as conservative and victim blaming. But it can also be seen as a response to the view of black athletes as little more than unreflexive dupes of an all-powerful system, which ignores the importance of agency. Gruneau (1983) has argued that sports must be examined within a theory that views human beings as active subjects who are operating within historically constituted structural constraints. Gruneau's reflexive theory rejects the simplistic views of sports as either a realm of absolute oppression or an arena of absolute freedom and spontaneity. Instead, he argues, it is necessary to construct an understanding of how and why participants themselves actively make choices and construct and define meaning and a sense of identity within the institutions that they find themselves.

None of these perspectives consider the ways that gender shapes men's definitions of meaning and choices. Within the sociology of sport, gender as a process that interacts with race and class is usually ignored or taken for granted—except when it is *women* athletes who are being studied. Sociologists who are attempting to come to grips with the experiences of black men in general, and in organized sports in particular, have almost exclusively focused their analytic attention on the variable "black," while uncritically taking "men" as a given. Hare and Hare (1984), for example, view masculinity as a biologically determined tendency to act as a provider and protector that is thwarted for black men by socioeconomic and racist obstacles. Staples (1982) does view masculinity largely as a socially produced script, but he accepts this script as a given, preferring to focus on black men's blocked access to male role fulfillment. These perspectives on masculinity fail to show how the male role itself, as it interacts with a constricted structure of opportunity, can contribute to locking black men into destructive relationships and lifestyles (Franklin 1984; Majors 1986).

This chapter will examine the relationships among male identity, race, and social class by listening to the voices of former athletes. I will first briefly describe my research. Then I will discuss the similarities and differences in the choices and experiences of men from different racial and social class backgrounds. Together, these choices and experiences help to construct what Connell (1987) calls "the gender order." Organized sports, it will be suggested, is a practice through which men's separation from and power over women is embodied and naturalized at the same time that hegemonic (white, heterosexual, professional-class) masculinity is clearly differentiated from marginalized and subordinated masculinities.

DESCRIPTION OF RESEARCH

Between 1983 and 1985, I conducted thirty open-ended, in-depth interviews with male former athletes. My purpose was to add a critical understanding of male gender identity to Levinson's (1978) conception of the "individual lifecourse"—specifically, to discover how masculinity develops and changes as a man interacts with the socially constructed world of organized sports. Most of the men I interviewed had played the U.S. "major sports"—football, basketball, baseball, track. At the time of the interview, each had been retired from playing organized sports for at least five years. Their ages ranged from twenty-one to forty-eight, with the median, thirty-three. Fourteen were black, fourteen were white, and two were Hispanic. Fifteen of the sixteen black and Hispanic men had come from poor or working-class families, while the majority (9 of 14) of the white men had come from middle-class or professional families. Twelve had played organized sports through high school, eleven through college, and seven had been professional athletes. All had at some time in their lives based their identities largely on their roles as athletes and could therefore be said to have had athletic careers.

MALE IDENTITY AND ORGANIZED SPORTS

Earlier studies of masculinity and sports argued that sports socializes boys to be men (Lever 1976; Schafer 1975). Here, boys learn cultural values and behaviors, such as competition, toughness, and winning at all costs, that are culturally valued aspects of masculinity. While offering important insights, these early studies of masculinity and sports suffered from the limiting assumptions of a gender-role theory that seems to assume that boys come to their first athletic experience as blank slates onto which the values of masculinity are imprinted. This perspective oversimplifies a complex reality. In fact, young boys bring an already gendered identity to their first sports experiences, an identity that is struggling to work through the developmental task of individuation (Chodorow 1978; Gilligan 1982). Yet as Benjamin (1988) has argued, individuation is accomplished, paradoxically, only through relationships with other people in the social world. So, although the major task of masculinity is the development of a "positional identity" that clarifies the boundaries between self and other, this separation must be accomplished through some form of connection with others. For the men in my study, the rule-bound structure of organized sports became a context in which they struggled to construct a masculine positional identity.

All of the men in this study described the emotional salience of their earliest experiences in sports in terms of relationships with other males. It was not winning and victories that seemed important at first; it was something "fun" to do with fathers, older brothers or uncles, and eventually with same-aged peers. As a man from a white, middle-class family said, "the most important thing was just being out there with the rest of the guys—being friends." A thirty-two-year-old man from a poor Chicano family, whose mother had died when he was nine years old, put it more succinctly:

> What I think sports did for me is it brought me into kind of an instant family. By being on a Little League team, or even just playing with kids in the neighborhood, it brought what I really wanted, which was some kind of closeness.

Though sports participation may have initially promised "some kind of closeness," by the ages of nine or ten, the less skilled boys were already becoming alienated from—or weeded out of—the highly competitive and hierarchical system of organized sports. Those who did experience some early successes received recognition from adult males (especially fathers and older brothers) and held higher status among peers. As a result, they began to pour more and more of their energies into athletic participation. It was only after they learned that they would get recognition from other people for being a good athlete—indeed, that this attention was contingent upon *being a winner*—that performance and winning (the dominant values of organized sports) became extremely important. For some, this created pressures that served to lessen or eliminate the fun of athletic participation (Messner 1987a, 1987b).

While feminist psychoanalytic and developmental theories of masculinity are helpful in explaining boys' early attraction to and motivations in organized sports, the imperatives of core gender identity do not fully determine the contours and directions of the life course. As Rubin (1985) and Levinson (1978) have pointed out, an understanding of the lives of men must take into account the processual nature of male identity as it unfolds through interaction between the internal (psychological ambivalences) and the external (social, historical, and institutional) contexts.

To examine the impact of the social contexts, I divided my sample into two comparison groups. In the first group were ten men from higher-status backgrounds, primarily white, middle-class, and professional families. In the second group were twenty men from lower-status backgrounds, primarily minority, poor, and working-class families. While my data offered evidence for the similarity of experiences and motivations of men from poor backgrounds, independent of race, I also found anecdotal evidence of a racial dynamic that operates independently of social class. However, my sample was not large enough to separate race and class, and so I have combined them to make two status groups.

In discussing these two groups, I will focus mainly on the high school years. During this crucial period, the athletic role may become a master status for a young man, and he is beginning to make assessments and choices about his future. It is here that many young men make a major commitment to—or begin to back away from—athletic careers.

Men From Higher-Status Backgrounds

The boyhood dream of one day becoming a professional athlete—a dream shared by nearly all the men interviewed in this study—is rarely realized. The sports world is extremely hierarchical. The pyramid of sports careers narrows very rapidly as one climbs from high school, to college, to professional levels of competition (Edwards 1984; Harris and Eitzen 1978; Hill and Lowe 1978). In fact, the chances of attaining professional status in sports are approximately 4/100,000 for a white man, 2/100,000 for a black man, and 3/1,000,000 for a Hispanic man in the United States (Leonard and Reyman 1988). For many young athletes, their dream ends early when coaches inform them that they are not big enough, strong enough, fast enough, or skilled enough to compete at the higher levels. But six of the higher-status men I interviewed did not wait for coaches to weed them out. They made conscious decisions in high school or in college to shift their attentions elsewhere—usually toward educational and career goals. Their decision not to pursue an athletic career appeared to them in retrospect to be a rational decision based on the growing knowledge of how very slim their chances were to be successful in the sports world. For instance, a twenty-eight-year-old white graduate student said:

> By junior high I started to realize that I was a good player—maybe even one of the best in my community—but I realized that there were all these people all over the country and how few will get to play pro sports. By high school, I still dreamed of being a pro—I was a serious athlete, I played hard—but I knew it wasn't heading anywhere. I wasn't going to play pro ball.

A thirty-two-year-old white athletic director at a small private college had been a successful college baseball player. Despite considerable attention from professional scouts, he had decided to forgo a shot at a baseball career and to enter graduate school to pursue a teaching credential. As he explained this decision:

> At the time I think I saw baseball as pissing in the wind, really. I was married, I was twenty-two years old with a kid. I didn't want to spend four or five years in the minors with a family. And I could see I wasn't a superstar; so it wasn't really worth it. So I went to grad school. I thought that would be better for me.

Perhaps most striking was the story of a high school student body president and top-notch student who was also "Mr. Everything" in sports. He was named captain of his basketball, baseball, and football teams and achieved All-League honors in each sport. This young white man from a middle-class family received attention from the press and praise from his community and peers for his athletic accomplishments, as well as several offers of athletic scholarships from universities. But by the time he completed high school, he had already decided to quit playing organized sports. As he said:

> I think in my own mind I kind of downgraded the stardom thing. I thought that was small potatoes. And sure, that's nice in high school and all that, but on a broad scale, I didn't think it amounted to all that much. So I decided that my goal's to be a dentist, as soon as I can.

In his sophomore year of college, the basketball coach nearly persuaded him to go out for the team, but eventually he decided against it:

> I thought, so what if I can spend two years playing basketball? I'm not going to be a basketball player forever and I might jeopardize my chances of getting into dental school if I play.

He finished college in three years, completed dental school, and now, in his mid-thirties, is again the epitome of the successful American man: a professional with a family, a home, and a membership in the local country club.

How and why do so many successful male athletes from higher-status backgrounds come to view sports careers as "pissing in the wind," or as "small potatoes"? How and why do they make this early assessment and choice to shift from sports and toward educational and professional goals? The white, middle-class institutional context, with its emphasis on education and income, makes it clear to them that choices exist and that the pursuit of an athletic career is not a particularly good choice to make. Where the young male once found sports to be a convenient institution within which to construct masculine status, the postadolescent and young adult man from a higher-status background simply *transfers* these same strivings to other institutional contexts: education and careers.

For the higher-status men who had chosen to shift from athletic careers, sports remained important on two levels. First, having been a successful high school or college athlete enhances one's adult status among other men in the community—but only as a badge of masculinity that is *added* to his professional status. In fact, several men in professions chose to be interviewed in their offices, where they publicly displayed the trophies and plaques that attested to their earlier athletic accomplishments. Their high school and college athletic careers may have appeared to them as "small potatoes," but many successful men speak of their earlier status as athletes as having "opened doors" for them in their present professions and in community affairs. Similarly, Farr's (1988) research on "Good Old Boys Sociability Groups" shows how sports, as part of the glue of masculine culture, continues to facilitate "dominance bonding" among privileged men long after active sports careers end. The college-educated, career-successful men in Farr's study rarely express overtly sexist, racist, or classist attitudes; in fact, in their relationships with women, they "often engage in expressive intimacies" and "make fun of exaggerated 'machismo' " (p. 276). But though they outwardly conform more to what Pleck (1982) calls "the modern male role," their informal relationships within their sociability groups, in effect, affirm their own gender and class status by constructing and clarifying the boundaries between themselves and women and lower-status men. This dominance bonding is based largely upon ritual forms of sociability (camaraderie, competition), "the superiority of which was first affirmed in the exclusionary play activities of young boys in groups" (Farr 1988, 265).

In addition to contributing to dominance bonding among higher-status adult men, sports remains salient in terms of the ideology of gender relations. Most men continued to watch, talk about, and identify with sports long after their own disengagement from athletic careers. Sports as a mediated spectacle provides an important context in which traditional conceptions of masculine superiority—conceptions recently contested by women—are shored up. As a thirty-two-year-old white

professional-class man said of one of the most feared professional
football players today:

> A woman can do the same job as I can do—maybe even be my boss. But
> I'll be *damned* if she can go out on the football field and take a hit from
> Ronnie Lott.

Violent sports as spectacle provide linkages among men in the project of the domination of women, while at the same time helping to
construct and clarify differences among various masculinities. The
preceding statement is a clear identification with Ronnie Lott *as a
man,* and the basis of the identification is the violent male body. As
Connell (1987, 85) argues, sports is an important organizing institution
for the embodiment of masculinity. Here, men's power over women
becomes naturalized and linked to the social distribution of violence.
Sports, as a practice, suppresses natural (sex) similarities, constructs
differences, and then, largely through the media, weaves a structure of
symbol and interpretation around these differences that naturalizes
them (Hargreaves 1986, 112). It is also significant that the man who
made the statement about Ronnie Lott was quite aware that he (and
perhaps 99 percent of the rest of the U.S. male population) was
probably as incapable as most women of taking a "hit" from someone
like Lott and living to tell of it. For middle-class men, the "tough guys"
of the culture industry—the Rambos, the Ronnie Lotts who are fear-
some "hitters," who "play hurt"—are the heroes who "prove" that "we
men" are superior to women. At the same time, they play the role of the
"primitive other," against whom higher-status men define themselves
as "modern" and "civilized."

Sports, then, is important from boyhood through adulthood for men
from higher-status backgrounds. But it is significant that by adolescence and early adulthood, most of these young men have concluded
that sports *careers* are not for them. Their middle-class cultural environment encourages them to decide to shift their masculine strivings in
more "rational" directions: education and nonsports careers. Yet their
previous sports participation continues to be very important to them in
terms of constructing and validating their status within privileged male
peer groups and within their chosen professional careers. And organized
sports, as a public spectacle, is a crucial locus around which ideologies
of male superiority over women, as well as higher-status men's superiority over lower-status men, are constructed and naturalized.

Men From Lower-Status Backgrounds

For the lower-status young men in this study, success in sports was not an added proof of masculinity; it was often their only hope of achieving public masculine status. A thirty-four-year-old black bus driver who had been a star athlete in three sports in high school had neither the grades nor the money to attend college, so he accepted an offer from the U.S. Marine Corps to play on their baseball team. He ended up in Vietnam, where a grenade blew four fingers off his pitching hand. In retrospect, he believed that his youthful focus on sports stardom and his concomitant lack of effort in academics made sense:

> You can go anywhere with athletics—you don't have to have brains. I mean, I didn't feel like I was gonna go out there and be a computer expert, or something that was gonna make a lot of money. The only thing I could do and live comfortably would be to play sports—just to get a contract—doesn't matter if you play second or third team in the pros, you're gonna make big bucks. That's all I wanted, a confirmed livelihood at the end of my ventures, and the only way I could do it would be through sports. So I tried. It failed, but that's what I tried.

Similar, and even more tragic, is the story of a thirty-four-year-old black man who is now serving a life term in prison. After a career-ending knee injury at the age of twenty abruptly ended what had appeared to be a certain road to professional football fame and fortune, he decided that he "could still be rich and famous" by robbing a bank. During his high school and college years, he said, he was nearly illiterate:

> I'd hardly ever go to classes and they'd give me Cs. My coaches taught some of the classes. And I felt, "So what? They *owe* me that! I'm an *athlete*! I thought that was what I was born to do—to play sports—and everybody understood that.

Are lower-status boys and young men simply duped into putting all their eggs into one basket? My research suggested that there was more than "hope for the future" operating here. There were also immediate psychological reasons that they chose to pursue athletic careers. By the high school years, class and ethnic inequalities had become glaringly obvious, especially for those who attended socioeconomically heterogeneous schools. Cars, nice clothes, and other signs of status were often unavailable to these young men, and this contributed to a situation in which sports took on an expanded importance for them in terms of constructing masculine identities and status. A white, thirty-six-year-old man from a poor, single-parent family who later played professional baseball had been acutely aware of his low-class status in his high school:

> I had one pair of jeans, and I wore them every day. I was always afraid of what people thought of me—that this guy doesn't have anything, that he's wearing the same Levi's all the time, he's having to work in the cafeteria for his lunch. What's going on? I think that's what made me so shy. . . . But boy, when I got into sports, I let it all hang out—[laughs]—and maybe that's why I became so good, because I was frustrated, and when I got into that element, they gave me my uniform in football, basketball, and baseball, and I didn't have to worry about how I looked, because then it was *me* who was coming out, and not my clothes or whatever. And I think that was the drive.

Similarly, a forty-one-year-old black man who had a twenty-year professional football career described his insecurities as one of the few poor blacks in a mostly white, middle-class school and his belief that sports was the one arena in which he could be judged solely on his merit:

> I came from a very poor family, and I was very sensitive about that in those days. When people would say things like "Look at him—he has dirty pants on," I'd think about it for a week. [But] I'd put my pants on and I'd go out on the football field with the intention that I'm gonna do a job. And if that calls on me to hurt you, I'm gonna do it. It's a simple as that. I demand respect just like everybody else.

"Respect" was what I heard over and over when talking with the men from lower-status backgrounds, especially black men. I interpret this type of respect to be a crystallization of the masculine quest for recognition through public achievement, unfolding within a system of structured constraints due to class and race inequities. The institutional context of education (sometimes with the collusion of teachers and coaches) and the constructed structure of opportunity in the economy made the pursuit of athletic careers appear to be the most rational choice to these young men.

The same is not true of young lower-status women. Dunkle (1985) points out that from junior high school through adulthood, young black men are far more likely to place high value on sports than are young black women, who are more likely to value academic achievement. There appears to be a gender dynamic operating in adolescent male peer groups that contributes toward their valuing sports more highly than education. Franklin (1986, 161) has argued that many of the normative values of the black male peer group (little respect for nonaggressive solutions to disputes, contempt for nonmaterial culture) contribute to the constriction of black men's views of desirable social positions, especially through education. In my study, a forty-two-year-old black man who did succeed in beating the odds by using his athletic scholarship to get a college degree and eventually becoming a successful professional said:

> By junior high, you either got identified as an athlete, a thug, or a book-worm. It's very important to be seen as somebody who's capable in some area. And you *don't* want to be identified as a bookworm. I was very good with books, but I was kind of covert about it. I was a closet bookworm. But with sports, I was *somebody;* so I worked very hard at it.

For most young men from lower-status backgrounds, the poor quality of their schools, the attitudes of teachers and coaches, as well as the antieducation environment within their own male peer groups, made it extremely unlikely that they would be able to succeed as students. Sports, therefore, became *the* arena in which they attempted to "show their stuff." For these lower-status men, as Baca Zinn (1982) and Majors (1986) argued in their respective studies of Chicano men and black men, when institutional resources that signify masculine status and control are absent, physical presence, personal style, and expressiveness take on increase importance. What Majors (1986, 6) calls "cool pose" is black men's expressive, often aggressive, assertion of masculinity. This self-assertion often takes place within a social context in which the young man is quite aware of existing social inequities. As the black bus driver, referred to earlier, said of his high school years:

> See, the rich people use their money to do what they want to do. I use my ability. If you wanted to be around me, if you wanted to learn something about sports, I'd teach you. But you're gonna take me to lunch. You're gonna let me use your car. See what I'm saying? In high school I'd go where I wanted to go. I didn't have to be educated. I was well-respected. I'd go somewhere, and they'd say, "Hey, that's Mitch Harris,[1] yeah, that's a bad son of a bitch!"

Majors (1986) argues that although "cool pose" represents a creative survival technique within a hostile environment, the most likely long-term effect of this masculine posturing is educational and occupational dead ends. As a result, we can conclude, lower-status men's personal and peer-group responses to a constricted structure of opportunity—responses that are rooted, in part, in the developmental insecurities and ambivalences of masculinity—serve to lock many of these young men into limiting activities such as sports.

SUMMARY AND CONCLUSIONS

This research has suggested that within a social context that is stratified by social class and by race, the choice to pursue—or not to pursue—an athletic career is explicable as an individual's rational assessment of the available means to achieve a respected masculine identity. For nearly all of the men from lower-status backgrounds, the status and respect that they received through sports was temporary—it did not translate into upward mobility. Nonetheless, a strategy of discouraging young black boys and men from involvement in sports is probably doomed to fail, since it ignores the continued existence of structural constraints. Despite the increased number of black role models in nonsports professions, employment opportunities for young black males have actually deteriorated in the 1980s (Wilson and Neckerman 1986), and nonathletic opportunities in higher education have also declined. While blacks constitute 14 percent of the college-aged (18-24 years) U.S. population, as a proportion of students in four-year colleges and universities, they have dropped to 8 percent. In contrast, by 1985, black men constituted 49 percent of all college basketball players and 61 percent of basketball players in institutions that grant athletic scholarships (Berghorn et al., 1988). For young black men, then, organized sports appears to be more likely to get them to college than their own efforts in nonathletic activities.

But it would be a mistake to conclude that we simply need to breed socioeconomic conditions that make it possible for poor and minority men to mimic the "rational choices" of white, middle-class men. If we are to build an appropriate understanding of the lives of all men, we must critically analyze white middle-class masculinity, rather than uncritically taking it as a normative standard. To fail to do this would be to ignore the ways in which organized sports serves to construct and legitimate gender differences and inequalities among men and women.

Feminist scholars have demonstrated that organized sports gives men from all backgrounds a means of status enhancement that is not available to young women. Sports thus serve the interests of all men in helping to construct and legitimize their control of public life and their domination of women (Bryson 1987; Hall 1987; Theberge 1987). Yet concrete studies are suggesting that men's experiences within sports are not all of a piece. Brian Pronger's (1990) research suggests that gay men approach sports differently than straight men do, with a sense of "irony." And my research suggests that although sports are important for men from both higher- and lower-status backgrounds, there are crucial differences. In fact, it appears that the meaning that most men give to their athletic strivings has more to do with competing for status among men than it has to do with proving superiority over women. How can we explain this seeming contradiction between the feminist claim that sports links all men in the domination of women and the research findings that different groups of men relate to sports in very different ways?

The answer to this question lies in developing a means of conceptualizing the interrelationships between varying forms of domination and subordination. Marxist scholars of sports often falsely collapse everything into a class analysis; radical feminists often see gender domination as universally fundamental. Concrete examinations of sports, however, reveal complex and multilayered systems of inequality: Racial, class, gender, sexual preference, and age dynamics are all salient features of the athletic context. In examining this reality, Connell's (1987) concept of the "gender order" is useful. The gender order is a dynamic process that is constantly in a state of play. Moving beyond static gender-role theory and reductionist concepts of patriarchy that view men as an undifferentiated group which oppresses women, Connell argues that at any given historical moment, there are competing masculinities —some hegemonic, some marginalized, some stigmatized. Hegemonic masculinity (that definition of masculinity which is culturally ascendant) is constructed in relation to various subordinated masculinities as well as in relation to femininities. The project of male domination of women may tie all men together but men share very unequally in the fruits of this domination.

These are key insights in examining the contemporary meaning of sports. Utilizing the concept of the gender order, we can begin to conceptualize how hierarchies of race, class, age, and sexual preference among men help to construct and legitimize men's overall power and privilege over women. And how, for some black, working-class, or gay men, the false promise of sharing in the fruits of hegemonic masculinity often ties them into their marginalized and subordinate statuses within hierarchies of intermale dominance. For instance, black men's development of what Majors (1986) calls "cool pose" within sports can be interpreted as an example of creative resistance to one form of social domination (racism); yet it also demonstrates the limits of an agency that adopts other forms of social domination (masculinity) as its vehicle. As Majors (1990) points out:

> Cool pose demonstrates black males' potential to transcend oppressive conditions in order to express themselves *as men*. [Yet] it ultimately does not put black males in a position to live and work in more egalitarian ways with women, nor does it directly challenge male hierarchies.

Indeed, as Connell's (1990) analysis of an Australian "Iron Man" shows, the commercially successful, publicly acclaimed athlete may embody all that is valued in present cultural conceptions of hegemonic masculinity—physical strength, commercial success, supposed heterosexual virility. Yet higher-status men, while they admire the public image of the successful athlete, may also look down on him as a narrow, even atavistic, example of masculinity. For these higher-status men, their earlier sports successes are often status enhancing and serve to link them with other men in ways that continue to exclude women. Their decisions not to pursue athletic careers are equally important signs of their status vis-à-vis other men. Future examinations of the contemporary meaning and importance of sports to men might take as a fruitful point of departure that athletic participation, and sports as public spectacle serve to provide linkages among men in the project of the domination of women, while at the same time helping to construct and clarify differences and hierarchies among various masculinities.

NOTE

1. "Mitch Harris" is a pseudonym.

REFERENCES

Baca Zinn, M. 1982. Chicano men and masculinity. *Journal of Ethnic Studies* 10:29-44.
Baca Zinn, M., L. Weber Cannon, E. Higginbotham, and B. Thornton Dill. 1986. The costs of exclusionary practices in women's studies. *Signs: Journal of Women in Culture and Society* 11:290-303.

Benjamin, J. 1988. *The bonds of love: Psychoanalysis, feminism, and the problem of domination.* New York: Pantheon.

Berghorn, F. J. et al. 1988. Racial participation in men's and women's intercollegiate basketball: Continuity and change, 1958-1985. *Sociology of Sport Journal* 5:107-24.

Brod, H. 1983-84. Work clothes and leisure suits: The class basis and bias of the men's movement. *M: Gentle Men for Gender Justice* 11:10-12, 38-40.

Brod, H. (ed). 1987. *The making of masculinities: The new men's studies.* Winchester, MA: Allen & Unwin.

Bryson, L. 1987. Sport and the maintenance of masculine hegemony. *Women's Studies International Forum* 10:349-60.

Chodorow, N. 1978. *The reproduction of mothering.* Berkeley: University of California Press.

Connell, R. W. 1987. *Gender and power.* Stanford, CA: Stanford University Press.

————. 1990. An Iron Man: The body and some contradictions of hegemonic masculinity. In *Sport, men, and the gender order: Critical feminist perspectives,* edited by M. A. Messner and D. S. Sabo. Champaign, IL: Human Kinetics.

Dunkle, M. 1985. Minority and low-income girls and young women in athletics. *Equal Pay* 5(Spring-Summer):12-13.

Edwards, H. 1971. The myth of the racially superior athlete. *The Black Scholar* 3 (November).

————. 1973. *The sociology of sport.* Homewood, IL: Dorsey.

————. 1984. The collegiate athletic arms race: Origins and implications of the Rule 480 controversy. *Journal of Sport and Social Issues* 8:4-22.

Eitzen, D. S., and D. A. Purdy. 1986. The academic preparation and achievement of black and white college athletes. *Journal of Sport and Social Issues* 10:15-29.

Eitzen, D. S. and N. B. Yetman. 1977. Immune from racism? *Civil Rights Digest* 9:3-13.

Farr, K. A. 1988. Dominance bonding through the good old boys sociability group. *Sex Roles* 18:259-77.

Franklin, C. W. II. 1984. *The changing definition of masculinity.* New York: Plenum.

————. 1986. Surviving the institutional decimation of black males: Causes, consequences, and intervention. In *The making of masculinities: The new men's studies,* edited by H. Brod. Winchester, MA: Allen & Unwin.

Gilligan, C. 1982. *In a different voice: Psychological theory and women's development.* Cambridge, MA: Harvard University Press.

Gruneau, R. 1983. *Class, sports, and social development.* Amherst: University of Massachusetts Press.

Hall, M. A. (ed). 1987. The gendering of sport, leisure, and physical education. *Women's Studies International Forum* 10:361-474.

Hare, N., and J. Hare. 1984. *The endangered black family: Coping with the unisexualization and coming extinction of the black race.* San Francisco, CA: Black Think Tank.

Hargreaves, J. A. 1986. Where's the virtue? Where's the grace? A discussion of the social production of gender through sport. *Theory, Culture and Society* 3:109-21.

Harris, D. S., and D. S. Eitzen. 1978. The consequences of failure in sport. *Urban Life* 7:177-88.

Hill, P., and B. Lowe. 1978. The inevitable metathesis of the retiring athlete. *International Review of Sport Sociology* 9:5-29.

hooks, b. 1984. *Feminist theory: From margin to center.* Boston: South End Press.

Kimmel, M. S. (ed.). 1987. *Changing men: New directions in research on men and masculinity.* Newbury Park, CA: Sage.

Leonard, W. M. II, and J. M. Reyman. 1988. The odds of attaining professional athlete status: Refining the computations. *Sociology of Sport Journal* 5:162-69.

Lever, J. 1976. Sex differences in the games children play. *Social Problems* 23:478-87.

Levinson, D. J. 1978. *The seasons of a man's life.* New York: Ballantine.

Majors, R. 1986. Cool pose: The proud signature of black survival. *Changing men: Issues in gender, sex, and politics* 17:5-6.

————. 1990. Cool pose: Black masculinity in sports. In *Sport, men, and the gender order: Critical feminist perspectives,* edited by M. A. Messner and D. S. Sabo. Champaign, IL: Human Kinetics.

Messner, M. 1985. The changing meaning of male identity in the lifecourse of the athlete. *Arena Review* 9:31-60.

————. 1987a. The meaning of success: The athletic experience and the development of male identity. In *The Making of masculinities: The new men's studies,* edited by H. Brod. Winchester, MA: Allen & Unwin.

————. 1987b. The life of a man's seasons: Male identity in the lifecourse of the athlete. In *Changing men: New directions in research on men and masculinity,* edited by M. S. Kimmel. Newbury Park, CA: Sage.

Pleck, J. H. 1982. *The myth of masculinity.* Cambridge: MIT Press.

Pronger, B. 1990. Gay jocks: A phenomenology of gay men in athletics. In *Sport, men, and the gender order: Critical feminist perspectives,* edited by M. A. Messner and D. S. Sabo. Champaign, IL: Human Kinetics.

Rubin, L. B. 1985. *Just friends: The role of friendship in our lives.* New York: Harper & Row.

Rudman, W. J. 1986. The sport mystique in black culture. *Sociology of Sport Journal* 3:305-19.

Sabo, D. 1985. Sport, patriarchy, and male identity: New questions about men and sport. *Arena Review* 9:1-30.

Sabo, D., and R. Runfola (eds.). 1980. *Jock: Sports and male identity.* Englewood Cliffs, NJ: Prentice Hall.

Schafer, W. E. 1975. Sport and male sex role socialization. *Sport Sociology Bulletin* 4:47-54.

Staples, R. 1982. *Black masculinity.* San Francisco, CA: Black Scholar Press.

Theberge, N. 1987. Sport and women's empowerment. *Women's Studies International Forum* 10:387-93.

Wellman, D. 1986. The new political linguistics of race. *Socialist Review* 87/88:43-62.

Wilson, W. J., and K. M. Neckerman. 1986. Poverty and family structure: The widening gap between evidence and public policy issues. In *Fighting poverty,* edited by S. H. Danzinger and D. H. Weinberg. Cambridge, MA: Harvard University Press.

Part II

Making a Living: Work, Occupational Structure, and Social Mobility

The main foci of this section are women's labor experiences as related to the pervasiveness of sexism, racism, and classism in the labor market, women's locations in the occupational structure, and hierarchical order in the workplace. Of primary importance is the relationship between women's positioning in society as structured by their dissimilar race, ethnic, and class backgrounds, their daily experiences trying to "make a living," and their striving for social mobility.

First, Barbara A. Zsembik and Chuck W. Peek's study in Chapter 5, "The Effect of Economic Restructuring on Puerto Rican Women's Labor Force Participation in the Formal Sector," provides compelling evidence of how economic change at the societal level shapes women's employment and personal life. Puerto Rican women's labor force participation resulted from increasing demand and expanded job opportunity in the formal economic sector due to export-led industrialization. Zsembik and Peek examined these women's return to work after the birth of their first child as the initial point of conflict between productive and reproductive work. The increased demand for women's labor brought about new forms of their involvement in work and family life and made it more difficult for them to forego wages and remain out of the labor force to devote themselves to domestic labor. Yet such a labor demand has failed to improve women's status in Puerto Rico because state policy continues to promote men as the primary breadwinners, perpetuating patriarchal ideology and limiting opportunities for women.

In Chapter 6, gender and race are systematically and quantitatively assessed by Wu Xu and Ann Leffler, who interpret effects of these structural factors on occupational prestige, segregation, and earnings.

They empirically demonstrate both the separate and the interactive effects of gender and race for White, Black, Asian American, and Hispanic men and women. Xu and Leffler found that race had a more powerful impact than gender on the occupational prestige enjoyed by workers but gender did affect prestige within particular racial groups. With regard to occupational segregation and earnings, the strongest effects are those of gender, though race effects were evident. The authors also reported correlations between occupational prestige and the percentage of each occupation composed of the various gender and racial groups, suggesting a joint impact of gender and race. This quantitative analysis lends support to the contention of many researchers that both gender and race must be considered in examining the American occupational structure.

Similarly, the relative salience of the three primary determinants of social inequality—class, race, and gender—is elucidated in Chapters 7 and 8. Whereas the comparative study by Elizabeth Higginbotham and Lynn Weber centers on the subjective experience of upward mobility, Segura's study focuses on both objective conditions and subjective aspects of occupational mobility.

In Chapter 7, "Moving Up With Kin and Community," Higginbotham and Weber identify some commonalities and differences in the ways that Black and White professional women experience certain aspects of the mobility process. Of particular importance is the authors' attempt to situate the experience of mobility within the context of social relations (e.g., of family, partners, children, kin, friends, and the wider community) and to examine the role of support for education. Some women in both groups had parents who never expected them to attend college and who gave them little emotional and financial support. A major difference between the two groups was that Black women learned that a career should take priority over marriage and that their mobility was a contribution to the uplift of the race more than an individual achievement. Moreover, Black women dealt with the unique interaction of racial and class bias in their experiences with mobility. They also reported feeling a much greater sense of debt to their family and friends and felt more in a position to give of themselves than did White women.

In Chapter 8, "Chicana and Mexican Immigrant Women at Work," Denise A. Segura demonstrates how both structural features of the labor market and social relations in the workplace as shaped by race, class, and gender affect these women's experiences and achievement of occupational mobility. In the segmented labor market that segregates along race and gender lines, Chicana and Mexican immigrant women obtained jobs with low pay and limited avenues for advancement and also encountered conflicting social relations at work. Their perceived upward mobility is derived from the *feeling* of having a better job in comparison to a local Chicano and Mexican working-class reference group. Sometimes, just having a stable job signified upward mobility to many of them. These women meet with contradictions when subjective feelings of mobility conflict with objective conditions and this subjectivity can become a rationale through which these women deal with the alienation they experience at work. This view can hinder their objective occupational mobility by keeping them from pursuing improved conditions for themselves and for their family.

The chapters included in this section illustrate how the main thesis and subthemes of the book unfold in the economy, the wage labor market, the occupational structure, and the work organization and how race, class, and gender affect employment, occupational achievement, mobility, and social relations at work and in other institutional settings. These thoughtful analyses exemplify the macro and micro linkages, underscoring the connectedness of women's objective circumstances and subjective experiences at work and in the larger society.

5 The Effect of Economic Restructuring on Puerto Rican Women's Labor Force Participation in the Formal Sector

BARBARA A. ZSEMBIK
CHUCK W. PEEK

In the early post-World War II years, the political elite of Puerto Rico, in collaboration with U.S. government officials and business interests, developed a series of legislative efforts designed to industrialize the island (Dietz 1986). Puerto Rico was transformed from an agricultural economy to one based on services and low-wage manufacturing, an export-oriented industrialization program known as Operation Bootstrap. Men (and some women) were displaced from the extractive industries, self-employment, and family enterprises, while expanding opportunities for employment in manufacturing and services drew women into the labor force (Safa 1985). Patriarchal and capitalistic pressures joined to establish an environment in which the labor demand for men was declining concomitant with an increase in the labor demand for women. The increased demand for women's labor resulted in new forms of women's participation in work and family life, making it more difficult for them to forego wages and remain out of the labor force for family considerations.

This research examines how changes in labor opportunities between 1950 and 1980 affected married women's labor force activity. We focus on the changes in the Puerto Rican formal economy stemming from the

AUTHORS' NOTE: We gratefully acknowledge the suggestions by *Gender & Society* reviewers.

industrialization program, recognizing that, as in other countries, women were neither excluded from the formal economy nor relegated to the edges of the informal economy (Elson and Pearson 1981; Safa 1986). We examine three hypotheses; whether women's labor force activity after childbirth responds to improving opportunities for women, declining opportunities for men, or the opportunities of the household. The effects of changes in labor opportunities in the formal economy yield different opportunity costs of a woman's labor force withdrawal and will be especially apparent after the birth of her first child, the initial point of conflict between women's work and parental roles.

OPPORTUNITY COSTS AND
OPPORTUNITY STRUCTURES

Opportunity costs, part of the price of children, are the potential wages foregone by women who leave the labor force to bear and raise children (Becker 1981; Mincer 1963). They reflect individual investments in education, training, and work experience before entry into parenthood. A woman who has higher opportunity costs is more likely to remain childless, to bear fewer children, and to otherwise minimize her time spent away from waged labor. Women who have lower opportunity costs will find it easier to withdraw from the labor force when work and family roles are incompatible, for example, immediately after the birth of a child. Between 1950 and 1980, the opportunity costs of Puerto Rican women rose due to higher levels of education and their increased participation in more career-structured white-collar occupations (Safa 1992). Opportunity costs are also determined by structural factors such as labor demand (Zsembik 1990) and the household division of labor (Mason and Palan 1981).

We focus our analysis on the role of the opportunity structure, or labor demand between 1950 and 1980, in shaping a woman's opportunity costs. Puerto Rico's industrialization process developed in two stages, each shaping the demand for women's and men's employment through changes in the number of jobs typically held by women and typically held by men (Acevedo 1990). The first stage of Operation Bootstrap, beginning in 1947, reflected policies that drew labor-intensive industries (Acevedo 1990). The availability of a cheap and abundant labor force and the favorable business terms offered to U.S. corporations, who faced little international competition, drew substantial industrial capital into Puerto Rico (Melendez 1993). The second stage of industrialization began in the early 1960s as industrial policy shifted to attract capital-intensive manufacturing and service industries (Acevedo 1990).

Examining the effect of opportunity structure on a woman's opportunity costs of childbearing yields three accounts of her labor force participation after childbirth. Higher opportunity costs, and the consequent press for a speedy return to work, may accrue when the demand for women's labor intensifies, the demand for men's labor eases, or when the household relies more heavily on the wife's labor relative to that of the husband's. One explanation suggests that an increasing demand for women's labor raises the level of income foregone with labor force withdrawal, even when the wages are low relative to those of men or those of women in economies that are more industrialized. A second explanation contends that the contracting demand for men's labor and resultant economic need may press women back into the labor force, regardless of women's opportunity structure. The third explanation assumes that the household considers the household wage options relative to other income-generating strategies. Households in which wives have stable wage opportunities and husbands have insecure wage streams will send the wife into the labor force.

Women's Expanding Labor Opportunities

The deliberate development of export-oriented industrialization increased the demand for female labor in the formal economy (Rios 1990; Safa 1985), contributing to the new international division of labor and a feminization of the labor force (Standing 1989). Employers in export-oriented industries selectively recruited women for their low wages (Nash 1983; O'Connor 1987; Rivera 1986; Safa 1985), relative docility (Rivera 1986; Safa 1986), and the belief that women have the patience and skills to do repetitive and detail-oriented tasks (Lim 1981; Rivera 1986). Manufacturing industries attracted to the island during both stages of industrialization included the producers of apparel and textiles, petrochemicals, pharmaceuticals, electronics, and professional and scientific instruments (Rios 1990). Analyses of decennial censuses (Presser and Kishor 1991) and annual employment data (Acevedo 1990) show that women's labor force participation declined during the 1950s, reflecting both women's typical transition from working in the primary sector to working in the tertiary sector (Boserup 1970; Durand 1975) and women's loss of jobs in the contracting tobacco and home needle-manufacturing industries (Rivera 1986). Yet the slight decline in women's labor force participation between 1950 and 1960 was concentrated in the early teenage and later adult years (Zsembik 1988). Labor force participation among women between the ages of eighteen and twenty-four, the ages at which most women bear their first child, increased in response to intensifying labor demand and increasing levels of education (Zsembik 1988). Despite the slight decline in labor force participation, women's share of all workers increased (Presser and Kishor 1991).

The sectoral shift in labor opportunities initially provided jobs in manufacturing to women with lower levels of education, then afforded proportionately more opportunities in the service sector to higher educated women. The substantial growth of the service sector generated demand for women's labor, largely due to growth in clerical and predominantly female professional occupations (Pico 1979; Presser and Kishor 1991; Safa 1980). Indeed, the growth in occupations such as clerical work, medical services and health technology, educational services and other service work accounted for over one-half of all occupations held by Puerto Rican women in 1970 and 1980 (Amott and Matthaei 1991). Women's labor force participation steadily increased from 20 percent in 1960 to 29 percent in 1980 (Presser and Kishor 1991; Rios 1990). The increase in women's labor force participation was concentrated among women between twenty and twenty-four, rising from around 30 percent in 1960 to more than 40 percent in 1980 (Zsembik 1988); it expanded women's share of the labor force from 24 percent to 37 percent (Presser and Kishor 1991; Rios 1990).

Our first hypothesis says that women in high-demand occupations will incur higher opportunity costs and return to work sooner than women employed in other occupations by providing the opportunity to earn a wage to more women. The relatively ample supply of affordable child-care workers, typically family members and women in the informal economy (Amott and Matthaei 1991), eases women back into the labor force after a birth. Earnings in manufacturing and services were significantly higher than those in the contracting industries (Baerga 1992), further increasing opportunity costs for women employed in expanding occupations. Industries in search of women's cheap labor may also offer incentives not captured in wages but that reinforce opportunity costs, such as insurance benefits and work schedules compatible with family demands. An additional impetus to return to work rests on the likelihood of increased autonomy of working women, reinforcing responses to higher opportunity costs.

Men's Contracting Labor Opportunities

An alternative explanation of women's return to work after childbirth emphasizes economic need rather than a preference for employment over family life (Safa 1992). Men were displaced from the extractive industries as Puerto Rico industrialized and many were pressured to take jobs in the northeastern United States (Dietz 1986; Morales 1986). Men's formal labor force participation declined from 71 percent in 1950 to 54 percent in 1980 (Presser and Kishor 1991; Rios 1990). The increasing proportion of women in the labor force between 1960 and 1980 stems more from the declining participation of men than from the increasing participation of women (Presser and Kishor 1991), which is consistent with reports that it is easier for women than for men to find jobs (Safa 1986). Our second hypothesis states that women whose husbands face contracting occupational opportunities are more likely to return to work after the birth of a child than are women whose husbands' opportunities are more stable, presuming that the pressure to return to work is primarily driven by financial need. For example, prior to 1959, women's annual earnings were less than men's, but thereafter the earnings gap was unusually narrow (Presser and Kishor 1991). Men in contracting occupations are less likely to earn a family wage, especially if job benefits are considered, encouraging women to return to work.

Household Opportunities

Wallerstein and Smith (1992) argue for a reconceptualization of the interrelationships among households, the workplace, and the state, maintaining that people are articulated into the economy not as individuals but as households. Because the household functions as an economic unit, one should not look at the labor force participation of individual household members as individual decisions but rather as a combination of needs and opportunities for all household members. By this reasoning, individual opportunity costs determined by labor demand, labor supply, or preferences for work over family roles are misleading because connections among household members and the dynamics of household decision processes are overlooked. Initial industrialization of an economy expands more readily when a large proportion of workers reside in semiproletarianized households (Wallerstein and Smith 1992), households that acquire income from a variety of nonwaged economic activities. They are less dependent on wage labor than are proletarianized households, are more likely to accept a low wage, and are more attractive to industries searching for cheap labor. In the initial stage of industrialization in Puerto Rico, households relied on a variety of income-generating strategies in addition to wage labor, a semiproletarianized household structure. Between 1940 and 1972, households increasingly depended on wages (Baerga 1992) and workers pressed for higher wages, encouraging industries to move to cheaper labor markets.

The state attempted to address the poverty of its population yet continued to support industries' need for low-wage labor by mediating the households' dependence on wages. Transfer payments accelerated in the 1970s, providing income support through welfare programs such as Social Security, health services, unemployment insurance, and food stamps (Baerga 1992; Bonilla and Campos 1981; Weisskoff 1985). The state subsidized industrialization through the development of a family planning program to reduce household size, yielding a larger supply of low-wage workers. State machinery promoted a large-scale sterilization program for women of reproductive age, often surreptitiously enacted and amid ambivalence among political factions and individual men and women (Ramirez de Arellano and Seipp 1983). Redefining opportunity costs reflects household wage income foregone because of a woman's labor force withdrawal after childbirth. Our third hypothesis states that Puerto Rican women whose husbands face a contracting opportunity structure and who themselves face an expanding opportunity structure will likely to return to work because of the joint occurrence of wage income activities imposed by their husbands' contracting and their own expanding opportunities.

DATA AND SAMPLE

We use data from the 1982 Puerto Rican Fertility and Family Planning Assessment (PRFFPA) to evaluate whether the balance between women's productive and reproductive lives shifts in response to improving opportunities for women, declining opportunities for men, or their combination. This island-wide, representative sample of reproductive-age women is well suited for our analytical task because of the information it contains on the occupation of each job held since the age of

TABLE 5.1 Descriptive Statistics for Analysis Variables: Puerto Rican Women Employed Before First Birth, 1950-1980

Variable	Mean	
Dependent variable		
Return to work within 12 months	0.64	
Background characteristics		
Urban residence	0.61	
Education	11.74	(3.69)[a]
Part-time work	0.08	
Age at first birth	23.38	(3.47)
Short second-birth interval	0.10	
Women's labor demand		
In growth occupation	0.79	
Men's labor demand		
In contracting occupation	0.11	
Education	11.84	(3.71)

SOURCE: *Puerto Rican Fertility and Family Planning Assessment* (N = 568).
a. Numbers in parentheses are standard deviations.

fifteen and the timing of each childbirth, job entry, and job exit. We restrict our analysis to women who were married or in a conjugal union at the time of the first birth to capture how changes in the labor demand of men and women affect women's lives. The sample is further restricted to women who worked before the birth of a first child to evaluate the return to work as opposed to the initial entry into the workplace. We cover the time of the greatest industrial expansion, between 1950 and 1980, historically bound by the earlier depression and by the later economic crisis caused by changing oil prices, return migration, and changing industrial policy. During this period of change, the women in this sample were making initial decisions that affected the balance between work and family lives.

Variables

Our dependent variable reflects the *return to work after a first birth.* This dichotomous variable is coded 1 for women who returned to work within one year of the birth of their first child and is coded 0 for those who did not (see Table 5.1 for the descriptive statistics).

Labor demand is measured as the percentage change in number of workers in an occupation over intercensal periods, calculated with U.S.

census tabulations of detailed occupations of the employed labor force. Women are assigned the code of 1 if their occupation prior to childbirth was expanding over the decade, reflecting an increasing *demand for women's labor,* and coded 0 otherwise. The declining *demand for men's labor* is measured in a similar fashion. Women are assigned the code of 1 if their mates' occupation was contracting and coded 0 otherwise. We include a measure of *men's level of completed education* to evaluate their market advantage in training. *Household opportunities* are measured as an interaction between the wife's and husband's opportunities. A household in which the wife works in an expanding occupation and the husband works in a contracting occupation, coded as 1, has a higher opportunity cost than a household with other combinations of individual opportunities, coded as 0.

Additional variables measure the labor supply factors of opportunity costs (*education* and *work experience*), the preference for working exclusively in the home, and the geographic distribution of labor demand in the formal economy. A woman's educational level is included to account for differential preference for productive life (work commitment) and investment in work skills. Part-time work, coded as 1, before a first birth serves as a proxy for labor supply and work experience.

The preference for working exclusively in the home is measured by the age of the woman at the birth of her first child and how soon afterward she bore a second child. *Age at first birth* reflects decisions to delay reproduction experiences to gain advantages in the productive arena. Women are inhibited from returning to work because of pregnancy with a second child; women who bore a second child within a year of the first (a short *second-birth interval*) are coded as 1. Urban areas contain many newly created jobs, more service and professional jobs, and offer more opportunities for women to engage child care. Women who resided in an *urban* area at the time of the first birth are coded as 1 and 0 otherwise.

Method

We estimate a series of nested logistic regression models to evaluate the effect of opportunity structure (see Table 5.2). The first model contains only the human-capital variables, the preference for family-work variables, and the geographic-residence variable. The second model examines the hypothesis that opportunity costs are determined by women's opportunity structure. The third model evaluates whether men's

TABLE 5.2 Effect of Women's, Men's, and Household Opportunities on Women's Return to Work Within One Year Following First Birth, 1950-1980

	Models			
Independent Variables	(1)	(2)	(3)	(4)
Respondent in growing occupation	—	.496*	.489*	.558*
Mate's education	—	—	.018	.018
Mate in contracting occupation	—	—	−.560*	−.236
Household: Wife in growing occupation and husband in contracting occupation	—	—	—	−.476
Education	.102***	.088**	.073*	.072*
Part-time employment	−1.219***	−1.227***	−1.253***	−1.262***
Age at first birth	.046	.039	.039	.039
Short birth interval	−.550⁽*⁾	−.589*	−.621*	−.622*
Urban residence	−.269	−.261	−.338⁽*⁾	−.336⁽*⁾
Intercept	1.391	1.424	1.341	1.374
Model χ^2	43.27	48.92	53.68	54.35
Model df	5	6	8	9
N	568	568	568	568

SOURCE: *Puerto Rican Fertility and Family Planning Assessment.*
$^{(*)}p \le .10$; $^*p \le .05$; $^{**}p \le .01$; $^{***}p \le .001$.

opportunity structure has an effect on a woman's opportunity cost of childbearing. If the coefficient for the wife's employment in an expanding occupation is not significant and the coefficient for the husband's employment in a contracting occupation is significant, we will conclude that a woman's return to work is dependent, in part, on opportunity costs incurred by her husband's labor opportunities. If opportunity costs are determined only by a woman's opportunity structure, then the only labor demand coefficient that will achieve significance will be the demand for women's labor. The final model tests the third hypothesis, that a woman's return to work is structured by the household economy. This model introduces an interaction between the husband's contracting opportunity structure and the wife's expanding opportunity structure as a measure of the household economic unit. If this term achieves signifi-

cance and the other labor demand variables do not, we will conclude
that household opportunities more strongly shape women's labor force
participation than individual opportunity structures.

RESULTS

The first model evaluates the supply-side opportunity costs of a
woman's reproductive activity (see Table 5.2). Women who invest in
education incur greater opportunity costs for remaining out of the labor
force, evident in their greater propensity to return to work within twelve
months of the birth of their first child. Women who invest in greater
work experience through full-time employment, rather than part-time
work, return to work soon after childbirth. The preference for family
work over market work in the formal economy is only marginally
related to the return to work. Working women who become mothers
early in life and women who delay childbearing are equally likely to
return to work. Women who bear their first child at younger ages are
less likely to be employed at any time during their reproductive years.
Women who bear a second child within a year of the first are less likely
to return to work. Some women may intend to bear their second child
soon after their first and remain out of the workforce to complete their
childbearing. Other women may become pregnant unintentionally yet
find it more difficult to integrate work and family roles while pregnant.
Urban residence at the time of the first birth is unrelated to a woman's
return to work.

Women's Labor Opportunities

The second model shows the effects of a woman's opportunity structure on her return to work and is a significantly better fit to the data than
the baseline model of supply-side opportunity costs. Higher opportunity
costs incurred in an expanding occupation serve to pull women back
into the labor force after the birth of a first child. The higher opportunity
costs associated with the demand for women's labor may coincide with
occupational sex segregation, producing a relative compatibility of
work and family roles in a number of the expanding occupations;
namely, nursing, teaching, and clerical work. Women who have higher
opportunity costs because of investment in higher education and full-
time work experience remain more likely to return to work. Although a

woman's age at first birth is not associated with continuing work activity, bearing a second child tends to keep a woman out of the formal economy.

Men's Labor Opportunities

The third model offers evidence that both the opportunity structure for men and women influences women's labor force participation after childbirth, a significantly better fit to the data than the model that included only women's labor demand. men's opportunity structure clearly helps to shape a woman's labor force participation after childbirth. Yet the coefficient of women's labor demand indicates that women also blend work and family roles in response to their own opportunity structure and are not returning to work solely in response to economic need. The variables measuring women's human capital remain significant, encouraging women to return to work. The preference for family work exerts an independent influence as women who bear a second child within a year of the first remain out of the labor force.

Contrary to expectations, a woman whose husband faces more tenuous job security, typically in extractive occupations, is significantly more likely to stay out of the labor force. Perhaps the initial contraction of the extractive industries compelled men with the least job security to migrate to the United States. The remaining jobs in the extractive industries then reflect relatively more employment and economic security. Alternatively, women may economically contribute to the household through participation in informal economy because the men's labor-intensive work schedules make it more difficult for their wives to simultaneously work in the formal economy and at home.

Although these couples may reside in rural areas, the geographic distribution of wage jobs cannot explain this unexpected finding; the effect of urban residence has been controlled. Urban residence becomes marginally significant when men's labor opportunities are considered, compared to its effect in the first two models. Yet the sign is the opposite direction than expected. Women who reside in rural areas at the time of their first birth are more likely to return to work than women in urban areas. Because this effect emerges when the effects of men's opportunity structure are included, women in urban areas may be turning to informal labor.

Household Opportunities

The household opportunity structure, measured with the interaction of husband's and wife's labor demand in model 4, does not appear to shape a woman's labor force participation after childbirth. Including household opportunity in the model does not result in a significant improvement over the model that includes both women's and men's labor demand acting independently. Women in households in which a woman's wage opportunities are strong and her husband's are slim are no more likely than women in other types of households to return to work. Moreover, the coefficient for men's opportunity structure is no longer significant, indicating that men's wage opportunities do not directly or indirectly affect a woman's labor force activity after childbirth. The coefficient for women's work opportunities, however, remains significant. Clearly, economic restructuring influences women's waged work primarily by generating labor demand for women.

DISCUSSION

The results of this analysis support the position that opportunity costs of remaining out of the labor force after the birth of a child are responsive to both the supply and demand factors governing women's participation in the formal economy. Individual demand factors appear more influential than the household demand factors, although data limitations render this more suggestive than conclusive. Conventional survey research of individuals rarely includes sufficient information on household dynamics to adequately compare models of individual actors to models of household strategies. The clear effect of labor demand, however mediated by the household, indicates that economic change at the societal level shapes a woman's life. Considerable debate remains over the effect of increased participation in the formal economy on women's status (Beneria and Sen 1981; Brydon and Chant 1989; Fernandez-Kelly 1986; Lim 1983).

The expanding demand for women's labor, even in low-wage occupations, may afford women the chance to gain greater economic independence and autonomy from husbands and fathers (Hartmann 1987). Consequently, young women will delay marriage and childbearing, bear fewer children in their lifetimes, and spend more time in the workforce (Hartmann 1987). Recent demographic trends are consistent with this changing gender ideology. Younger cohorts of Puerto Rican women are marrying at later ages, bearing their first child at later ages, and are more likely to be employed before childbearing begins. Safa (1992) contends that Puerto Rican women's increased contribution to the household economy underlies an emergent, more egalitarian relationship between husbands and wives (Safa 1990, 1992); moreover, the increasing participation of Puerto Rican women in the productive arena has solidified the feminist movement (Mergal 1993).

Yet the increased demand for women's labor does not necessarily improve women's status as persistent patriarchal pressures at the societal level continue to favor policies that promote men as the primary breadwinners and as industrial capitalism holds both men and women hostage to footloose industries. First, women may have gained advantages in the household as a result of men's contracting opportunities rather than of women's expanding opportunities (Baca Zinn 1987; Kuhn and Bluestone 1987), leading some Puerto Ricans to anticipate the ultimate destruction of the marital and familial institutions. Puerto Rican officials have voiced concern about social problems that are presumed to inevitably arise in a society that inhibits men from assuming the principal provider role and have accordingly developed policies designed to reduce men's unemployment (Rios 1990). If Puerto Rican policy successfully attracts employment opportunities that favor men, Puerto Rican women may be driven out of the labor force and lose their newly acquired autonomy. Giele (1992) contends that the "lack of female power at the higher levels can work as a disincentive to female productivity and reinforce the skewed reward system that privileges men and overburdens women" (p. 7).

The persistence of patriarchal forces at the societal level is further demonstrated in poor Latin American women's social movements (Safa 1990). Women are pressing the state, not specific industries, to meet their demands for public services and improved human rights. Safa asserts that these movements are partially responsible for Latin American women's increased awareness of their gender subordination and holds hope that it will translate into a long-term trend.

Second, prevalent jobs tend to be low-wage jobs, susceptible to relocation to ever-cheaper labor markets, that do not lift women from relative impoverishment. Reliance on footloose industries for women's employment produces only a fleeting liberation as women and their families remain economically vulnerable to the threat of corporate flight (Safa 1990). Puerto Rico already has lost jobs, as wages and international competition grows, to nearby Caribbean countries and to the Pacific Rim. Dietz and Pantojas-Garcia (1993) suggest that this is the final stage of the postwar restructuring, generating *maquiladoras* or "twin plants." The more labor-intensive segments of production in garment and electronics assembly shift in a continual search for cheap labor, yet Puerto Rico thus far has succeeded in maintaining the finishing and packaging process for exports to the United States.

The Puerto Rican economy continues to depend on U.S. funding; U.S. firms provide job opportunities and the federal government provides income-maintaining transfer payments. Intensifying international competition thrusts foreign investment into a habitual search for cheap labor, often finding it in the more peripheral Pacific Rim. Puerto Rico's shift toward the economic center relative to other Third World countries, but persistent semiperipheral placement relative to the U.S. economy, indicates that well-paying, secure jobs for women and men will remain scarce. The deepening global economic crisis foreordains Puerto Rican women's and men's continued dependence on industrial capital's need for women's cheap labor, maintaining women as a last colony (Acosta-Belen and Bose 1990).

REFERENCES

Acevedo, L. D. 1990. Industrialization and employment: Changes in the patterns of women's work in Puerto Rico. *World Development* 18:231-55.

Acosta-Belen, E., and C. E. Bose. 1990. From structural subordination to empowerment: Women and development in Third World contexts. *Gender & Society* 4:299-320.

Amott, T. L., and J. A. Matthaei. 1991. *Race, gender, and work: A multicultural economic history of women in the United States.* Boston: South End.

Baca Zinn, M. 1987. Structural transformation and minority families. In *Women, households, and the economy,* edited by L. Benaria and C. R. Stimpson. New Brunswick, NJ: Rutgers University Press.

Baerga, M. del Carmen. 1992. Puerto Rico: From colony to colony. In *Creating and transforming households: The constraints of the world-economy,* coordinated by J. Smith and I. Wallerstein. Cambridge, UK: Cambridge University Press.

Becker, G. 1981. *A treatise on the family.* Cambridge, MA: Harvard University Press.

Beneria, L., and G. Sen. 1981. Accumulation, reproduction and women's role in economic development. *Signs* 7:279-98.

Bonilla, F., and R. Campos. 1981. A wealth of poor: Puerto Ricans in the new economic order. *Daedalus* 110:133-76.

Boserup, E. 1970. *Women's role in economic development.* New York: St. Martin's.

Brydon, L., and S. Chant. 1989. *Women in the Third World: Gender issues in rural and urban areas.* New Brunswick, NJ: Rutgers University Press.

Dietz, J. L. 1986. *Economic history of Puerto Rico: Institutional change and capitalist development.* Princeton, NJ: Princeton University Press.

Dietz, J. L., and E. Pantojas-Garcia. 1993. Puerto Rico's new role in the Caribbean: The high finance/maquiladora strategy. In *Colonial dilemma: Cultural perspectives on contemporary Puerto Rico*, edited by E. Melendez and E. Melendez. Boston: South End.

Durand, J. D. 1975. *The labor force in economic development*. Princeton, NJ: Princeton University Press.

Elson, D., and R. Pearson. 1981. Nimble fingers make cheap workers: An analysis of women's employment in Third World export manufacturing. *Feminist Review* 7:87-107.

Fernandez-Kelly, M. P. 1986. Introduction. In *Women's work: Development and the division of labor by gender*, edited by E. Leacock, H. I. Safa, and contributors. New York: Bergin & Garvey.

Giele, J. Z. 1992. Promise and disappointment of the modern era: Equality for women. In *Women's work and women's lives: The continuing struggle worldwide*, edited by H. Kahne and J. Z. Giele. Boulder, CO: Westview.

Hartmann, H. I. 1987. Changes in women's economic and family roles in post-World War II United States. In *Women, households, and the economy*, edited by L. Beneria and C. R. Stimpson. New Brunswick, NJ: Rutgers University Press.

Kuhn, S., and B. Bluestone. 1987. Economic restructuring and the female labor market: The impact of industrial change on women. In *Women, households, and the economy*, edited by L. Beneria and C. R. Stimpson. New Brunswick, NJ: Rutgers University Press.

Lim, L. Y. C. 1981. Women's work in multinational electronics factories. In *Women and technological change in developing countries*, edited by R. Dauber and M. L. Cain. Boulder, CO: Westview.

———. 1983. Capitalism, imperialism, and patriarchy: The dilemma of Third-World women workers in multinational factories. In *Women, men, and the international division of labor*, edited by J. Nash and M. P. Fernandez-Kelly. Albany: State University of New York Press.

Mason, K. O., and V. T. Palan. 1981. Female employment and fertility in peninsular Malaysia: The maternal role incompatibility hypothesis reconsidered. *Demography* 18:549-75.

Melendez, E. 1993. Colonialism, citizenship, and contemporary statehood. In *Colonial dilemma: Cultural perspectives on contemporary Puerto Rico*, edited by E. Melendez and E. Melendez. Boston: South End.

Mergal, M. 1993. Puerto Rican feminism at a crossroad: Challenges at the turn of the century. *Colonial dilemma: Cultural perspectives on contemporary Puerto Rico*, edited by E. Melendez and E. Melendez. Boston: South End.

Mincer, J. 1963. Market prices, opportunity costs, and income effects. In *Measurement in economics: Studies in mathematical economics and econometrics in memory of Yehuda Grunfeld*. Stanford, CA: Stanford University Press.

Morales, J. 1986. *Puerto Rican poverty: We just had to try elsewhere*. New York: Praeger.

Nash, J. 1983. The impact of the changing international division of labor on different sectors of the labor force. In *Women, men, and the international division of labor*, edited by J. Nash and M. P. Fernandez-Kelly. Albany: State University of New York Press.

O'Connor, D. C. 1987. Women workers and the changing international division of labor in microelectronics. In *Women, households, and the economy,* edited by L. Beneria and C. R. Stimpson. New Brunswick, NJ: Rutgers University Press.

Pico, I. 1979. The history of women's struggle for equality in Puerto Rico. In *The Puerto Rican woman,* edited by E. Acosta-Belen. New York: Praeger.

Presser, H. B., and S. Kishor. 1991. Economic development and occupational sex segregation in Puerto Rico: 1950-1980. *Population and Development Review* 17:53-85.

Ramirez de Arellano, A., and C. Seipp. 1983. *Colonialism, Catholicism and contraception in Puerto Rico.* Chapel Hill: University of North Carolina Press.

Rios, P. N. 1990. Export-oriented industrialization and the demand for female labor: Puerto Rican women in the manufacturing sector, 1952-1980. *Gender & Society* 4:321-37.

Rivera, M. 1986. The development of capitalism in Puerto Rico and the incorporation of women into the labor force. In *The Puerto Rican woman,* edited by E. Acosta-Belen. New York: Praeger.

Safa, H. I. 1980. Class consciousness among working class women in Latin America: Puerto Rico. In *Sex and class in Latin America: Women's perspectives on politics, economics, and the family in the Third World,* edited by J. Nash and H. I. Safa. New York: J. F. Bergin.

————. 1985. Female employment in the Puerto Rican working class. In *Women and change in Latin America,* edited by J. Nash, H. I. Safa, and contributors. South Hadley, MA: Bergin & Garvey.

————. 1986. Runaway shops and female employment: The search for cheap labor. In *Women's work: Development and the division of labor by gender,* edited by E. Leacock, H. I. Safa, and contributors. New York: Bergin & Garvey.

————. 1990. Women's social movements in Latin America. *Gender & Society* 4:353-70.

————. 1992. Development and changing gender roles in Latin America and the Caribbean. In *Women's work and women's lives: The continuing struggle worldwide,* edited by H. Kahne and J. Z. Giele. Boulder, CO: Westview.

Standing, G. 1989. Global feminization through flexible labor. *World Development* 17:1077-96.

Wallerstein, I., and J. Smith. 1992. Households as an institution of the world-economy. In *Creating and transforming households: The constraints of the world-economy,* coordinated by J. Smith and I. Wallerstein. Cambridge, UK: Cambridge University Press.

Weisskoff, R. 1985. *Factories and food stamps.* Baltimore: Johns Hopkins University Press.

Zsembik, B. A. 1988. A question of balance: The employment of Puerto Rican Women during their reproductive years. Ph.D. diss., University of Texas at Austin.

————. 1990. Labor market structure and fertility differences among Puerto Rican women: The effects of economic and social policies on opportunity costs. *Population Development and Policy Review* 9:133-49.

6 Gender and Race Effects on Occupational Prestige, Segregation, and Earnings

WU XU
ANN LEFFLER

THEORETICAL BACKGROUND

It is well documented that all societies recognize some sort of gender differentiation and that most or all exhibit some level of gender stratification—a rank ordering of men and women that signifies the unequal distribution of power and the distribution of resources. In the United States, as the rate of female labor force participation has risen, social scientists have paid increasing attention to women's position in the labor force. Of special interest is the continuing pattern of women's concentration in occupations with low wages, low prestige, and high gender segregation—although the proportion of women in the labor force has markedly increased. Similar patterns are known to characterize the labor force experiences of various racial minorities. But theories attempting to explain women's disadvantaged position in the labor market tend not to place equal emphasis on racial patterns, while those analyzing race tend not to give equal attention to gender (King 1990). As a result, the interactive impacts of race and gender on labor force experience are unclear. In this chapter, we examine three classic foci of labor force analysis: occupational segregation, earnings, and

AUTHORS' NOTE: We are grateful to Christine E. Bose, Deborah King, Doris Wilkinson, and the anonymous reviewers of this work for their comments. We also thank Dair L. Gillespie for her advice about theory and Luis M. C. Paita for his advice about data analysis. An earlier version of this work was presented at the 1990 American Sociological Association meeting.

prestige. After reviewing the literature about gender and race effects on each, we present our own effort to explore gender and race impacts.

Although explanations of gender effects on various occupational characteristics differ (e.g., Blumberg 1978; England 1984; Glenn 1987; Kanter 1975; Madden 1985; Marini 1989; Sokoloff 1987), researchers agree that gender affects occupational segregation (Bielby and Baron 1986; Fox and Hesse-Biber 1984; Jacobs 1989; Malveaux 1982; Tienda, Smith, and Ortiz 1987; Waite 1981), earnings (Russell et al. 1989; Smith 1977; Wagman and Folbre 1988), and prestige (Bose and Rossi 1983; Powell and Jacobs 1983; Tyree and Hicks 1988). Race effects on occupational characteristics have an even more venerable standing in the literature (Allen and Farley 1986).

When race and gender have been examined together, the results have been intriguing. For example, with respect to the joint impact of race and gender on *occupational segregation,* Glenn (1987) highlights the impact of race on racial-ethnic women. Sokoloff emphasizes both race and gender, suggesting that Black women work in the bottom strata of female-stratified jobs (1987). Concerning *earnings differentials,* Blumberg (1978) argues, "Sex is a greater penalty than race when it comes to earnings" (p. 105). Steel, Abeles, and Card (1982) report that sex appears to be a strong direct determinant of occupational achievement. Marini (1989) agrees and states, "There is a large sex difference in earnings in all racial groups" (p. 345). Sorenson, too, emphasizes gender, reporting that occupational segregation by race is not a significant factor influencing earnings except for White men (1989). England et al. (1988, 544) report their findings of "pay discrimination against men and women in predominantly female occupations." Studies of *occupational prestige* tend to examine gender more often than they examine race. Findings often indicate that the gender composition of occupations has a significant effect on prestige ratings (Bose and Rossi 1983; England 1979; Powell and Jacobs 1983; Powers and Holmberg 1978). Women receive less prestige for their work than do men (Tyree and Hicks 1988). However, Bose and Rossi (1983) suggest that the significant impact of gender composition on prestige can be seen only in the most prestigious occupations. Examining the effects of race on prestige, Sampson and Rossi (1975) find that White households receive higher prestige scores than Black ones. A rare and notable effort to investigate gender and race prestige differences simultaneously is put forth by Sullivan (1984), who reports that gender-based prestige differences exist among Cuban and

Mexican immigrants, while race-based differences characterize White women and Hispanic immigrant women.

However, since studies have tended to examine different pools of occupations with respect to the occupational characteristics of segregation, earnings, and prestige and since race and gender usually are not examined together, the specific interlinked impacts of race and gender on different characteristics of the same occupations remain unclear (Mason 1986). For example, the notion of "double jeopardy" has been widely theorized but rarely examined empirically. King (1988) questions the implication of the double jeopardy assumption that relationships among various discriminations are simply and constantly additive and calls for an empirical effort to determine the issue.

Besides a lack of sufficient research about the joint impacts of race and gender on different characteristics of the same occupations, studies are often limited to a small set of specific racial comparisons, for example, White versus Black (McLanahan, Sorensen, and Watson 1989; Smith 1977; Williams and Rodeheaver 1989) or White versus Black and/or Hispanic (Kelly and Garcia 1988; Marini 1989; Segura 1989; Stephens, Oser, and Blau 1980; Tienda, Smith, and Ortiz 1987). Asian American women have been largely excluded from gender/race analyses of segregation, earnings, and prestige. Nor have various gender/race combinations been contrasted with a single comparison group. In short, the literature suggests gaps in our understanding of race and gender effects on particular occupational characteristics. In order to bridge some of these gaps in literature, this study examines some of the interlinked relations of gender and race on the occupational characteristics of prestige, segregation, and earnings.

To do this, we pool data about occupational prestige, segregation, and earnings. We use White men as the comparison group for each gender/race combination and we use a variety of gender/race combinations: White men, White women, Black men, Black women, Asian American men, Asian American women, Hispanic men, and Hispanic women. We have selected the racial categories that are most populous in the labor force. However, it is important to keep in mind that each racial category includes a wide array of groups, masking great status differences between groups within it. The general racial categories are used here because the data available to us do not provide sufficiently detailed information to permit separate analysis of the groups within categories. The sole alterations we have made in census taxonomies are changing its 1980 "Spanish origin" label to "Hispanic" and its "Asian and Pacific Islander" label to "Asian American" to reflect contemporary usages. It is also important to keep in mind that gender/race effects on occupational characteristics and interpretations of these effects change over time. Thus, for example, in the 1950s research literature, race seemed to be the category that primarily organized occupational earnings. In the 1980s, while debates raged over race versus class effects on life chances, gender received more attention as an occupational stratifier.

METHODS AND DATA

Occupational Prestige

Interest in prestige has been given a central role in sociology by its connection with status in Weber's famous tripartite conception of inequality (Gerth and Mills 1946). Occupational prestige is usually conceptualized in the literature as a matter of collective subjective consensus concerning occupational status. National Opinion Research Council (NORC) prestige scores are the benchmark prestige studies in terms of securing subjective ranking of a large number of occupations (Miller 1991). This chapter, however, employs the prestige standing of occupations reported by Bose and Rossi (1983), because Bose and Rossi deliberately selected occupations for their study that were particularly useful for looking at gender issues. Compared with NORC scores, Bose and Rossi's prestige study highlighted gender-incumbency effects of stereotyped "men and women's occupations" on prestige, which makes Bose and Rossi's scores more suitable for gender-related research. While Bose and Rossi considered racial effects on the behavior of prestige rating, race was not their main focus. Bose and Rossi chose 108 occupations, mainly on the basis of probabilities constructed to reflect their gender compositions. They then asked respondents subjectively to rate the social standing of each job on a scale of 1 (low) to 9 (high). These raw scores were converted via a linear transformation to the standard prestige metric of 0 (low) to 100 (high) used by NORC. Respondents were obtained through block quota sampling of Baltimore households. Although Bose and Rossi asked respondents to assess prestige when the gender of the job holder was specified, as well as when it was not, only the latter prestige scores are used here.

Occupational Segregation

In order to examine correlations between prestige scores and gender and racial clustering in occupations, the present analysis is restricted to occupations that have the same titles in Bose and Rossi's (1983) reports of prestige scores and the tabulations of the 1980 U.S. census. Bose and Rossi used 1960 census occupational titles, and many changes have occurred in nomenclature and job duties since then. We retained only those occupations we judged closely analogous in both their 1960 and their 1980 names and duties. From these, we discarded any for which information about gender and race distributions was unavailable. The result was a set of 52 occupations out of Bose and Rossi's original 108 and out of 503 in the reports of the 1980 census.

Unfortunately, the need to exclude occupations for which some data were unavailable means that our analysis cannot be generalized to the whole labor force. First, gender/race distributions are somewhat different here than in the overall labor force in 1980. Because Bose and Rossi (1983) selected occupations according to gender composition, our data include a higher percentage of women (58%) than in the 1980 U.S. census (43%). The racial composition in this study, however, is similar to that in the 1980 U.S. census. Because of our own needs to match census occupations with those of Bose and Rossi and to address gender/race effects, two major occupational categories in the 1980 U.S. census —executive/administrative/managerial and farming/forestry/fishing— are not represented here (see U.S. Bureau of the Census 1983). Thus, given the data currently available, the price of analyzing gender/race effects on prestige, segregation, and earnings in the same occupations is sacrificing generalizability. The importance of the topic, however, suggests that exploratory work like ours may be useful in inspiring further research.

Earnings

In order to minimize the effects of unemployment and underemployment on earnings comparisons, our analysis of earnings is restricted to full-time, year-round workers. Of the 52 occupations we used for the segregation analyses, we were able to obtain sufficient information on gender and race earnings for 29 of them to permit comparisons across gender/race groups. These 29 occupations are the basis for our earnings

TABLE 6.1 Mean Prestige Across 52 Occupations, by Gender/Race Group

	White	Black	Asian American	Hispanic
Men	50.7	37.8	55.9	40.7
		$\overline{X}$ Men = 49.0	$\overline{X}$ Women = 47.4	
Women	48.5	42.1	48.3	41.2
	$\overline{X}$ White = 49.4	$\overline{X}$ Black = 40.5	$\overline{X}$ Asian American = 51.3	$\overline{X}$ Hispanic = 41.0

SOURCE: U.S. Bureau of the Census (1984, Table 278).

analyses. (The detailed procedure of selecting occupations for this study can be obtained from the authors.)

RESULTS

Occupational Prestige

To what degree do workers' different gender and race characteristics affect their chances of holding occupations with different prestige levels? To assess the prestige levels at which each gender/race group of workers finds itself, we weighted Bose and Rossi's (1983) prestige scores of 52 occupations by how many workers actually occupied each job according to the 1980 census. Table 6.1 reports the results as mean occupational prestige scores for each gender/race group. It also reports weighted means between genders across races and between races across genders.

These means suggest that race influences the occupational prestige level a worker is likely to occupy more than gender does. Black men and Hispanic men have the lowest mean scores (37.8 and 40.7) of all gender/race groups. White women have the highest mean occupational prestige (48.5), followed by Asian American women (48.3), Black (42.1), and Hispanic women (41.2). Although across race women's mean prestige is lower than men's (47.4 vs. 49.0), this difference is far less than weighted prestige means for race groups across gender. However, an examination of variations within each race reveals an interaction of race and gender in which gender affects some race groups far more powerfully than others. Thus, while the prestige gap between

TABLE 6.2 Indices of Occupational Segregation[a] for Each Gender/
Race Group Among 52 Occupations

| | Index of Segregation | |
Race/Gender	Men	Women
White	00.0[b]	71.9
Black	31.4	69.8
Asian American	34.8	69.8
Hispanic	22.3	72.6

SOURCE: U.S. Bureau of the Census (1984, Table 278).
a. The formula for the Index of Segregation is $IS = \frac{1}{2} \Sigma \mid r_{ja} - r_{ia} \mid$, where r_j stands for the percentage of occupational distribution for each race/gender group and r_i stands for the percentage of occupational distribution for white men.
b. White men are the comparison group in this table.

Asian American men and women is 7.6, it is 4.3 for Blacks, 2.2 for Whites, and 0.5 for Hispanics. Gender evidently affects the prestige fates of Asian American workers more than those of other race groups, especially Hispanics.

Occupational Segregation

To what extent is the part of the labor force this chapter examines clustered by gender and race? Specifically, how much are various gender/race groups segregated in particular occupations compared to White men? To examine this question, we report indices of segregation in Table 6.2. These indices address the percentage of workers in each gender/race group needing to change jobs in order to mirror the distribution across occupations of White men.

In these indices of segregation, gender outweighs race as a determinant of labor force concentration. To match White male distributions across our 52 occupations, approximately 72 percent of the White women, 70 percent of the Black women, 70 percent of the Asian American women, and 73 percent of the Hispanic women in the sample would need different jobs. On the other hand, approximately 31 percent of the Black men in the sample would need different jobs, compared to 35 percent of Asian American men and 22 percent of Hispanic men. Thus, when segregation alone is examined, the gender gap is wider than the race gap, although clearly both gender and race affect occupational distributions.

TABLE 6.3 Correlations of Occupational Prestige Scores and Gender/
Race Compositions of 52 Selected Occupations

	Correlation Coefficient	
Race/Gender	Men	Women
White	.27*	−.08
Black	−.49**	−.30*
Asian American	.26	.00
Hispanic	−.41**	−.42**

SOURCE: U.S. Bureau of the Census (1984, Table 278).
*p ≤ .05, two-tailed test; **p ≤ .01, two-tailed test.

Occupational Segregation and Prestige

A more complex picture emerges than that for prestige or segregation, however, once we examine the occupations in which workers are segregated in terms of the prestige of these occupations. Table 6.3 reports correlations between occupational prestige and the percentage of each occupation composed of the various gender/race groups.

These data suggest the joint impact of race and gender, except for the two Asian American groups. The significant positive correlation for White males indicates that the more exclusively an occupation is composed of White men, the higher its prestige. The proportions of occupations that are composed of Black or Hispanic workers of either gender are significantly negatively related to prestige. The distribution of White women is negatively related to occupational prestige, but not significantly. Prestige is correlated positively with the distribution of Asian American men, but not significantly. The lack of association between prestige and occupational clustering for Asian American men and women may reflect the selectivity of immigration among Asian Americans. For instance, the need for nursing professionals in American job markets has provided more opportunities for immigrants from Asia, especially from the Philippines (Asis 1991).

The way that prestige and segregation interact can be seen by examining the occupational distribution of each gender/race group. Table 6.4 indicates into which of our 52 occupations each gender/race group was most likely to fall, according to the 1980 census.

White and Asian American men are most likely to be concentrated within the higher prestige jobs. White men are the most concentrated group in 10 of the top 26 occupations; Asian American men, in 6. By contrast, the next highest scoring groups hold positions in 4 of the 26 highest prestige occupations (White women) and 3 of the top 26 (Black women), sharing between them an additional modal spot in the eleventh-ranking administrative assistant occupation. In contrast, White men are not the most concentrated group in any of the lowest prestige occupations ($N = 26$). Rather, Black men, Hispanic men, and Hispanic women each hold 6 of these positions, while Black women hold 4.

Examining the specific occupational and prestige distribution of each group, we can see that some occupations usually labeled as "men's jobs" (e.g., physician, lawyer, and janitor) are not men's jobs regardless of race. Further, occupations labeled as "women's jobs" (e.g., registered nurse, secretary, and housekeeper) are not equally distributed across different racial women's groups. Consequently, while approximately 38 percent of Asian American men, 22 percent of White men, and 22 percent of Asian American women find themselves in the 10 highest prestige occupations, only about 13 percent of White women do; the figures are lower for Hispanic men (11%), Black women (10%), Black men (9%), and Hispanic women (8%).

Earnings and Prestige

Next, we ask how the earnings of each gender/race group compare with those of White men. In order to control for underemployment and unemployment, which are known to affect the gender/race groups differently, we examine full-time, year-round workers only. Group earnings expressed as percentages of White male earnings are reported in Table 6.5.

With respect to earnings, gender effects are more discernible than race effects. Among full-time, year-round workers in the occupations sampled, Black, Asian American, and Hispanic men earn an average of approximately 84 percent to 94 percent of what White men make. White, Black, Asian American, and Hispanic women, on the other hand, report earnings that average approximately 66 percent to 77 percent of White men's earnings. There is no overlap between these gender means. Every race group of women earns less on the average than any race group of men.

The ordering of race groups varies slightly by gender. Among men, Asian Americans most nearly approach White male earnings, followed

(text continues on page 120)

TABLE 6.4 Percentage of Individuals in Each Occupation, by Prestige of Occupation, Race, and Gender

Prestige Rank	Occupation	Prestige Score	Men				Women				Total in Labor Force
			White	Black	Asian American	Hispanic	White	Black	Asian American	Hispanic	
1	Physician	95.8	2.71	0.75	12.51†	1.96	0.25	0.15	2.96	0.26	1.28
2	Lawyer	90.1	3.42†	0.67	1.07	0.83	0.37	0.19	0.24	0.19	1.48
3	Professor	90.1	3.00	1.10	5.99†	1.13	1.22	0.70	1.43	0.72	1.86
4	Architect	88.8	0.73	0.19	1.51†	0.46	0.05	0.01	0.09	0.04	0.31
5	Electrical engineer	79.5	2.30	0.58	5.53†	0.86	0.08	0.07	0.17	0.07	0.95
6	Registered nurse	75.0	0.36	0.39	0.77	0.31	6.44	4.19	11.09†	2.56	3.76
7	Sociologist	74.7	0.01	0.01	0.02†	0.00	0.01	0.00	0.01	0.00	0.01
8	Accountant	71.2	4.69	1.64	7.74†	2.18	0.20	1.38	4.07	1.35	2.95
9	Secondary teacher	70.2	2.82†	1.50	1.20	1.08	2.56	2.03	1.10	1.26	0.71
10	Office manager	68.3	1.98†	1.92	1.73	1.73	1.83	1.78	1.27	1.62	1.88
11	Administrative assistant	67.8	0.94	0.84	1.19	0.78	1.38†	1.38†	1.30	1.27	1.19
12	Elementary teacher	65.4	4.16	3.30	2.22	2.10	8.91	9.34†	4.74	4.96	6.79
13	Stationary engineer	64.5	0.93†	0.69	0.82	0.52	0.02	0.02	0.01	0.02	0.39
14	Social worker	63.2	1.00	1.83	1.03	1.35	1.31	2.71†	0.97	1.54	1.32
15	Clinical technician	63.1	0.39	0.57	1.65	0.46	0.88	0.92	2.45†	0.62	0.71
16	Artist	62.8	0.20†	0.11	0.19	0.19	0.10	0.03	0.07	0.05	0.14
17	Electrician	62.5	4.40†	1.95	2.14	2.69	0.06	0.08	0.06	0.08	1.75
18	Insurance agent	62.5	3.23†	1.27	1.90	1.20	0.76	0.52	0.54	0.46	1.66
19	Police officer	58.3	2.85†	2.22	1.00	1.79	0.11	0.21	0.04	0.12	1.22
20	Practical nurse	56.4	0.09	0.21	0.14	0.09	1.95	3.44†	1.50	1.46	1.26
21	Dental assistant	54.8	0.02	0.03	0.08	0.02	0.82†	0.27	0.57	0.81	0.45
22	Carpenter	53.5	8.16†	3.88	3.20	7.54	0.09	0.10	0.06	0.11	3.27
23	Stenographer	52.6	0.06	0.03	0.04	0.04	0.41†	0.10	0.42	0.30	0.25
24	Secretary	51.3	0.34	0.29	0.43	0.29	21.09†	10.04	10.13	14.86	11.50

#	Occupation									
25	Bookkeeper	50.0	1.35	0.90	2.91	1.31	9.18†	3.09	6.76	5.43	5.43
26	Toolmaker	48.4	1.45†	0.40	0.37	0.62	0.02	0.02	0.01	0.02	0.56
27	Welder	46.8	4.69	4.77	2.69	7.02†	0.19	0.30	0.11	0.32	2.12
28	Telephone operator	46.2	0.17	0.28	0.18	0.25	1.32	1.78†	0.64	1.27	0.87
29	Typist	44.9	0.13	0.30	0.37	0.27	3.25	4.85†	3.53	4.24	2.08
30	Auto mechanic	44.9	6.57	4.49	4.69	6.96†	0.05	0.07	0.05	0.08	2.70
31	Data-entry keyer	44.6	0.18	0.33	0.56	0.30	1.62	2.67	3.35†	2.24	1.12
32	Postal clerk	42.3	1.06	0.25	1.66†	1.14	0.36	1.47	0.44	0.32	0.79
33	Truck driver (heavy)	40.1	11.60	15.74†	2.77	11.10	0.19	0.25	0.05	0.19	5.09
34	Hairdresser	39.4	0.48	0.30	0.39	0.73	2.57	1.50	1.91	2.94†	1.62
35	Sales worker, shoe	35.9	0.33	0.33	0.26	0.50†	0.34	0.16	0.16	0.30	0.32
36	Cashier	35.6	1.99	2.02	3.76	2.86	7.42	6.16	6.65	8.36†	5.10
37	File clerk	34.0	0.37	0.63	0.64	0.43	1.03	1.77†	1.12	1.56	0.82
38	Dress cutter	33.3	0.03	0.06	0.02	0.08†	0.02	0.04	0.02	0.05	0.03
39	Hospital aide	29.5	0.86	3.41	1.18	1.26	4.73	14.10†	4.39	5.89	3.85
40	Bookbinder	28.2	0.09	0.07	0.08	0.11	0.08	0.07	0.05	0.13†	0.08
41	Textile machine operator	27.9	1.65	4.08	2.44	4.28	5.29	10.09	12.23	15.37†	4.42
42	Truck driver (light)	26.9	3.34	3.74	1.80	4.17†	0.18	0.12	0.06	0.17	1.52
43	Shoe repairer	26.0	0.14	0.16	0.18	0.35†	0.05	0.03	0.03	0.08	0.09
44	Housekeeper	25.3	0.01	0.06	0.05	0.04	0.20	1.12	0.41	1.15†	0.20
45	Stock clerk	24.4	2.55	3.35†	2.68	2.91	1.01	1.08	0.89	1.03	1.70
46	Waiter/waitress	22.1	1.07	1.14	5.28	2.61	6.62†	2.25	6.44	4.53	4.05
47	Short-order clerk	21.5	0.30	0.37†	0.33	0.35	0.13	0.21	0.09	0.09	0.21
48	Laundry worker	14.7	0.00	0.00	0.04†	0.00	0.01	0.02	0.01	0.02	0.01
49	Janitor	12.5	9.23	21.52†	8.22	16.30	1.84	5.89	1.91	4.06	5.84
50	Maid/houseman	10.3	0.72	3.31	1.50	2.61	1.31	0.73	3.33	5.26†	1.82
51	Vehicle washer	8.3	0.66	1.51†	0.49	1.36	0.09	0.19	0.08	0.15	0.38
52	Parking lot attendant	8.0	0.17	0.53†	0.36	0.46	0.01	0.02	0.02	0.03	0.10
	Total	100	100	100	100	100	100	100	100	100	100

SOURCE: U.S. Bureau of the Census (1984, Table 278).
†Indicates the most concentrated race/gender group in each occupation.

TABLE 6.5 Earnings of Full-Time Year-Round Workers as Percentages of White Men's Earnings by Occupational Prestige and Gender/Race Group

Prestige Rank	Occupation	Prestige Score	Men				Women			
			White	Black	Asian American	Hispanic	White	Black	Asian American	Hispanic
1	Physician	95.8	100.0	74.6	90.3	89.3	39.2	34.6	59.9	53.5
2	Professor	90.1	100.0	84.6	100.9	89.9	70.0	65.5	76.0	66.7
3	Architect	88.8	100.0	83.1	98.9	93.0	68.3	76.1	74.2	71.3
4	Electrical engineer	79.5	100.0	85.7	99.8	91.4	75.4	66.5	79.2	74.4
5	Registered nurse	75.0	100.0	93.5	107.7	89.4	89.7	91.7	100.3	91.7
6	Accountant	71.2	100.0	79.4	84.9	82.5	61.3	61.9	67.8	59.0
7	Secondary teacher	70.2	100.0	90.3	106.0	88.3	77.9	76.9	92.9	72.5
8	Office manager	68.3	100.0	82.7	90.9	78.8	60.5	63.3	66.6	58.5
9	Elementary teacher	65.4	100.0	90.6	106.4	88.0	75.5	72.0	95.1	67.6
10	Social worker	63.2	100.0	88.0	96.6	87.0	80.5	78.1	86.3	74.9
11	Clinical technician	63.1	100.0	87.1	109.1	95.3	74.1	73.9	95.9	74.0
12	Electrician	62.5	100.0	83.7	106.2	83.9	63.7	64.1	52.9	60.0
13	Insurance agent	62.5	100.0	77.7	89.6	85.8	62.5	61.8	69.7	62.5

14	Police officer	58.3	100.0	96.8	101.9	99.9	74.7	83.6	69.2	71.2
15	Practical nurse	56.4	100.0	102.3	96.5	99.2	87.6	94.6	103.3	89.7
16	Carpenter	53.5	100.0	81.7	119.7	85.4	69.8	61.3	59.6	68.9
17	Secretary	51.3	100.0	68.5	79.2	72.4	64.9	64.4	72.7	63.6
18	Bookkeeper	50.0	100.0	80.1	85.2	79.7	64.7	65.4	73.4	63.9
19	Toolmaker	48.4	100.0	84.3	86.4	84.4	60.0	60.5	98.5	41.9
20	Welder	46.8	100.0	89.1	74.6	86.3	64.9	65.4	67.7	54.3
21	Telephone operator	46.2	100.0	70.2	67.6	63.9	60.6	63.0	66.4	56.3
22	Auto mechanic	44.9	100.0	86.1	113.4	89.3	79.8	75.2	92.5	84.7
23	Data-entry keyer	44.6	100.0	74.4	78.8	79.4	64.1	65.1	70.8	64.7
24	Cashier	35.6	100.0	80.5	87.5	76.8	61.5	58.7	67.3	58.4
25	File clerk	34.0	100.0	71.4	81.1	71.4	58.2	57.9	62.4	55.1
26	Hospital aide	29.5	100.0	91.2	112.8	96.6	72.2	77.1	88.9	72.3
27	Textile machine operator	27.9	100.0	84.7	83.9	80.7	67.5	64.8	65.4	62.1
28	Waiter/waitress	22.1	100.0	86.8	85.1	97.9	65.8	67.2	75.9	64.8
29	Janitor	12.5	100.0	81.5	93.4	84.6	64.9	60.7	70.1	59.9
	Mean		100.0	83.8	94.3	85.9	68.3	68.0	76.6	66.2

SOURCE: U.S. Bureau of the Census (1984, Table 281).

by Hispanics, with Blacks close behind. Among women, too, Asian Americans most nearly approximate White male earnings; White women come next, followed closely by Blacks and then Hispanics.

Almquist (1987, 1989) stresses the importance of comparing women with men in their own racial group. Comparing within-race earnings here, we find that Black women make approximately 81 percent of what Black men make. Asian American women make approximately 81 percent of what Asian American men make. Hispanic women make approximately 77 percent of what Hispanic men make, while White women make approximately 68 percent of what White men make. Within race, the largest gender gap in earnings is between White men and White women. Marini's (1989) analysis of White, Black, and Hispanic women's earnings reaches similar conclusions.

Is there a relationship between occupational prestige and relative earnings of each gender/race group compared to White male earnings? Correlations between occupational prestige and earnings disparities from White men were tested; these relationships are positive but nonsignificant in our data.

DISCUSSION AND CONCLUSIONS

The occupations examined here were those for which data were available by race and gender on occupational prestige, segregation, and earnings. Findings suggest that gender and race seem to have different impacts on these occupational characteristics. Had we examined only segregation or only full-time year-round earnings, the effects of gender would have seemed far more powerful than those of race. On occupational prestige, in contrast, the main impact seems to be racial, although gender affects prestige within particular racial groups. And when segregation is considered in terms of the prestige levels to which it allocates groups, both race and gender effects can be seen. Evidently race and gender differentially affect somewhat different characteristics of the occupations examined. Furthermore, when different occupational characteristics are examined jointly, a different picture appears than when they are examined separately.

Cautions about these conclusions are in order. First, our data do not mean that racial impacts are weak, even with respect to occupational characteristics where effects seemed weak here. For instance, it may be that Black and Asian American women's growing similarities to White women's earning patterns in this data partly reflect longer work histories on the part of the former two groups (Chow 1987; Fox and Hesse-Biber 1984; Smith 1977). If this is true, then Black and Asian American women must accumulate more labor force seniority to arrive at the same earnings point as less experienced White women. Furthermore, the need to exclude from our sample occupations for which data on prestige, the gender/race composition of the labor force, and earnings were unavailable means that no generalizations can be drawn about the overall labor force.

What forces shape the differential relationships of race and gender to different occupational characteristics? Recent works on gender and race stratification cogently explore explanatory theories that can be applied to those with disadvantaged positions in the labor market, ranging from theories that deal with the formation and characteristics of the labor supply, such as human capital, status attainment, and sex-role socialization theories, to dual-labor market and Marxist/feminist approaches that deal primarily with labor demand (England and McCreary 1987; England et al. 1988; Marini 1989). The data on which this chapter is based do not allow an examination of these themes: The data are meant to elaborate the worth of a gender/race focus on an array of occupational characteristics, not to explore forces at work in the wider labor force. However, future research on the latter question may wish to consider Hill Collins's (1990) warning that no current models "capture the intersection of race and gender in explaining Black women's social class location" (p. 45).

Many researchers have pointed to the need for considering both gender and race in examining the occupational structure (King 1990). Our findings strongly support that call. With respect to the set of occupational characteristics examined here, to consider either gender or race alone would be to overlook ways in which they exhibit different joint impacts on different occupational characteristics.

REFERENCES

Allen, Walter R., and Reynolds Farley. 1986. The shifting social and economic tides of Black America, 1950-1980. In *Annual review of sociology*. Vol. 12, edited by R. H. Turner and J. F. Short, Jr. Palo Alto, CA: Annual Reviews.

Almquist, Elizabeth M. 1987. Labor market gender inequality in minority groups. *Gender & Society* 1:400-14.

————. 1989. The experiences of minority women in the United States: Intersections of race, gender, and class. In *Women: A feminist perspective.* 4th ed., edited by Jo Freeman. Mountain View, CA: Mayfield.

Asis, Maruja Milagros B. 1991. To the United States and into the labor force: Occupational expectations of Filipino and Korean immigrant women. Papers of the East-West Population Institute, Honolulu, HI.

Bielby, William T., and James N. Baron. 1986. Men and women at work: Sex segregation and statistical discrimination. *American Journal of Sociology* 91:759-99.

Blumberg, Rae Lesser. 1978. *Stratification: Socioeconomic and sexual inequality.* Dubuque, IA: Brown.

Bose, Christine E., and Peter H. Rossi. 1983. Gender and jobs: Prestige standings of occupations as affected by gender. *American Sociological Review* 48:316-30.

Chow, Esther Ngan-ling. 1987. The development of feminist consciousness among Asian American women. *Gender & Society* 1:284-99.

England, Paula. 1979. Women and occupational prestige: A case of vacuous sex equality. *Signs: Journal of Women in Culture and Society* 5:252-65.

————. 1984. Socioeconomic explanations of job segregation. In *Comparable worth and wage discrimination,* edited by H. Remick. Philadelphia: Temple University Press.

England, Paula, George Farkas, Barbara Stanek Kilbourne, and Thomas Dou. 1988. Explaining occupational sex segregation and wages: Findings from a model with fixed effects. *American Sociological Review* 53:544-58.

England, Paula, and Lori McCreary. 1987. Gender inequality in paid employment. In *Analyzing gender: A handbook of social science research,* edited by Beth B. Hess and Myra Marx Ferree. Newbury Park, CA: Sage.

Fox, Mary Frank, and Sharlene Hesse-Biber. 1984. *Women at work.* Mountain View, CA: Mayfield.

Gerth, H. H., and C. Wright Mills. 1946. *From Max Weber: Essays in sociology.* New York: Oxford University Press.

Glenn, Evelyn Nakano. 1987. Racial ethnic women's labor: The intersection of race, gender, and class oppression. In *Hidden aspects of women's work,* edited by C. Bose, R. Feldberg, and N. Sokoloff with the Women and Work Research Group. New York: Praeger.

Hill Collins, Patricia. 1990. *Black feminist thought: Knowledge, consciousness, and the politics of empowerment.* Boston: Unwin Hyman.

Jacobs, Jerry A. 1989. Long-term trends in occupational segregation by sex. *American Journal of Sociology* 95:160-73.

Kanter, Rosabeth Moss. 1975. Women and the structure of occupations: Explorations in theory and behavior. In *Another voice: Feminist perspectives on social life and social science,* edited by M. Millman and R. M. Kanter. Garden City, NY: Anchor.

Kelly, M. Patricia Fernández, and Anna M. Garcia. 1988. Invisible amidst the glitter: Hispanic women in the Southern California electronics industry. In *The world of women's work,* edited by Anne Statham, Eleanor M. Miller, and Hans O. Mauksch. Albany: State University of New York Press.

King, Deborah. 1988. Multiple jeopardy, multiple consciousness: The context of a Black feminist ideology. *Signs: Journal of Women in Culture and Society* 14:42-72.

————. 1990. Comments on papers. Talk delivered at the American Sociological Association annual meetings. Washington, DC.

Madden, Janice Fadding. 1985. The persistence of pay differentials: The economics of sex discrimination. In *Women and work: An annual review.* Vol. 1, edited by L. Larwood, A. H. Stromberg, and B. A. Gutek. Beverly Hills, CA: Sage.

Malveaux, Julianne M. 1982. Moving forward, standing still: Women in white collar jobs. In *Women in the workplace,* edited by P. A. Wallace. Boston: Auburn House.

Marini, Margaret Mooney. 1989. Sex differences in earnings in the United states. In *Annual review of sociology.* Vol. 15, edited by W. R. Scott and J. Blake. Palo Alto, CA: Annual Reviews.

Mason, Karen Oppenheim. 1986. The status of women: Conceptual and methodological issues in demographic studies. *Sociological Forum* 1:284-300.

McLanahan, Sara S., Annemette Sorensen, and Dorothy Watson. 1989. Sex differences in poverty, 1950-1980. *Signs: Journal of Women in Culture and Society* 15:102-22.

Miller, Delbert C. 1991. *Handbook of research design and social measurement.* 5th ed. Newbury Park, CA: Sage.

Powell, B., and J. A. Jacobs. 1983. Sex and consensus in occupational prestige ratings. *Sociology and Social Research* 67:392-404.

Powers, Mary G., and Joan J. Holmberg. 1978. Occupational status scores: Changes introduced by the inclusion of women. *Demography* 15:183-204.

Russell, Anne M., Donna Ruffini, Dorian Burden, Shirley Chan, Roxane Farmanfarmaian, Janette Scandura, Jill Werman, and Laurel Touby. 1989. The Tenth Annual Working Woman Salary Survey. *Working Woman* 14:71-79.

Sampson, William A., and Peter H. Rossi. 1975. Race and family social standing. *American Sociological Review* 40:201-14.

Segura, Denise A. 1989. Chicana and Mexican immigrant women at work: The impact of class, race, and gender on occupational mobility. *Gender & Society* 3:37-52.

Smith, James P. 1977. The convergence to racial equality in women's wages. In *Women in the labor market,* edited by C. B. Lloyd, E. S. Andrews, and C. L. Gilroy. New York: Columbia University Press.

Sokoloff, N. 1987. What's happening to women's employment: Issues for women's labor struggles in the 1980s-1990s. In *Hidden aspects of women's work,* edited by C. Bose, R. Feldberg, and N. Sokoloff with the Women and Work Research Group. New York: Praeger.

Sorenson, Elaine. 1989. Measuring the effect of occupational sex and race composition on earnings. In *Pay equity: Empirical inquiries,* edited by R. T. Michael, H. I. Hartmann, and B. O'Farrel. Washington, DC: National Academy Press.

Steel, Lauri, Ronald P. Abeles, and Josefina J. Card. 1982. Sex differences in the patterning of adult roles as a determinant of sex differences in occupational achievement. *Sex Roles* 8:1009-24.

Stephens, Richard C., George T. Oser, and Zena Smith Blau. 1980. To be aged, Hispanic, and female: The triple risk. In *Twice a minority: Mexican American women,* edited by Margarita B. Melville. St. Louis, MO: C. V. Mosby.

Sullivan, Teresa A. 1984. The occupational prestige of women immigrants: A comparison of Cubans and Mexicans. *International Migration Review* 18:1045-62.

Tienda, M., S. A. Smith and V. Ortiz. 1987. Industrial restructuring, gender segregation, and sex differences in earnings. *American Sociological Review* 52:195-210.

Tyree, A., and R. Hicks. 1988. Sex and the second moment of occupational distributions. *Social Forces* 66:1028-37.

U.S. Bureau of the Census. 1983. *Census on population and housing, 1980: Public-use micro-data sample technical documentation.* Washington, DC.

———. 1984. *The 1980 Census of Population: Detailed population characteristics* (United States summary). Washington, DC: GPO.

Wagman, Barnet, and Nancy Folbre. 1988. The feminization of inequality: Some new patterns. *Challenge* 31:56-59.

Waite, Linda J. 1981. Occupational segregation. *Population Bulletin* 36:26-29.

Williams, James L., and Daniel G. Rodeheaver. 1989. Changes in the social visibility and prominence of black and white women from 1925-1988. *Sociology and Social Research* 73:107-13.

7 Moving Up With Kin and Community: Upward Social Mobility for Black and White Women

ELIZABETH HIGGINBOTHAM
LYNN WEBER

> My parents always expected me to go to college. In my elementary school in
> Mississippi, we had split-terms. Schools were closed in the fall so that students
> could go in the fields and pick cotton. I remember thinking, "If there is any way to
> get out of this field, I'm gonna take it." At the end of October, I would go back to
> school, but other children would still be working in the fields. And I thought,
> "There's got to be a way to help people do better." That's when I started thinking
> about going to college.
>
> —Earnstein Washington, Social Worker[1]
> (Interviewed, Summer 1986)

When women and people of color experience upward mobility in
America, they scale steep structural as well as psychological barriers.
The long process of moving from a working-class family of origin to
the professional-managerial class is full of twists and turns: choices
made with varying degrees of information and varying options; critical
junctures faced with support and encouragement or disinterest, rejec-

AUTHORS' NOTE: The research reported here was supported by National Institute for
Mental Health Grant MH38769, coprincipal investigators Elizabeth Higginbotham and Lynn
Weber. We wish to thank the special issue editors, the editor, and the two anonymous review-
ers for their suggestions and comments. We also appreciate Anne Eisenberg, Laura Harris,
Laurie Powell, and Mary Beth Snapp for their assistance.

tion, or active discouragement; and interpersonal relationships in which basic understandings are continuously negotiated and renegotiated. It is a fascinating process that profoundly shapes the lives of those who experience it, as well as the lives of those around them. Social mobility is also a process engulfed in myth. One need only pick up any newspaper or turn on the television to see that the myth of upward mobility remains firmly entrenched in American culture: With hard work, talent, determination, and some luck, just about anyone can "make it."

As Strauss (1971) notes, those who are upwardly mobile must raise work to primacy in their self-definition, take on a new reference group, embrace middle-class values and aspirations, and spend time with "the right people." To accomplish this, working-class men are expected to distance themselves from their families and friends—a process facilitated by male socialization, which emphasizes independence, detachment, and rational (economically motivated) decision making.

The study of the subjective experience of mobility ceased in the early 1970s, just as the largest ever influx of upwardly mobile individuals began to enter the professional managerial middle class. In just one generation, professional, managerial, and administrative positions increased from 15 percent to 30 percent of the labor force (Ehrenreich and Ehrenreich 1979; Vanneman and Cannon 1987). This expansion of middle-class positions also accompanied the civil rights and women's movements, which brought down many race and gender barriers to occupational attainment and upward class mobility. Because of these shifts in the occupational structure and breakdowns in some race and gender barriers, more White women and people of color (especially of the baby boom generation) have experienced upward social mobility in the post-World War II period than at any time in this century (Fossett, Galle, and Kelley 1986).

The broad goal of this chapter is to reopen the study of the contexts of mobility by examining the subjective experience of upward class mobility among Black and White women of the baby boom generation. Two recent studies have begun to explore these mobility issues with regard to White men and teenagers (Ryan and Sackrey 1984; Steinitz and Solomon 1986). In this chapter, we seek to begin to lay a foundation for future explorations into the ways that race and gender shape the class experience of upward mobility.

The image of the isolated and detached experience of mobility that we have inherited from past scholarship is problematic for anyone seeking to understand the process for women or people of color. Twenty years of scholarship in the study of both race and gender has taught us the importance of interpersonal attachments to the lives of women (cf. Miller 1986) and a commitment to racial uplift among people of color (cf. Anthony 1980; Collins 1990; Gilkes 1983). For example, recent research on White women presents a picture of the female experience that emphasizes commitment, interdependence, and affiliations —especially with family. Far from a willingness to distance self from family for the greater goal of "making it," social relationships are viewed as the core of women's lives (Gilligan 1982).

The psychologist Miller (1986, 83) notes:

> Women stay with, build on, and develop in the context of attachments and affiliations with others. Indeed, women's sense of self becomes very much organized around being able to make and then to maintain affiliations and relationships. Eventually, for many women the threat of disruption of an affiliation is perceived not as a loss of a relationship but as something closer to a total loss of self.

McAdoo (1978) suggests that lacking wealth, the greatest gift a Black family has been able to give to its children has been the motivation and skills to succeed in school. Aspirations for college attendance and professional positions are stressed as *family* goals, and the entire family may make sacrifices and provide support. Likewise, recent scholarship on women of color (Collins 1990) notes that Black women have long seen the activist potential of education and have sought it as a cornerstone of community development—a means of uplifting the race. When women of color or White women are put at the center of the analysis of upward mobility, it is clear that different questions will be raised about social mobility and different descriptions of the process will ensue.

This study seeks to bring race and gender into the study of the subjective experience of upward social class mobility. Specifically, we seek to identify some commonalities and differences in the ways that Black and White women experience certain key relational aspects of the mobility process. First, we examine their relationships with family as reflected in parental expectations and supports for education, occupation/career, and marriage and children. Second, we explore the women's sense of debt and obligation to family and friends. Finally, we explore some ways that mobile women's experiences are situated within the larger communities—both Black and White.

RESEARCH METHODS

Research Design

These data are from a study of full-time employed middle-class women in the Memphis metropolitan area. This research is designed to explore the processes of upward social mobility for Black and White women by examining differences between women professionals, managers, and administrators who are from working- and middle-class backgrounds—that is, upwardly mobile and middle-class stable women. In this way, we isolate subjective processes shared among women who have been upwardly mobile from those common to women who have reproduced their family's professional-managerial class standing. Likewise, we identify common experiences in the attainment process that are shared by women of the same race, be they upwardly mobile or stable middle class. Finally, we specify some ways in which the attainment process is unique for each race-class group.

Sample

The population of interest was defined as women of the "baby boom" cohort (i.e., 25 to 40 years of age at the time of the study) who were college graduates who went to college directly from high school or within two years of graduation and who were currently working full-time as professionals, managers, or administrators—that is, in "middle-class" occupations (Vanneman and Cannon 1987). (For a discussion of the rationale for selecting these groups, see Cannon, Higginbotham, and Leung 1988.)

As is the case with many studies of special categories of women, there was no way to sample randomly the population who fit the preceding study parameters. We employed a quota sample that was stratified by three dimensions of inequality: race, class background of the respondent, and the gender composition of her occupation. Each dimension was operationalized into two categories: Black and White, raised working class/upwardly mobile and raised middle class/middle-class stable, and female-dominated and male-dominated. Twenty-five cases were selected for each of the eight cells of this $2 \times 2 \times 2$ design. For purposes of this research, data are analyzed by race and class background only.

Instrument

Data were gathered in face-to-face focused life-history interviews, lasting 2½ to 3 hours each. The research instrument contained many items, including schooling experiences from elementary school through college; early family experiences; perceived barriers to attainment and social support networks at critical mobility junctures (from high school to college, immediately after college, in graduate school); current work situation (including perceived job stress, location in the administrative hierarchy, job rewards, perceptions of discrimination, obstacles to attainment); integration of work and personal life (including social support networks); and general well-being and physical health, life events, and mental health.

Measurement

In this research, we rely on a model of social class basically derived from the work of Poulantzas (1974), Braverman (1974), Ehrenreich and Ehrenreich (1979), and elaborated in Vanneman and Cannon (1987). These works explicate a basic distinction between social class and social status. Classes represent bounded categories of the population, groups set in a relation of opposition to one another by their roles in the capitalist system. The middle class, or professional-managerial class, is set off from the working class by the power and control it exerts over workers in three realms: economic (power through ownership), political (power through direct supervisory authority), and ideological (power to plan and organize work; Poulantzas 1974; Vanneman and Cannon 1987).

In contrast, education, prestige, and income represent social statuses —hierarchically structured relative rankings along a ladder of economic success and social prestige. Positions along these dimensions are not established by social relations of dominance and subordination but, rather, as rankings on scales representing resources and desirability. In some respects, they represent both the justification for power differentials vested in classes and the rewards for the role that the middle class plays in controlling labor.

Our interest is in the process of upward social class mobility, moving from a working-class family of origin to a middle-class destination— from a position of working-class subordination to a position of control over the working class. Lacking inherited wealth or other resources, those working-class people who attain middle-class standing do so primarily by obtaining a college education and entering a professional, managerial, or administrative occupation. Thus we examine carefully the process of educational attainment not as evidence of middle-class standing but as a necessary part of the mobility process for most working-class people.

Likewise, occupation alone does not define the middle class, but professional, managerial, and administrative occupations capture many of the supervisory and ideologically based positions whose function is to control workers' lives. Consequently, we defined subjects as *middle class* by virtue of their employment in either a professional, managerial, or administrative occupation as specified in Braverman (1974), Ehrenreich and Ehrenreich (1979), and Vanneman and Cannon (1987; see Cannon, Higginbotham, and Leung 1988 for exceptions). Classification of subjects as either professional or managerial-administrative was made on the basis of the designation of occupations in the U.S. Bureau of the Census's (1983) "Detailed Population Characteristics: Tennessee." Managerial occupations were defined as those in the census categories of managers and administrators; professionals were defined as those occupations in the professional category, excluding technicians, whom Braverman (1974) contends are working class.

Upwardly mobile women were defined as those women raised in families where neither parent was employed as a professional, manager, or administrator. Typical occupations for working-class fathers were postal clerk, craftsman, semi-skilled manufacturing worker, janitor, and laborer. Some working-class mothers had clerical and sales positions, but many of the Black mothers also worked as private household workers. *Middle-class stable* women were defined as those women raised in families where *either* parent was employed as a professional, manager, or administrator. Typical occupations of middle-class parents were social worker, teacher, and school administrator as well as high-status professionals such as attorneys, physicians, and dentists.

Data Analysis

In the following section we present a set of responses to questions regarding the family, friend, and community relationships of upwardly mobile and middle-class stable Black and White women. Each of the questions provided a dichotomous response, yes or no, and then asked subjects to elaborate on their answers. Table 7.1 contains frequencies and percentages of yes or affirmative responses for each question by each of the four race-class background groups: Black and White, upwardly mobile and middle-class stable. Since percentages add to 100, data on no or negative responses are not included. For each question, chi-square statistics are presented for three analyses: (1) a four-category independent variable including all race and class categories, labeled *Total;* (2) a race effect obtained by collapsing class categories; (3) a class effect obtained by collapsing race categories. In addition to these data, quotes from respondents that explicate the responses are also presented, along with some responses to open-ended questions.

RESULTS

Relationships With Family

Family Expectations for Educational Attainment

Four questions assess the expectations and support among family members for the educational attainment of the subjects. First, "Do you recall your father or mother stressing that you attain an education?" *Yes* was the response of 190 of the 200 women. Each of the women in this study had obtained a college degree, and many have graduate degrees. It is clear that for Black and White women, education was an important concern in their families (see Table 7.1, row 1).

The comments of Laura Lee, a 39 year-old Black woman who was raised middle class, were typical:

> Going to school, that was never a discussable issue. Just like you were born to live and die, you were going to go to school. You were going to prepare yourself to do something.

It should be noted, however, that only 86 percent of the White working-class women answered yes, compared to 98 percent of all other groups. Although this difference is small, it foreshadows a pattern where White women raised in working-class families received the least support and encouragement for educational and career attainment.

"When you were growing up, how far did your father expect you to go in school?" While most fathers expected college attendance from their daughters, differences also exist by class of origin. Only 70 percent of the working-class fathers, both Black and White, expected their daughters to attend college. In contrast, 94 percent of the Black middle-class and 88 percent of the White middle-class women's fathers had college expectations for their daughters.

When asked the same question about mother's expectations, 88 percent to 92 percent of each group's mothers expected their daughters to get a college education, except the White working-class women, for whom only 66 percent of mothers held such expectations. In short, only among the White working-class women did a fairly substantial propor-

TABLE 7.1 Family Supports for Educational and Occupational Achievement by Race and Class Background

	Black		White					
	Upwardly Mobile	Middle-Class Stable	Upwardly Mobile	Middle-Class Stable	N	Total (χ^2)	Race (χ^2)	Class (χ^2)
Parents stressed need for an education	98% (49)	98% (49)	86% (43)	98% (49)	200	11.37**	3.79*	3.79*
Father expected college education	69% (33)	94% (46)	70% (32)	88% (44)	193	15.00**	0.15	14.44**
Mother expected college education	88% (44)	88% (44)	66% (33)	92% (45)	199	15.15*	3.05	5.98*
Family provided emotional support for college	64% (32)	86% (43)	56% (28)	70% (35)	200	11.31**	3.37	7.57**
Financial aid from family for college	56% (28)	90% (45)	62% (31)	88% (44)	200	23.91**	0.10	23.99**
Parents stressed need for an occupation	94% (47)	94% (47)	56% (28)	70% (35)	200	31.74**	19.02**	1.45
Family encouraged respondent to think about career	56% (28)	60% (30)	40% (20)	52% (26)	200	4.49	2.88	1.28
Parents stressed marriage as primary life goal	6% (3)	4% (2)	22% (11)	18% (9)	200	10.74*	12.00**	0.48

132

Never married	34% (17)	24% (12)	20% (10)	34% (17)	200	3.77	0.16	0.16
Feeling of owing kin	86% (43)	74% (37)	46% (23)	68% (34)	200	19.53**	12.26**	1.71
Balance of obligations to kin					190	17.85**	2.77	10.19**
Gave > received	31% (15)	4% (2)	15% (7)	10% (5)				
Received > gave	31% (15)	48% (22)	27% (13)	40% (19)				
Gave = received	39% (18)	48% (22)	58% (28)	50% (24)				
Balance of obligations to friends					196	11.19	8.48**	0.39
Gave > received	33% (16)	24% (12)	15% (7)	16% (8)				
Received > gave	0% (0)	4% (2)	10% (5)	8% (4)				
Gave = received	67% (33)	72% (36)	75% (36)	76% (37)				

NOTE: Numbers in parentheses represent the number of people in each group.
*$p \leq .05$; **$p \leq .01$.

tion (about one-third) of both mothers and fathers expect less than a college education from their daughters. About 30 percent of Black working-class fathers held lower expectations for their daughters, but not the mothers; virtually all middle-class parents expected a college education for their daughters.

Sara Marx is a White, 33-year-old director of counseling raised in a rural working-class family. She is among those whose parents did not expect a college education for her. She was vague about the roots of attending college:

> It seems like we had a guest speaker who talked to us. Maybe before our exams somebody talked to us. I really can't put my finger on anything. I don't know where the information came from exactly.

"Who provided emotional support for you to make the transition from high school to college?" While 86 percent of the Black middle-class women indicated that family provided that support, 70 percent of the White middle class, 64 percent of the Black working class, and only 56 percent of the White working class received emotional support from family.

"Who paid your college tuition and fees?" Beyond emotional support, financial support is critical to college attendance. There are clear class differences in financial support for college. Roughly 90 percent of the middle-class respondents and only 56 percent and 62 percent of the Black and White working-class women, respectively, were financially supported by their families. These data also suggest that working-class parents were less able to give emotional or financial support for college than they were to hold out the expectation that their daughters should attend.

Family Expectations for Occupation or Career

When asked, "Do you recall your father or mother stressing that you should have an occupation to succeed in life?" racial differences appear. Ninety-four percent of all Black respondents said yes. In the words of Julie Bird, a Black woman middle-class-raised junior high school teacher:

> My father would always say, "You see how good I'm doing? Each generation should do more than the generation before." He expects me to accomplish more than he has.

Ann Right, a 36-year-old Black attorney whose father was a janitor, said:

> They wanted me to have a better life than they had. For all of us. And that's why they emphasized education and emphasized working relationships and how you get along with people and that kind of thing.

In contrast, only 70 percent of the White middle-class and 56 percent of the White working-class women indicated that their parents stressed that an occupation was needed for success. Nina Pentel, a 26-year-old White medical social worker, expressed a common response: "They said 'You're going to get married but get a degree, you never know what's going to happen to you.' They were pretty laid back about goals."

When the question focuses on a career rather than an occupation, the family encouragement is lower and differences were not significant but similar patterns emerged. We asked respondents, "Who, if anyone, encouraged you to think about a career?" Among Black respondents, 60 percent of the middle-class and 56 percent of the working-class women answered that family encouraged them. Only 40 percent of the White working-class women indicated that their family encouraged them in their thinking about a career, while 52 percent of the White middle-class women did so.

Mary Ann Tidwell, a White woman raised working class in the rural South, is now an environmental manager. She has a B.A. and an M.A. in physics. Despite the scarcity of women in her occupation, Mary Ann's experiences getting there were not unusual for working-class women of this era. In high school, Mary Ann excelled in science and math, yet her parents held very traditional expectations for her:

> They wanted me to be a teacher, be married, have grandkids for them, and live near home. They wanted me to attend school so that I could support myself in case I . . . ended up with a husband leaving me. My brothers were encouraged to have a *big* career, be something *big!* Mine was to have financial independence. They expected the same grades from us but they didn't expect a career-daughter.

Dawn Jones, a 33-year-old White attorney from a working-class family, described her parents' feelings:

> They felt that ideal life is something that does not encourage the woman to have a demanding professional career. It is asking for trouble. . . . During

that time everything was presumed, "you'll do well in school, you go to college, you'll have a family." I was totally unprepared for what my life has been, really.

When working-class White women seek to be mobile through their own attainments, they face conflicts. Their parents encourage educational attainment, but when young women develop professional career goals, these same parents sometimes become ambivalent. This was the case with Elizabeth Marlow, who is currently a public interest attorney —a position her parents never intended her to hold. She described her parents' traditional expectations and their reluctance to support her career goals fully.

> My parents assumed that I would go college and meet some nice man and finish, but not necessarily work after. I would be a good mother for my children. I don't think that they ever thought I would go to law school. Their attitude about my interest in law school was, "You can do it if you want to, but we don't think it is a particularly practical thing for a woman to do."

Elizabeth is married and has three children, but she is not the traditional housewife of her parents' dreams. She received more support outside the family for her chosen lifestyle.

Although Black families are indeed more likely than White families to encourage their daughters to prepare for careers, like White families, they frequently steer them toward highly visible traditionally female occupations, such as teacher, nurse, and social worker. Thus many mobile Black women are directed toward the same gender-segregated occupations as White women.

For example, Lynn Johnson was encouraged by her working-class mother to get a degree in education, but instead, she majored in economics and never told her mother until graduation day. She described her encounter.

> Momma said, "Be a teacher." That's all she wanted me to do. She came to my graduation from Regional College and she got my degree, and it said *Bachelor of Science in Economics.* Momma said, "Girl, what are you gonna teach? They don't teach Economics, . . . and you can't type either!" I said, "That's right Momma, I sure can't." "Well, I want to see you get a job with this!" She threw that degree back at me. Oh, she was *so mad!* She has since learned better, but initially she was really hurt, because she thought my only option was to teach.

Marriage

Although working-class families may encourage daughters to marry, they recognize the need for working-class women to contribute to family income or to support themselves economically. To achieve these aims, many working-class girls are encouraged to pursue an education as preparation for work in gender-segregated occupations. Work in these fields presumably allows women to keep marriage, family, and child rearing as life goals while contributing to the family income and to have "something to fall back on" if the marriage does not work out. This interplay among marriage, education, financial need, and class mobility is complex (Joslin 1979).

We asked, "Do you recall your mother or father emphasizing that marriage should be your primary life goal?" While the majority of all respondents did not get the message that marriage was the *primary life goal,* Black and White women's parents clearly saw this differently. Virtually no Black parents stressed marriage as the primary life goal (6% of the working class and 4% of the middle class) but significantly more White parents did (22% of the working class and 18% of the middle class).

Some White women said their families expressed active opposition to marriage, such as Clare Baron, a working-class-raised nursing supervisor, who said, "My mother always said, 'Don't get married and don't have children!' "

More common responses recognized the fragility of marriage and the need to support oneself. For example, Alice Page, a 31-year-old White middle-class-raised librarian, put it this way:

> I feel like I am really part of a generation that for the first time is thinking, "I don't want to have to depend on somebody to take care of me because what if they say they are going to take care of me and then they are not there? They die, or they leave me or whatever." I feel very much that I've got to be able to support myself and I don't know that single women in other eras have had to deal with that to the same degree.

While White working-class women are often raised to prepare for work roles so that they can contribute to family income and, if necessary, support themselves, Black women face a different reality. Unlike White women, Black women are typically socialized to view marriage separately from economic security, because it is not expected that marriage will ever remove them from the labor market. As a result,

Black families socialize all their children—girls and boys—for self-sufficiency (Clark 1986; Higginbotham and Cannon 1988).

Lou Nelson's response was typical of the Black working-class women. She said:

> I can truly remember my parents saying "I want you to go to school and get your degree, get you a job, then get married if you choose to." It was always a case of you being in a position to get married if you choose to marry and not having to rely on a man to provide you with food and clothing and things of that sort. They said, "Always be able to take care of yourself."

In fact, fairly substantial numbers of each group had never married by the time of the interview, ranging from 20 percent of the White working-class to 34 percent of the Black working-class and White middle-class respondents. Some of the women were pleased with their singlehood, like Alice Page, who said:

> I am single by choice. That is how I see myself. I have purposely avoided getting into any kind of romantic situation with men. I have enjoyed going out but never wanted to get serious. If anyone wants to get serious, I quit going out with him.

Other women expressed disappointment and some shock that they were not yet married. When asked about her feeling about being single, Sally Ford, a 32-year-old White manager, said:

> That's what I always wanted to do: to be married and have children. To me, that is the ideal. I want a happy, good marriage with children. I do not like being single at all. It is very, very lonesome. I don't see any advantages to being single. None!

SENSE OF OBLIGATION

Subjective Sense of Debt to Kin and Friends

McAdoo (1978) reports that upwardly mobile Black Americans receive more requests to share resources from their working-class kin than do middle-class Black Americans. Many mobile Black Americans feel a "social debt" because their families aided them in the mobility process and provided emotional support. When we asked the White women in the study the following question: "Generally, do you feel you owe a lot for the help given to you by your family and relatives?" many were perplexed and asked what the question meant. In contrast, both the working- and middle-class Black women tended to respond immediately that they felt a sense of obligation to family and friends in return for the support they had received. Black women, from both the working class and the middle class, expressed the strongest sense of debt to family, with 86 percent and 74 percent, respectively, so indicating. White working-class women were least likely to feel that they owed family (46%), while 68 percent of White middle-class women so indicated. In short, upwardly mobile Black women were almost twice as likely as upwardly mobile White women to express a sense of debt to family.

Linda Brown, an upwardly mobile Black woman, gave a typical response, "Yes, they are there when you need them." Similar were the words of Jean Marsh, "Yes, because they have been supportive. They're dependable. If I need them I can depend upon them."

One of the most significant ways in which Black working-class families aided their daughters and left them with a sense of debt related to care for their children. Dawn March expressed it thus:

They have been there more so during my adult years than a lot of other families that I know about. My mother kept all of my children until they were old enough to go to day care. And she not only kept them, she'd give them a bath for me during the daytime and feed them before I got home from work. Very, very supportive people. So, I really would say I owe them for that.

Carole Washington, an upwardly mobile Black woman occupational therapist, also felt she owed her family. She reported:

I know the struggle that my parents have had to get me where I am. I know the energy they no longer have to put into the rest of the family even though they want to put it there and they're willing. I feel it is my responsibility to give back some of that energy they have given to me. It's self-directed, not required.

White working-class women, in contrast, were unlikely to feel a sense of debt and expressed their feelings in similar ways. Irma Cox, part owner of a computer business, said, "I am appreciative of the values my parents instilled in me. But I for the most part feel like I have done it on my own." Carey Mink, a 35-year-old psychiatric social worker, said, "No, they pointed me in a direction and they were supportive, but I've done a lot of the work myself." Debra Beck, a judge, responded, "No, I feel that I've gotten most places on my own." And finally, Phyllis Coe, a library administrator, stated:

> No. Growing up in a family, I don't think it's that kind of a relationship—that's their job. I feel that way with my son. I certainly love him but I don't want him ever to be in a position to think he owes me.

The sense of balance or imbalance in one's interpersonal relationships with family and friends can be a source of comfort or stress. Carrington (1980, 266) found that the sense of debt can contribute to depression among Black professional women:

> Depressed black women express strong needs to nurture and "take care of" significant others in their lives—spouses and children. They also feel guilty when engaging in self-enhancing activities, either professionally or personally, that do not directly or indirectly include their families. This sense of guilt is particularly observed in depressed black women who are upwardly mobile.

To examine this issue we asked, "In terms of your obligations to your family and relatives, do you feel you've: given more help than you received, received more help than you've given, or given about the same as you've received?" Responses varied by race and class. For all groups except the Black working-class women, about one-half felt that they had given equal to what they had received; there was some sort of balance in family relationships. When perceived imbalance existed, it was mostly that the women felt they received more than they gave. Again the rather striking exception is Black working-class-raised women, 31 percent of whom feel they have given more than they have received from family. Some comments from this group illustrate the point.

Rose Hill, a 40-year-old professor who was raised working class, said: "I feel that in many respects I'm stronger in terms of emotional and financial well-being than most of my family and I feel an obligation to give it back."

Jenny Well, a college administrator, recalled an incident that was typical of how she frequently gave more to her family than she received.

For example, our aunt died. All the nieces and nephews were going to buy flowers—a spray from us. I ended up paying for it, okay? And all of them made a lot more money than I do. And I felt used. That happens a lot of times. We all come up with an idea, but to make sure the idea goes through, Jenny's always stuck with it.

Mary Chapel, a married 35-year-old corporate director with three children, said:

I've given more than I received. Because it is almost as if I'm the backbone of the family in my father's absence. I'm the person that all of them come to. My sister in New York comes to me, my sister in Memphis comes to me, my mother comes to me, everybody, even my friends come to me. It's as if I've moved in to take the place that my father vacated when he passed.

We also asked, "In terms of your obligations to your friends, do you feel you've given more help than you received, received more help than you've given, or given about the same as you've received?" Since friends are chosen, it is not surprising that the balance of obligations with friends is more likely to be equal for all groups. Interestingly, however, Black women are most likely to feel that they give more than they receive, even to friends.

In addition to being the backbone of her family, Mary Chapel is also a key person in her friendship network. She reported:

Well, not so much in terms of giving money but certainly giving them my time. I don't care what it is, day or night, if they want to see me or talk to me, I think it is really important. And I don't turn around and ask them to do the same for me because I don't need that kind of external support. I don't need to go outside of my family to ask for help.

RELATIONS TO THE COMMUNITY

Commitment to Community

The mainstream "model of community stresses the rights of individuals to make decisions in their own self interest, regardless of the impact on the larger society" (Collins 1990, 52). This model may explain relations to community of origin for mobile White males but cannot be generalized to other racial and gender groups. In the context of well-recognized structures of racial oppression, America's racial-ethnic communities develop collective survival strategies that contrast with the individualism of the dominant culture but ensure the community's survival (Collins 1990; Stack 1974; Valentine 1978). McAdoo (1978) argues that Black people have *only* been able to advance in education and attain higher status and higher paying jobs with the support of the wider Black community, teachers in segregated schools, extended family networks, and Black mentors already in those positions. This widespread community involvement enables mobile people of color to confront and challenge racist obstacles in credentialing institutions, and it distinguishes the mobility process in racial-ethnic communities from mobility in the dominant culture. For example, Lou Nelson, now a librarian, described the support she felt in her southern segregated inner-city school. She said:

> There was a closeness between people and that had a lot to do with neighborhood schools. I went to Tubman High School with people that lived in the Tubman area. I think that there was a bond, a bond between parents, the PTA. . . . I think that it was just that everybody felt that everybody knew everybody. And that was special.

Family and community involvement and support in the mobility process means that many Black professionals and managers continue to feel linked to their communities of origin. Lillian King, a high-ranking city official who was raised working class, discussed her current commitment to the Black community. She said:

> Because I have more opportunities, I've got an obligation to give more back and to set a positive example for Black people and especially for Black women. I think we've got to do a tremendous job in building self-esteem and giving people the desire to achieve.

Judith Moore is a 34-year-old single parent employed as a health investigator. She has been able to maintain her connection with her community and that is a source of pride.

> I'm proud that I still have a sense of who I am in terms of Black people. That's very important to me. No matter how much education or professional status I get, I do not want to lose touch with where I've come from. I think that you need to look back and that kind of pushes you forward. I think the degree and other things can make you lose sight of that, especially us Black

folks, but I'm glad that I haven't and I try to teach that [commitment] to my son.

For some Black women, their mobility has enabled them to give to an even broader community. This is the case with Sammi Lewis, a working-class-raised woman who is a director of a social service agency. She said, "I owe a responsibility to the entire community and not to any particular group."

There are also questions about the depth of mainstream individualism within the White community. Recent scholarship on mobility experiences of White youth in the Northeast demonstrates that some share a commitment to educational attainment but do not necessarily want to take on all the trappings of the middle class. Steinitz and Solomon (1986) discuss how many of their White respondents want to become somebody, but "they do not want to become different kinds of people, nor do they want to separate themselves from those they now know and love" (p. 30). They value their connections with others and are people who believe "that development through relationships is the critical role to maturity, [and] who hold that responsibility to others is necessary to the realization of self" (p. 13).

In our study as well, the White working-class-raised women represented a spectrum. Some discussed primary responsibility to the nuclear family, like Sara Marx, a 33-year-old director of counseling. When asked about the similarities between her life and her parents' lives, Sara remarked:

> There is a definite loyalty to partners. We have a good communication within the family. I think my parents have more of a non-verbal communication and my husband and I have a more verbal communication. Honesty, work ethic—we both think we should work hard to get things to make us comfortable.

Sally Ford, a 33-year-old single woman raised working class and now employed as a manager for a manufacturing company, was taught to look beyond the family. When reporting similarities with her parents, Sally noted: "They taught me a tremendous sense of responsibility in terms of what you owe to the world and your fellow man and community. We have that in common." Sally's parents were active in social organizations and community issues and she has followed that path.

Crossing the Color Line

Mobility for people of color is complex because in addition to crossing class lines, mobility often means crossing racial and cultural ones as well. Since the 1960s, people of color have increasingly attended either integrated or predominantly White schools. Only mobile White ethnics have a comparable experience of simultaneously crossing class and cultural barriers, yet even this experience is qualitatively different from that of Black and other people of color. White ethnicity can be practically invisible to White middle-class school peers and coworkers, but people of color are more visible and are subjected to harsher treatment. Our research indicates that no matter when people of color first encounter integrated or predominantly White settings, it is always a shock. The experience of racial exclusion cannot prepare people of color to deal with the racism in daily face-to-face encounters with White people.

For example, Lynn Johnson was in the first cohort of Black students at Regional College, a small private college in Memphis. The self-confidence and stamina Lynn developed in her supportive segregated high school helped her withstand the racism she faced as the first female and the first Black to graduate in economics at Regional College. Lynn described her treatment:

> I would come into class and Dr. Simpson (the economics professor) would alphabetically call the roll. When he came to my name, he would just jump over it. He would not ask me any questions, he would not do anything. I stayed in that class. I struggled through. When it was my turn, I'd start talking. He would say, "Johnson, I wasn't talking to you" [because he never said *Miss* Johnson]. I'd say, "That's all right, Dr. Simpson, it was my turn. I figured you just overlooked me. I'm just the littlest person in here. Wasn't that the right answer?" He would say, "Yes, that was the right answer." I drove him mad, I really did. He finally got used to me and started to help me.

In southern cities, where previous interaction between Black and White people followed a rigid code, adjustments were necessary on both sides. It was clear to Lynn Johnson and others that college faculty and students had to adapt to her small Black cohort at Regional College.

Wendy Jones attended a formerly predominantly White state university that had just merged with a formerly predominantly Black college.

This new institution meant many adjustments for faculty and students. As a working-class person majoring in engineering, she had a rough transition. She recalled:

> I had never gone to school with White kids. I'd always gone to all Black schools all my life and the Black kids there [at the university] were snooty. Only one friend from high school went there and she flunked out. The courses were harder and all my teachers were men and White. Most of the kids were White. I was in classes where I'd be the only Black and woman. There were no similarities to grasp for. I had to adjust to being in that situation. In about a year I was comfortable where I could walk up to people in my class and have conversations.

For some Black people, their first significant interaction with White people did not come until graduate school. Janice Freeman described her experiences:

> I went to a Black high school, a Black college and then worked for a Black man who was a former teacher. Everything was comfortable until I had to go to State University for graduate school. I felt very insecure. I was thrown into an environment that was very different—during the 1960s and 1970s there was so much unrest anyway—so it was extremely difficult for me.

It was not in graduate school but on her first job as a social worker that Janice had to learn to work *with* White people. She said, "After I realized that I could hang in school, working at the social work agency allowed me to learn how to work *with* White people. I had never done that before and now I do it better than anybody."

Learning to live in a White world was an additional hurdle for all Black women in this age cohort. Previous generations of Black people were more likely to be educated in segregated colleges and to work within the confines of the established Black community. They taught in segregated schools, provided dental and medical care to Black communities, and provided social services and other comforts to members of their own communities. They also lived in the Black community and worshiped on Sunday with many of the people they saw in different settings. As the comments of our respondents reveal, both Black and White people had to adjust to integrated settings, but it was more stressful for the newcomers.

SUMMARY AND CONCLUSIONS

Our major aim in this research was to reopen the study of the subjective experience of upward social mobility and to begin to incorporate race and gender into our vision of the process. In this exploratory work, we hope to raise issues and questions that will cast a new light on taken-for-granted assumptions about the process and the people who engage in it. The experiences of these women have certainly painted a different picture from the one we were left some twenty years ago. First and foremost, these women are not detached, isolated, or driven solely by career goals. Relationships with family of origin, partners, children, friends, and the wider community loom large in the way they envision and accomplish mobility and the way they sustain themselves as professional and managerial women.

Several of our findings suggest ways that race and gender shape the mobility process for baby boom Black and White women. Education was stressed as important in virtually all of the families of these women; however, they differed in how it was viewed and how much was desired. The upwardly mobile women, both Black and White, shared some obstacles to attainment. More mobile women had parents who never expected them to achieve a college education. They also received less emotional and financial support for college attendance from their families than the women in middle-class families received. Black women also faced the unique problem of crossing racial barriers simultaneously with class barriers.

There were fairly dramatic race differences in the messages that the Black and White women received from family about what their lives should be like as adults. Black women clearly received the message that they needed an occupation to succeed in life and that marriage was a secondary concern. Many Black women also expressed a sense that their mobility was connected to an entire racial uplift process, not merely an individual journey.

White upwardly mobile women received less clear messages. Only one-half of these women said that their parents stressed the need for an occupation to succeed, and 20 percent said that marriage was stressed as the primary life goal. The most common message seemed to suggest that an occupation was necessary, because marriage could not be counted on to provide economic survival. Having a career, on the other hand, could even be seen as detrimental to adult happiness.

Upward mobility is a process that requires sustained effort and emotional and cognitive, as well as financial, support. The legacy of the image of mobility that was built on the White male experience focuses on credentialing institutions, especially the schools, as the primary place where talent is recognized and support is given to ensure that the talented among the working class are mobile. Family and friends are virtually invisible in this portrayal of the mobility process.

Although there is a good deal of variation in the roles that family and friends play for these women, they are certainly not invisible in the process. Especially among many of the Black women, there is a sense that they owe a great debt to their families for the help they have received. Black upwardly mobile women were also much more likely to feel that they give more than they receive from kin. Once they have achieved professional managerial employment, the sense of debt combines with their greater access to resources to put them in the position of being asked to give and of giving more to both family and friends. Carrington (1980) identifies some potential mental health hazards of such a sense of debt in upwardly mobile Black women's lives.

White upwardly mobile women are less likely to feel indebted to kin and to feel that they have accomplished alone. Yet even among this group, connections to spouses and children played significant roles in defining how women were mobile, their goals, and their sense of satisfaction with their life in the middle class.

These data are suggestive of a mobility process that is motivated by a desire for personal, but also collective, gain and that is shaped by interpersonal commitments to family, partners and children, community, and the race. Social mobility involves competition but also cooperation, community support, and personal obligations. Further research is needed to explore fully this new image of mobility and to examine the relevance of these issues for White male mobility as well.

NOTE

1. This and all the names used in this chapter are pseudonyms.

REFERENCES

Anthony, Bobbie. 1980. Parallels, particularities, problems, and positive possibilities related to institutional sexism and racism. *Women's Studies Quarterly* 3:339-46.

Blau, Peter, and Otis D. Duncan. 1967. *The American occupational structure.* New York: Wiley.

Braverman, Harry. 1974. *Labor and monopoly capital.* New York: Monthly Review Press.

Cannon, Lynn Weber, Elizabeth Higginbotham, and Marianne L. A. Leung. 1988. Race and class bias in qualitative research on women. *Gender & Society* 2:449-62.

Carrington, Christine. 1980. Depression in Black women: A theoretical appraisal. In *The Black woman*, edited by La Frances Rodgers Rose. Beverly Hills, CA: Sage.

Clark, Reginald. 1986. *Family life and school achievement*. Chicago: University of Chicago Press.

Ehrenreich, Barbara, and John Ehrenreich. 1979. The professional-managerial class. In *Between labor and capital*, edited by Pat Walker. Boston: South End Press.

Fossett, Mark A., Omer R. Galle, and William R. Kelley. 1986. Racial occupational inequality, 1940-1980: National and regional trends. *American Sociological Review* 51:421-29.

Gilkes, Cheryl Townsend. 1983. Going up for the oppressed: The career mobility of Black women community workers. *Journal of Social Issues* 39:115-39.

Gilligan, Carol. 1982. *In a different voice: Psychological theory and women's development*. Cambridge: Harvard University Press.

Higginbotham, Elizabeth, and Lynn Weber Cannon. 1988. *Rethinking mobility: Towards a race and gender inclusive theory*. Research Paper no. 8. Center for Research on Women, Memphis State University.

Hill Collins, Patricia. 1990. *Black feminist thought: Knowledge, consciousness, and the politics of empowerment*. Boston: Routledge.

Joslin, Daphne. 1979. *Working-class daughters, middle-class wives: Social identity and self-esteem among women upwardly mobile through marriage*. Doctoral dissertation, New York University.

McAdoo, Harriette Pipes. 1978. Factors related to stability in upwardly mobile Black families. *Journal of Marriage and the Family* 40:761-76.

Miller, Jean Baker. 1986. *Towards a new psychology of women*. 2d ed. Boston: Beacon.

Poulantzas, Nicos. 1974. *Classes in contemporary capitalism*. London: New Left Books.

Ryan, Jake, and Charles Sackrey. 1984. *Strangers in paradise: Academics from the working class*. Boston: South End Press.

Stack, Carol. 1974. *All our kin*. New York: Harper & Row.

Steinitz, Victoria Anne, and Ellen Rachel Solomon. 1986. *Starting out: Class and community in the lives of working-class youth*. Philadelphia: Temple University Press.

Strauss, Anselm. 1971. *The context of social mobility*. Chicago: Aldine.

U.S. Bureau of the Census. 1983. Detailed population characteristics: Tennessee. Census of the Population, 1980. Washington, DC: GPO.

Valentine, Bettylou. 1978. *Hustling and other hard work*. New York: Macmillan.

Vanneman, Reeve, and Lynn Weber Cannon. 1987. *The American perception of class*. Philadelphia: Temple University Press.

8 Chicana and Mexican Immigrant Women at Work: The Impact of Class, Race, and Gender on Occupational Mobility

DENISE A. SEGURA

Occupational Mobility—or improvement in job status and income—can be impeded by social and structural features of the labor market, familial responsibilities, and individual characteristics. This chapter examines the effects of labor market structure and social relations at work on the early occupational choices of a selected sample of Chicana and Mexican immigrant women[1] occupationally segregated in clerical, service, and operative jobs—jobs at which a majority of women of Mexican origin work.

Occupational segregation by gender constrains the employment options of all women (Bergmann 1974, 1984; Bielby and Baron 1986; Hartmann 1976). Racial and ethnic segmentation within typical women's jobs further constrains the employment options of women of color (Malveaux and Wallace 1987, Segura 1984, Stolz 1985). Malveaux and Wallace (1987) and Dill, Cannon, and Vanneman (1987) demonstrate that, given the preponderance of women of color in the lowest-paying women's jobs, gender is only one barrier to advancement. With respect

AUTHOR'S NOTE: This work is a revised version of a paper presented at the American Sociological Association Annual Meeting, Chicago, IL, 1987. I would like to thank Tomás Almaguer, Arlie R. Hochschild, Beatríz M. Pesquera, and Maxine Baca Zinn for their constructive comments on earlier drafts. I also appreciate the careful editing and suggestions of Judith Lorber.

to Chicanas, Segura (1986a, 1986b) argues that the interaction among lower-class status, ethnicity, and gender limits human capital acquisition and channels minority women into lower- echelon jobs that offer few opportunities for advancement.

In light of the dual dimension of occupational segregation, this chapter subdivided gender-specific jobs by race and compared barriers to occupational mobility of Chicanas and Mexicanas employed in jobs with an overrepresentation of White women (White-female-dominated jobs) with those employed in jobs with an overrepresentation of minority-group women (minority-female-dominated jobs). White women's share of the total U.S. labor force is 34.97 percent. Jobs in which White women are overrepresented include secretaries (88.84 percent White women), receptionists (82.7 percent), waitresses (79.64 percent), bank tellers (79.16 percent; Dill et al. 1987, 32). Jobs that have disproportionately large numbers of either Latinas or Black women, who constitute 2.14 percent and 4.8 percent, respectively, of the U.S. labor force, include sewing-machine operatives (13.49 percent Latina and 12.83 percent Black women) and teacher's aides (10.07 percent Latina and 14.87 percent Black women; Dill et al. 1987, 28-29).

In addition to their structural properties, class, race, and gender shape individual social relations. Dill (1983) and Davis (1981), for example, argue that the recent feminist overemphasis on the power of the social construction of gender often ignores critical class and race antagonisms between White women employers and Black employees. The character of workplace interaction has strong effects on an individual's labor market experiences and opportunities for promotion. How the actions and attitudes of coworkers and supervisors from one class, race, or gender are perceived and acted upon by women from different backgrounds is important to consider in analyses of job entries, job exits, and occupational mobility. The character of these social relations reinforces or challenges labor market stratification along class, race, and gender lines.

In analyzing the interplay between labor market structure and women's occupational mobility, I examined work dynamics that impede and facilitate job advancement. I also delved into the meaning of occupational mobility, highlighting both its objective and subjective dimensions. Within these contexts, I suggest that perceptions of upward mobility affect individual mobility in particular and labor market stratification in general. Thus jobs characterized in labor research as dead-end, low paying, and without prestige may be viewed by Chicana and Mexicana women as decent or even "better" jobs vis-à-vis jobs held by members of their reference groups or, most important, their own occupational expectations. This subjective dimension of occupational mobility can restrict women's job aspirations and reinforce the limited labor market position of Chicana and Mexicana women. This chapter reports the ways in which the interaction among class, race, and gender affects each woman's employment experiences and options for mobility.

RESEARCH DESIGN

Sample Selection

A sample of twenty Chicanas and twenty resident Mexican immigrant women were selected from the 1978-1979 or 1980-1981 cohorts of an adult education and employment-training program located in the San Francisco Bay Area. This program placed the respondents into jobs typically filled by women and racial-ethnic minorities. From the student rosters of these years, I compiled a list of forty-nine Mexicanas or Chicanas who had been placed by the agency. I was able to locate and interview forty women. The other nine potential respondents were not available for interviews because they had either returned to Mexico or had moved to unknown locations.

Table 1 provides a breakdown of the initial jobs secured by the forty respondents of this study. In all, 55 percent of the women secured jobs where nearly all of their coworkers were women of color. Another 42 percent obtained jobs where their coworkers and supervisors were predominantly White women. Only one woman obtained a job where most of her coworkers were men.

Sample Characteristics

All but one Mexicana and one Chicana grew up in families they described as poor or working class. Half of the Mexicanas had fathers who had worked on farmland belonging to the extended family in Mexico, one father had been a teacher, and the rest had been employed as manual laborers. Most of their mothers had not worked outside the home. Of the Mexicanas, 40 percent had less than a primary school education and 60 percent had finished elementary school. All but three

TABLE 8.1 Initial Jobs of Chicana and Mexicana Respondents[a]

Type of Job	Chicanas	Mexicanas
(White-female-dominated)		
Clerical jobs	65%	20%
Data entry clerk	(1)	(1)
Office assistant	(1)	(1)
Operations clerk	(1)	(0)
Receptionist	(4)	(1)
Sales clerk	(3)	(1)
Teller	(2)	(0)
Utility clerk	(1)	(0)
(Minority-female-dominated)		
Service jobs	35%	30%
Bilingual instructional aide	(2)	(0)
Child care worker	(2)	(1)
Hotel maid	(2)	(2)
Kitchen helper	(0)	(2)
Waitress	(1)	(1)
Operative jobs	0%	45%
Production worker	—	(6)
Seamstress	—	(3)
(Male-dominated)	0%	5%
Paint filler	—	(1)
Total	(20)	(20)

a. These classifications are based on the respondents' reports of the race and gender composition of their coworkers. Nationally, some of these jobs may be more diverse ethnically (Dill et al., 1987).

of the Mexicanas had obtained a high school equivalency diploma by the time they finished the training program. Their average age was 33.5 years.

With one exception, the Chicanas' fathers had worked in factory jobs, in the service sector as janitors and waiters, or as farm workers. A majority of the Chicana respondents had mothers who worked outside of the home, usually in low-paying service and clerical jobs. Slightly over half of the Chicanas had not finished high school. By the time they finished the training program, only five did not have either a high school diploma or its equivalent. Their average age was 27.5 years.

More Mexicanas than Chicanas were married but the Chicanas were more likely to be single heads of household. When they entered the training program, 20 percent of the Chicanas and 65 percent of the Mexicanas were married. Twenty-five percent of the Chicanas and 10 percent of the Mexicanas were single parents heading a household. Fifty-five percent of the Chicanas and 25 percent of the Mexicanas were single without dependents. At the time of their interviews, 30 percent of the Chicanas and 70 percent of the Mexicanas were married. Thirty-five percent of the Chicanas and 20 percent of the Mexicanas were single heads of household. Thirty-five percent of the Chicanas and 10 percent of the Mexicanas were single without dependents. In the time period under study, only seven Chicanas and two Mexicanas were not responsible for dependent children. Married or single-parent Chicanas averaged 1.3 dependent children, whereas Mexicanas averaged 2.4 children.

Interview Methods

The data for this study came from intensive interviews I conducted between October 1984 and July 1985. During the previous five years I had become familiar with the local Chicano and Mexicano communities as a junior high school teacher and as a parent with children at the child care center used by many of my future informants' families. In addition, I had established a good relationship with the training program by giving numerous employment workshops for their clients. All of these activities helped establish my credibility in the community. Such credibility is important inasmuch as Chicana and Mexicana women can be reluctant to be interviewed, given their vulnerability to the hostile inquiries of immigration officials and other public agencies (Solorzano-Torres 1987; Zavella 1987). Moreover, Chicanas and Mexicanas are likely to feel more comfortable talking to someone who is known within their social network than to an unknown researcher (Baca Zinn 1980; Zavella 1987). Finally, the quality of the interview data and the reliability is enhanced when the researcher is knowledgeable and integrated into the community under study (Baca Zinn 1979; Delgado-Gaitan 1987).

My familiarity with the local community enabled me to have shorter, more focused interviews than researchers in unfamiliar terrain. Each interview was informal and usually took place in the respondent's home. Six women were interviewed at the training program at their own request. The interviews were open-ended and based on an interview guide developed early in the research. I did not administer a questionnaire but asked general questions that became more specific in the course of the interview. I sought to gather detailed information about each woman's career and life aspirations, expectations, education, employment experiences, and family lives.

All but five interviews were tape recorded and transcribed. I took extensive notes during the nontaped interviews. Each interview lasted three to four hours. All of the Mexicanas preferred to be interviewed in Spanish (interlaced with English); the Chicanas were interviewed in English.

Findings

At the time of this study, the Mexicana and Chicana respondents were not well integrated into the social mainstream. Until they entered the labor force, the Mexicanas' contact with White men and women had occurred mainly in public-service agencies. The Mexicanas had approached work believing that race, gender, and class differences were not as important to job advancement as productivity. The Chicana respondents, however, believed that an individual's race, gender, and class were just as likely as productivity to impede or enhance advancement. These differences were a source of considerable friction between the Mexicanas and Chicanas when their paths crossed in the training program and on the job. From the interviews, I identified and analyzed the factors that actually impeded or facilitated the upward occupational mobility of the forty Chicana and Mexicana respondents.

Occupational Mobility

In this study, fourteen of the forty interviewed women improved their job status. Of the Chicanas, nine were promoted within White-female-dominated clerical jobs (e.g., from clerical assistant to first two grades of word processor). Subsequently one of these nine Chicanas secured a male-dominated mail carrier job. Of the Mexicanas, three were promoted in White-female-dominated clerical jobs. Later, one of them obtained a mail carrier job. One Mexicana was promoted in a minority-female-dominated service job, and one in a male-dominated operative job. A majority of the women interviewed did not improve their occupational status in the four to six years under review. Slightly over three-fourths of the twenty-six occupationally stable women worked in minority-female-dominated service jobs, such as teacher's aides in bilingual programs, child-care workers, waitresses in small Mexican restaurants, domestic workers, and production workers in private industry. The other six occupationally stable women worked in White-female-dominated clerical occupations. All but two of the fourteen upwardly mobile women had worked in White-female-dominated jobs, mainly in banking and as civil service secretaries. Two of these women later entered high-paying, male-dominated jobs (mail carrier). One woman was promoted from paint filler to line foreman in a male-dominated job, and one woman went from hotel maid to assistant housekeeper manager in a minority-female-dominated job.

More Chicanas (43 percent) than Mexicanas (26 percent) were occupationally mobile. The differences in their occupational mobility were not due to education, since most of the women had high school diplomas or the equivalent, nor were they due to fluency in English, since several Mexicanas with limited English advanced in English-only work settings. Individual characteristics cannot explain why some respondents were occupationally mobile and others were not. Better explanatory variables were labor market structure and differences in the work experiences of those women in White-female-dominated jobs compared with the work experiences of those in minority-female-dominated jobs.

Labor-Market Structure and Work Experiences

There were critical differences in earnings, working conditions, job ladders, and social relations at work for respondents working in White-female-dominated jobs compared with those employed in minority-female-dominated jobs.

With respect to wages, women working full-time in minority-female-dominated jobs earned, on the average, about $250 less per month than women in White-female-dominated jobs. Women employed full-time in either female segment of the labor market earned between $800 and $1,000 less per month than the few women who had moved into male-dominated jobs.

Women employed in minority-female-dominated jobs were more vulnerable to economic fluctuations than women in White-female-dominated jobs. Compared to those with year-round clerical jobs dominated by White women, production workers and hotel workers, in particular, reported numerous seasonal layoffs or tenuous job circumstances. Women employed in minority-female-dominated jobs reported greater physical distress, even danger at work, than did women working in White-female-dominated jobs. Women in male-dominated jobs also reported great physical stress but their pay was much higher. Women employed in minority-female-dominated jobs earned only 58 percent of the earnings of women in male-dominated jobs, despite the fact that both faced physical hazards such as heavy lifting, noise, and toxic fumes.

The respondents who worked in White-female-dominated clerical jobs in large organizations reported having clear and recognizable avenues for promotion. Osterman defines such job ladders as "limited and strictly defined ports of entry and well-marked progression paths" (1983, 352). Women working in jobs where virtually all of their coworkers were women of color did not recognize job ladders or declared that there weren't any to recognize.

Conditions of Upward Mobility in White-Female-Dominated Jobs

While job ladders existed in most clerical jobs, the criteria for advancement were problematic. In some jobs, occupational mobility hinged on objective criteria; in other jobs, subjective criteria shaped mobility. Civil service clerical workers reported that objective measures, primarily test scores, usually determined job advancement. Other clerical workers (primarily in banks, department stores, and small factories) indicated that pleasing supervisors, being a "hard worker," and getting along well with coworkers were key elements of job advancement.

Social relations at work were enormously important to the upward mobility and continued employment of the respondents in White-female-dominated jobs. The degree to which a woman could understand and adapt to the "culture of the firm" had a significant impact on her occupational mobility. Among the clerical workers in the White-female-dominated labor market—a majority of whom had entered their jobs through affirmative action—there was a high level of antagonism between the respondents and their coworkers and supervisors.

Chicana or Mexicana newcomers to White-female dominated jobs generally passed through a stage of feeling unwelcomed by their women coworkers and by their supervisors, who tended to be White women or men. Their racial or class backgrounds, coupled with their special mode of entry—affirmative action—produced lengthy periods of social ostracism.

A majority of the respondents interpreted their alienation at work as the price of gaining access to jobs outside their traditional milieu. As one Mexicana employed as a senior data entry clerk said:

> It has been difficult to get used to working here. The atmosphere is very different [from Mexico]. The customs are different. There is little conversation beyond "hi." Only with their friends do they say more. I realize that these feelings usually happen when one enters a new job. But usually the novelty wears off. For me it has never worn off. The atmosphere still seems very cold. I have thought that perhaps it is the language. But I don't know . . . perhaps it's being Latina. The few Latinas they've had there—all of them leave.

Her feeling of "not belonging" in an environment lacking other women of color was corroborated by many of the other respondents. Similar feelings hampered them from becoming integrated into important work networks or from engaging in social activities, such as office parties, that attract favorable notice from supervisors and coworkers.

The sense of isolation the women in White-female-dominated jobs reported reflected not only racial differences but class differences as well. As a Chicana receptionist in an all-White department at a local college described it:

> With my coworkers it was difficult. It was a very stuffy environment there at the college. But everyone there, they were from a totally different class. They were more into themselves and others like them—you know, more upper class. So I guess I couldn't relate to them. They used to talk about things I didn't know anything about. I felt really out of place. After I'd been there three years I'd reached the top level—for me. Then I got called to the post office. When I told my supervisors that I was leaving, she was shocked [laughs with a wicked gleam in her eye]. She said, "Why don't we try for a promotion?" I said, "It's kind of late for that." You see, I'd been trying to transfer and be promoted for about two years.

A working-class background can set a woman apart from her coworkers because her "presentation of self"—her choice of words, her mannerisms, and her way of dressing—may vary significantly from the workplace norm. As one Chicana clerical supervisor in a large bank said:

When I first got to the bank, I felt like everybody was staring at me with my feathered hair and khakis [pants]. They got my friend to quit with all their behind-the-back racist comments about Mexicans, but I just ignored them and did my job. I knew my rights. I knew they couldn't deny me promotions because I wore my hair a certain way [laughed uncertainly].

"Your hair isn't feathered now," I interjected.

Yes. Well, I got a new supervisor who helped me out. . . . I cut my hair a while back and started wearing nicer, more professional clothes. I think that helped me get this last promotion.

This change in supervisors kept her on the job not only by teaching her important work skills but also by encouraging her to work hard and by recommending her to other bank supervisors. With the supervisor's sponsorship, this Chicana became mobile in the clerical segment of the banking world.

The experiences of these and other isolated and alienated working-class Chicana and Mexicana women I interviewed disclosed important but subtle barriers to occupational mobility that are rooted in social class, ethnicity, and the dynamics of the firm. They felt uncomfortable and experienced rejection from coworkers and supervisors because of their lack of familiarity with white-collar work. They felt extremely self-conscious about their accents—a condition that was not helped by coworkers who spoke slowly to them in tones normally reserved for children. While these coworkers may have had the best of intentions, the condescending manner in which they offered the Latinas assistance reinforced the insecurity many of these women felt as they worked in jobs where few Latinas were employed.

While supportive supervisors helped two women adjust to the social and work requirements of their jobs and the alien culture of the firm, these women were not trained or encouraged to advance in their jobs until their first supervisors were replaced. Because their new supervisors had not been involved in the initial affirmative action hires of each woman or their strained periods of adjustment, they accepted them as members of the unit and gave them workloads and training commensurate with their seniority in the workplace.

Lack of such supervisory support posed the greatest obstacle to upward occupational mobility for the women interviewed. Few of them enjoyed supervisory support in their first jobs, and two-thirds of the occupationally mobile women became more successful in their second or third jobs by obtaining supervisory support for the training necessary for promotions.

The respondents said they consciously cultivated supervisory support and friendships (or tolerance, at the least) among coworkers. They differed on how long a time period they felt should elapse before they might reasonably give up on establishing rapport with supervisors and coworkers. Of the sixteen clerical workers who reported hostility directed at them, nine left their job within a year. The seven women who did not leave their jobs had higher tolerance levels because of the dire socioeconomic circumstances of their families. In general, women responsible for households tended to endure poor working conditions much longer than either single women or women with husbands in full-time, year-round jobs.

Conditions of Upward Mobility in Minority-Female-Dominated Jobs

Promotions and pay increases in minority-female-dominated jobs hinged on a combination of factors, which included individual productivity, seniority, and a supervisory job opening—a rare occurrence, according to the respondents. Only one respondent, a Mexicana, advanced occupationally in a minority-female-dominated job. After two years, she was promoted to assistant housekeeping manager in an elegant, medium-sized (145-room) hotel and supervised fifteen maids. The previous assistant manager had worked in that job for over ten years; being present when such a position opens up can be a matter of luck.

Chicanas and Mexicanas working in minority-female-dominated jobs did not report feeling socially isolated by coworkers. Women in these jobs socialized with one other during break times; they celebrated birthdays and various cultural holidays. The major complaints these women voiced concerned physical conditions at work, not the social aspects of employment. Recent evidence on cannery work culture and Chicanas corroborates this finding (Zavella 1987).

The relatively comfortable social relations Chicanas and Mexicanas experienced in these jobs, however, reinforced their occupational segregation in this race- and gender-specific segment of the secondary labor market. These jobs did not have recognized promotion ladders and were paid less than White-female-dominated jobs. Typically, women employed full-time in White-female-dominated clerical jobs earned between $980 and $1,360 monthly in 1985. Women employed full-time in minority-female-dominated operative jobs earned between $700 and $1,000 monthly in 1985 (U.S. Department of Labor, Bureau of Labor Statistics, 1985).

SUBJECTIVE AND OBJECTIVE MOBILITY

Actual job advancement did not occur for a majority of the respondents; nevertheless, over half of the nonmobile women averred that they worked in "better" jobs. This belief points to a subjective dimension of occupational mobility that can complement or conflict with actual job advancement.

In this study, a majority of the respondents *felt* upwardly mobile. They evaluated job success according to the type of job they thought they would get as a worker in the U.S. labor market, the earnings they thought they would earn as an adult worker, and whether their current job was better than jobs held by members of their reference groups. If their current job met any one of these conditions, the respondent considered herself to be occupationally mobile—even if actual wages or working conditions had not improved from the first to the current job. It is important to note, however, that the respondents who were the economic mainstays of their household rarely considered themselves occupationally mobile at the subjective level.

Not surprisingly, feelings of mobility emanated from actual improvement in wages and working status. As one Mexicana said:

> After I passed my GED [high-school equivalency diploma], my hope was to get a job earning about $4.50 an hour but full-time. Because that was the best salary I had earned. When the paint company told me it would be $5.00 an hour I was ecstatic. But the job was very hard—very physical. My back always ached.

Even though she did not like the working conditions or limited chances for advancement in her male-dominated job, it paid better than her previous job as a restaurant hostess. Since she had never believed that she could secure a job paying over $4.50 an hour, especially in a male-dominated arena, she surpassed both her objective and subjective criteria for occupational mobility.

At other times, women felt mobile even though they had not actually improved their job status from their first to their present job. A Chicana employed as a bilingual instructional aide said:

> I have a good job—a better job. Six years ago, who was I—a woman without education until I went to [the training program]. Of course, I wish I could work full-time so that I could earn more. But, when I look around me and see all the Mexicans and Latinos struggle to be employed, I thank God I have a good job!

Even though her job had fluctuating hours and lacked advancement opportunities, she felt successful when she considered the limited options of similarly situated Mexican and Latino workers. Over half of the Mexicanas felt mobile when they secured a job in the formal labor market if others in their reference group were largely confined to the informal world of work (e.g., baby-sitters, housecleaners). As one woman said, "I sew—but the Mexican woman here is most often appreciated for her ability to clean and take care of children."

In some instances, the subjective dimension of occupational mobility conflicted with the quest for actual job advancement. A case in point is a Chicana who worked as a dental assistant, with fluctuating hours and limited vacation and health benefits:

> I became a dental assistant. The only reason I left that place was the problems my boss had. It was really good. And it was something that I had gotten—that I a *Chicana* [her emphasis] had gotten by myself and without a [high school] diploma!

Her previous job as a bank bookkeeper and her subsequent job as a department-store cosmetic representative offered better pay, benefits, and promotional opportunities; yet she firmly believed that she had reached her occupational apex as a dental assistant because in her social world, Chicanas without high school diplomas did not obtain such jobs. Her belief that a dental assistant job represented "success" probably kept her in this job longer than the pay and working conditions warranted and deterred her from exploring better employment options until she had to leave it.

The interplay between subjective and objective dimensions of occupational mobility is important to consider in labor market analyses of groups such as Mexican-origin women who, historically, have been confined to employment in the secondary sector. At one level, subjective feelings of occupational mobility help explain why a large portion of the study sample appeared content with low-paying jobs with few avenues for actual job advancement. Actual job advancement was confined to movement into White-female-dominated jobs or into working-class male-dominated jobs via affirmative action.

CONCLUSION

The experiences of the women in this study demonstrate how both structural features of the labor market and social relations at work, shaped by class, race, and gender, affect occupational mobility. Employment in jobs occupationally segregated by gender and race restricted opportunities for advancement. Among the respondents, promotional opportunities were greater in White-female-dominated jobs than in minority-female-dominated jobs. The ethnicity and social class background of the respondents, however, often separated them from White coworkers and supervisors, since they seemed to be from different social worlds. Further obstructing positive relationships in the workplace was the fact that the respondents had penetrated the White-female-dominated work world through affirmative action.

In addition to the barriers to occupational mobility each woman experienced at work, a conceptualization of mobility legitimized their participation in secondary-sector jobs. Subjective mobility—the feeling of occupational betterment—is a concept whose content is rooted in the class, race, and gender of the respondents. For women whose life experiences and those of their reference groups have not led them to aspire to professional careers, employment in a stable job signified upward mobility. In addition, women who were unsure whether or not they could obtain *any* job felt mobile when they entered the labor force. In this sense, subjective mobility emanates from a woman's evaluations of her employment expectations as well as the successes and failures of her reference group.

Ironically, subjective feelings of mobility can hinder objective occupational mobility because it is a rationale through which women can control the alienation they experience at work. As long as women feel mobile upon gaining access to low-paying jobs with limited advancement because they are in the formal labor market, their actual job advancement will be limited. Moreover, if women like these respondents are made to feel unwelcome or unworthy when they work outside of their traditional milieu, their occupational mobility will remain largely subjective.

NOTE

1. In this chapter, *Chicano/a* refers to people of Mexican descent born in the United States or raised there since early childhood (before the age of six). *Mexicano/a* refers to resident immigrants from Mexico. For analytic purposes, Mexicanas are separated from Chicanas. The term *women of Mexican origin* includes both Chicanas and Mexican immigrant women. *Latino/a* and *Hispanic* are broader terms often used by U.S. state agencies to refer to persons of Spanish and Latin American heritage; 60 percent of all Hispanics in the United States are of Mexican origin. For additional information on the origins and use of the term *Chicano/a,* especially its political implications, see Tienda (1981), Penalosa (1970), and Barrera (1979).

REFERENCES

Baca Zinn, M. 1979. Field research in minority communities: Ethical, methodological, and political observations by an insider. *Social Problems* 27:209-19.

———. 1980. Employment and education of Mexican-American women: The interplay of modernity and ethnicity in eight families. *Harvard Educational Review* 50:47-62.

Barrera, M. 1979. *Race and class in the Southwest: A theory of racial inequality.* Notre Dame, IN: University of Notre Dame Press.

Bergmann, B. 1974. Occupational segregation, wages and profits when employers discriminate by race or sex. *Eastern Economic Journal* 1:103-10.

———. 1984. Trends in occupational segregation by sex and race, 1960-1981. In *Sex segregation in the workplace: Trends, explanations and remedies,* edited by B. F. Reskin. Washington, DC: National Academy Press.

Bielby, W. T., and J. N. Baron. 1986. Men and women at work: Sex segregation and statistical discrimination. *American Journal of Sociology* 91:759-99.

Davis, A. Y. 1981. *Woman, race and class.* New York: Vintage.

Delgado-Gaitan, C. 1987. Mexican adult literacy: New directions for immigrants. In *Becoming literate in English-as-a-Second Language: Advanced in research and theory,* edited by S. Goldman and H. Trueba. Norwood, NJ: Ablex.

Dill, B. Thornton. 1983. Race, class, and gender: Prospects for an all-inclusive sisterhood. *Feminist Studies* 9:131-50.

Dill, B. Thornton, L. W. Cannon, and R. Vanneman. 1987. *Pay equity: An issue of race, ethnicity and sex.* Washington, DC: National Commission on Pay Equity (February).

Hartmann, H. 1976. Capitalism, patriarchy and job segregation by sex. In *Women and the workplace,* edited by M. Reagan and B. Reagan. Chicago: University of Chicago Press.

Malveaux, J., and P. Wallace. 1987. Minority women in the workplace. In *Women and work: Industrial Relations Research Association Research volume,* edited by Karen S. Koziara, M. Moskow, and L. Dewey Tanner. Washington, DC: Bureau of National Affairs.

Osterman, P. 1983. Employment structures within firms. *British Journal of Industrial Relations* 20:349-60.

Penalosa, F. 1970. Toward an operational definition of the Mexican American. *Aztlan: Chicano Journal of the Social Sciences and the Arts* 1:1-12.

Segura, D. A. 1984. Labor market stratification: The Chicana experience. *Berkeley Journal of Sociology* 29:57-91.

————. 1986a. Chicanas and triple oppression in the labor force. In *Chicana voices: Intersections of class, race and gender,* National Association for Chicano Studies, Conference Proceedings. Austin: Center for Mexican American Studies, University of Texas, Austin.

————. 1986b. Chicanas and Mexican immigrant women in the labor market: A study of occupational mobility and stratification. Unpublished Ph.D. dissertation, University of California, Berkeley.

Solorzano-Torres, R. 1987. Female Mexican immigrants in San Diego County. In *Women on the U.S.-Mexico border: Responses to change,* edited by V. L. Ruiz and S. Tiano. Boston, MA: Allen & Unwin.

Stolz, B. A. 1985. *Still struggling: America's low-income working women confronting the 1980's.* New York: Lexington.

Tienda, M. 1981. The Mexican American population. In *Non-metropolitan American in transition,* edited by A. H. Hawley and S. M. Mazie. Chapel Hill: University of North Carolina Press.

U.S. Department of Labor, Bureau of Labor Statistics. 1985. *Employment and earnings.* Washington, DC: Government Printing Office (January).

Zavella, P. 1987. *Women's work and Chicano families: Cannery workers of the Santa Clara Valley.* Ithaca, NY: Cornell.

Part III

Getting By: Gender Relations, Family, and Community

Works in this section examine how different groups of women experience family life. Analyzing feminist and racial revisions of family scholarship, Maxine Baca Zinn in Chapter 9, "Family, Feminism, and Race in America," demonstrates the need to address racial stratification in order to embrace the experience of White families as well as racial ethnic families. She raises the question: "What does including race have to offer the study of the family?" She argues that, in addition to class and gender hierarchies, racial stratification is among the major macrostructural forces that situate families both in specific social locations and in relation to social institutions which allocate resources. Two other macrostructural processes, industrialization and deindustrialization, interacting with class and gender, have produced certain racial patternings in family and household formation. Theories of family have largely ignored the new knowledge about race, labor, and family formation. Baca Zinn's analysis of historical transformation of the family offers examples of the importance of race in theorizing about family life in American society.

In Chapter 10, "Overcoming Patriarchal Constraints," Pierrette Hondagneu-Sotelo examines how gender shapes the migration and settlement experiences of Mexican immigrant women and men. Her primary concern is that the analytic primacy of the household in the migration literature has been highly inadequate because it has not considered gender. She also wants to know how gender relations in Mexican immigrant families have been shaped by the migration process. She argues that the events responsible for immigrant families becoming less patriarchal go beyond resource theories and are very different from those posited by acculturation models. She contends that the partial dismantling of patriarchy arises from new patterns of behavior induced by the arrangements of family migration and that migration itself has become a gendered process.

Comparing the experiences of families in which the husbands departed prior to 1965 to those in which they departed after 1965, Hondagneu-Sotelo discovered that lengthy spousal separations, access to community social networks, and husbands' ability to gain legal status in the U.S. altered patterns of patriarchal authority, gender relations, the traditional gendered household division of labor, and the conditions of daily life. Such structural changes were indicative of the fluid character of patriarchal relations in Mexican immigrant families. The women were able to challenge, dissuade, subvert, and diminish patriarchal control in a new societal setting. This induced a trend toward more egalitarian conjugal relations after their settlement in the U.S. This study of Mexican immigrant women's lives and their struggles for family survival contributes profoundly to our understanding of women's agency as a source of resistance and empowerment.

The effects of migration on gender roles and power are also the focus of Nazli Kibria's work in Chapter 11, "Power, Patriarchy, and Gender Conflict in the Vietnamese Immigrant Community." Based on her ethnographic study of Vietnamese immigrants recently settled in the U.S., Kibria explores how women's groups and networks play an important role in the exchange of social and economic resources among households and in the mediation of disputes between women and men in the family. Like Hondagneu-Sotelo's study, Kibria's work shows how the notion of "bargaining with patriarchy" is a direct outcome of migration. Kibria's first argument was that the "old" patriarchal bargains constructed in Vietnam might now be renegotiated, given the shift in resources between women and men resulting from the migration process. Her second argument is that Vietnamese women's community groups in the U.S., as sources of exchange and support, constrained male authority within acceptable limits, to roles as guardians of the family and supporters of particular women's interests. Her third argument is that this kind of support from networks is limited and that the women's community ultimately upheld and affirmed traditional gender-role ideology and behavior. As such, says Kibria, the views of the women are not unlike those of many current U.S. anti-feminists who fear shifting gender relationships as a threat to their economic security and parental authority over their children. In sum, her research suggests that the dialectical effects of migration on gender relations must be understood as highly uneven and shifting in quality, often resulting in gains for women in certain spheres and losses in others.

In Chapter 12, "Activist Mothering," Nancy A. Naples reports her observations concerning the cross-generational continuity of community work performed by Black women and Latinas with different social and cultural histories who live and work in low-income communities. She investigates the complex ways in which gender, race-ethnicity, and class contribute to the social construction of mothering. Although White women and women of color may both describe their motivation for community work as an extension of their gender identities, Nancy Naples uncovers the fact that their differing standpoints, shaped by race-ethnicity, class, sexual orientation, and region of residence, influence how they define their families' and communities' needs as well as the political strategies they adopt to meet these differing needs. Questioning definitions of mothering that are derived from biological and legal expressions, Naples argues for the importance of community-based caregiving and race-uplifting work for the family and the community by various women's groups. The community workers that she studied defined "activist mothering" as comprising all actions that address the needs of their children and community, including social activism. Naples contends that the analysis of activist mothering provides a new conceptualization of the interacting nature of labor, politics, and mothering.

Naples's research challenges the idea of separate spheres, showing the complexity of the connections among political activism, mothering, community work, and paid work. Her careful analysis reveals the inseparability of paid and unpaid work and of production and social reproduction and reconceptualizes power as also existing in the private sphere, in which the homeplace may serve as "a site of resistance."

As a whole, these chapters highlight diverse women's experiences as derived from their different sociopolitical and cultural histories and the extent to which they perceive sexism, racism, and economic exploitation. The foci of "overcoming patriarchal constraints," "activist mothering," and gender discord in families and across generations vividly capture the various ways in which race, class, and gender are experienced and yet how commonalities become apparent. Gender relations have been and will continue to be shaped and modified as diverse groups of women and men seek to balance their work, family, and community lives.

9 Family, Feminism, and Race in America

MAXINE BACA ZINN

Rapid social changes have often besieged families. Much of the contemporary crisis in American family life is related to larger socioeconomic changes. Upheavals in the social organization of work have created a massive influx of women into the labor force. At the same time, the removal of certain kinds of work have left millions of workers without jobs. Both kinds of change have affected the well-being of American families.

As debates about the context and consequences of family change reach heightened proportions, the racial ethnic[1] composition of the United States is undergoing dramatic shifts. Massive waves of immigration from Latin America and Asia are posing difficult issues for a society that clings stubbornly to its self-image of the melting pot. Changes in fertility and immigration patterns are altering the distribution of Whites and people of color, and at the same time, creating a nation of varied racial ethnic groups. In many cities and communities, Blacks, Hispanics, Asians, and Native Americans outnumber the White population. Their families are distinctive not only because of their ethnic heritage but because they reside in a society where racial stratification continues to shape family resources and structures in important ways. The changing demography of race in the United States presents compelling challenges to family sociology.

AUTHOR'S NOTE: Some of the ideas in this article were presented in *Diversity in Families,* first and second editions (Baca Zinn, M. and D. S. Eitzen, Harper and Row, 1987 and 1990). I thank Margaret L. Andersen, Bonnie Thornton Dill, and Judith Lorber for their contributions.

Questions about what is happening to families in the United States and how this country's racial order is being reshaped are seldom joined. Yet they are more closely related than either popular or scholarly discourse on these topics would suggest. The national discussion about the erosion of inner-city Black and Latino families has not been applied to our understanding of the family in general. Although many sources of this crisis are rooted in new forms of race and class inequality in America, the empirical data can sharpen our theoretical understanding of "the family" and its relationship to wider social forces. Instead of marginalizing minority families as special cultural cases, it is time to bring race into the mainstream of our thinking about family life in America.

For the past two decades, family scholarship has been in the throes of revision. Both feminist revisions (for reviews see Andersen 1989; Gerstel and Gross 1987; Glenn 1987; Komorovsky 1988; Thorne 1982) and revisions of scholarship on families of racial ethnic groups (for reviews see Allen 1978; Baca Zinn 1982/83; Mirande 1977; Mullings 1986a; Ramirez and Arce 1981; Staples and Mirande 1980; Wilkinson 1987) have given us new perspectives, approaches, and explanations of American family life in this society. In contrast to discussions of the family two decades ago, issues of gender stratification are paramount today. Issues of racial stratification, however, have received little theoretical attention. While feminist scholarship has had a great impact on analysis of the family, revisionist research on minority families continues to be marginalized, absent even from much feminist scholarship. Without a framework for incorporating race and ethnicity into models of "the family," feminist reformulations cannot be inclusive.

In this chapter, I take a step toward incorporating race into the feminist revision of the concept of the family. One of this chapter's aims is to show that research on racially and ethnically diverse families can make an essential contribution to the study of the family. The intent is not to provide a theory of racial stratification and family life but to raise issues about the extent to which racial formation is a meaningful category for analyzing family experience.

THE FEMINIST RE-VISION

Feminist challenges to traditional family theory have been accomplished by decomposing the family—that is, by breaking the family into constituent elements so that the underlying structures are exposed. In

doing so, feminists have brought into relief three aspects of that structure: ideologies that serve to mystify women's experiences as wives and
mothers, hierarchical divisions that generate conflict and struggle
within families, and the multiple and dynamic interconnections between households and the larger political economy (Glenn 1987, 358).
An understanding of family dynamics has been transformed by exposing gender as a fundamental category of social relations both within and
outside the family (Andersen 1989).

First evolved as a critique of functionalism and its emphasis on roles,
the crucial impact of feminist scholarship on family research has been
to recast the family as a system of gender stratification. Because roles
neglect the political underpinnings of the family, feminists have directed attention outside the family "to the social structures that shape
experience and meaning, that give people a location in the social world,
and that define and allocate economic and social rewards" (Hess and
Ferree 1987, 11). Once feminist scholars made it clear that gender roles
are not neutral ways of maintaining order in family and society but
benefit some at the expense of others, virtually everything about the
family looked different. As Bridenthal (1982) said:

> Put another way, feminists have opened up a whole new vista by asking
> not what do women do for the family? (an older question) but what does
> the family do *for* women? What does it do *to* women? Whom does the
> family organization serve best and how? (pp. 231-32)

Rather than viewing the family as a unit shaped only by affect or
kinship, we now know that families are settings in which people with
different activities and interests often come into conflict with one
another.

The last point has had important ramifications for thinking about
diversity and family life. Feminists have challenged the monolithic
ideology of the family that elevated the traditional nuclear family with
a breadwinner husband and a full-time homemaker wife as the only
legitimate family form. We now give equal weight to the varied family
structures and experiences that are produced by the organization of the
economy, the state, and other institutions (Thorne 1982, 2). Some of
these alternative family structures and living arrangements are non-
marital cohabitation, single-parent households, extended kinship units
and expanded households, dual-worker families, commuter marriages,
gay and lesbian households, and collectives.

REVISIONS IN RACE-RELATIONS SCHOLARSHIP

The revisioning of American scholarship on racial ethnic families different from those of the White middle class has run a similar but not intersecting course with feminist scholarship. Like feminist scholarship, this revisioning began with a critique of functionalist accounts of racially and ethnically diverse families as dysfunctional units that acted as barriers to their groups' mobility (Staples and Mirande 1980). The sociology of the family has been noted for its absence of a strong tradition of theory and for being heavily normative, moralistic, and mingled with social policy and the social objectives of various action groups (Morgan 1975, 3). Nowhere is this tendency more apparent than in its treatment of racial ethnic families in the United States.

The model of the backward and culturally deviant minority family originated within the sociology of race relations in the United States and its then guiding framework of assimilation and modernization. The preoccupation in race relations with "traditional" and "modern" social forms fit well with family sociology's preoccupation with the nuclear family, its wage-earner father, and domestic-caretaker mothers. Minorities and others whose family patterns differed from the ideal were explained as cultural exceptions to the rule. Their slowness to acculturate and take on the normal patterns of family development left them behind as other families in American society modernized. They were peripheral to the standard family and viewed as problems because of their failure to adopt the family patterns of the mainstream.

The "social problems" origin of family studies in the nineteenth century also contributed to this perspective. Family study as a new field emerged out of a deep concern for the need to solve such problems as rising divorce rates and the effects of slavery and industrialization on the family (Thomas and Wilcox 1987, 82). Social reforms of the times favored the modern family as a way of combating social problems, a belief that remains widely held in American society, if not in American family sociology.

Mainstream American sociology thus supported popular ideology by legitimizing the marginalization of racial ethnic groups in the social hierarchy. As cultural holdovers in a modernizing world, minority families were relegated to the sidelines with no relevance to the core of family theory. Scholars of various disciplines have long refuted this culturally deviant model of family, arguing that alternative family patterns do not reflect deviance, deficiency, or disorganization and that alternative family patterns are related to but not responsible for the social location of minorities. Revisionist approaches have emphasized the structural conditions giving rise to varied family forms, rather than the other way around. Differences in family patterns have been reinterpreted as adaptations to the conditions of racial inequality and poverty, often as sources of survival and strength (see, for example, Billingsley 1968; Glenn 1983; Griswold del Castillo 1984; Gutman 1976; Hill 1972; Ladner 1971; Stack 1974; Wagner and Shaffer 1980).

ASSESSING THE REVISIONS

The feminist revisioning of the family and the revisioning of studies of families in race relations scholarship have common origins. Both gained momentum as critiques of functionalism by an emergent critical sociology. The family was an important starting point in the development of women's studies, Black studies, and Chicano studies. In each of these areas, study of the family represented a vital thread in the evolution of critical scholarship. Both bodies of scholarship locate family experience in societal arrangements that extend beyond the family and allocate social and economic rewards. Both begin with the assumption that families are social products and then proceed to study their interrelationships with other social structures. Just as feminist theories have reconceptualized the family along a gender axis of power and control, racial ethnic family scholarship has reconceptualized the family along the axis of race, also a system of power and control that shapes family life in crucial ways.

Because they both locate family experience in societal arrangements extending beyond the family, these two streams of revisionist scholarship fall within the "radical critical" tradition. Although they are not commonly identified with this framework (see Osmond 1987, 119), they do adopt basic assumptions, major premises, and general directions of this approach.

Despite such fundamental similarities in their intellectual roots, the feminist revision and the racial ethnic studies revision have not been combined nor have they had the same impact on theories of the family. Feminist scholarship with its gender-as-power theme has had a far greater impact. Especially noteworthy in this regard has been the application of certain feminist insights to studies of minority families. In fact, gender-as-power and the racial division of labor have become key themes of recent studies of racial ethnic families. Glenn's study of

Japanese families (1986) and Zavella's study of Chicano families (1987) are particularly meaningful because they explore the close connections between the internal dynamics of women's family lives and economic conditions as they are bound up in broader systems of class and race inequality.

Studying the intersection of gender, race, and class in minority families has enormously enhanced family scholarship. Now, in studying racial ethnic families, we routinely examine race and gender as interacting hierarchies of resources and rewards that condition material and subjective experiences within families (see, for example, Almquist 1987).

Interacting race, class, and gender ideologies have shaped prevailing models of minority families, appearing even in the culturally deviant explanations of racial ethnic families. As Collins (1989) explains, the new version of this argument is that because minority women and men do not follow dominant notions of masculinity and femininity, they are responsible for their subordinate class placement in society. As Bridenthal (1981) has put it:

> Black people have been called matriarchal (ruled by the mother) and Chicano families have been called patriarchal (ruled by the father). These supposedly opposite family structures and relationships have been blamed for the failure of many members of each group to rise to a higher socioeconomic level. In other words, black and Chicano families have been blamed for the effect of racial discrimination. (p. 85)

While revisionist research on racial ethnic families has incorporated many feminist insights, the reverse has not occurred. Knowledge about racial stratification has not been incorporated into much feminist research on the family, and race enters the discussion of family life only when minority families are concerned.

To be fair, feminist literature on the family does recognize the societal context of inequality that gives rise to distinctive family forms. Feminist rethinking of the family has dropped the cultural *deviant* perspective. But for the most part, it retains a *cultural* perspective. Most contemporary feminist thought takes great care to underscore class, race, and gender as fundamental categories of social organization, but when it comes to family patterns, race and ethnicity are used as elements of culture, not social structure. Descriptions of cultural diversity do not explain why families exhibit structural variations by race. While it is true that many family lifestyles are differentiated by ethnicity, structural patterns differ because social and economic conditions produce and may even require diverse family arrangements. Although the family nurtures ethnic culture, families are not the product of ethnic culture alone.

RACIAL INEQUALITY AND FAMILY LIFE

Feminist revision has been reluctant to grapple with race as a power system that affects families throughout society and to apply that understanding to "the family" writ large. As Glenn (1987) says, "Systematically incorporating hierarchies of race and class into feminist reconstruction of the family remains a challenge, a necessary next step in the development of theories of family that are inclusive" (p. 368).

Social Location and Family Formation

In our quest to understand the structural sources of diversity in family life, we must examine all of the "socioeconomic and political arrangements and how they impinge on families" (Mullings 1986a, 13). Like class and gender hierarchies, racial stratification is a fundamental axis of American social structure. Racial stratification produces different opportunity structures that shape families in a variety of ways. Marriage patterns, gender relations, kinship networks, and other family characteristics result from the social location of families, that is, where they are situated in relation to societal institutions allocating resources.

Thinking about families in this way shifts the theoretical focus from cultural diversity or "ethnic lifestyles" of particular groups to race as a major element of hierarchical social relations that touches families throughout the social order (Omi and Winant 1986, 61). Racial stratification is a basic organizing principle in American society even though the forms of domination and discrimination have changed over time. Omi and Winant use the term "racial formation" to refer to the process by which social, economic, and political forces determine the content and import of racial categories and by which they are in turn shaped by racial meanings (1986, 61). As racial categories are formed and transformed over time, the meanings, practices, and institutions associated with race penetrate families throughout the society.

Social categories and groups subordinate in the racial hierarchy are often deprived of access to social institutions that offer supports for family life. Social categories and groups elevated in the racial hierarchy have different and better connections to institutions that can sustain families. Social location and its varied connection with social resources thus have profound consequences for family life.

If families are to be conceptualized in a way that relates them to social, historical, and material conditions, then racial stratification cannot be ignored. We are forced to abandon conventional notions that racial ethnic diversity is a cultural phenomenon best understood at the microstructural level. Instead of treating diversity as a given or as a result of traditions alone, we must treat racial stratification as a macrostructural force situating families in ways requiring diverse arrangements. These macrostructural forces can be seen in two periods of economic upheaval in the United States—industrialization and the current shift from manufacture to information and services. In both of these transitions, the relationship between families and other institutions has been altered. Despite important differences, these economic transformations have produced new relations among individuals, families, and labor systems that have had profound effects on family development throughout American society. Industrialization and deindustrialization are not neutral transformations that touch families in uniform ways. Rather, they manifest themselves differently in their interaction with race and gender, and both periods of transition reveal racial patterning in family and household formation. The theme of historical variation has become increasingly accepted in family studies, but theories of the family have largely ignored the new knowledge about race, labor, and family formation.

INDUSTRIALIZATION AND FAMILY STRUCTURE

The past two decades of historical research on the family have revealed that industrialization has had momentous consequences for American families because of massive changes in the way people have made a living. The industrial revolution changed the nature of work performed, the allocation of work responsibilities, and the kind of pay, prestige, and power that resulted from various positions in the economy. The effect of industrialization on American family life was uneven. Instead of a linear pattern of change in which families moved steadily to a more modern level, the pattern of change was checkered (Hareven 1987). Labor force exploitation produced various kinds of family and household adaptations on the part of slaves, agricultural workers, and industrial workers.

Both class and race were basic to the relations of production in the United States in this period. Race was intertwined with class; populations from various parts of the world were brought into the labor force at different levels, and racial differences were utilized to rationalize exploitation of women and men (Mullings 1986b, 56). European ethnics were incorporated into low-wage industrial economies of the north, while Blacks, Latinos, Chinese, and Japanese filled labor needs in colonial labor systems of the economically backward regions of the west, southwest, and the south. These colonial labor systems, while different, created similar hardships for family life.

All these groups had to engage in a constant struggle for both immediate survival and long-term continuation of family and community, but women's and men's work and family patterns varied considerably within different racial labor structures, with fundamentally different social supports for family life. Dill (1988) has compared patterns of White families in nineteenth-century America with those of racial ethnics and identified important racial differences in the social supports for family life. She finds that greater importance was accorded European American families by the wider society. As primary laborers in the reproduction and maintenance of family life, these women were acknowledged and accorded the privileges and protections deemed socially appropriate to their family roles. While this emphasis on family roles denied these women many rights and privileges and seriously constrained their individual growth and development, it also revealed public support for White women's family roles. Women's reproductive labor was viewed as an essential building block of the family. Combined with a view of the family as the cornerstone of the nation, this ideology produced experiences within the White dominant culture very different from those of racial ethnics (Dill 1988, 418). Because racial ethnic men were usually unable to earn a "family wage," their women had to engage in subsistence and income-producing activities both in and out of the household. In addition, they had to struggle to keep their families together in the face of outside forces that threatened the integrity of their households (Glenn 1987, 53-54).

During industrialization, class produced some similarities in the family experiences of racial ethnic women and those of White working-class immigrants. As D. E. Smith (1987) has argued, working-class women during this period were often far removed from the domestic ideal. The cults of domesticity and true womanhood that proliferated during this period were ideals attained more frequently by those European American women whose husbands were able to earn enough to support their families (Mullings 1986b, 50).

This ideal was not attainable by Blacks, Latinos, and Asian Americans, who were excluded from jobs open to White immigrants. For example, in most cities, the constraints that prevented Black men from earning a family wage forced Black married women into the labor market in much greater proportions than White immigrant women. By 1880, about 50 percent of Black women were in the labor force, compared with 15 percent of White women (Degler 1980, 389). Furthermore, the family system of the White working class was not subject to institutional assaults, such as forced separation, directed against Black, Latino, and Chinese families (Glenn 1987, 73).

Racial ethnic women experienced the oppressions of a patriarchal society but were denied the protections and buffering of a patriarchal family. Their families suffered as a direct result of the labor systems in which they participated. Since they were a cheap and exploitable labor force, little attention was given to their family and community life except as it related to their economic productivity. Labor, and not the existence or maintenance of families, was the critical aspect of their role in building the nation. They were denied the social and structural supports necessary to make their families a vital element in the social order (Dill 1988, 418). Nevertheless, people take conditions that have been thrust upon them and out of them create a history and a future (Mullings 1986b, 46). Using cultural forms where possible and creating new forms where necessary, racial ethnics adapted their families to the larger social order. These adaptations were not exceptions to the rule; they were instead variations created by mainstream forces. One family type was not standard and the others peripheral. Different forms existed at the same time.

Once we recognize how racial stratification has affected family formation, we can understand why the idealized family was not a luxury shared by all. At the same time, we can see how some idealized family patterns were made possible because of the existence of alternative family forms and how all of these are products of the social and economic conditions of the times. Although Blacks, Mexicanos, and Asians were excluded from industrial work, all three groups helped build the agricultural and industrial base for subsequent industrial development. New ways of life and new family patterns sprang from industrialization. As Mullings (1986b) says, "It was the working class and enslaved men and women whose labor created the wealth that allowed the middle class and upper middle class domestic life styles to exist" (p. 50).

DEINDUSTRIALIZATION AND FAMILIES

Vast changes in the social organization of work are currently transforming the American family across class and race groups. Not only are women and men affected differently by the transformation of the economy from its manufacturing base to service and high technology, but women and men in different racial categories are experiencing distinctive changes in their relationship to the economy. This transformation is profoundly affecting families as it works with and through race and gender hierarchies.

In the current American economy, industrial jobs traditionally filled by men are being replaced with service jobs that are increasingly filled by women. Married White women are now entering the labor force at a rate that, until recently, was seen exclusively among women of color (J. Smith 1987, 16). The most visible consequences of the increased labor force participation among White women include declining fertility and changes in marriage patterns. American White women are delaying marriage and childbearing and having fewer children over their lifetimes, living alone or as heads of their own households—living with neither parents nor husbands (Hartmann 1987, 36). The new economy is reshaping families as it propels these women into the labor force.

In minority communities across America, families and households are also being reshaped through new patterns of work and gender roles. The high level of female-headed families among Blacks and Hispanics (especially Puerto Ricans) is the outgrowth of changes in the larger economy. The long-term decline in employment opportunities for men is the force most responsible for the growth of racial ethnic families headed by women. Wilson's (1987) compelling work has shown that the shortage of Black men with the ability to support a family makes it necessary for many Black women to leave a marriage or forego marriage altogether. Adaptation to structural conditions leaves Black women disproportionately separated, divorced, and solely responsible for their children.

Families throughout American society are being reshaped by economic and industrial change: "The shifting economy produces and even demands diverse family forms—including, for example, female headed households, extended kinship units, dual career couples, and lesbian collectives" (Gerstel and Gross 1987, 7). Families mainly headed by women have become permanent in all racial categories in America, with the disproportionate effects of change most visible among Blacks and Latinos. While the chief cause of the increase in female-headed households among Whites is the greater economic independence of White women, the longer delay of first marriage and the low rate of remarriage among Black women reflects the labor force problems of Black men (Wilson and Neckerman 1986, 256). Thus race creates different routes to female headship, but Whites, Blacks, and Latinos are all increasingly likely to end up in this family form.

CONCLUSION

Knowing that race creates certain patterns in the way families are located and embedded in different social environments, we should be able to theorize for all racial categories. Billingsley (1988) suggests that the study of Black families can generate important insights for White families: Families may respond in a like manner when impacted by larger social forces. To the extent that White families and Black families experience similar pressures, they may respond in similar ways, including the adaptation of their family structures and other behaviors. With respect to single-parent families, teenage childbirth, working mothers, and a host of other behaviors, Black families serve as barometers of social change and as forerunners of adaptive patterns that will be progressively experienced by the more privileged sectors of American society.

While such insights are pertinent, they should not eclipse the ways in which racial meanings inform our perceptions of family diversity. As social and economic changes produce new family arrangements, alternatives—sometimes called "family pluralism"—are granted greater legitimacy. Yet many alternatives that appear new to middle-class White Americans are actually variant family patterns that have been traditional within Black and other minority communities for many generations. Presented as the new lifestyles of the mainstream, they are, in fact, the same lifestyles that have in the past been deemed pathological, deviant, or unacceptable when observed in Black families (Peters and McAdoo 1983, 228).

In much popular and scholarly thinking, alternatives are seen as inevitable changes, new ways of living that are part of an advanced society. In other words, they are conceptualized as products of the mainstream. Yet such alternatives, when associated with racial ethnic groups, are judged against a standard model and found to be deviant. Therefore, the notion of family pluralism does not correctly describe the family diversity of the past or the present. Pluralism implies that alternative family forms *coexist* within a society. In reality, racial meanings create a hierarchy in which some family forms are privileged and others are subordinated, even though they are both products of larger social forces.

Treating race as a basic category of social organization can make the feminist reconstruction of the family more inclusive. The implications of this approach are also provocative and uncomfortable because they challenge some of our basic sociological and feminist assumptions about how families in different races (and classes) are related to the larger society, to each other, and how they are all changing as a result of ongoing social and economic changes. These are important issues for social scientists, policymakers, and others to ponder, understand, and solve.

NOTE

1. The term *racial ethnic* refers to groups labeled as races in the context of certain historical, social, and material conditions. Blacks, Latinos, and Asian Americans are racial groups that are formed, defined, and given meaning by a variety of social forces in the wider society, most notably distinctive forms of labor exploitation. Each group is also bound together by ethnicity, that is, common ancestry and emergent cultural characteristics that are often used for coping with racial oppression. The concept racial ethnic underscores the social construction of race and ethnicity for people of color in the United States.

REFERENCES

Allen, W. 1978. Black family research in the United States: A review, assessment and extension. *Journal of Comparative Family Studies* 9:167-89.

Almquist, E. M. 1987. Labor market gender inequality in minority groups. *Gender & Society* 1:400-414.

Andersen, M. 1989. Feminism and the American family ideal. Paper presented at the Eastern Sociological Society annual meeting, Baltimore.

Baca Zinn, M. 1982/83. Familism among Chicanos: A theoretical review. *Humboldt Journal of Social Relations* 101:224-38.

Baca Zinn, M., and D. S. Eitzen. 1987. *Diversity in American families.* New York: Harper & Row.

———. 1990. *Diversity in families.* 2d ed. New York: Harper & Row.

Billingsley, A. 1968. *Black families in White America.* Englewood Cliffs, NJ: Prentice Hall.

———. 1988. The impact of technology on Afro-American families. *Family Relations* 7:420-25.

Bridenthal, R. 1981. The family tree: Contemporary patterns in the United States. In *Household and kin,* edited by A. Swerdlow, R. Bridenthal, J. Kelly and P. Vine. Old Westbury, NY: Feminist Press.

———. 1982. The family: The view from a room of her own. In *Rethinking the family,* edited by B. Thorne and M. Yalom. New York: Longman.

Collins, P. Hill. 1989. A comparison of two works on Black family life. *Signs* 14:875-84.

Degler, C. 1980. *At odds: Women and the family in America from the revolution to the present.* New York: Oxford University Press.

Dill, B. Thornton. 1988. Our mother's grief: Racial ethnic women and the maintenance of families. *Journal of Family History* 13:415-31.

Gerstel, N., and H. E. Gross, eds. 1987. *Families and work.* Philadelphia: Temple University Press.

Glenn, E. Nakano. 1983. Split household, small producer, and dual wage earner: An analysis of Chinese-American family strategies. *Journal of Marriage and the Family* 45:35-46.

———. 1986. *Issei, nesei, war bride: Three generations of Japanese American women in domestic service.* Philadelphia: Temple University Press.

———. 1987. Racial ethnic women's labor: The intersection of race, gender and class oppression. In *Hidden aspects of women's work,* edited by C. Bose, R. Feldberg, and N. Sokoloff. New York: Praeger.

Griswold del Castillo, R. 1984. *La familia.* Notre Dame, IN: University of Notre Dame Press.

Gutman, H. 1976. *The Black family in slavery and freedom, 1750-1925.* New York: Pantheon.

Hareven, T. 1987. Historical analysis of the family. In *Handbook of marriage and the family,* edited by M. B. Sussman and S. Steinmetz. New York: Plenum.

Hartmann, H. I. 1987. Changes in women's economic and family roles in post World War II United States. In *Women, households and the economy,* edited by L. R. Beneria and C. R. Stimpson. New Brunswick, NJ: Rutgers University Press.

Hess, B., and M. M. Ferree. 1987. Introduction. In *Analyzing gender,* edited by B. Hess and M. M. Ferree. Newbury Park, CA: Sage.

Hill, R. 1972. *The strengths of Black families.* New York: Emerson-Hall.

Komorovsky, M. 1988. The new feminist scholarship: Some precursors and polemics. *Journal of Marriage and the Family* 50:585-93.

Ladner, J. 1971. *Tomorrow's tomorrow: The Black woman.* New York: Doubleday.

Mirande, A. 1977. The Chicano family: A reanalysis of conflicting views. *Journal of Marriage and the Family* 39:737-56.

Morgan, D.H.J. 1975. *Social theory and the family.* London: Routledge & Kegan Paul.

Mullings, L. 1986a. Anthropological perspectives on the Afro-American family. *American Journal of Social Psychiatry* 6:11-16.

———. 1986b. Uneven development: Class, race and gender in the United States before 1900. In *Women's work,* edited by E. Leacock, H. I. Safa, and contributors. New York: Bergin & Garvey.

Omi, M., and H. Winant. 1986. *Racial formation in the United States.* London: Routledge & Kegan Paul.

Osmond, M. Withers. 1987. Radical-critical theories. In *Handbook of marriage and the family,* edited by M. B. Sussman and S. Steinmetz. New York: Plenum.

Peters, M., and H. P. McAdoo. 1983. The present and future of alternative lifestyles in ethnic American cultures. In *Contemporary families and alternative lifestyles,* edited by E. D. Macklin and R. H. Rubin. Beverly Hills, CA: Sage.

Ramirez, O., and C. H. Arce. 1981. The contemporary Chicano family: An empirically based review. In *Explorations in Chicano psychology,* edited by A. Baron, Jr. New York: Praeger.

Smith, D. E. 1987. Women's inequality and the family. In *Families and work,* edited by N. Gerstel and H. E. Gross. Philadelphia: Temple University Press.

Smith, J. 1987. Transforming households: Working-class women and economic crisis. *Social Problems* 34:416-36.

Stack, C. 1974. *All our kin.* New York: Harper & Row.

Staples, R., and A. Mirande. 1980. Racial and cultural variations among American families: A decennial review of the literature on minority families. *Journal of Marriage and the Family* 40:157-73.

Thomas, D. L., and J. E. Wilcox. 1987. The rise of family theory. In *Handbook of marriage and the family,* edited by M. B. Sussman and S. Steinmetz. New York: Plenum.

Thorne, B. 1982. Feminist thinking on the family: An overview. In *Rethinking the family,* edited by B. Thorne and M. Yalom. New York: Longman.

Wagner, R. M., and D. M. Shaffer. 1980. Social networks and survival strategies: An explanatory study of Mexican-American, Black and Anglo female family heads in San Jose, California. In *Twice a minority: Mexican American women,* edited by M. Melville. St. Louis, MO: C. V. Mosby.

Wilkinson, D. 1987. Ethnicity. In *Handbook of marriage and the family,* edited by M. B. Sussman and S. Steinmetz. New York: Plenum.

Wilson, W., and K. M. Neckerman. 1986. Poverty and family structure: The widening gap between evidence and public policy issues. In *Fighting poverty,* edited by S. H. Danziger and D. Weinberg. Cambridge, MA: Harvard University Press.

Wilson, W. J. 1987. *The truly disadvantaged.* Chicago: University of Chicago Press.

Zavella, P. 1987. *Women's work and Chicano families.* Ithaca, NY: Cornell University Press.

10 Overcoming Patriarchal Constraints: The Reconstruction of Gender Relations Among Mexican Immigrant Women and Men

PIERRETTE HONDAGNEU-SOTELO

Patriarchy is a fluid and shifting set of social relations in which men oppress women, in which different men exercise varying degrees of power and control, and in which women resist in diverse ways (Baca Zinn et al. 1986; Collins 1990; hooks 1984; Kandiyoti 1988). Given these variations, patriarchy is perhaps best understood contextually. This chapter examines family stage migration from Mexico to the United States, whereby husbands precede the migration of their wives and children, and it highlights how patriarchal gender relations organize migration and how the migration process reconstructs patriarchy.

The process of family stage migration diminishes patriarchy but it does not do so uniformly. In this case study, the time period of male migration and settlement distinguishes between two groups. Men who departed prior to 1965 were more likely to live initially in predominantly male communities, to endure a longer period of time in the United States without their wives and families, and eventually to obtain

AUTHOR'S NOTE: An earlier version of this work was presented at the 1991 American Sociological Association meeting in Cincinnati, OH. I would like to thank Nazli Kibria, Michael Messner, Barrie Thorne, Maxine Baca Zinn, and the anonymous reviewers for their helpful comments on earlier drafts of this work, and I would like to acknowledge the Business and Professional Women's Foundation and the Center for U.S.-Mexican Studies at the University of California at San Diego for partially supporting the research and writing on which this work is based.

legal status, unlike a later cohort of undocumented immigrant men;[1] this differentially modified the obstacles their wives would face in migration. Women and men do not enter the migration process equally, but given the diverse historical and social contexts in which migration occurs, women in the same culture and in similar circumstances may encounter different types of patriarchal obstacles and, hence, improvise different responses to migration. Distinct migration trajectories culminate in the creation of different types of gender relations once the families settle in the United States. Patriarchy is neither a monolithic nor a static construct, even within a group sharing similar class and racial-ethnic characteristics.

Gender relations in ethnic families are typically explained as culturally determined, as derivative from either "traditional" or "modern" values. Revisionist scholarship on Latino families challenges this acculturation perspective by considering the effects of structural economic, political, and social factors in shaping relative resources (Baca Zinn 1980, 1990; Pessar 1984). This chapter continues in that tradition but with a slightly different twist. The alterations in patriarchal behavior are attributable neither to the adoption of feminist ideology nor of "modern" values, as the acculturation model posits, nor to women's enhanced financial contributions to the family economy, but to arrangements induced by the migration process itself.

While the causes of this U.S.-bound Mexican immigration can be identified in macro-level structural rearrangements in Mexico and the United States (Massey et al. 1987), the manner in which people respond to these macrostructural transformations is shaped by gender. Since gender is relational, the analysis considers both women's and men's experiences during the spousal separations. What women do during the spousal separations ultimately affects their husbands and vice versa.

HOUSEHOLDS AND MIGRATION WITHOUT GENDER?

When I began my research, I entered the field with a set of guiding assumptions derived from the migration literature promoting the analytic primacy of the household (Dinerman 1978; Pessar 1982; Selby and Murphy 1982; Wood 1982). Several key assumptions, fundamentally economic ones, typify this approach, and in order to understand my alternative conceptual framework proposed for the study of migration, it is useful to review these tenets. First, the household is defined as a contained *unit* composed of kin-related persons who share a set amount of land, labor, capital, and social resources, such as immigrant network ties. Migration is perceived as a responsive *adaptation,* one pursued when the household's consumption needs outstrip locally available resources. Finally, the model assumes the operation of householdwide calculation—that family members together devise household *strategies* that guide migration.

Family and household members do not necessarily act as a unit. Divergent and conflicting interests over migration may coexist within the household unit, although these differences might be masked by family members' attempts to forge an appearance of family unity (Rouse 1989). The major point, however, is that family interests and individual interests—especially women's and men's—do not always mesh. This observation suggests that the study of women's and men's migration might be better understood within a paradigm that acknowledges the power relations operating within the family or household unit. Patriarchal authority and constraints, as well as contention and resistance to patriarchy, shape family migration decisions.

Focusing on patriarchal constraints and negotiations improves upon the conception of migration derived from a monolithic household model. This alternative approach not only captures the divergent strategies employed by women and men within any given household or family but highlights as well the diverse strategies and resources employed by women in similar but different contexts. While an older cohort of women whose husbands had migrated achieved migration by persuading their husbands, a more recent group of women in similar circumstances were more likely to rely on subversion of patriarchal authority. The household model captures only unitary household strategies and implicitly assigns women heterogeneous (e.g., dependent, passive) roles in migration. Finally, while the household model sees migration as an adaptive measure in which families or households secure resources, the focus on patriarchal constraints examines the search for resources as they occur in the dynamic arena of family politics.

An exclusive focus on the household risks ignoring the significance of broader kin and non-kin networks. Immigrants are experts at developing social networks that reduce migration's financial and social costs and risks by providing the new migrant with valuable information, job contacts, and other resources. Recent studies of Mexican immigration highlight the importance of these social infrastructures in facilitating, channeling, and maintaining migration flows (Massey et al. 1987; Mines 1981; Portes and Bach 1985). While men have been identified as the "pioneers" of these networks (Mines 1981), research has not explored women's place in these social relations. Operating under the implicit assumption of the household model—that all resources, including social ones, are shared equally among household and family members, studies imply that married women automatically benefit from their husbands' social resources and expertise (Kossoudji and Ranney 1984; Massey et al. 1987; Mines 1981).[2] The analysis developed in this chapter underscores the manner in which gendered immigrant networks facilitate or limit migration opportunities for Mexican women and men. Men and women in the same family may use different network resources, sometimes at cross purposes. These networks are significant for both migration processes and settlement outcomes.

SETTLEMENT AND
EMERGENT GENDER RELATIONS

A second area of inquiry concerns the type of gender relations immigrant newcomer families establish in the United States. The stereotypical view maintains that Mexican immigrant families are characterized by extreme machismo. This image consists of a caricaturelike portrait of excessively tyrannical men and submissive women. It is based not only on the notion that immigrants preserve intact cultural traditions but also on the belief that machismo is "traditional" among Mexican families. Research, however, does not support the claim that all contemporary Mexican and Chicano families are characterized by a uniformly extreme type of patriarchy (Baca Zinn 1980; Cromwell and Ruiz 1979; Guendelman and Perez-Itriaga 1987; Kelly and Garcia 1990; Segura 1988; Ybarra 1982, 1988; Zavella 1987), although patriarchal ideologies and divisions of labor certainly endure (Baca Zinn 1980; Peña 1991; Zavella 1987).

Conversely, there is an emerging view that sees Mexican immigrant families becoming less patriarchal because of American cultural influences. This view, I believe, is correct in its assessment of the general trend toward more egalitarian gender relations among Mexican immigrants but incorrect in its explication of why this arises. According to the acculturation perspective, changes in conjugal roles in ethnic families derive from the influence of modern cultural values, not structural arrangements. Research, however, shows that Latino families may adopt increasingly egalitarian gender behavior while still retaining elements of traditional culture (Baca Zinn 1980). The Mexican immigrants who participated in this case study not only identified themselves as *Mexicanos,* but moreover, they lived extremely segregated, encapsulated lives, characterized by limited contact with Anglos, so the changes do not appear to be due to any "Americanization" or "modernizing" acculturation process.

A more satisfactory analysis of this issue departs from a model based on relative control over resources and contributions to the family economy (Blood and Wolfe 1960; Blumberg 1984, 1991; Blumstein and Schwartz 1983). Research by feminist scholars in various racial-ethnic communities suggests that the increase in immigrant women's economic contributions to the family economy, concomitant with immigrant men's declining economic resources, accounts for the diminution of male dominance in the family (Kibria 1990; Lamphere 1987; Pessar 1984, 1986).

Although gender relations in Mexican immigrant families become less patriarchal, they do so in a heterogeneous fashion. The forces responsible for these transformations go beyond resource equations and are very different from those posited by the acculturation model. The analysis developed in this chapter focuses on a dimension that is generally overlooked—behavioral changes initiated by the migration process itself. I argue that the partial dismantling of patriarchy arises from new patterns of behavior induced by the arrangements of family stage migration. In light of this analysis, migration becomes a gendering process. These changes do not occur uniformly, and the analysis contrasts two groups that are distinguished by the historical period of migration and by length of spousal separation due to migration. Once families were reunited, these spousal separations and the context in which they occur were fundamental in shaping new gender relations.

Insights drawn from the early stages of field research and from the feminist literature led me to focus on two dimensions of patriarchal gender relations that shape migration: the changing balance of power and authority in the family and access to community social networks. After a description of the research, the discussion focuses on the place of gender in organizing family stage migration and follows through with an analysis of how this particular social route of migration induces transformations in gender relations.

DESCRIPTION OF RESEARCH

This chapter is based on a case study encompassing forty-four adult women and men in twenty-six families. I began research in a San Francisco Bay-area community in November 1986, just as the Immigration Reform and Control Act passed,[3] and I engaged in eighteen months of continuous, intensive social interaction using participant observation and in-depth interviews. Whenever possible, I interviewed husbands and wives separately; interviews were tape-recorded and fully transcribed with nearly all forty-four individuals. All interviews and interactions occurred in Spanish; the quotes appearing in this chapter are verbatim translations selected from the transcripts.

Sample

Conventional random sampling techniques are not feasible when researching an undocumented immigrant population in the United States (Cornelius 1982), so I chose a nonrandom snowball sample. I met some of the respondents during the period spanning 1979 to 1982, when I had worked in the community. It was, however, primarily my participation in various community organizations during the field research for this project and extensive personal reciprocity that enabled me to elicit study participants. These involvements allowed me to maintain relationship continuity with respondents. Since I was primarily interested in undocumented settlement, I chose subjects who had resided in the United States for a minimum of three years.[4] Twenty-two of the twenty-six families were undocumented when I met them, although many of them became candidates for amnesty-legalization.

The ten couples discussed in this chapter were mostly middle-aged when I interviewed them. Women's ages ranged from 30 to 73, the men's from 33 to 73.[5] With the exception of one couple, they all had children. Respondents' level of education ranged from no schooling to secondary school, preparing two men for work as rural schoolteachers and another for a job as a bookkeeper in Mexico. Prior to their husbands' migration to the United States, most of the women had not worked outside the home.

In spite of the undocumented legal status that many of the subjects maintained for years, they had stabilized their residency and, to some extent, their employment in California. The men generally worked as janitors, gardeners, or restaurant employees, and the women as domestic workers. These occupations do not necessarily represent nationwide trends in Mexican immigrant employment but reflect the structure of employment opportunities for Latino immigrants in this particular metropolitan area.

A small sample and qualitative methods were chosen for this study in order to develop an explanation of processes as they occur at the microstructural level. The analysis offered in this chapter is concerned with explaining how family stage migration arises in the context of domestic patriarchy and how it elicits diverse outcomes in gender relations, rather than with predicting future patterns of migration or generalizing the findings to all Mexican undocumented immigrants.

FAMILY STAGE MIGRATION

Direct labor recruitment of Mexican men by U.S. employers, dating back to the nineteenth century and the *bracero* program, a temporary contract labor program established by the United States and Mexico between 1942 and 1964, institutionalized family stage migration. Although these programs provided historical precedent, the interviews and the discussions that I conducted with husbands and wives reveal the significance of patriarchal gender relations and ideologies in shaping family stage migration.

In all of the families in which men preceded their wives, patriarchal forms of authority prevailed, so that migration decisions did not arise as part of a unified family or household strategy. Generally, husbands unilaterally decided to migrate with only token, superficial regard for their wives' concerns and opinions. Women were not active decision-making participants. When I asked the men about their initial departure and their wives' responses, they were generally reluctant to present information that implied family conflict over migration. While some men admitted that their wives reacted unenthusiastically, they claimed that their wives agreed or, at worst, were resigned to the situation because of economic need. Typical of their responses was one man's comment: "How could she disagree? My brother was here [in the United States], and things were going well for him."

When I asked the women to recall these scenarios, many of them reported having been vehemently opposed to their husbands' migration. The principal reason was fear of their husbands' desertion, of becoming a *mujer abandonada* (an abandoned woman). One woman, speaking of her home town in Mexico, estimated that "out of ten men who come here [United States], six return home. The others who come here just marry another woman and stay here, forgetting their wives and children in Mexico." Women feared that their husbands' migration would signal not a search for a better means of supporting the family but escape from supporting the family. Their husbands' migration promised an uncertain future for them and for the children who would remain behind; therefore, women tended to respond negatively to their husbands' departure.

Even so, few women were in a position to voice this opposition. Some of them were young—teen brides when their husbands began their long migration careers. In retrospect, these women recognized that they were not accustomed to disagreeing with or even questioning their husbands' judgment. Dolores Avila, who was initially left behind with an infant and who gave birth to a second child while her husband was in the United States, recalled: "I had to believe that he knew what was best for us, that he knew how to advance our situation." Other women expressed their opposition in silence, through prayer. Several women reported that they implored God to have the border patrol capture their husbands and send them back home. While their prayers were sometimes answered, the men stayed home only briefly before departing once again. Other women initially supported their husbands' decision to migrate in the hope that U.S. remittances and savings would alleviate economic needs; as time passed, these women became opposed to their husbands' lengthy sojourns.

The husbands' departures initiated lengthy spousal separations, ranging from one year to sixteen years.[6] The ten couples discussed in this chapter were separated an average of nearly six years. During these periods, the men usually returned to Mexico for visits. In many of the families, spousal separations induced significant transformations in conjugal relations. The following discussion examines the dynamics through which this occurred.

The Women Who Stay Behind:
New Rewards and New Burdens

Remittances sent by migrant husbands arrived sporadically and in smaller amounts than anticipated. While store credit and loans from kin provided emergency relief, these sources could not be relied upon indefinitely. In response to extreme financial urgencies and in spite of structural limitations on employment, women devised income-earning activities compatible with their child-rearing responsibilities. The most common solution was informal-sector employment, usually vending or the provision of personal services, such as washing and ironing, which they performed in their homes. These women, especially those with young children, worked intensively. Often, it was precisely these conditions that prompted women to migrate. A study of women who fit the pattern of family stage migration found that all fourteen women in the sample reported pursuing migration to end the burden of being the sole head of household (Curry-Rodriquez 1988, 51).

Although these expanded activities and responsibilities were onerous, the women discovered unanticipated rewards during these spousal separations. Women provided a substantial portion of family resources, and they became more competent at performing multiple roles as they honed new skills, such as budgeting or public negotiation. A cluster of studies conducted in Mexico and among Mexican immigrant women in the United States suggests that these conditions foster women's autonomy, esteem, and role expansion (Ahern, Bryan, and Baca 1985; Baca and Bryan 1985; Curry-Rodriquez 1988; González de la Rocha 1989; Mummert 1988). As Teresa Ibarra, a woman whose husband migrated to California while she remained behind in a small town in Michoacan caring for five children, explained:

> When he came here [to the United States], everything changed. It was different. It was me who took the responsibility for putting food on the table, for keeping the children clothed, for tending the animals. I did all of these things alone, and in this way, I discovered my capacities. And do you know, these accomplishments gave me satisfaction.

Earning and administering an autonomous income did not automatically translate into greater power for women. These women administered budgets with negligible disposable income, an experience characterized more by the burden of stretching scarce resources than by holding the reigns of economic power (Benería and Roldán 1987, 120). Paradoxically, the men migrated north for economic reasons, to fulfill breadwinner responsibilities and to save money to purchase a house, buy land, or pay debts. Yet in the United States the men encountered—especially in this particular metropolitan area of California—an extremely high cost of living and low wages, which their "illegal" status only exacerbated. This situation hindered the accumulation of savings and remittances, and over time, the women resented their husbands' shunning of familial responsibilities, especially with so few economic resources returning in the form of remittances.

REMITTANCES

I don't know whether they earned a little or nothing, but that was what they sent.

As the preceding quote suggests, the small amount of money that husbands sent home, and women's ignorance about where the entirety of men's U.S. income was spent, fueled women's discontent. Several women strongly suspected that their husbands squandered the money frivolously on other women and in bars. The husbands' migration aggravated a situation in which women performed a disproportionate share of household reproduction tasks and men controlled the greatest share of income. Although men migrated in order to support their families better, they were less accountable to their families while in the United States than if they had not gone north and less accountable than the women who stayed behind.

Men's absences from the home enhanced their ability to withhold from their wives information on the exact amount of their earnings, a practice not uncommon among poor, working-class families in Mexico (Benería and Roldán 1987). This meant that the men could spend a greater share of their earnings on personal pleasures, if they were so inclined. In informal conversations, many women and men, respondents as well as other immigrants in the community, insinuated that many men prefer the life of an independent migrant, free of the constraints and daily responsibilities imposed by a wife and children. Without admitting these motives as his own, Luis Bonilla, a husband and father who remained apart from his wife and six children for two years, explained why he believes men wish to defer their families' migration to the United States:

For many husbands it's just not convenient for their wives to come here. Sometimes they don't want their families to come here because they feel more liberated alone here. When a man is by himself, he can go anywhere he pleases, do anything he chooses. He can spend money as he wants. Instead of sending them $400, he can send them $300 and spend the other $100 on what he wants. He's much freer when the family is in Mexico.

Women resented both the extra burdens imposed on them by men's absence from family obligations and the small amount of remittances. As one woman remarked, "The entire burden falls on one, and that isn't fair." For women such as Isabel Barrios, whose husband's first departure in 1950 initiated a fourteen-year separation before she and their seven children joined him, this anger became an impetus for migration:

> He would leave and come back, and sometimes he would leave for three years, four years. Every time that he returned home to visit I became pregnant, and I had children, and more children, as they say, "fatherless children." The check that they [migrant husbands] send, that's very different than being a father. Because as the priest at San Cristobal Church says, they are fathers only by check. They are fathers who in reality have not helped raise the children until they [children] arrive here, something for which I fought hard. . . . Because in reality, I didn't want them to be raised only by myself. I had to work to earn money, and I had to raise the children alone. It was exhausting.

Most of the men remained steadfastly opposed to their wives' and families' migrating. Conjugal struggles, some lasting several years, ensued. How, then, did the women successfully challenge their husbands' authority to achieve family reunification and migration? The men who began their migrant careers prior to 1965 faced a set of circumstances very different from those faced by men who began migrating after 1965. Consequently, the wives of husbands who went north prior to 1965 faced patriarchal constraints different from those faced by the wives of a later cohort of migrant husbands, and the following section contrasts the experiences of these groups.

PERSUADING PATRIARCHY

Because of changing U.S. immigration legislation, many of the pre-1965 cohort of migrant men had obtained legal status by the 1970s. In order to do likewise, the women needed their husbands' cooperation and formal assistance. To legally migrate, then, the women needed first to persuade their husbands into helping them. Women accomplished this by using family—in-laws, kin, and especially teenage sons and daughters—to help convince the men. Raymundo Carbajal, for example, for years had resisted the migration of his wife and six children, but he finally conceded when their eldest daughter joined forces with her mother. The daughter pointed out that she and her older siblings were approaching twenty-one, and after that age, they would not be eligible to obtain legal status through their father. In the Avila family, in which the children were still young, in-laws helped Dolores convince her husband Marcelino to reunite the family by telling him that the children needed to grow up with their father present. In families with sons, this was perceived as imperative; Arturo Barrios, the father of seven boys, conceded to his family's migration, and years later acknowledged that "boys need their fathers." Family members and kin pressured husbands into assisting with family migration; the wives and teenage children often agreed in advance that their employment earnings would contribute to family income in the United States.

The long separations fostered by the men's solo sojourns diminished the hegemony of the husbands' authority and increased women's autonomy and influence in the family. This enabled the women to develop their own migrant agendas. The women who endured these long spousal separations seemed to develop the greatest sense of autonomy and social power; they used this in advancing their goal of migration. Sidra Galvan, now seventy-three, recalled how she had stubbornly persisted in convincing her husband over the years:

> A lot of time had passed, and he always gave excuses. But after he came back that time [after deportation], I saw no good reason why I should not go too. . . . He always said it was too dangerous for women to cross, but his boss was going to fix his papers, so now he had not one pretext.

These women pursued their personal goal of migration by persuading and urging their husbands to help them go north.

The wives of men who began their migrant careers before 1965 relied on a more limited range of resources than did the wives of the later post-1965 cohort. Specifically, the absence of a significant representation of Mexican immigrant women in the United States denied them access to assistance from other immigrant women, leaving them more or less dependent on male kin, especially spouses. It is also important to note that because the men could easily obtain legal status, their wives expected to obtain U.S. legal status through their husbands. These women were placed in a position of persuading or negotiating with their husbands in order to achieve migration. Until the mid-1970s, women gained leverage in these spousal negotiations with their husbands through the support of family members in Mexico and reliance on resources such as their jobs, their expected U.S. earnings, and in one case, even literacy skills.

SUBVERTING PATRIARCHY
THROUGH WOMEN'S NETWORKS

For a more recent cohort of undocumented immigrant men, those who began their migrant sojourns after 1965, obtaining legal status easily was no longer a viable option. Consequently, their wives were not dependent on obtaining legal status through their husbands. This effectively removed the women's need to gain their husbands' approval for migration.

By the 1970s and 1980s, women who wanted to migrate to the United States after their husbands and against their husbands' wishes were more likely to rely on the direct assistance of other migrant women to subvert or challenge their husbands' opposition to migration. Women's migrant networks work much the same as the men's migrant networks, with one exception: They provide prospective migrant women assistance in persuading their husbands to allow them to go north or in achieving migration without the husbands' knowledge. Immigrant women already in the United States assisted their sisters, mothers, and friends in this manner, helping them to write letters to their husbands or helping them to formulate convincing arguments about their earning potential in the United States. Teresa Ibarra, for example, recalled that she initially migrated with the help of a friend who had U.S. migration experience:

> Well, I came with this friend, because for years I had suffered from that illness in the eyes [migraine headaches]. So my friend had gone back there [Mexico]. . . . She would say to me, "They'll cure you in the United States, they'll cure you over there," and in that way, she encouraged me to go. And she told me to write to him so I could go. She stayed in Mexico for three months, and during those three months I kept writing him, to see if I could go, until he finally gave in.

When husbands resisted, women's networks made material forms of assistance available to circumvent men's power. Women lent each other money to cover travel costs and "coyote" or smuggler fees, sometimes unbeknownst to the men. In some cases, separate income funds covered spouses' migration costs; sometimes husbands, much to their chagrin, did not learn of their wives' and children's migration until after the fact.[7]

A case in point is the Bonilla family. In 1974 Tola Bonilla, an illiterate woman, managed with the help of a friend, to write letters to her husband in California, asking that he either return home or bring her and the children to the United States. Luis Bonilla ignored his wife's pleas, so Tola secretly borrowed money from her mother and sister, both of whom worked in California, and after Luis had unexpectedly arrived home for a brief visit due to an expulsion by the Immigration and Naturalization Service (INS), she used these funds to go north. She accompanied him when he departed, yet separate income funds covered their migration costs. Tola was pregnant at the time, and at her insistence, they took the eldest son and youngest daughter. Once in the United States, she saved part of her earnings and borrowed money from a friend to bring the remaining four children. She did this secretly: "Luis didn't know they were coming. He became very angry when they called from Tijuana, but by then it was too late. They were practically here." Tola Bonilla's migration and accomplishment in bringing her children north against her husband's will depended on the encouragement and financial assistance that she received from her mother and sister, her teen daughter's support and willingness to stay behind and care for the younger children, and help from her new friend in California.

The experiences of these migrant women suggest that when women are not accorded legitimate or institutional power, they may resort to subversion of legitimate authority. Two conditions are necessary for women to challenge their husband's authority. One is a sense of social power and autonomy, derived from the processes induced by the lengthy spousal separations. Studies conducted in Mexico by Ahern et al. (1985) and González de la Rocha (1989) demonstrate that as women assume expanded roles and tasks while their husbands are in the United States, they develop an enhanced sense of empowerment and decision-making capacity. As Curry-Rodriquez (1988, 52) notes, this ability to act independently appears to be the "by-product" of migration. Without this transformative process, set in motion by the husbands' migration, it is unlikely that women would have developed and actively pursued their own migration intentions.

The other important factor, one that appears to have become increasingly important since the 1970s, is access to women's network resources. Migration, as noted earlier, depends on social resources and these were less available to women in the 1950s and 1960s when as one woman recalled, "it wasn't customary for women to cross [the border] without papers." By the 1970s women were "illegally" migrating and joining undocumented migrant husbands, and they no longer relied exclusively on their husbands' formal cooperation and assistance, as did the wives of the *bracero*-era men who had obtained legal status. In this sense, the husbands' illegal status helped to further erode their patriarchal authority in the family. Since more women had migrated and settled in immigrant communities in California by the 1970s, there was a greater pool of social resources available to women than during the 1950s and 1960s.

CONJUGAL RELATIONS IN THE UNITED STATES: MEN'S EXPERIENCES AND DIMINISHING PATRIARCHY

The migration process discussed earlier affected relations between wives and husbands once families were reunited in the United States. Two indicators of patriarchy are considered here: the household division of labor and patterns of decision making and authority. In those families in which the husbands first migrated prior to 1965, an unorthodox, more egalitarian gender division of labor emerged when the families were reunited. In order to understand why this happened, we must examine the men's experiences during the spousal separations.

Many of these long-term sojourning migrant husbands lived in what we might call "bachelor communities." These consisted of all-male residences, usually small apartments, shared by a number of migrant men. As few as two or three men, and sometimes as many as fifteen or twenty, shared a residence. In this context, men learned to do household chores that traditionally in U.S. or Mexican culture, men are not supposed to do. Men learned to cook, clean, iron, and shop for groceries. Most of them also held restaurant jobs, where they worked busing tables, washing dishes, preparing food, and in one case, cooking; these work experiences also widened their repertoire of domestic kitchen skills.

Symbolically, tortillas perhaps best represent Mexican food, and their preparation is traditionally women's work. Yet in these bachelor residential quarters, many of the men in the United States during the 1950s and 1960s learned to make tortillas. As one man related: "There were no tortillas for sale then [1950s] as there are now. So I learned to make tortillas and to cook food too."

Most striking was how proud some of these men were about their newly acquired repertoire of domestic skills. Marcelino Avila, who first came north in 1957, four years before his wife and two children, recalled:

> Back in Mexico, I didn't know how to prepare food, iron a shirt or wash my clothes. I only knew how to work, how to harvest. But when I found myself with certain urgencies here, I learned how to cook, iron my clothes and everything. I learned how to do everything that a woman can do to keep a man comfortable. And the custom stayed with me. . . . I now know how to prepare American food and Mexican food, while back in my country I didn't know to cook at all. Necessity forced me to do things which I had previously ignored.

Once reunited with their spouses in the United States, the domestic skills that men were forced to learn in their wives' absence often continued to be exercised. Based on what I observed during my visits to their homes, what these couples told me, and in some cases, on what I heard from neighbors, these families appear to maintain a more nontraditional division of household labor than other Mexican immigrant families that I visited. Men did part of the cooking and housework, they unselfconsciously assumed the role of host in offering me food and beverages, and in some cases, men continued to make tortillas on weekends and special occasions. These changes are modest if we judge them by ideal standards of feminist egalitarianism, but they are significant if we compare them to normative patriarchal practices.

One Sunday afternoon, while I interviewed Rebecca Carbajal, she and I sat at the large dining table while her husband Raymundo made soup and flour tortillas from scratch. When the soup and tortillas were prepared, he joined us, and commenting on his activities, he said, without a touch of sarcasm, "This is exactly how we are, this is how we live, just as you see us." He even boasted that he was a more talented cook than his wife. Manuel Galvan, at age seventy-three, rose to squeeze fresh orange juice for himself and his wife before taking his morning walk to a nearby donut shop, where he met with a small group of men for coffee and gossip. The women also held higher expectations for their husbands' activities in the domestic sphere. Isabel Barrios, for example, complained that by comparison with her grown sons, her husband was deficient, as he had never changed dirty diapers, neither in the United States nor in Mexico. Dolores Avila testified that her husband had changed babies' diapers after the family migrated, and in the current Avila household, it is Marcelino who takes primary responsibility for household chores, such as washing and ironing clothes, vacuuming, and cooking.

In those families in which husbands began their migrant sojourn prior to 1965, these new arrangements arose as a result of the long spousal separations and the small, isolated settlement communities characterized by the relative scarcity of women who would typically perform domestic household chores. Meanwhile, the wives had grown more independent and assertive during the long spousal separations. They were no longer accustomed or always willing to act subserviently before their husbands.

In families in which the men began their migrant sojourns after 1965, daily housework arrangements were not radically transformed once the families were reconstituted in the United States. In these families, the men did not perform a significant amount of housework. Although most of the wives held jobs outside the home, the men still expected their wives to wait on them and to take primary responsibility for cooking and cleaning. Most of the women did so.

The Bonilla family arrangements illustrate this pattern. When Tola Bonilla returned home in the late afternoon from cleaning other people's houses, she set about cleaning her own home, laundering, and cooking. On two occasions when I was invited for dinner, Tola cooked and served the meals but did not eat, and she sat down with a glass of juice only after she had served us, claiming that eating heavy food at night made her ill. I felt awkward discussing community organizational tactics with Luis while Tola assumed a subordinate position on the sidelines. Although the Bonillas advocated, in my eyes, a progressive social agenda, their household division of labor remained conservative and patriarchal. Although both Luis and Tola had adopted the rhetoric of gender equality—part of the curriculum they learned in church-sponsored weekend marriage encounters—in practice, their daily activities did not challenge women's subordination. Similar inequities were apparent in the Ibarra, Macias, Gandara, and Duarte families—all of whom had migrated since the mid-1960s.

The continuation of a traditional gender division of labor among this group is, I believe, rooted in the conditions of migration. The post-1965 migrant men migrated a fewer number of times and for shorter periods before their families joined them. In the United States, the post-1965 migrant men countered and lived in a flourishing Mexican immigrant community that included both men and women, as well as entire families. They were more likely to live with kin or, in some instances, in amorous relationships with other women than in an all-male dwelling. Despite the absence of their wives, the post-1965 group of migrant men were not impelled to learn traditional "women's work," because they lived in residences where other women—kin, wives of the men who invited them to stay, or in some cases, "girlfriends"—performed these tasks. Traditional expectations that delegate domestic tasks to women were often reinforced by kinship obligations.

When husbands and wives were reunited, an orthodox gender division of household labor was generally reinstated. Yet traditional forms of patriarchy were not reconstituted in precisely the same form as they had existed prior to migration. Women did not relinquish the decision-making power and authority that they had established during their husbands' sojourns. Women often participated fully in major family decisions regarding the disciplining and rearing of teenage children, whether or not to take in boarders, and how to spend hard-earned savings. Blanca Macias, for example, meticulously cared for her home and family, but when her husbands' brothers arrived to stay for an indefinite period of time, taxing her already-significant cooking and cleaning responsibilities, she balked and ultimately convinced her husband to tell his brothers that they could no longer stay. In addition to working as a domestic, Teresa Ibarra cleaned, cooked, and laundered in her own household of thirteen people, which included three boarders living in the garage, yet she successfully resisted her husband's attempts to remove their juvenile delinquent son permanently from the home.

CONCLUSION

Patriarchal gender relations organize family stage migration, and migration reorganizes gender relations. Men's authority within families and men's access to migrant network resources favor husbands' initial departure. Yet their departure rearranges gender relations in the family; as women assume new tasks and responsibilities, they learn to act more assertively and autonomously. This new sense of social power and later, for another cohort of migrant wives, additional access to women's network resources enable the wives to migrate.

The unitary household model cannot explain these changes, because it does not recognize power relations between women and men sharing the same household. Women praying for the border patrol to capture their husbands and families in which spouses rely on different network resources and on separate income funds to cover their migration costs call into question assumptions about "household migration strategies" and the universality of shared household resources. While some women are coerced into migration by their husbands, this process is characterized more by contention than by household harmony.

Once the families are reunited in the United States, migration and resettlement processes elicit transformations in patriarchal gender relations. During the spousal separations, women often learn to act independently, and men, in some cases, learn to cook and wash dishes. In other instances, they learn to concede to their wives' challenges to their authority. These behaviors are not readily discarded when the spouses are reunited. Not only is migration shaped by gender relations, but perhaps more important, the migration process experienced by those who pursue family stage migration forges new gender relations. In this sense, migration is both gendered and gendering.

What are the implications for this new sector of U.S. society? While it is too hasty to proclaim that gender egalitarianism prevails in interpersonal relations among Mexican undocumented immigrants, there is a significant trend in that direction. This egalitarianism is indicated by the emergence of a more egalitarian household division of labor and by shared decision-making power. Women still have less power than men but they generally enjoy more than they previously did in Mexico. The stereotypical image of machismo in Mexican immigrant families is contradicted by the daily practices of families discussed in this chapter. With the diminution of patriarchal gender relations, women gain power and autonomy, and men lose some of their authority and privilege. These gains and losses are reflected in the women's near-unanimous preference for permanent settlement in the United States and in men's desire for return migration—a finding that echoes Pessar's (1986) data on Dominicans in New York City. Men's desire to return to Mexico is also rooted in their loss of public status once in the United States, where their class position, racial-ethnic category, and often legal status further erode their ability to exert patriarchal privileges. Patriarchal authority is not entirely undermined, but the legitimacy of men's unchallenged domination in the family diminishes through processes induced by family stage migration.

NOTES

1. The differences in these migration trajectories are related to the establishment since the late 1960s of permanent immigrant settlement communities in the United States, a

phenomenon shaped in part by the legacy of the *bracero* program, the maturation of immigrant social networks, passage of the 1965 Amendments to the Immigration and Nationality Act (Pub. Law 414), and the diversification of labor demand for Mexican immigrants in the United States.

2. Kossoudji and Ranney (1984, 1141) do acknowledge that since the 1970s, young single Mexican women have developed new immigrant networks.

3. The Immigration Reform and Control Act (IRCA), enacted in November 1986, included major provisions in the areas of employment and legalization for undocumented immigrants in the United States.

4. Other studies (Chavez, Flores, and Lopez-Garza 1989; Massey et al. 1987) also use the three-year residency criterion as an indicator of long-term Mexican immigrant settlement.

5. The case study also included families who migrated together as a unit, as well as unmarried women and men, most of whom later formed some type of family in the United States.

6. Occasionally, spousal separations were more lengthy. In one family, not included in the analysis here, spousal separation numbered thirty-one years. That husband was eventually joined by some of the adolescent and young adult children; although his wife had migrated and temporarily resided in the United States, she had returned to live in Mexico.

7. In Curry-Rodriquez's (1988) study, separate income funds were more common than not in sustaining family stage migration. In that study, eleven of the fourteen women reported that they, without assistance from their husbands, made their own travel arrangements and raised the money to cover migration documents (p. 52).

REFERENCES

Ahern, Susan, Dexter Bryan, and Reynaldo Baca. 1985. Migration and la mujer fuerte. *Migration Today* 13(1): 14-20.

Baca, Reynaldo, and Bryan, Dexter. 1985. Mexican women, migration and sex roles. *Migration Today* 13(3): 14-18.

Baca Zinn, Maxine. 1980. Employment and education of Mexican American women: The interplay of modernity and ethnicity in eight families. *Harvard Educational Review* 50:47-62.

———. 1990. Family, feminism, and race in America. *Gender & Society* 4:68-82.

Baca Zinn, Maxine, Lynn Weber Cannon, Elizabeth Higginbotham, and Bonnie Thornton Dill. 1986. The costs of exclusionary practices in women's studies. *Signs: Journal of Women in Culture and Society* 11:290-303.

Benería, Lourdes, and Martha Roldán. 1987. *The crossroads of class and gender.* Chicago: University of Chicago Press.

Blood, Robert O., and Donald M. Wolfe. 1960. *Husbands and wives.* New York: Free Press.

Blumberg, Rae Lesser. 1984. A general theory of gender stratification. In *Sociological theory 1984,* edited by Randall Collins. San Francisco: Jossey-Bass.

———. 1991. Introduction: The "triple overlap" of gender stratification, economy and the family. In *Gender, family, and economy: The triple overlap,* edited by Rae Lesser Blumberg. Newbury Park, CA: Sage.

Blumstein, Philip, and Pepper Schwartz. 1983. *American couples: Money, work, and sex.* New York: William Morrow.

Chavez, Leo R., Estevan T. Flores, and Marta Lopez-Garza. 1989. Migrants and settlers: A comparison of undocumented Mexicans and Central Americans in the United States. *Frontera norte* 1:49-75.

Cornelius, Wayne A. 1982. Interviewing undocumented immigrants: Methodological reflections based on fieldwork in Mexico and the United States. *International Migration Review* 16:378-411.

Cromwell, R. E., and R. A. Ruiz. 1979. The myth of macho dominance in decision-making with Mexican and Chicano families. *Hispanic Journal of Behavioral Sciences* 1:355-73.

Curry-Rodriquez, Julia E. 1988. Labor migration and familial responsibilities: Experiences of Mexican women. In *Mexicanas at work in the United States,* edited by Margarita B. Melville. Mexican American Studies Monograph no. 5. Houston, TX: University of Houston.

Dinerman, Ina. 1978. Patterns of adaptation among households of U.S.-bound migrants from Michoacan, Mexico. *International Migration Review* 12:485-501.

González de la Rocha, Mercedes. 1989. El poder de la ausencia: Mujeres y migracion en una comunidad de Los Altos de Jalisco. Paper presented at XI Coloquio de antropologia e historia regionales, Zamora, Michoacan, Mexico.

Guendelman, Sylvia, and Auristela Perez-Itriaga. 1987. Double lives: The changing role of women in seasonal migration. *Women's Studies* 13:249-71.

hooks, bell. 1984. *Feminist theory: From margin to center.* Boston: South End Press.

Hill Collins, Patricia. 1990. *Black feminist thought.* Boston: Unwin Hyman.

Kandiyoti, Deniz. 1988. Bargaining with patriarchy. *Gender & Society* 2:274-90.

Kelly, M. Patricia Fernández, and Anna M. Garcia. 1990. Power surrendered, power restored: The politics of work and family among Hispanic garment workers in California and Florida. In *Women, politics, and change,* edited by Louise A. Tilly and Patricia Gurin. New York: Russell Sage.

Kibria, Nazli. 1990. Power, patriarchy, and gender conflict. *Gender & Society* 4:9-24.

Kossoudji, Sherrie A., and Susan I. Ranney. 1984. The labor market experience of female migrants: The case of temporary Mexican migration to the U.S. *International Migration Review* 18:1120-43.

Lamphere, Louise. 1987. *From working daughters to working mothers.* Ithaca, NY: Cornell University Press.

Massey, Douglas, S., Rafael Alarcon, Jorge Durand, and Humberto González. 1987. *Return to Aztlan: The social process of international migration from Western Mexico.* Berkeley: University of California Press.

Mines, Richard. 1981. *Developing a community tradition of migration: A field study in rural Zacatecas, Mexico, and California settlement areas.* Monographs in U.S.-Mexico Studies no. 3. La Jolla: University of California San Diego, Program in U.S.-Mexican Studies.

Mummert, Gail. 1988. Mujeres de migrantes y mujeres migrantes de Michoacan: Nuevo papeles para las que se quedan y para les que se van. In *Movimientos de poblacion en el occidente de Mexico,* edited by Thomas Calvo and Gustavo Lopez. Mexico, DF: Centre d'études mexicaines et centramericaines and El colegio de Mexico.

Peña, Manuel. 1991. Class, gender, and machismo: The "treacherous-woman" folklore of Mexican male workers. *Gender & Society* 5:30-46.

Pessar, Patricia. 1982. The role of households in international migration and the case of U.S.-bound migration from the Dominican Republic. *International Migration Review* 16:342-64.

———. 1984. The linkage between the household and workplace in the experience of Dominican women in the U.S. *International Migration Review* 18:1188-1212.

———. 1986. The role of gender in Dominican settlement in the United States. In *Women and change in Latin America,* edited by June Nash and Helen Safa. South Hadley, MA: Bergin & Garvey.

Portes, Alejandro, and Robert L. Bach. 1985. *Latin journey: Cuban and Mexican immigrants in the United States.* Berkeley: University of California Press.

Rouse, Roger. 1989. Mexican migration to the United States: Family relations in the development of a transnational migrant circuit. Ph.D. diss., Stanford University.

Segura, Denise A. 1988. Familism and employment among Chicanas and Mexican immigrant women. In *Mexicanas at work in the United States,* edited by Margarita B. Melville. Mexican American Studies Monograph no. 5. Houston, TX: University of Houston.

Selby, Henry A., and Arthur D. Murphy. 1982. *The Mexican urban household and the decision to migrate to the United States.* ISHI Occasional Papers in Social Change no. 4. Philadelphia: Institute for the Study of Human Issues.

Wood, Charles. 1982. Equilibrium and historical-structural perspectives in migration. *International Migration Review* 16:298-319.

Ybarra, Lea. 1982. Marital decision-making and the role of machismo in the Chicano family. *De colores* 6:32-47.

———. 1988. Separating myth from reality: Socio-economic and cultural influences on Chicanas and the world of work. In *Mexicanas at work in the United States,* edited by Margarita B. Melville. Mexican American studies Monograph no. 5. Houston, TX: University of Houston.

Zavella, Patricia. 1987. *Women's work and Chicano families: Cannery workers of the Santa Clara Valley.* Ithaca, NY: Cornell University Press.

11 Power, Patriarchy, and Gender Conflict in the Vietnamese Immigrant Community

NAZLI KIBRIA

Women maximize resources within patriarchal systems through various strategies (Collier 1974; di Leonardo 1987; Wolf 1972). Kandiyoti (1988) has suggested that women's strategies reveal the blueprint of what she calls the "patriarchal bargain," that is, the ways in which women and men negotiate and adapt to the set of rules that guide and constrain gender relations. The notion of "bargaining with patriarchy" suggests that both men and women possess resources with which they negotiate to maximize power and options within a patriarchal structure. The bargaining is asymmetric, for as long as patriarchy is maintained, women's power and options will be less than those of men in the same group.

The analysis of women's strategies, with its potential to reveal processes of negotiation between men and women, may also shed light on the dynamics of change in gender relations. Social transformations, such as those implied by modernization and migration, often entail important shifts in the nature and scope of resources available to women and men (Lamphere 1987; Pessar 1984). A period of intense renegotiation between women and men may thus ensue, as new bargains based on new resources are struck. Indeed, the fundamental rules of the

AUTHOR'S NOTE: This work is a revised version of a paper presented at the 1988 Eastern Sociological Society Annual Meeting, Philadelphia. I would like to thank Greg Brooks, Suzy Nguyen, Elizabeth H. Pleck, and Susan Silbey for their helpful comments on earlier drafts. The skillful editing and suggestions of Judith Lorber have contributed to a final version of the work.

previous system of gender relations may come into question, as the social worlds of men and women undergo change. However, when patriarchal structures remain in place despite certain changes, limited transformations in the relations between women and men may occur without deep shifts in men's power and authority.

This chapter examines the organization and activities of the informal community life of Vietnamese immigrant women in the United States. Data are drawn from an ethnographic study of a community of Vietnamese refugees in Philadelphia. Through research on the women's social groups and networks, I explored the effects of migration on women's roles in the family and community and the collective strategies forged by women to cope with male authority in the family.

Settlement in the United States has increased opportunities for the growth of Vietnamese women's power because their economic contributions to the family economy have grown while those of men have declined. Women use their new resources to cope more effectively with male authority in the family. However, male authority is not openly challenged. Because there are important advantages for women in maintaining the old "bargain" between men and women, Vietnamese women have tried to maintain the patriarchal family structure.

RESEARCH DESIGN

Using participant-observation and in-depth interviews, I studied twelve Vietnamese households located in a low-income, inner-city area of Philadelphia from 1983 to 1985 (Kibria 1993). Interviews were conducted with fifteen women and sixteen men, all of whom were members of the households composing the core sample.

The twelve households were located in close proximity to each other, within a radius of ten blocks. They ranged in size from three to nineteen members, with a median number of seven. Study participants had been in the United States for three to five years. Of the forty-six adults, thirty-two had lived in the urban areas of southern and central Vietnam prior to leaving the country. The men had often been in the South Vietnamese army or worked in small businesses and middle-level government administrative and clerical occupations. The women had engaged in farming and commercial activities or a variety of odd jobs in the informal urban economy, such as selling goods in the bazaar and working in restaurants and laundries.

All of the households had experienced a decline in their socioeconomic status with the move to the United States, especially when compared to their situation in Vietnam before the political changes of 1975. At the time of the study, the economic situation of the study participants was generally marginal and precarious, a finding that is supported by other studies of post-1978 Vietnamese arrivals to the United States (Gold and Kibria 1993; Haines 1987; Rumbaut 1989). In 1984, over 30 percent of the men in the households of the study were unemployed. Of the men who were employed, over half worked in low-paying, unskilled jobs in the urban service sector or in factories located in the outlying areas of the city. The women tended to work periodically at jobs in the informal economic sector as well as in the urban service economy. Eight of the households had members who collected public assistance payments (Kibria 1989).

The family economy, a system of pooling and exchanging material resources within family groups, was an important strategy by which the Vietnamese households coped with these economic uncertainties and difficulties (Finnan and Cooperstein 1983; Gold 1989; Haines, Rutherford, and Thomas 1981).

Another important sphere of economic cooperation was the informal, women-centered social groups and networks in the community. I use the term *social group* to refer to clusters of people who gathered together on a regular, if not frequent, basis. These groups had a stable core membership that usually included kin but were by no means exclusive to family members. Over the course of a year, I attended and observed the informal gatherings of seven social groups in women's homes as well as in Vietnamese-owned service establishments (ethnic grocery stores, restaurants, hairdressers) where the women worked. I gained access to each of the seven groups through my relationships with members of the study households. The women's groups included members of these households and others in the community.

The study of the women's social groups revealed the complex and powerful role of Vietnamese women in their ethnic community. The women's community was organized around two central activities: the distribution and regulation of the exchange of resources among households and the mediation of domestic tensions and disputes. Through these activities, the women's groups were an important source of collective power and support for women. However, the power of the women's groups was "unofficial" in nature and limited by the structural and ideological boundaries of the patriarchal family system. In their involvement in family conflicts, the women's groups often tried to protect the interests of individual women who were in conflict with male authority in the family. Yet they did so in ways that did not challenge, but rather reaffirmed, traditional Vietnamese ideology concerning the family and gender roles.

THE EFFECTS OF MIGRATION: OLD STRATEGIES AND NEW RESOURCES

The traditional Vietnamese family was modeled on Confucian principles. In the ideal model, households were extended, and the family was structured around the patrilineage or the ties of the male descent line (Keyes 1977; Marr 1976). Women were married at a young age and then entered the household of their husband's father. The young bride had minimal status and power in the household until she produced sons (Johnson 1983; Kandiyoti 1988; Lamphere 1974; Wolf 1972). The patriarchal bargain in this setting was one in which women expected significant rewards in their old age from allegiance and deference to the patrilineal family system. The power and resources of women in the patrilineal extended household tended to vary across the life cycle. While young brides were subservient to both men and older women in the household, older women held a position of some power and status (cf. Wolf 1974).

There were also resources available to Vietnamese women in traditional rural society that could be used to cope with male authority in the family and community. According to recollections of my informants, in rural Vietnam, women's neighborhood groups were an important source of informal power. Women were able, through gossip, to affect the reputations of men and women in the community. However, in rural Vietnam, the influence of the women's groups was curbed and limited by powerful male organizations, such as village political and legal bodies, as well as the patrilineal descent group (Hendry 1954; Hickey 1964; Keyes 1977).

Women in rural Vietnam also had some access to economic resources through their involvement in village commerce and business. Women often sold food and other goods at the village market and many played an important role in the family business (Hendry 1954; Hickey 1964; Nguyen Van Vinh 1949). But while such activities may have enhanced the resources and bargaining power of women in the family, there is little evidence that they weakened the fundamental economic subordination and dependence of women on men.

The social and economic bases of the traditional system of gender relations were deeply affected by the social turmoils in Vietnam of the 1950s and 1960s, which also transformed the lives of the participants of this study. War and urbanization eroded the structure of the patrilineal extended household. Within the cities, the households that survived retained their extended character but they were less centered on patrilineal ties and incorporated a wider array of kin. For many Vietnamese, economic survival in the cities was precarious (Beresford 1988, 57). However, many Vietnamese from middle-class backgrounds, such as the participants in this study, were able to take advantage of the expansion of middle-level positions in the government bureaucracy and army. Such occupational opportunities were fewer for women; they engaged in informal income-generating activities or worked in low-level jobs in the growing war-generated service sector in the cities (Beresford 1988; Nyland 1981; Thrift and Forbes 1986). As in rural Vietnam, most women remained dependent on men for economic support.

War and migration to the cities thus served to weaken the patrilineal extended household—the structural core of the traditional patriarchal system. However, because the middle-class status of the families depended in large part on the incomes of the men, the threat of economic impoverishment sustained the ideals of the traditional family system and men's authority in the family. Women feared the economic consequences of male desertion, a not uncommon occurrence, especially when men were on military duty for extended periods. The "bargain" between women and men that emerged in this setting was one in which women deferred to men's authority in exchange for economic protection.

In the United States, the social context of gender relations was both similar to and different from that of modern, urban South Vietnam. The most important difference was that the relative economic resources of men and women had shifted. As in Vietnam, women continued to engage in a variety of income-generating activities, including employment in informal and low-level, urban, service-sector jobs. In contrast to Vietnam, however, the economic contributions of men had declined significantly. In Vietnam, the men held jobs that enabled them to maintain a middle-class standard of living for their families. In the United States, many Vietnamese men faced unemployment or had low-paying unstable jobs that did not usually enable them to support a family. Compounding the men's economic problems has been a widespread sense of powerlessness and alienation from the institutions of the dominant American society. The shifts in the resources of women and men that have accompanied the migration process have thus created the potential for a renegotiation of the patriarchal bargain.

THE WOMEN'S COMMUNITY: STRATEGIES
OF POWER AND RESPONSES TO CHANGE

The women's social groups were formed around household, family, and neighborhood ties. Groups had a stable set of regular members, ranging in size from six to ten women. The boundaries of groups were fluid and open, with participation in group activities generally unrestricted to women in the ethnic community. The groups had heterogeneous membership, including women of varied ages and social backgrounds, and the Vietnamese women in the community tended to participate in the gatherings and activities of several social groups. Such overlapping membership in the groups led to connections of both a direct and indirect nature among women across the community. The groups were thus at the core of social networks of women that extended throughout the area.

A woman's membership in a group, regardless of the extent of her involvement, signified an obligation to participate in exchange activities with others in the group and connecting network. Exchange was a central and perhaps the most visible activity of the women's community, in ways similar to those in low-income, urban, black communities (Martin and Martin 1978; Stack 1974). Women exchanged food and material goods of various sorts, as well as services and tasks such as child care and cooking. They exchanged information on such issues as where to get "good buys" on food and other items for the family. They also shared knowledge on available jobs and income-generating opportunities in the area, as well as how to cope with and maximize gains from various institutions (e.g., welfare and social service agencies, hospitals, and schools). For both men and women in the community, the exchange networks of the Vietnamese women represented a highly valued material and informational resource.

Besides their involvement in exchange activities, the women's groups also played an important part in strategies for coping with familial male authority, often playing a pivotal role in supporting and protecting women who were in conflict with the men in their family. In traditional Vietnamese society, the principle of male authority was expressed in the cultural and legal acceptance of wife beating (Marr 1976; Ta Van Tai 1981). In three of the study households, physical assaults by men on women in the family were a regular occurrence, thus suggesting that wife beating continues among the Vietnamese in the United States. However, in the United States, the Vietnamese women's groups play an important moderating role in situations of domestic violence, protecting women from the excesses of the patriarchal family system, as shown by the following:

Several women were gathered at Dao's house. Dao brought up the situation of her older sister Thu. She said she hadn't wanted to talk about it before . . . but everyone here was family. Now it was so bad she had to talk about it. Thu's husband (Chau) was hitting her very much. The other day, Dao had to take Thu to the hospital, when Chau had hit Thu on the face. One of the women says, "What about Chau's brother? Does he say anything?"

Dao replies that the brother had told Chau to stop it. But nobody really cared about what the brother said, certainly Chau didn't. The brother was very old. He did nothing but eat and sleep. And he hardly talked to anyone anymore, he was so sad to leave Vietnam. Dao starts crying, saying that if her parents were here, they could help Thu.

Dao's neighbor says that maybe Thu should leave the husband. That wasn't a bad thing to do, when the husband was so bad, the woman should leave the husband. Chau didn't even take care of the children. He wasn't a good father. He also hit the children. Even the smallest one, who was only three years old. No good father would do that.

Dao says that yes, that was true, Chau wasn't a good father. He also didn't like to work and have a job. Thu talked about leaving Chau, but she was scared. She thought maybe Chau would come after her and the children and do something bad to them. One of the women says, "My brother, he's Chau's friend. I'll talk to my brother and he'll tell Chau to be good, and not make trouble for Thu." Several other women mention people they know who are in some way associated with Chau. They all say they will talk to these people about Chau. Someone says, "Thu is a good woman. She wants to take care of her children, her family. Chau, he's no good." (Fieldnotes)

Dao's social network was an important source of support for Thu. Largely through gossip, the women were able to bring pressures to bear on Thu's husband. Chau found his reputation throughout the community affected by the rapidly disseminated judgments of the women's group.

In conversations with a number of men and women in the community, I found that Chau had been ostracized not only by the women but also by male friends and relatives. Chau left the city to join a cousin in California. There were no legal divorce proceedings, but the marriage had been dissolved in the eyes of the Vietnamese community. Thu and her children continued to live in the city, receiving help and support from family and friends. Chau, in contrast, severed almost all relationships in the area.

The preceding example shows how the women collectively helped to bring male authority back into its acceptable limits. The women's group supported Thu in breaking ties with the husband, a course of action that conflicted with the values and norms of family solidarity and female propriety. Marital separation or divorce is a stigma among the recently arrived Vietnamese in the United States, particularly for women. But in Thu's case, the women created an interpretation of the situation in which the man was at fault. The judgment or "message" of the women's group was that the principle of male authority had been abused, contradicting other central familial values. The women interpreted Thu's actions so that she was not seen as violating family and gender norms. Women emerged in this situation as both guardians of the family and as supporters of a particular woman's interests.

There were other instances in which women collectively stepped in to protect the interests of women who were in conflict with men in the family, most often husbands. These situations involved not only domestic violence but also disputes between women and men over various sorts of household decisions. In one case that I observed, a young woman named Lien was supported by female kin and friends in her decision to seek employment despite the objections of her husband. After completing six months of training in haircutting, Lien had had her second child. She planned to leave the baby in the care of her aunt while she worked as a hairdresser in Chinatown. Lien's husband objected to her plans, feeling that it was important for her to stay at home with the baby. While Lien agreed that it was preferable for her to remain at home, she argued that her husband's frequents bouts of unemployment made it necessary for her to go out and work.

With the support of other women in the community, Lien's aunt intervened in the couple's dispute in a powerful fashion. At a gathering of friends, Lien's aunt discussed how she had "had a talk" with Lien's husband in which she had emphasized that Lien was not deviating from traditional women's roles but merely adapting out of necessity to economic circumstances:

> I told him that Lien should take care of the baby, that is the right way. But this is America and we have a different kind of life now. If Lien doesn't work, then the children won't get good food, good clothes . . . the welfare money is not enough. I explained to him that she's not being a bad mother, she's working for the children.

The women at the gathering accepted the interpretation of the situation presented: that Lien was acting in conformity with the dictates of traditional gender roles. Because of the gossip that ensued, Lien's husband found himself under community pressure to accept Lien's decision to work outside the home.

In another case women mobilized community opinion against a man who forbade his wife to see her brother, whom he disliked. Ha, a woman in her early thirties, had been living in the city with her husband and their children. Some time ago, Ha's brother and his four children had arrived in the city from the refugee camp to join Ha. Ha described the household atmosphere as tense and uncomfortable during this time. Her husband, Le, was in "a bad mood," as he was not able to find a suitable job. Le and Ha's brother had been fighting constantly over small matters. Because of these problems, after a stay of two months, the brother and his children moved to another apartment in the area.

Ha went over to see her brother frequently, usually every other day. Ha often cooked for her brother's children, and she sometimes lent her brother small amounts of money. Le resented Ha's involvement in her brother's life and eventually told her to stop visiting them. Ha became incensed and told women kin and friends that she would divorce Le if he did not allow her to take care of her brother:

> I told my friends and Le's sister that I don't want to stay with Le. They said I must stay with Le because it's not good for me and my children to leave. They talked to me a lot about it. And then Le's sister said that Le was bad to tell me not to see my brother. All my friends said that was right, that my brother was like Le's brother, Le must understand that. Le changed after that. Because his sister talked to him, everyone talked to him. He knows that everyone will think he's bad if he tells me to not see my brother.

In this case the women's community "stepped in," both to discourage Ha from leaving the marriage and to change Le's behavior and attitude toward Ha's relationship with her brother. The women were able to muster considerable support for their position. Because of the women's actions, Le felt social pressures from both his family and the community to allow Ha to maintain her relationship with her brother. The women constructed an interpretation of the situation such that Le was seen to be violating the foremost value of family solidarity.

While extremely powerful, the women's groups were not always successful in their interventions in family disputes. In one such case, a women's group supported a member named Tuyet in her efforts to dissuade her husband from purchasing an expensive car with the family savings. Tuyet told women friends that the purchase of the car would significantly postpone their plans to buy a house. Despite the gossip that followed and the women's collective disapproval of his actions, Tuyet's husband went ahead with the purchase. His decision to ignore the women's community was influenced perhaps by his stable and favorable employment situation, which reduced his sense of economic dependency on the women's resources. However, while Tuyet's social group was unsuccessful in deterring the purchase of the car, their judgments did serve to cause Tuyet's husband to reconsider and delay his purchase.

In all of these cases, the process by which the women's community attempted to influence the outcome of the disputes was similar. The women's groups derived influence from their ability to interpret situations, define who was right or wrong, and impose these interpretations through gossip and the threat of ostracism. In the process of generating collective interpretations of situations, women drew on the symbols and values of the traditional family ideology to provide legitimacy for their actions and opinions. The judgments of the women were often effective sanctions, as both men and women in the ethnic community valued the economic and social resources available to them through the women's exchange networks.

THE NEW PATRIARCHAL BARGAIN

The collective strategies of the women for coping with male authority reveal some aspects of the new patriarchal bargain being generated by migration. The power exerted by the women's groups over the behavior of men and women in the Vietnamese immigrant community reflects the decline in men's social and economic resources. But while the women's groups use their enhanced power to support the struggles of individual women with male authority in the family, they are careful not to disturb the traditional boundaries of family and gender relations.

In their activities, the women's groups constantly displayed concern for upholding and preserving elements of the relationship they had had with men and the family system prior to settlement in the United States. For example, the women's groups did not support women in their conflicts with men in the family when they had violated traditional sexual norms. In one case, a widow had developed a reputation for sexual promiscuity. In the second case, a woman had left her husband for a man with whom she had been having an affair for several months. In both cases, the women's groups disparaged and isolated the two women, and in the second case, provided support to the husband. In general, the women's groups judged harshly those women who failed to show a high degree of commitment to "keeping the family together" or to the norms of behavior appropriate to wives and mothers. The women would mobilize their community resources to sanction and enforce these normative codes by withholding resources from offenders.

Anything that threatened to disrupt the fundamental structure and ideological coherence of the family was unacceptable to the women's community. Repeatedly during my research, the Vietnamese women talked of the threat presented by the familial and sexual values of the dominant American culture to their family system. Thus, when asked about the greatest drawback of living in the United States, women often expressed fears concerning children's defection from the traditional family system:

> The biggest problem of living here is that it's difficult to teach your children how to be good and to have good behavior. The children learn how to be American from the schools, and then we don't understand them and they don't obey us. The customs here are so different from our culture. The children learn about sex from TV. Maybe American parents think that's OK but for me that's not OK because I know the children will learn bad behavior (*hu*) from watching TV. Also, I worry about when my children grow older they won't ask me my opinion about when they have girlfriends and they get married.

Another expression of the conflicts about the dominant American culture felt by the women was their ambivalence about the protection from domestic violence offered to them by the American legal system. While many women felt positively about the illegality of wife beating in American society, there was also widespread concern that the intervention of the law into family life detracted from the authority and rights of parents to discipline their children as they chose (cf. Pleck 1983).

Besides the decline of parental authority, there was another consequence of Vietnamese assimilation into American culture that women feared: the desertion of men from the family. Both the economic protection of men and the officially sanctioned authority of parents over children were aspects of the premigration patriarchal bargain that women viewed as attractive and beneficial for themselves, and they would often use the resources and power available to them through their community groups and networks in an attempt to preserve these aspects of the old "bargain," as illustrated by the following situation:

> Ly told me her sister-in-law Kim's daughter, 15-year-old Mai, was thought to be mixing with American boys at school. Ly thought Kim was "making too much fuss about it," as Mai was "really a good, smart girl who's not going to get into trouble." This afternoon, in the restaurant where Kim worked, the regular crowd of five or six women gathered around a couple of tables, chatting and drinking tea and bittersweet coffee. Kim, quite suddenly, started crying and dabbing her eyes with a napkin. Everyone's attention focused on Kim, who then talked of how she didn't know what to do with her children who were on the streets all the time, she couldn't keep her eye on them continually because she worked all the time. Especially Mai, who was growing up to be a woman now, she was always playing on the streets, sometimes until late at night. And she didn't take care of her younger brothers and sisters, and didn't do any of the housework, instead always wanting money to go and buy the latest fashions.
>
> An elderly white-haired women wearing traditional dress and seated at the next table piped in loudly about how this was what happened to all the children when they came here, they became like American children, selfish and not caring about their family. The other women then talked of how they all had similar problems, that children here just didn't listen to their parents and family. One said, "You should make her behave right, otherwise she'll be sorry later. She's not an American girl, she's Vietnamese." There were murmurs of agreement. (Fieldnotes)

In this case, a women's group supported a member's authority as a parent. In the process of doing so, the group upheld and affirmed traditional notions of appropriate female conduct. Following this incident, the women's group also carefully watched and supervised Mai's activities in an attempt to support her mother's concerns actively.

The new patriarchal bargain emerging in the United States is thus one in which women use their heightened resources to cope more effectively with male authority. But there is also a concern for maintaining the old modes of accommodation between women and men and the traditional ideological relationships within the family.

CONCLUSIONS

This study showed how the Vietnamese women's groups, using the resources that had become available to them as a result of migration and that were necessary to their families' survival, challenged male authority. But they did not use their newly acquired resources to forge a radical restructuring of the old patriarchal bargain. In many ways, the women remained attached to the old male-dominant family system that called for female deference and loyalty because it offered them economic protection and allowed them to continue their officially sanctioned authority over the younger generation.

The social losses incurred by the Vietnamese men with settlement in the United States have enhanced women's collective power. Their exchange networks have come to assume an important source of economic security and family survival. Moreover, the women's groups have become an important, if not the primary, agent of negotiation between the Vietnamese community and "outside" institutions, such as hospitals and welfare agencies. As a result, the men defer to the moral judgments of the women's community in part because many cannot afford to be cut off from these resources. In sum, the Vietnamese women's community in the United States is continuous with the past in its basic organization and activities but it is now operating in a social context that enhances its status and power.

The women's status and power, however, are not great enough to transform gender relations in the Vietnamese immigrant community radically. While the economic resources of the women have risen, compared to those of the men, they are seen as too limited to sustain the economic independence of women from men and so the women continue to value the promise of male economic protection. In short, the difficult economic environment and the continued material salience of family ties in the United States help preserve the attraction and meaning of the traditional patriarchal bargain for women, although in a tempered form.

Migration to the United States has thus had a complex, somewhat contradictory, impact on the status of Vietnamese immigrant women. On the one hand, migration has weakened men's control over economic and social resources and allowed women to exert greater informal family power. At the same time, the precarious economic environment has heightened the salience of the family system and constrained the possibilities for radical change in gender relations. For the moment, the patriarchal family system is too valuable to give up as it adds income earners and extends resources. Another appeal of the traditional family system for women is the status-related privileges that are promised to them—in particular, the authority to wield considerable influence over the lives of the young.

Thus, because they expected to gain important economic and status benefits from allegiance to the traditional family system, by and large, the Vietnamese women of the study were a conservative force in the community, deeply resistant to structural changes in family and gender relations. In this regard, the responses of the Vietnamese women are not unlike views expressed by many women supporters of the current antifeminist movement in the United States, who see shifts in gender relations as a threat to their economic security (Chafetz and Dworkin 1987; Ehrenreich 1982; Klatch 1987).

The experiences of these Vietnamese women also suggest that women may, in a selective manner, take advantage of the resources that have become available to them as a result of the very social transformations they resist. These new resources strengthen women's capacity to cope effectively with male authority; as long as the men need the women's economic and social resources, their ability to resist the collective interventions of women is limited. At the same time, the women themselves fight to hold back the social consequences of migration, in particular the cultural incursions into the family that cause the undermining of their own authority over their children.

The "bargain" between the Vietnamese women and men that has been described here is highly unstable and tenuous in quality. The ability of women collectively to sanction the behavior of men rests on the dependence of men on the economic and social resources of women. If there is little economic progress in the situation of the Vietnamese men in the future, then a fundamental appeal of the traditional patriarchal bargain for women, that is, the promise of men's economic protection, may become far less compelling. Male authority may then be openly challenged, paving the way for a radical restructuring of gender relations. In such a situation, the traditional family structure may further erode— without the material support of men, women may find their traditional status and authority over the younger generation difficult to sustain.

Alternatively, the Vietnamese men may gain economic and social resources in the future, in which case they are likely to reinstate their authority over women. A rise in the economic status of these Vietnamese families has other implications as well. As I have described, the women's strategies for coping with male authority are collective in nature, closely tied to the presence of a distinct and highly connected ethnic community that allows for the growth of women's social networks. A rise in the economic status of the Vietnamese families may be accompanied by movement into the outlying areas of the city and the subsequent geographic dispersal of the Vietnamese ethnic community. Such changes would have serious implications for the ability of the Vietnamese women to forge the kind of powerful community life that I have described in this chapter. Thus, somewhat ironically, the assimilation of the Vietnamese into dominant American economic and social structures may indicate both a major shift from the traditional Vietnamese patriarchal family system and a reassertion of the economic and social bases of male authority in the family. Recent scholarship on the effects of modernization and migration on women's lives has seriously questioned the prior assumption that these processes are uniformly liberating for women (Morokvasic 1984; Ybarra 1983). My research on Vietnamese immigrant women suggests that the effects of migration on gender relations must be understood as highly uneven and shifting in quality, often resulting in gains for women in certain spheres and losses in others.

REFERENCES

Beresford, M. 1988. *Vietnam: Politics, economics, society.* London: Pinter.

Chafetz, J., and A. Dworkin. 1987. In the face of threat: Organized antifeminism in comparative perspective. *Gender & Society* 1:33-60.

Collier, J. 1974. Women in politics. In *Women, culture and society,* edited by M. Rosaldo and L. Lamphere. Palo Alto, CA: Stanford University Press.

di Leonardo, M. 1987. The female world of cards and holidays: Women, families and the work of kinship. *Signs* 12:440-54.

Ehrenreich, B. 1982. Defeating the ERA: A right-wing mobilization of women. *Journal of Sociology and Social Welfare* 9:391-98.

Finnan, C. R. and R. Cooperstein. 1983. *Southeast Asian refugee resettlement at the local level.* Washington, DC: Office of Refugee Resettlement.

Gold, S. 1989. Differential adjustment among immigrant family members. *Journal of Contemporary Ethnography* 17:408-34.

Gold, S., and N. Kibria. 1993. Vietnamese refugees and blocked mobility. *Asian and Pacific Migration Journal* 2:1-30.

Haines, D. 1987. Patterns in Southeast Asian refugee employment: A reappraisal of the existing research. *Ethnic Groups* 7:39-63.

Haines, D., D. Rutherford, and P. Thomas. 1981. Family and community among Vietnamese refugees. *International Migration Review* 15:310-19.

Hendry, J. B. 1954. *The small world of Khanh Hau.* Chicago: Aldine.

Hickey, G. C. 1964. *Village in Vietnam.* New Haven, CT: Yale University Press.

Johnson, K. A. 1983. *Women, the family and peasant revolution in China.* Chicago: University of Chicago Press.

Kandiyoti, D. 1988. Bargaining with patriarchy. *Gender & Society* 2:274-91.

Keyes, C. F. 1977. *The golden peninsula.* New York: Macmillan.

Kibria, N. 1989. Patterns of Vietnamese women's wagework in the U.S. *Ethnic Groups* 7:297-323.

———. 1993. *Family tightrope: The changing lives of Vietnamese Americans.* Princeton, NJ: Princeton University Press.

Klatch, R. E. 1987. *Women of the new right.* Philadelphia: Temple University Press.

Lamphere, L. 1974. Strategies, cooperation and conflict among women in domestic groups. In *Women, culture and society,* edited by M. R. Rosaldo and L. Lamphere. Stanford, CA: Stanford University Press.

———. 1987. *From working daughters to working mothers.* Ithaca, NY: Cornell University Press.

Marr, D. G. 1976. The 1920's women's rights debate in Vietnam. *Journal of Asian Studies* 35:3.

Martin, E. P., and J. M. Martin. 1978. *The Black extended family.* Chicago: University of Chicago Press.

Morokvasic, M. 1984. Birds of passage are also women. *International Migration Review* 18:886-907.

Nguyen Van Vinh. 1949. *Savings and mutual lending societies (ho).* Southeast Asia Studies, Yale University.

Nyland, C. 1981. Vietnam, the plan/market contradiction and the transition to socialism. *Journal of Contemporary Asia* 11:426-28.

Pessar, P. R. 1984. The linkage between the household and workplace in the experience of Dominican women in the U.S. *International Migration Review* 18:1188-1212.

Pleck, E. H. 1983. Challenges to traditional authority in immigrant families. In *The American family in social-historical perspective,* edited by M. Gordon. New York: St. Martin's.

Rumbaut, R. G. 1989. Portraits, patterns and predictors of the refugee adaptation process: Results and reflections from the IHARP panel study. In *Refugees as immigrants: Cambodians, Laotians and Vietnamese in America,* edited by D. W. Haines. Totowa, NJ: Rowman & Littlefield.

Stack, C. 1974. *All our kin: Strategies for survival in a Black community.* New York: Harper & Row.

Ta Van Tai. 1981. The status of women in traditional Vietnam: A comparison of the Le dynasty (1428-1788) with the Chinese codes. *Journal of Asian History* 15:97-145.

Thrift, N., and D. Forbes. 1986. *The price of war: Urbanization in Vietnam, 1954-1985.* London: Allen & Unwin.

Wolf, M. 1972. *Women and the family in rural Taiwan.* Palo Alto, CA: Stanford University Press.

———. 1974. Chinese women: Old skills in a new context. In *Women, culture and society,* edited by M. Rosaldo and L. Lamphere. Palo Alto, CA: Stanford University Press.

Ybarra, L. 1983. Empirical and theoretical developments in studies of the Chicano family. In *The state of Chicano research on family, labor and migration studies,* edited by A. Valdez. Stanford, CA: Stanford Center for Chicano Research.

12 Activist Mothering:
Cross-Generational Continuity in
the Community Work of Women From
Low-Income Urban Neighborhoods

NANCY A. NAPLES

Black feminist scholarship of the last decade challenges the traditional definitions of mothering that derive from white, middle-class perspectives (Collins 1990, 1991a; hooks 1984; King 1988). Chicana and Puerto Rican feminist writers also call attention to the limitations of such analyses for capturing the meaning and practice of mothering in different racial-ethnic[1] communities (see, e.g., Acosta-Belén 1986; Moraga 1981). By comparing the experiences of African American women and Latinas (predominantly Puerto Rican women) from New York City and Philadelphia, this chapter further demonstrates the ways that knowledge generated from the standpoint of women from different classes and racial-ethnic backgrounds transforms our understanding of mothering. The analysis draws on in-depth interviews with community workers hired in antipoverty programs funded by the Economic Opportunity Act of 1964. The women identified for the study continued to

AUTHOR'S NOTE: Two different versions of this work were presented at the annual meeting of the American Anthropological Association, Phoenix, Arizona, November 1988, and the annual meeting of the Society for the Study of Social Problems, Cincinnati, Ohio, August 1991. I am grateful to the women whose stories are represented here for their willingness to share their experiences. I also thank Sandra Morgen, Cynthia J. Truelove, Doris Wilkinson, Maxine Baca Zinn, Esther Ngan-ling Chow, and three anonymous reviewers for helpful suggestions on earlier drafts. I owe a special debt to Nina E. Fortin (1949-87) for her ongoing support during the research. She is greatly missed.

223

work as unpaid or paid community workers in 1984 and 1985 when the interviews took place.

Analysis of the community work of African American women and Latinas living and working in low-income neighborhoods provides an opportunity to examine the social construction of mothering and the significance of the cross-generational continuity of "activist mothering" for their communities. The findings of this research challenge analyses of women's work that separate paid and unpaid work or social reproduction from so-called productive labor and show the interlocking and reinforcing connections between political activism, mothering, community work, and paid labor (also see Naples 1991a, 1991b).

RACIAL-ETHNIC AND CLASS DIFFERENCES IN WOMEN'S COMMUNITY WORK

Women's community-based activities have historically involved unpaid work in churches, schools, child-care programs, hospitals, and recreation centers. Recent historical research by feminist writers stresses the role of black women in the struggle to provide social services, education, and health care to low-income residents (see, e.g., Giddings 1984; Gordon 1991; Hine 1990; Jones 1985). Latinas, Native American women, and Asian American women also have a long tradition of community-based work designed to protect and improve the lives of their "people" (see, e.g., Acosta-Belén 1986; Glenn 1986; Green 1990; Hewitt 1990). However, until recently, most of the literature on social reform, charity work, the settlement house movement, and contemporary civic work in voluntary associations focused on the work of white, middle- and upper-income women (see, e.g., Daniels 1988; Kaminer 1984; Sklar 1985). When we turn our attention to the community-based work of African American women, Latinas, and other women of color, we are forced to reconceptualize our understanding of community work, political activism, mothering, and by extension, our analyses of labor.

McCourt (1977) describes working-class white women's motivation for community work as an extension of their self-definitions as women and mothers. Gilkes (1980) also found that black women's community-based political activism developed out of their mothering practices. However, while white women and women of color may describe their motivation for community work as an extension of their gender identities, their differing standpoints shaped by race-ethnicity, class, sexual orientation, and region of residence influence how they define their family's and community's needs as well as the political strategies they adopt to accomplish their differing goals (see Gilkes 1988; Hine 1990; Morgen and Bookman 1988; Naples 1991b; Sacks 1987; Susser 1988). For example, as Gordon (1991, 31) demonstrates, African American women's welfare reform activism differed from white women's work in claiming "leadership" on behalf of their whole people.

Collins (1991a) describes the broad-based nature of mothering in the black community and highlights the work of "community othermothers" who help build community institutions and fight for the welfare of their neighbors. She argues that the activities of "other-mothers," who form part of the extended kinship networks in the black community, pave the way for the political activism of community othermothers (also see Stack 1974; Troester 1984). According to Collins (1991a), "A substantial portion of Black women's status in African American communities stems not only from their roles as mothers in their own families but from their contributions as community othermothers to Black community development as well" (p. 170).

Black women's struggle against racism infuses their mothering practices inside and outside their "homeplace" (hooks 1990, 41). Lessons carved out of the experiences of "everyday racism" (Essed 1990, 144) contribute to mothering practices that include "handing down the knowledge of racism from generation to generation" (Carothers 1990). The author bell hooks refers to this practice in her discussion of homeplace as "a set of resistance." She explains, "Working to create a homeplace that affirmed our beings, our blackness, our love for one another was necessary resistance" (1990, 46). She also argues that "any attempts to critically assess the role of black women in liberation struggle must examine the way political concern about the impact of racism shaped black women's thinking, their sense of home, and their modes of parenting" (1990, 46).

Latinas also fight against discrimination and the oppressive institutions that shape their daily lives, and consequently, as mothers they model strategies of resistance for their children as self-conscious or un-self-conscious practices (see, e.g., Moraga 1981). This chapter offers an opportunity to compare the perspectives of African American women with Latinas who "mother" in relatively similar class contexts but who bring different cultural experiences to their motherwork.

METHODOLOGICAL CONSIDERATIONS

In order to place the study in a specific historical context, the sample was limited to community workers who had found paid employment through the antipoverty programs in New York City or Philadelphia funded by the Economic Opportunity Act of 1964 (U.S. Congress 1964). The legislation provided support for neighborhood-based community action agencies that would be directed and staffed by the poor. The emphasis on "maximum feasible participation" of the poor inadvertently acknowledged the value of the community work performed by low-income women who subsequently found employment in the antipoverty programs.[2]

For this study of community work, I interviewed a total of forty-two workers who were living in low-income communities when they were hired by the antipoverty programs. Of the forty-two, twenty-six were African American, ten were Puerto Rican, one was Dominican, four were White European American, and one was Japanese American. This chapter is based on the personal narratives of the twenty-six African American women, ten Puerto Rican women, and one Dominican woman who were living in a low-income community when they were hired by an antipoverty program. The sample of community workers differed in terms of the community work positions held at the time of the interview (see Table 12.1).[3]

The study starts from the personal narratives of the activists themselves. This approach is informed by feminist scholarship, which is interested in "documenting women's experience and observing the patterns found in looking at gender as a category of social experience" (Andersen 1988, 15) in the context of each woman's specific social location (Amott and Matthaei 1991). The open-ended interview developed for this study included the creation of an oral history with special emphasis on family background, employment, community work, motherwork, political activities and political analyses, and a description of changes that the women saw in their community and their visions for the future.[4] Each interview was audiotaped and transcribed and, subsequently, analyzed for recurring themes and patterns. Themes and patterns were compared across narratives. This approach offered a "context in which to examine the development of political consciousness" (Mohanty 1991, 33) as well as an opportunity to explore conflicts and tensions in the community workers' self-definition (also see Ginsburg 1989). This grounded theory method "stresses discovery and

TABLE 12.1 Employment Status of African American and Latina Community Workers at Time of Interview

	African American Women		Latinas	
	N	Percentage	N	Percentage
Director, community agency	6	23.1	1	9.1
Area coordinator, PAAC[a]	7	26.9	0	0.0
Program director, community agency	1	3.8	3	27.3
Outreach, intake, or I&R worker[b]	5	19.2	1	9.1
Administrator, citywide agency	3	11.5	2	18.2
Other community work	1	3.8	3	27.3
Retired	2	7.7	0	0.0
Unemployed	1	3.8	1	9.1
Total	26	99.8	11	100.1[c]

a. PAAC is the acronym for Philadelphia Area Action Commission, the antipoverty agency in Philadelphia.
b. I&R worker = information and referral worker, PAAC.
c. Total exceeds 100 percent because of rounding.

theory development" through "systematic efforts to check and refine emerging categories" (Charmaz 1983, 111). The concept of activist mothering was generated through close reading and rereading of the narratives developed through the interview.

THEORETICAL CONSIDERATIONS

The traditional definition of *mothering* that refers to nurturing work with children who are biologically or legally related and cared for within the confines of a bounded family unit (see Chodorow 1978) failed to capture the community workers' activities and self-perceptions of their motherwork. The term *activist mothering* better expresses the complex ways in which the African American and Latina community workers made sense of their own activities. The analysis of activist mothering provides a new conceptualization of the interacting nature of labor, politics, and mothering—three aspects of social life usually analyzed separately—from the point of view of women whose motherwork has often been ignored or pathologized (Moynihan 1967) in sociological analyses.

Traditional academic practices fragment social life and falsely separate paid work from social reproduction, activism from mothering, and family from community. A close reading of the community workers' oral history reveals the inseparability of these so-called separate spheres of social life. For example, when we begin with a definition of work circumscribed by wage labor, many of the community workers' activities fall from view (Gilkes 1988; Naples 1991a). When we adopt a definition of *politics* that is limited to voting behavior, membership in political clubs or parties, and running for public office, the political practice of the community workers is obscured (Gilkes 1988; Morgen and Bookman 1988; Naples 1991b; Susser 1988). The development of the concept of activist mothering demonstrates the power of knowledge generated from "self-defined, subjugated standpoints" to decenter dominant frameworks (Collins 1991b, 377). The following discussion illustrates the themes that emerged as aspects of activist mothering in the community work of African American women and Latinas who were living and working in low-income communities in New York City and Philadelphia.

MOTIVATIONS FOR COMMUNITY WORK

The women interviewed for this study described their community work as a logical result of their desire to improve the lives of their family and neighbors. Most women interviewed described myriad community problems that sparked their initial community activism. Twenty of the African American women and ten of the Latinas became involved in community work as they confronted specific problems in their neighborhoods ranging from health care, housing, and sanitation to crime and safety. For most of the women, concern for their geographic community overlapped with concern for their racial-ethnic community; therefore, they also described their community work in terms of their interest in promoting the rights of African Americans or Puerto Ricans or Hispanics. The variety of issues they addressed in their communities required their participation in a wide array of specific political strategies, including testifying at public hearings, organizing voter registration drives and educational forums, leading public protests, performing legal advocacy, and speaking before community groups and the media.

The four African American women and three Latinas who did not have children at the time of the interview traced their motivations for community work to a variety of community-based concerns. For example, Francine Evans started her community work because of concern for the deteriorating housing conditions in her neighborhood. Her work on housing problems in her community led her to advocate for an improved court system, because she found that "the judges ruled with the land-lords." Angela Garcia, along with Francine Evans and the other African American women who did not have children, also explained their initial development as community workers through church-related activities. An additional fifteen African American community workers said their work with the church, as one worker explained, "was a catalyst for a lot of the things I do now." Ann Robertson said that her initial involvement in church work eventually helped her develop the skills she applied as a community worker. However, it was her parents' participation in church activities that first prompted her own church involvement as well as her other community work.

Thirty of the thirty-seven community workers had children at the time of the interview. All the women with children said that for the most part, a large portion of their community work derived from concern for their children's well-being. Rita Martinez was an assistant teacher in a community child-care program earning $8,000 a year at the time of the interview. She married at age eighteen and had three children. Rita's apprehension over her youngest child's emotional development led to her involvement in a community-based child care program that in turn, gave her the opportunity to enhance her own personal growth and pursue her career goal as a teacher. Through her subsequent involvement in the antipoverty program, Rita also developed a broader analysis of parents' rights that in turn, informed her unpaid and paid community work practice. This overlap of mothering practices, political activism, and community work is a defining feature of activist mothering identified throughout the personal narratives.

Defining Activist Mothering

When we explore the community workers' description of the activities they performed in their role as mothers, significant differences emerge between their mothering practices and the dominant ideology of mothering as limited to nurturing work for children who are biologically or legally related. The broadened understanding of mothering practices is a major component of activist mothering. Ten of the thirty women with children described their first community work activity as a response to the problems with the quality of their children's education. For example, Wilma North said her community work in Central Harlem started with her dissatisfaction with the educational quality of her children's school. However, she continued to fight for "anything that had to do with the betterment of [my] community and the welfare of those children going to the elementary school" long after her own children graduated.

Activist mothering not only involves nurturing work for those outside one's kinship group but also encompasses a broad definition of actual mothering practices. The community workers defined *good mothering* to comprise all actions, including social activism, that addressed the needs of their children and community. Wilma served as president of the community block council in her neighborhood for several years. She believed that her group was successful because "each time there was a meeting, we were there. We were testifying about one thing or another. We did all kinds of things—anything for the betterment of that community—we went before the zoning boards, we went before the school boards." In addition to testifying before public officials, all the community workers participated in public protests and demonstrations for improved community services, increased resources, and expansion of community control. Ann Robertson, for example, described her involvement in protests against the city-run hospital in her Manhattan neighborhood and for welfare rights and improved housing as well as for expanded child-care services and community control of the public schools. Ann's narrative of police resistance against the parents' organizing for community control of their schools illustrates the interlocking nature of the so-called separate spheres of family, community, and the state in her community work. She vividly recalled, "I was quite active [in demonstrations] . . . and one day we had a meeting [in the school] . . . and they shot right into the school house. We had several of our people get their heads beat up." The community workers' ideas concerning their identities as mothers or community caretakers shaped their motivation for community work to a certain extent. Once they became active in community work, their experiences and acts of resistance defied the dominant definition of *motherhood* as emphasizing work performed within the private sphere of the family or in face-to-face interaction with those in need.

Racism, Poverty, and Community Work

Racial discrimination was one of the consistent themes expressed by all the African American and Latina community workers, and struggles against racism formed a basic undercurrent for most of their community work. Maria Calero, a program director for a citywide nonprofit agency in New York City, remembered the problems with police brutality in her Harlem community and also emphasized that "Hispanics had enormous problems getting registered to vote because you had to pass a test" that presumed a certain facility with written English. Her awareness of the "relations of ruling" (Smith 1987) was heightened when she gave birth to her first child and began to investigate the high school drop-out rate and how racist teachers had lower expectations for Hispanic children.

Ann Robertson was a single head of her household who described a complex of factors that motivated her community activism. She learned very quickly how personal troubles were politically constituted. Ann described difficulties she encountered as a mother living in a tenement in a low-income neighborhood. Lack of heat, water leaks, and mice and rats roaming her apartment—all contributed to her determination to fight against the conditions under which low-income people were forced to live. When her son died of pneumonia, she said, "It just triggered me off!" She reported:

> What had happened is wrong! All the little babies that were born that year died that winter in those houses, except one little boy. And we took the babies to Metropolitan Hospital, and they bathed the babies in alcohol and gave them some aspirin and told us to take them home. And I started fighting them, the Health Department, and others, to get heat in the house, and other things like that. I knew that it didn't have to be like that. There's no reason that my children or anybody else's had to live like that. So when my kids started school I tried to organize the parents.

Ann was a recognized community leader in Harlem before she was paid for community work. When she began as a paid community worker, it related directly to her previous unpaid activities with parents in East Harlem. In 1965 she took a job as a receptionist with a community action agency in Harlem while performing unpaid community work. When she had to miss her job for a week, the woman who filled in for her did not want to give up the position, so Ann said she "just began doing my natural thing out there in the community." She remained on the payroll as a community worker and, she explained, "just continued in the day-to-day struggles of the schools and got involved in trying to get a drug program in Harlem Hospital, wherever I saw a need." Ann's story vividly demonstrates the inadequacy of an analysis that separates paid from unpaid community work and family-based labor.

The blurring of community work and family-based labor by these women frequently meant opening their homes to those in need. Ethel Pearls described how she invited young people, especially those with children, who had no other place to live or who were having difficulties in their own homes to stay with her and her family. Ethel's own children were now grown and out of the house. She continued to offer her home to others, even after she was laid off from her paid community work position. She said that "they always tell me I had a household of people and if anybody just doesn't have anywhere to stay, they come back here." Ethel introduced me to a young woman staying in her house and explained:

> She's trying to find someplace to stay. I got bedrooms, so until she gets herself straightened out, she and her baby [are] here. I could never have a fancy house, I guess, but my house is usable. Some people have homes that aren't livable . . . I don't have anything fancy—I couldn't because everybody just comes along sometimes and just wants to talk and I don't want to say to them: "Don't sit there." . . . I'm 60 years old now, and God has been good to me—I don't think I've lost anything by trying to help.

The preceding examples are illustrative of the broadened definition of mothering that infuses the community work of the women in this study. For many, this continued the activist mothering practices that they witnessed as children in their parents' home.

EARLY CHILDHOOD EXPERIENCES AS GROUNDS FOR COMMUNITY WORK

The African American women and Latinas interviewed uniformly identified many experiences with racism, which included some of their earliest childhood memories. For the four Latinas who moved to New York City from Puerto Rico or the Dominican Republic, their lack of facility with English enhanced their encounters of racism. Maria Calero had married young, was divorced, and had three children. Her first paid job was as a factory worker. Maria was born in the Dominican Republic and moved to New York City with her family as a teenager. Shortly after she arrived in this country she recalls being "called nigger for the first time." She "hardly spoke the language" and was unprepared for the racism she found. She recalled:

I remember feeling that I was not a part of the society at all. . . . I had come to this country when I was fifteen so my experience was different from those Hispanic women that were raised and went to school here. I came from a homogeneous society . . . to a society that strongly discriminated.

Anna Montalvo also confronted the pain of racism when she and her family first moved to this country. She could not speak English when she entered the first grade. Once day when she had to go to the bathroom, the teacher told her that "if I couldn't ask her in English, I couldn't be excused." Anna wet her pants and "was totally mortified." When she told her parents, they went in the next day "to straighten out the teacher." Anna said she received "a more valuable education" from her parents than she "was getting within the confines of the establishment walls." Anna's discussion of the lessons she learned from her parents parallels Collins's (1990, 208) emphasis on "concrete experience as a criterion of meaning" in "Afrocentric feminist epistemology" (p. 206). It also illustrates that, while it may not be limited to the African American community, the practice of using "concrete experience as a criterion of meaning" has different historical and cultural meaning for members of varying racial-ethnic groups.

Parents as Role Models

Many of the African American and Latina community workers attributed their success as community workers to their parents, who helped them understand and confront the discrimination they faced in the wider social environment. The community workers were especially angry about the racial discrimination their parents encountered. It is clear from the women's personal narratives that these perceptions had profound effects on their commitment to community work. Anna Montalvo discussed how her father's job opportunities were limited by his ethnic background. Anna's father was an experienced accountant in Puerto Rico. When he moved to New York City, he could not get a job in his field because "even though he spoke English, he had a heavy accent," Anna explained. Consequently, he was employed as a factory worker during the day and a watchman at night. Anna recalled:

It had an impact on me because I could not understand why he could not work in his field. That left an impression on me and also a reality that stayed with me, and I think it was the genesis that in one way or the other I had to be involved in helping my community in whatever way.

While Anna's parents did not participate in"establishment" political activities, such as political clubs or electoral politics, she reported that they discussed politics in the home and modeled strategies of resistance to the racism and classism in the surrounding environment. Ann Robertson's earliest memories were of a household that was always open to others in need. Ann believed that her parents' example helped shape her concern for others in her community. Ann recounted:

> One thing I saw within my home . . . my parents would have food to share with somebody, be it a child or an adult. And I remember many a night we would be woken up and I would sleep in the living room because somebody [needed] my bed.

Ann's experience as a child resembled that of Ethel Pearls's children. In both homes, family and friends, as well as strangers, were welcome if they needed a place to stay or food to eat. Historians of the black family point out the importance of resource sharing for the survival of low-income people (Giddings 1984; Jones 1985), and data from this study reveal the continuity of this practice among low-income women in contemporary urban neighborhoods (also see Stack 1974). This practice is not limited to the African American community. The Latinas in this study were also taught the importance of sharing resources with others in their community, a practice they took into their own activist mothering.

Mothers' Activist Mothering

Many of the workers' mothers provided, as one worker stated, a "strong foundation" for their desire to serve their community. A total of seventeen mothers were described by their daughters as informal caretakers in their communities. Five (or 45 percent) of the Latinas and twelve (or 46 percent) of the African American women said their mothers were involved in a variety of helping activities in their neighborhoods. These activities included taking neighbors to the hospital, helping to care for the elderly, advocating for increased child-care programs, fighting school officials to improve educational opportunities for young people, struggling with landlords and police officials to improve the housing and safety conditions in their community, and interpreting for non-English-speaking residents.

At the time of the interview, Carmen Hernandez was director of the same education program in East Harlem that had employed her as a bus driver in 1969. Carmen characterized her mother, who is still very active in her neighborhood, as "a frontier community person" who fought for other children's rights as well as her own. Carmen recounted:

> Back in the '50s and early '60s, when it wasn't right for parents to get involved, to be in the classrooms and to question teachers, she was doing that. She'd ask: "Why?" "How come?" "Give me a reason." "I won't take it just because you said it." "Show it to me." "Let me read it so I can understand what's going on, because verbally that doesn't connect with me." . . . And she used to do things like that. And I used to look at her and she got her point across. And she would fight for different children's rights, and she didn't care whose child it was.

Carmen's description of her mother as an activist and "a frontier community person" mirrors Collins's (1990) account of how black women's broad-based mothering practices contribute to their role as "community othermothers." Among the many lessons Carmen learned from her mother's activist mothering was the importance of questioning and "dialogue in assessing knowledge claims" as well as the "ethic of caring" (Collins 1990, 212, 215).

Mothers also taught their daughters how to create and sustain community ties. These community-building and sustaining skills became one foundation upon which the daughters developed as community workers in their own right. Josephine Carson was in her early fifties and worked in a program for the elderly in her East Harlem community, earning an annual salary of $18,000 in 1985. Josephine learned from her mother's example how important informal networks are to the survival of low-income people like herself. Josephine's mother was a schoolteacher in Georgia but could not find a job in her field when she moved to New York City in 1929. Her mother had recently died, but Josephine continued to feel her mother's spirit with her. She explained:

> There are a lot of things I do, and I get tickled because I think about her and what she would have done, and I know just what she would have done with a lot of stuff. She was a very bright woman. Everybody in the community came to her for anything—if they had problems with bills, if they

had problems with burying somebody that lived somewhere else, they'd
come to my mother. My mother knew all the funeral directors and she knew
all the ministers in the churches and she knew everybody. . . . She'd always
know who to call. And they'd use her almost like for community counseling. I'm serious! My mother's house was always like a [revolving] door.

Josephine decided to accept a paid position for which she at first thought
she was unqualified. When, during the job interview, the members of
the board of directors of the new community-based agency told her the
names of some of the people with whom she would be in contact through
the position, she found that she knew everyone they mentioned. She
took the job and through it she reaffirmed her connection to the community. The networking skills she learned from her mother helped
Josephine in her own community work, enhanced her success as a paid
worker, and increased her feelings of personal connection with other
members of her community. Josephine's experience further demonstrates the blurring between family-based experiences, paid labor, and
social reproductive work.

The community workers modeled activist mothering for their own
children, often with unintended influence on their political socialization. Maria Calero said her oldest daughter is "a real activist" who
attended "lots of community meetings" with her mother when she was
growing up. Maria enthusiastically shared:

I really love her. I really respect her. And we disagree, we have political
disagreements. She's much more idealistic than I am. She's very theoretical. She has a very harsh view of the United States and its policies. I think
that I was much more a romantic . . . [about] this country.

Like Maria, Carmen Rodriguez believed that her children learned from
her example and continued her community work legacy. She explained
that they "saw me working and how I got involved . . . I was an inspiration!" She believed that she was especially influential in her daughter's life: "And that's why my daughter, I feel, she's very active, she's
even more active than me, because she's already started and she's very
young, and I've encouraged this in her."

The community workers challenged traditional notions of gender and
mothering in their work and served as models for their children as well
as others in their community. All of the women interviewed held onto
a strong sense of their personal power and, for many, the example given

by other activist mothers helped strengthen their belief, already established by their own mothers, in their power to affect change in their
communities. They bequeathed this legacy to their children through
their words, actions, and lifelong commitment.

TENSIONS BETWEEN COMMUNITY
WORK AND FAMILY-BASED LABOR

The intricate relationship between community work and family-
based labor also generated tension between a worker's caretaking responsibilities for her own children and her caretaking work in the
community.[5] Some of the women expressed regret that the extensive
hours they spent on community work took them away from their children. Pat Martin, for example, regretted the time she lost with her
children, especially her youngest child. Her husband had a steady
blue-collar job when she started as an unpaid community worker outside the home. Pat became interested in taking a paid community work
position. She had two children when she accepted a paid community
work position, and she gave birth to another child while working for a
community action agency. She became "so involved in what was going
on in the community" that she was unable to spend much time with her
children. She said she would have been unable to engage in community
work without the support of her daughter's aunt, who babysat for her
during the day. The paid community work position quickly became vital
to the economic survival of Pat's family. Her husband lost his job as a
skilled laborer and accepted a job as a driver that paid very little.
Consequently, the salary from community work helped to keep her
family out of poverty. Pat's story again illustrates the overlap between
family-based labor and community work as well as the contradictions
that result from overlapping demands.

Tensions between family-based and community work were further
strained when paid work took the worker from her home community. A
total of three African American women and three Latinas accepted
higher paying positions outside their communities; five of these six
women had children. They encountered two of the most common difficulties faced by employed women with children—the lack of quality
child care and the inflexibility of employers who refused to recognize
the child-care needs of their employees. As a single parent, Maria
Colero could not live with the uncertainties and low pay of neighbor-

hood-based community work. She accepted a "professional position" in a city agency.[6] She recalled:

> I had no day care for my son. . . . Finally, I found day care on the upper west side [of Manhattan]. . . . I would take two buses to be at the day care by a quarter to nine in the morning. My boss then had a real position about "feminists" and would say . . . that I had to be a professional, that my circumstances were of no importance to him. I had to be at my job at nine o'clock in the morning so whether [my son] was clinging or not, I had to leave [him].

Maria's paid work experience enhanced her sense of personal and political power. Yet she also said that it took away from the original enthusiasm that motivated her community work. In her desire to increase her family's economic resources and advance her "professional" career, she "became uninspired by the job" and increasingly alienated from her personal goals. Her experience of alienation affected how she related to her children. She felt that the position she accepted in order to increase her ability to support her family directly interfered with her emotional and physical availability to her three children.

Josephine Carson, on the other hand, shifted her site of work from non-community-based factory work to community work that enabled her to remain more involved in the care of her seven children. Josephine's next position was as a school aide. She left this job when her youngest child was born but continued unpaid community work. Through this work, she learned about the antipoverty programs and applied for a paid community work position. She accepted a job as an assistant supervisor in the community action agency in her neighborhood and was promoted to supervisor three months later. The community work position that Josephine Carson accepted was only a few blocks away from her home. Her previous jobs as factory worker, cashier, and school aide did not offer her the same challenge that the community work position provided. She gained a wide range of additional experiences. She designed programs, provided direct services to her community, spoke in public, and at one point, supervised a staff of twelve. For Josephine, the community-based work enhanced her availability to her children as well as her self-esteem.

The community workers' self-confidence and feelings of empowerment grew through their community work. On the other hand, they also related a deep sense of loss for the time spent away from their families.

Fortunately, the African American and Latina community workers were situated within an extensive network of "othermothers" (Troester 1984) who assisted them with their child-care needs and supported their community work. All of the community workers with children mentioned the importance of other women in their lives who helped them negotiate the complex demands of unpaid and paid community work and parental responsibilities. The contradictions that arose from the community workers' negotiation of family-based labor, unpaid community work, and paid work further expose how the so-called separate spheres of social life are braided in and through the social relations of community.

THE SOCIAL PRODUCTION
OF ACTIVIST MOTHERING

As Ruddick (1989, 17) argues, "maternal thinking" derives from "maternal practice," from the "demands . . . imposed on anyone doing maternal work." However, Ruddick's analysis remains bounded by a limited definition of family-based work. While she demonstrates that "maternal practice" influences women's disproportionate support for a "politics of peace," she neglects class, racial-ethnic, historic, and regional dimensions of social experience that also shape "maternal practice" and may contribute to different forms of political activism (also see Morgen and Bookman 1988). The community workers whose lives were shaped by experiences of racism, sexism, and poverty learn to mother as activists fighting in their homes and communities against the debilitating and demoralizing effects of oppression. When we limit our analysis of mothering practices to those activities that occur within the confines of a nuclear family, we miss the material conditions that contribute to differing family forms as well as the social construction of gender and mothering. For example, experiences of racism constituted the community workers' first encounters with justice in North American society. These experiences informed the antiracist mothering practices they utilized within their own homes and served as a basic target for community work.

Similarity between Latina and African American community workers also emanates from their social location in low-income communities. As residents of low-income communities, many of the women described how the deteriorating conditions of their communities as well as the inadequate education and health services that threatened their children's growth and development fostered a commitment to community work. Their own mothers helped interpret experiences with racism and classism and instilled in their daughters a belief in their ability to overcome these obstacles. Their fathers also contributed to the cross-generational continuity of activist mothering. Therefore, the conceptualization of activist mothering challenges essentialist interpretations of mothering practices.

Furthermore, significant differences between the African American and Latina community workers were derived from their different social and cultural histories. Latinas differed in the extent to which sexism was perceived to circumscribe their community work. While the African American women reported numerous experiences with sexism, Latinas were more likely to emphasize the ways in which sexism inhibited their ability to engage in community work to the extent that they desired. Many felt that the male-dominated institutions of the Hispanic community kept women from assuming more leadership positions. Latinas also reported a range of experiences with sexism in their personal relationships. Rita Martinez's husband was also active in community activities, serving on several boards of directors of community-based agencies. He initially resisted his wife's interest in community work and rarely assisted her in the home. The conflict over her community work put a strain on Rita's marriage. She explained the difficulty in terms of contrasting cultural expectations between herself and her husband:

> I became so involved that I would go from work, and then go home, feed the kids, and then come back and go for a meeting. And it was hard because I had to take my kids with me everywhere. [My husband] was active in this community and he did a lot of organizing tenement housing buildings and he had to go to their meetings, so we were never home together. And then when he was, I wasn't. And I would ask for him to baby sit. And he would say, "But I never see you!" . . . What happened was that it was all right for him to do it because he's a Puerto Rican. In terms of Puerto Ricans, they're very macho. The woman is in the house, the man is not in the house, so that was a conflict. And we needed a lot of discussion. . . . But I think after awhile it did us good. He knew I was doing it for the children.

In contrast, Gloria Alvarez described her Puerto Rican husband as extremely supportive. She related:

I've been married to my husband for twenty-three years. . . . My daughters love him. And I know how good he is. But anything that I am very active in, he's with me. He's supportive of everything that I do. He says I'm a fighter. . . . And he gives me suggestions. He helps. He doesn't mind the hours. He believes in what I'm doing.

The contrast between Rita's and Gloria's husbands' support for their wives' community work illustrates the danger in generalizing about sexist practices within the Puerto Rican community. While there may exist gendered cultural patterns within a racial-ethnic group, analyses of the concrete practices of specific members may reveal a wide variety of experiences that do not correspond with the stereotypical view. Analyses of gender inequities within a specific racial-ethnic group need to remain sensitive to the diversity of actual practices that shape women's lives.

As a result of their activist mothering, the community workers played a crucial role in the continued survival of their own communities (also see Gilkes 1988; Susser 1988). Their goal was to see their communities grow, thrive, and become self-sufficient beyond their lifetimes. The older women in the study expressed a desire to scale down their community work activities but believed they could not do so unless there were others to replace them in the community. Some women feared that younger people were unwilling or unable to continue the tradition of community work necessary to sustain their communities. Ruth Parker, at age fifty-three, said she was "getting a little pooped" from negotiating the demands of unpaid and paid community work but was concerned that young people were not showing interest in their communities. She feared that the future of the struggle for civil rights and equality might be in danger unless younger people took up the torch from older community workers. Angela Garcia also expressed concern about the future of leadership in the struggle for equity in this society. However, Angela did see new leadership developing among Puerto Rican women in New York City in the mid-1980s. What made her even more excited was that she saw "a development of a consciousness of women in [her] community, a definite consciousness." Angela pointed to the National Conference of Puerto Rican Women and the Hispanic Women's Center in New York City as evidence that Puerto Rican women are "getting [their] act together."

TRANSFORMING SOCIAL KNOWLEDGE

This analysis of activist mothering highlights the need for expanded definitions of labor. Community work was low paid, offered little opportunity for advancement, and was highly unstable. In spite of this, many of the community workers chose to remain in community-based positions. Those who obtained professional credentials, such as a college or master's degree, often turned down jobs that offered higher salaries and professional visibility in citywide agencies. Of the three African American and seven Latina community workers who received a bachelor's, master's, or higher degree while performing paid community work, only four subsequently accepted positions in citywide agencies outside their communities. In addition, all of the community workers remained active as unpaid community workers during their tenure as paid workers, and most, if physically able, continued to serve their communities after retirement. Since the economic viability of low-income communities had deteriorated over the fifteen to twenty years since they first accepted paid community work, their jobs were even more demanding in the mid-1980s. Given the apparent "irrationality" demonstrated by these women in relation to pay and career advancement, the traditional literature on the sociology of work and occupations provides only a limited framework for an analysis of women's community work in low-income communities.

In order to correct the limited notion of class and labor associated with orthodox Marxist theorizing, feminists in the dual-systems tradition argued for greater significance to be accorded activities defined as social reproduction (Hartmann 1981). However, the separation of productive from social reproductive labor reproduces the gendered division of labor within sociological analyses and prevents a socially contextualized appreciation of the ways that women, in particular, make sense of their own activities. For the community workers, their paid work formed one component of their mothering practices, just as their mothering practices formed one component of their labor. For all the women in this study, paid labor was woven intricately with their commitment to the social reproduction of a more just and humane society. In fact, it was frequently impossible to determine which activities composed unpaid community work and which ones were exclusively related to their paid community work. Rather than start with a separation between productive labor and social reproduction, this analysis of activist mothering reveals the inseparability of paid labor from social reproduction and highlights the ways in which race-ethnicity and class as well as gender inform mothering practices. Analysis of the community workers' personal narratives keenly discloses the limitations of dominant sociological paradigms for explicating the interlocking nature of race, class, and gender. Just as the community workers did not separate their identities as women from their class background or racial-ethnic communities (also see Gilkes 1988; Susser 1988), so must sociological theorists resist fragmenting social life into artificially disconnected areas of analysis.

NOTES

1. Following Glenn (1991) and Amott and Matthaei (1991), I use the term *race-ethnicity* to avoid the biological determinism associated with the concept of *race* and to highlight more accurately the cultural background of the community activists.

2. See Naples (1991a) for a discussion of the contradictions that result from the incorporation of women from low-income communities into the state as paid community workers.

3. For further detail on sampling procedures and demographics of the sample of the women from low-income communities, see Naples (1991a, 1991b).

4. The interviews ranged from 1½ to 4 hours, included one or more separate sessions, and were conducted between 1984 and 1985. All names used are pseudonyms. Maria Calero, Angela Garcia, Carmen Hernandez, and Anna Montalvo are the pseudonyms for the Latina community workers; and Josephine Carson, Francine Evans, Wilma North, Pat Miller, Ruth Parker, Ann Robertson, and Ethel Pearls are the pseudonyms for the African American women included in this chapter.

5. In addition to the tension between home-based mothering and activist mothering, there are many psychological and social costs paid by the community workers as a consequence of daily struggles against sexism, racism, and poverty. Scott (1991) explores some of these costs in her study of African American women titled *The Habit of Surviving*.

6. See Naples (1991a) for a discussion of the contradictions of professionalization in the community action agencies in New York City and Philadelphia.

REFERENCES

Acosta-Belén, E., ed. 1986. *The Puerto Rican woman's perspectives on culture, history, and society.* New York: Praeger.

Amott, T. L., and J. A. Matthaei. 1991. *Race, gender, and work: A multicultural economic history of women in the United States.* Boston: South End Press.

Andersen, M. L. 1988. *Thinking about women: Sociological and feminist perspectives.* New York: Macmillan.

Carothers, S. C. 1990. Catching sense: Learning from our mothers to be Black and female. In *Uncertain terms: Negotiating gender in American culture,* edited by F. Ginsburg and A. Lowenhaupt Tsing. Boston: Beacon.

Charmaz, K. 1983. The grounded theory method: An explication and interpretation. In *Contemporary field research: A collection of readings,* edited by R. M. Emerson. Prospect Heights, IL: Waveland.

Chodorow, N. 1978. *The reproduction of mothering: Psychoanalysis and the sociology of gender.* Berkeley: University of California Press.

Collins, P. Hill. 1990. *Black feminist thought: Knowledge, consciousness, and the politics of empowerment.* Boston: Unwin Hyman.

———. 1991a. The meaning of motherhood in Black culture. In *The Black family: Essays and studies,* edited by R. Staples. Belmont, CA: Wadsworth.

———. 1991b. On our own terms; Self-defined standpoints and curriculum transformation. *NWSA Journal* 3:367-81.

Daniels, A. Kaplan. 1988. *Invisible careers: Women civic leaders from the volunteer world.* Chicago: University of Chicago Press.

Essed, P. 1990. *Everyday racism: Reports from women of two cultures.* Claremont, CA: Hunter House.

Giddings, P. 1984. *When and where I enter: The impact of Black women on race and sex in America.* New York: William Morrow.

Gilkes, C. Townsend. 1980. "Holding back the ocean with a broom": Black women and community work. In *The Black woman,* edited by L. Rodgers-Rose. Beverly Hills, CA: Sage.

———. 1988. Building in many places: Multiple commitments and ideologies in Black women's community work. In *Women and the politics of empowerment,* edited by A. Bookman and S. Morgen. Philadelphia: Temple University Press.

Ginsburg, F. 1989. Dissonance and harmony: The symbolic function of abortion in activists' life stories. In *Interpreting women's lives: Feminist theory and personal narratives,* edited by the Personal Narratives Group. Philadelphia: Temple University Press.

Glenn, E. Nakano. 1986. *Issei, Nisei, war bride: Three generations of Japanese women in domestic service.* Philadelphia: Temple University Press.

———. 1991. White women/women of color: Historical continuities in the racial division of women's work. Paper presented at the American Sociological Association, annual meetings, Cincinnati, OH, 24 August.

Gordon, L. 1991. *Black and white visions of welfare: Women's welfare activism, 1890-1945.* Madison, WI: Institute for Research on Poverty.

Green, R. 1990. American Indian women: Diverse leadership for social change. In *Bridges of power: Women's multicultural alliances,* edited by L. Albrecht and R. M. Brewer. Philadelphia: New Society.

Hartmann, H. I. 1981. The unhappy marriage of Marxism and feminism: Towards a more progressive union. In *Women and revolution,* edited by L. Sargent. Boston: South End Press.

Hewitt, N. A. 1990. Charity or mutual aid?: Two perspectives on Latin women's philanthropy in Tampa, Florida. In *Lady bountiful revisited: Women, philanthropy, and power,* edited by K. D. McCarthy. New Brunswick, NJ: Rutgers University Press.

Hine, D. Clark. 1990. "We specialize in the wholly impossible": The philanthropic work of Black women. In *Lady bountiful revisited: Women, philanthropy, and power,* edited by K. D. McCarthy. New Brunswick, NJ: Rutgers University Press.

hooks, b. 1984. *Feminist theory: From margin to center.* Boston: South End Press.

———. 1990. *Yearning: Race, gender, and cultural politics.* Boston: South End Press.

Jones, J. 1985. *Labor of love, labor of sorrow: Black women, work, and the family, from slavery to the present.* New York: Vintage.

Kaminer, W. 1984. *Women volunteering: The pleasure, pain, and politics of unpaid work from 1830 to the present.* Garden City, NY: Doubleday.

King, D. K. 1988. Multiple jeopardy, multiple consciousness: The context of a Black feminist ideology. *Signs: Journal of Women in Culture and Society* 14:42-72.

McCourt, K. 1977. *Working class women and grass roots politics.* Bloomington: Indiana University Press.

Mohanty, C. Talpade. 1991. Introduction to cartographies of struggle: Third World women and the politics of feminism. In *Third World women and the politics of feminism,* edited by C. Talpade Mohanty, A. Russo, and L. Torres. Bloomington: Indiana University Press.

Moraga, C. 1981. La guera. In *This bridge called my back: Writings by radical women of color,* edited by C. Moraga and G. Anzaldúa. Watertown, MA: Persephone.

Morgen, S. 1988. "It's the whole power of the city against us!: The development of political consciousness in a health care coalition." In *Women and the politics of empowerment,* edited by A. Bookman and S. Morgen. Philadelphia: Temple University Press.

Morgen, S., and A. Bookman. 1988. Rethinking women and politics: An introductory essay. In *Women and the politics of empowerment,* edited by A. Bookman and S. Morgen. Philadelphia: Temple University Press.

Moynihan, D. P. 1967. *The Negro family: The case for national action.* Washington, DC: GPO.

Naples, N. A. 1991a. Contradictions in the gender subtext of the War on Poverty: Community work and resistance of women from low-income communities. *Social Problems* 38:316-32.

———. 1991b. "Just what needed to be done": The political practice of women community workers in low-income neighborhoods. *Gender & Society* 5:478-94.

Ruddick, S. 1989. *Maternal thinking: Toward a politics of peace.* New York: Ballantine.

Sacks, K. Brodkin. 1987. *Caring by the hour: Women, work, and organizing at Duke Medical Center.* Urbana: University of Illinois Press.

Scott, K. Y. 1991. *The habit of surviving.* New York: Ballantine.

Sklar, K. Kish. 1985. Hull House in the 1890's: A community of women reformers. *Signs: Journal of Women in Culture and Society* 10:658-77.

Smith, D. E. 1987. *The everyday world as problematic: A feminist sociology.* Toronto: University of Toronto Press.

Stack, C. 1974. *All our kin: Strategies for survival in a Black community.* New York: Harper & Row.

Susser, I. 1988. Working-class women, social protest, and changing ideologies. In *Women and the politics of empowerment,* edited by A. Bookman and S. Morgen. Philadelphia: Temple University press.

Troester, R. 1984. Turbulence and tenderness: Mothers, daughters and "othermothers" in Paule Marshall's *Brown Girl, Brownstones. Sage: A Scholarly Journal on Black Women* 1:13-16.

U.S. Congress. House. 1964. Economic Opportunity Act of 1964, Public Law 88-452, 88th Cong., 2d sess.

Part IV

Transforming Reality: Consciousness, Political Activism, and Social Change

Feminist thinking about the importance of women as social agents and the politics of their empowerment through community activism, social movements, and policy change are illustrated in this section. Although the contents, emphases, and strategies of feminist consciousness and political activism vary depending on the specific social location of women, ongoing attempts to challenge the existing social order are evident.

Esther N. Chow's study of Asian American women's feminist consciousness blends with the constraints of race and class that Bernice McNair Barnett next describes as characterizing southern African American women leaders in the civil rights movement. Each catalyst for and limitation on the evolution of a feminist consciousness and political involvement further documents the shared ties among women of different races, ethnic backgrounds, and economic classes.

In Chapter 13, "The Development of Feminist Consciousness Among Asian American Women," Chow specifically analyzes how the intersection of race, class, and gender has shaped the lived experience of Asian American women historically, affecting the ways in which they develop feminist consciousness and the degree of their political activism. Her concept of feminist consciousness is one that is rooted not only in gender identity and order but also in racial and class structure. Chow also focuses on how the dialectics of multiple forces of oppression based on racial discrimination, economic exploitation, and male dominance in Asian American communities and the larger society generate cross-group allegiances and conflicting pressures. These dialectics shape the development of feminist consciousness and political participation among Asian American women in their communities during different historical times.

Surmounting the invisibility of southern Black women who played heroic and valuable roles in the civil rights movement is the major task undertaken by Bernice McNair Barnett in Chapter 14. She questions the traditional notion of leadership, "men led, but women organized." Significantly for theory-building, Barnett redefines the concept of leadership and argues that it is multidimensional and grounded in structural and historical settings. Her work demonstrates how the "triple constraints" of gender, race, and class structured Black women's leadership and participation in the civil rights movement. Although seldom recognized as leaders, these Black women were often the ones who initiated protests, selected strategies and tactics, and mobilized other resources necessary for successful collective action. Her work validates the paramount importance of working-class women at the grass-roots level who assume roles that "represent profiles in courage and suggest that they were *leaders* in their communities, *leaders* in the day-to-day fight against various forms of oppression, and *leaders* in the modern civil rights movement."

Both Chapter 15 by Cynthia Deitch and Chapter 16 by Kim M. Blankenship place their respective policy analyses of the 1964 Civil Rights Act's Title VII and of the Equal Pay Act of 1963 in historical and societal contexts. Deitch and Blankenship suggest a reconceptualization encompassing a *gendered, racist, and capitalist state* to understand how the state intervenes in race, class, and gender conflicts in a fragmented way, having differential impacts on women and racial-ethnic groups. Both authors describe the triumphs and the contradictions of the passage of these laws.

These policy analyses vary in their foci, approaches, and assessments. Whereas Deitch focuses on Title VII of the Civil Rights Act, Blankenship compares Title VII to the Equal Pay Act—one aimed at racial and the other at sex discrimination. Using a textual analysis, Deitch shows that when both the dominant and the oppositional discourses tend to construct "women," "Black," and "labor" as separate and distinct categories or constituencies, their underlying interconnections are distorted. Part of the task of a feminist analysis of interlocking systems is to deconstruct that discourse. Deitch's discussion fundamentally challenges current feminist state theories for not accounting for the racial character of the state and also takes issue with race and class theories that leave out gender. Her research is situated within the perspective that the state is not race-, class-, or gender-neutral. Her main premise is that the dichotomy of equality and difference and the analogy between race and gender have long dominated the discourse on women's rights in the U.S. This tradition has helped White women but marginalized Black women.

Deitch's insightful work illustrates that although race, class, and gender are all significant in shaping state action, they are not necessarily equally salient in determining specific policy outcomes. She points out that the mere fact that race, class, and gender interlock does not always mean that they are mutually reinforcing. In the case of Title VII of the 1964 Civil Rights Act, outlawing employment discrimination, state action expanding women's rights was proposed by the opponents of civil rights. Although Title VII supposedly benefits women, it does so within a framework that also reinforces women's subordination. Title VII invokes the interests of White women and racially disadvantaged men and at the same time limits racially marginalized women's rights. Finally, Deitch contends that the ways in which race, class, and gender intersect in shaping state action or oppositional movement politics are not constant or static. The dynamics between feminists and labor on the issue of the Equal Rights Amendment as well as the dynamics between women's rights and civil rights groups on issues of employment shifted significantly after passage of Title VII.

In Chapter 16, "Bringing Gender and Race In: U.S. Employment Discrimination Policy," Blankenship examines how race and sex discrimination bills confronted some of the problems facing American postwar capitalism yet simultaneously reinforced women's dependence on men in families. In theorizing about the state, Blankenship, like Deitch, critiques traditional class analyses for ignoring the gendered nature of public policy and also challenges the reliance of feminist state theory on a family wage ideology that historically has not applied to African American families. Blankenship argues that the Equal Pay Act and Title VII of the Civil Rights Act instituted two distinctive perspectives on employment discrimination and consequently two distinct systems for enforcement, one established for sex and the other for race discrimination.

Essentially, the resulting bifurcated discrimination policy fit the business needs of postwar capitalism in the U.S., the family wage ideology, and the position of African American men in families. During this period, employment discrimination threatened to impede not just the progress of capitalism but men's power in the family. As such, employment discrimination policy attempted to reestablish male familial power, an effort that took different strategies depending on race. Basically, the equal pay bill blocked women's access to a family wage by ensuring that men would not lose jobs to the cheap labor of women and thus lose their positions as heads of household. Similarly, race discrimination legislation was a way to challenge the low wages, high unemployment, and poverty rates among people of color, particularly African Americans, while relieving the squeeze on the tight primary sector labor market. It also represented a way to promote men of color as heads of families. In essence, the legislation was an effort to secure the family wage for men to reinforce male hegemony in both Black and White families. Though women of color were covered by both bills, they were the focus of neither.

In conceptualizing race, class, and gender as interlocking systems, authors of these chapters specify how they actually operate in affecting women's consciousness, leadership, and political activism in various historical contexts.

13 The Development of Feminist Consciousness Among Asian American Women

ESTHER NGAN-LING CHOW

Like other women of color, Asian American women as a group have neither been included in the predominantly white middle-class feminist movement, nor have they begun collectively to identify with it (Chia 1983; Chow 1989; Dill 1983; Loo and Ong 1982; Yamada 1981). Although some Asian American women have participated in social movements within their communities or in the larger society, building ties with white feminists and other women of color is a recent phenomenon for Asian American women. Since Asian American women are a relatively small group in the United States, their invisibility and contribution to the feminist movement in the larger society may seem insignificant.[1] Furthermore, ethnic diversity among Asian American women serves as a barrier to organizing and makes it difficult for these women to identify themselves collectively as a group. Because approximately 66 percent of Asian American women are foreign-born, their lack of familiarity with the women's movement in the United States and their preoccupation with economic survival limit their feminist involvement. The use of demographic factors such as size, ethnic diversity, and nativity, without an examination of structural conditions, such as gender, race, class, and culture, will not permit an adequate understanding of the extent of feminist activism of Asian women in the United States.

AUTHOR'S NOTE: Special thanks are given to Rita Kirshstein, Sherry Gorelick, Margaret Andersen, and Brett Williams for their constructive comments and suggestions on the early versions of this work.

251

What are the social conditions that have hindered Asian American women from developing a feminist consciousness, a prerequisite for political activism in the feminist movement? From a historical and structural perspective, this chapter argues that the feminist consciousness of Asian American women has been limited by their location in society and social experiences. A broader perspective is needed to understand the development of feminist consciousness among Asian American women who are subject to cross-group pressures.

The intent of this chapter is primarily conceptual, describing how gender, race, and class intersect in the lives of Asian American women and how their experiences as women have affected the development of feminist consciousness. The ideas are a synthesis of legal documents, archival materials, and census statistics; participant observation in the civil rights movement, feminist movement, Asian American groups, and Asian American organizations since the mid-1960s; interviews and conversations with Asian American feminists and leaders; and letters, oral histories, ethnic newspapers, organizational newsletters, films, and other creative writings by and about Asian American women.

GENDER CONSCIOUSNESS: PRECURSOR OF FEMINIST CONSCIOUSNESS

Gender consciousness is an awareness of one's self as having certain gender characteristics and an identification with others who occupy a similar position in the sex-gender structure. In the case of women, an awareness of femaleness and an identification with other women can lead to an understanding of gender power relations and the institutional control and socialization processes that create and maintain these power relations (Weitz 1982). Ultimately, gender consciousness can bring about the development of feminist consciousness and the formation of group solidarity necessary for collective action in the struggle for gender equality (Christiansen-Ruffman 1982; Green 1979; Houston 1982).

Being female, awareness of gender roles, and identification with other women are the major ingredients in building gender consciousness. However, it is necessary to understand the social contexts in which the gender consciousness of Asian American women has developed. Domination by men is a commonly shared oppression for Asian American women. These women have been socialized to accept their devaluation, restricted roles for women, psychological reinforcement of gender stereotypes, and a subordinate position within Asian communities as well as in the society at large (Chow 1985). Within Asian communities, the Asian family (especially the immigrant one) is characterized by a hierarchy of authority based on gender, age, and generation, with young women at the lowest level, subordinate to the father-husband-brother-son. The Asian family is also characterized by well-defined family roles, with father as breadwinner and decision maker and mother as compliant wife and homemaker. While they are well protected by the family because of their filial piety and obedience, women are socially alienated from their Asian sisters. Such alienation may limit the development of gender and feminist consciousness and render Asian women politically powerless in achieving effective communication and organization, and in building bonds with other women of color and white feminists.

In studying the majority of women activists who participated in various movements for oppressed groups, Blumberg (1982) found that participation in these movements affected the development of gender consciousness among women, which later, because of sexism in the movements, was transformed into a related but distinctive state of awareness—a feminist consciousness. For Asian American women, cross-group allegiances can hinder or facilitate the development of feminist consciousness and expand it into a more universal view. Women who consider racism and classism to be so pervasive that they cannot embrace feminism at the same level may subordinate women's rights to other social concerns, thus limiting the development of feminist consciousness. Women who are aware of the interlockings of multiple oppressions and who advocate taking collective action to supersede racial, gender, and class differences may develop a feminist consciousness that transcends gender, racial, and class boundaries.

AWAKENING FEMINIST CONSCIOUSNESS

In the wake of the civil rights movement in the early 1960s and the feminist movement in the mid-1960s, Asian American women, following the leads of black and Hispanic women, began to organize (Chow 1989; Ling and Mazumdar 1983; Lott and Pian 1979; Wong 1980). Initially, some better educated Asian American women formed women's groups to meet personal and family needs and to provide services to their respective organizations and ethnic communities. These groups, few in number and with little institutionalized leadership, were traditional and informal in nature and usually supported philanthropic concerns (Wong 1980). While there had been a few sporadic efforts to organize Asian American women around specific issues that did not center on women's concerns particularly (e.g., the unavailability or high cost of basic food, Angel Island, the World War II internment of Japanese Americans), these attempts generally lacked continuity and support, and the organization of Asian American women was limited as a political force. Nevertheless, these activities, as stepping stones for future political activism, allowed Asian American women to cultivate their gender consciousness, to acquire leadership skills, and to increase their political visibility.

In the late 1960s and early 1970s, many Asian American women activists preferred to join forces with Asian American men in the struggle against racism and classism (Fong 1978; Wong 1980; Woo 1971). Like black and Hispanic women (Cade 1970; Dill 1983; Fallis 1984; Hepburn et al. 1977; hooks 1984; Terrelonge 1984), some Asian American women felt that the feminist movement was not attacking racial and class problems of central concern to them. They wanted to work with groups that advocated improved conditions for people of their own racial and ethnic background or people of color, rather than groups oriented toward women's issues (Fong 1978; Wong 1980; Woo 1971), even though they may have been aware of their roles and interests and even oppression as women.

As Asian American women became active in their communities, they encountered sexism. Even though many Asian American women realized that they usually occupied subservient positions in the male-dominated organizations within Asian communities, their ethnic pride and loyalty frequently kept them from public revolt (Woo 1971). More recently, some Asian American women have recognized that these organizations have not been particularly responsive to their needs and concerns as women. They also protested that their intense involvement did not and will not result in equal participation as long as the traditional dominance by men and the gendered division of labor remain (Wong 1980). Their protests have sensitized some men and have resulted in changes of attitudes and treatment of women, but other Asians, both women and men, perceived them as moving toward separatism.

Asian American women are criticized for the possible consequences of their protests: weakening of the male ego, dilution of effort and resources in Asian American communities, destruction of working relationships between Asian men and women, setbacks for the Asian

American cause, co-optation into the larger society, and eventual loss of ethnic identity for Asian Americans as a whole. In short, affiliation with the feminist movement is perceived as a threat to solidarity within their own community. All these forces have restricted the development of feminist consciousness among Asian American women and their active participation in the feminist movement. (For the similar experience of black women, see hooks 1984.)

Other barriers to political activism are the sexist stereotypes and discriminatory treatment Asian American women encounter outside their own communities. The legacy of the Chinese prostitute and the slave girl from the late nineteenth century still lingers. American involvement in Asian wars continues to perpetuate the image of Asian women as cheap whores and exotic sexpots (e.g., images such as "Suzie Wong" for Chinese women, the "geisha girl" in the Japanese teahouse, the bar girls in Vietnam). The "picture bride" image of Asian women is still very much alive, as U.S. soldiers and businessmen brought back Asian wives from China, Japan, Korea, Vietnam and Southeast Asia, with the expectation that they would make perfect wives and homemakers. In the last few years, a systematic importation through advertisements in newspapers and magazines of Asian "mail-order brides" has continued their exploitation as commodities and has been intensively protested by many Asian American communities. Mistreatment, desertion, divorce, and physical abuse of Asian wives and war brides have been major concerns for Asian American women (Kim 1977). The National Committee Concerned with Asian Wives of U.S. Servicemen was specifically organized to deal with these problems.

The interlocking of race, class, and gender simultaneously forms the multiple systems of domination and meaning that shape the life experience and conscious development of Asian American women and, at the same time, creates dialectical forces that affect their identity politics, social alliance, and political empowerment. Lee (1971, 119) reported interviews with two Asian American feminists who reflected the mixed feelings of many Asian American women. One woman, Sunni, said:

> We are *Asian* women. Our identity is *Asian,* and this country recognizes us as such. We cannot afford the luxury of fighting our Asian counterparts. We ought to struggle for Asian liberation first, and I'm afraid that the "feminist" virtues will not be effective weapons. There is no sense in having only women's liberation while we continue to suffer oppression as Asians. (Lee 1971, 119)

Another woman, Aurora, took the opposite view:

> History has told us that women's liberation does not automatically come
> with political revolutions; Asian liberation will not necessarily bring Asian
> women's liberation. . . . We ought to devote our energies to feminism
> because a feminist revolution may well be the only revolution that can bring
> peace among people. (Lee 1971, 119)

When Asian American women began to recognize injustice and
became aware of their own strengths as women, some developed a
feminist consciousness, giving top priority to the fight against sexism
and for women's rights. Some sought to establish women's caucuses
within existing Asian American organizations (e.g., the Organization of
Chinese American Women), while others attempted to organize separately outside of the male-dominated Asian American organizations
(e.g., the Organization of Pan American Women and the National
Network of Asian and Pacific Women).

Asian American women began to organize formally around women's
issues in the early 1970s. Yet many of these groups were short-lived
because of lack of funding, grass-roots support, membership, credible
leadership, or strong networking. Those that endured included women's
courses and study groups sponsored by Asian American studies programs on college and university campuses, multilingual and multicultural service programs in women's health or mental health centers (e.g.,
the Asian Pacific Health Project in Los Angeles and the Asian Pacific
Outreach Center in Long Beach, the Pacific Asian Shelter for Battered
Women in Los Angeles), and writers' groups (Pacific Asian American
Women's Writers West).

A few regional feminist organizations have been formally established
and are in the process of expanding their influence and building up their
networks from the grass-roots level to the national one. These organizations include the National Organization of Pan Asian Women, the
National Network of Asian and Pacific Women, Asian American
Women United, the Philipino Women's League, the Filipino American
Women Network, the Vietnamese Women Association, and the Cambodian Women for Progress, Inc.[2] These feminist organizations aim to
advance the causes of women and racial and ethnic minorities, to build
a strong Asian sisterhood, to maximize the social participation of Asian
American women in the larger society, and to effect changes through
collective efforts in education, employment, legislation, and informa-

tion. The active participants in these feminist organizations are mostly middle-class Asian women, college students, professionals, political activists, and a few working-class women (Wong 1980).

RACIAL CROSS-PRESSURES

Joining the white feminist movement is a double-edged sword, for Asian American women experience oppression not only as women in a society dominated by men but also as minorities facing a variety of forms of racism that are not well understood by white feminists (Chia 1983; Chow 1982; Fujitomi and Wong 1976; Kumagai 1978; Loo and Ong 1982). The structural racism of American institutions, which limits access to resources, opportunities, prestige, privileges, and power, affects all the racial and ethnic minority groups of which Asian American women are a part (Chow 1989; Dill 1983; Hepburn et al. 1977; LaRue 1976; Loo and Ong 1982; Palmer 1983; Wong et al. 1979).

Legal restrictions, as one form of racism, were used to exploit cheap labor, to control demographic growth, and to discourage family formation by Asians. These restrictions also hindered the development of gender consciousness and political power among Asian American women. Since the mid-1850s, the legal and political receptivity to Asian Americans, both men and women, has been low in the United States (Elway 1979; Pian 1980). The U.S. immigration policies generally emphasized imported cheap labor and discouraged the formation of family unity. Some laws specifically targeted Asian American women. As early as the 1850s, the first antiprostitution law was passed in San Francisco, barring traffic of Chinese women and slave girls. The Naturalization Act of 1870 and the Chinese Exclusion Act of 1882 forbade the entry of Chinese laborers and their wives. In 1921, a special act directed against Chinese women kept them from marrying American citizens. The Exclusion Act of 1924 extended these restrictions to other Asians. It did not allow alien-born wives to enter the United States, but their children could come. This act thus separated many families until the passage of the Magnuson Act in 1943. The Cable Act of 1932 stipulated that American-born Chinese women marrying foreign-born Asians would lose their U.S. citizenship, although they could regain it through naturalization later. The passage of anti-miscegenation laws (e.g., the California Anti-Miscegenation Law in 1906), ruled unconstitutional by the U.S. Supreme Court in 1967, barred marriage between whites and "Mongolians" and laborers of Asian origins, making it impossible for Asians to find mates in this country. As a result, bachelor communities mainly consisting of single Asian men became characteristic of many Asian groups, especially the Chinese (Glenn 1983).

In spite of political pressures, repressive immigration laws, and restrictive and discouraging economic hardships, a few Asian women did come to the United States. Chinese women came in the 1850s, followed by Japanese women, who came during the late 1890s, and Filipino and Korean women who migrated in the early part of the twentieth century. These women were "picture brides," merchant wives, domestics, laborers, and prostitutes. In the popular literature they were generally portrayed as degraded creatures, cheap commodities, and sex objects who took jobs from whites, spread disease and vice, and corrupted the young. Descriptions of their sexist, racist, and economically deprived living conditions reveal a personal and private resistance marked by passive acceptance, suppression of feelings, silent protest, withdrawal, self-sacrifice, and hard work (Aquino 1979; Gee 1971; Jung 1971; Louie 1971; Wong 1978; Yung 1986).

The repressive immigration laws were repealed after World War II, and the number of Asian families immigrating to the United States increased. By 1980, the sex ratio was balanced for the first time in the history of this racial and ethnic group. Women now constitute 51 percent of the Asian American population (U.S. Bureau of the Census 1993). Although many of the repressive laws that conspired to bar the sociopolitical participation of Asian American men and women have changed, the long-term effect of cultural, socioeconomic, and political exploitation and oppression are still deeply felt, and there are new forms of discrimination and deprivation. The passage of the Immigration Reform and Control Act of 1986, setting restricted immigration quotas for family members of Asian American and Hispanic Americans, recalls earlier repressive legislation. As long as legal circumstances restrict the immigration of the mothers, daughters, and sisters of the Asian American women in the United States, the full development of their gender and feminist consciousness will be hampered.

The long history of racism in the United States has left its mark on feminism. Some Asian American women feel repelled by the racial composition, insensitivity, and lack of receptivity of some white women in the feminist movement (Fong 1978; Yamada 1981). They argue that white feminists do not fully understand or include issues and problems that Asian American women confront. White feminists are not aware of or sympathetic to the differences in the concerns and priorities of Asian

American women. Without understanding the historically and socially constructed experience of Asian American women, some white feminists have been impatient with the slow progress toward feminism of Asian American women.

Although some degree of acceptance of Asian American women and of women of color by certain segments of the white feminist movement has occurred, many problems remain (Bogg 1971; Dill 1983; Hepburn et al. 1977; hooks 1984; Lee 1971). Ideological acceptance does not necessarily lead to full structural receptivity. Conscious and rigorous efforts have not been made by many of those active in white feminist organizations to recruit Asian American women and other women of color openly, to treat them as core groups in the movement, and to incorporate them in the organizational policy and decision-making levels. Palmer (1983) points out that ethnocentrism is a major reason that feminist organizations treat race and class as secondary and are not fully accepting of women of color. hooks (1984) is critical of a feminist movement based on the white women who live at the center and whose perspectives rarely include knowledge and awareness of the lives of women and men who live at the margin. Dill (1983, 131) states, "Political expediency drove white feminists to accept principles that were directly opposed to the survival and well-being of blacks in order to seek to achieve more limited advances for women." The same is true for Asian American women.

Inconsistencies between attitudes and behavior of white women are highly evident in the "token" membership of minority women in some feminist organizations, which indicates simply a superficial invitation to join. For women of color, these frustrations of not being included in the "white women's system" run parallel to those experiences of white women who try to break into the "old boy's network." Consequently, Asian American women feel more comfortable making allies with women of color (e.g., the National Institute for Women of Color) than with their white counterparts. While there are interethnic problems among Asian American women and between them and other women of color, social bonding and group allegiance are much more readily established, and common issues are more easily shared on the basis of race, ethnicity and class. A separate movement for women of color may be a viable alternative for the personal development of Asian American women and other women of color and for their struggle for liberation and social equality.

ECONOMIC CONDITIONS
AND CLASS CLEAVAGES

Economic exploitation and class cleavages also account for the limited development of feminist consciousness and political activism among Asian American women. American capitalism demands cheap labor and the economic subordination of certain groups, resulting in a dual or split labor market. Certain minorities, primarily blacks, Mexican Americans, and Asian Americans, are treated as internal colonized groups exploited culturally, politically, and economically (Almquist 1984; Blauner 1972; Bonacich 1972).

Asian American women have lived in racially segregated internal colonies such as Chinatown, Little Tokyo, and Little Saigon. They have experienced social isolation, ghettoization, poverty, and few opportunities for personal growth and emancipation. Limited resources and lack of access to information, transportation, and social services have made them rely on their families for support and protection. They must also work to maintain them financially. Although there are some subgroup variations, the labor force participation of Asian American women is higher than the U.S. population in general (U.S. Bureau of the Census 1993). Many of them have worked in the secondary labor market sector, which is characterized by long working hours, low pay, and low prestige. According to the 1990 census, Asian Americans/Pacific Islanders tend to have a higher rate of families living below the poverty level than the U.S. general population (11.6 percent in contrast to 10 percent respectively), with Hmong, Cambodians, and Laotians experiencing poverty rates two to five times higher than other Asian American groups (U.S. Bureau of the Census 1993).

Cultural values that emphasize hard work and that place a stigma on idleness prevent Asian American women from not working and going on welfare even though they may be in need of public assistance. Asian American households generally have a greater number of multiple breadwinners per family than the general U.S. population. The financial burdens on many Asian American women pressure them to continue struggling for economic survival for the good of their families, sacrificing their own interests, and suppressing their feelings and frustrations even in the face of gender, class, and racial discrimination. They have little time to examine the implications of their economic situations; they do not fully understand the dynamics of class position; and they are not likely to challenge the existing power structure.

How economic and class conditions intersect with gender and race simultaneously to hinder feminist consciousness and political activism is evident for Chinese working-class women living in Chinatowns in many cities. Subject to the impact of internal colonization, their work world is an ethnic labor market, offering few good jobs, low pay, long hours, limited job advancement, and relative isolation from the larger society. The film *Sewing Woman* (Dong 1982) vividly describes the ways in which a working-class Chinese woman attempts to balance her family, work, and community responsibilities. Unionization of garment factor workers in Chinatown is only the beginning of a long process of political struggle for these women.[3]

In a study of Chinatown women, Loo and Ong (1982) identify the major reasons for the lack of integration of these working-class women into the feminist movement. First, Chinatown women do not relate comfortably to people outside their ethnic subgroup, which produces social distancing and alienation. Second, Chinatown women face varied problems, so no political movement that addresses only one of these will claim their allegiance. Third, although the women's movement aims to improve conditions for all women, the specific concerns of Chinatown's women are often not those of the women's movement. For instance, health, language, and cultural adjustment are major issues for low-income immigrant women. These are not the foci of the women's movement. Fourth, Loo and Ong demonstrate that the psychological profile of Chinatown women is not that of political activists. Chinatown women lack a sense of personal efficacy or control over outcomes in their lives, do not have a systematic understanding of the structural and cultural elements of a society that produces sexism, and tend to blame themselves for social problems. And finally, Chinatown women perceive themselves as having more in common with Chinatown men than with white middle-class women.

Although class cleavages exist among Asian American women, political allegiance is easily achieved because of racial bonding. Initially, highly educated and professional, middle-class Asian American women organized politically and involved themselves in the feminist movement, in some cases organizing Asian American women's groups (Wong 1980). Although some of these groups may tend to advance middle-class interests, such as career mobility, there have also been efforts to incorporate the needs of working-class Asian American women. Because race and ethnicity cut across classes and provide a base for political identification, economic barriers are much easier to overcome among Asian American women than between them and white women. Nevertheless, working-class Asian American women have engaged in their struggle and resistance in everyday life. There is still a great need to address issues concerning working-class Asian American women and to politically empower them through organizing.

CONCLUSION

Paradoxically, Asian American women (like other women of color) have much to gain from the white feminist movement; yet they have had a low level of participation in feminist organizations. Since feminist consciousness is a result as well as a source of feminist involvement, Asian American women have, by and large, remained politically inviable and powerless. The development of feminist consciousness for Asian American women cannot be judged or understood through the experience of white women. Conversely, white women's understanding and definition of feminist consciousness needs to incorporate the perspective of women of color. The same cross-pressures that hinder the political development of women of color could be a transcending political force that includes gender with their other consciousness and thus broadens political activism. It is concluded that Asian American women have to come to terms with their multiple identities and social locations and define feminist issues from the interlocking of these multiple dimensions. By incorporating race, class, and ethnicity issues along with gender, a transcendent feminist consciousness that goes beyond these boundaries may develop and a more inclusive sisterhood may be accomplished.

NOTES

1. According to the 1990 Census, there are 7.3 million Asian Americans and Pacific Islanders in this country, constituting 2.9 percent of the total U.S. population. Women constitute 51 percent of the total Asian American and Pacific Islanders population in the United States. For short, Asian American is used to include these two major groups in this paper.

2. *Philipino* and *Filipino* are acceptable terms used to describe people from the Philippines and can be used interchangeably. The U.S. Bureau of Census has used the term *Filipino* since 1900. Now *Filipino* is a commonly used term for the group and it also can be found in *Webster's Dictionary*.

3. Personal discussion with the union representative in Local 23-25 of the ILGWU in New York Chinatown.

REFERENCES

Almquist, Elizabeth M. 1984. Race and ethnicity in the lives of minority women. In *Women: A feminist perspective,* edited by Jo Freeman. 3rd ed. Palo Alto, CA: Mayfield.

Aquino, Belinda A. 1979. The history of Philipino women in Hawaii. *Bridge* 7:17-21.

Blauner, Robert. 1972. *Racial oppression in America.* New York: Harper & Row.

Blumberg, Rhoda Lois. 1982. Women as allies of other oppressed groups: Some hypothesized links between social activism, female consciousness, and feminism. Paper presented at the Tenth World Congress of the International Sociological Association, August 16-22, Mexico City.

Bogg, Grace Lee. 1971. The future: Politics as end and as means. In *Asian women,* edited by Editorial Staff. Berkeley, CA: University of California Press.

Bonacich, Edna. 1972. A theory of ethnic antagonism: The split labor market. *American Sociological Review* 37:547-559.

Cade, Toni. 1970. *The black woman.* New York: Mentor.

Chia, Alice Yun. 1983. Toward a holistic paradigm for Asian American women's studies: A synthesis of feminist scholarship and women of color's feminist politics. Paper presented at the Fifth Annual Conference of the National Women's Studies Association, Columbus, OH.

Chow, Esther Ngan-ling. 1982. *Acculturation of Asian American professional women.* Washington, DC: Department of Health and Human Services, National Institute of Mental Health.

―――. 1985. Acculturation experience of Asian American women, In *Beyond sex roles,* edited by Alice G. Sargent. 2nd ed. St. Paul, MN: West.

―――. 1989. The women's liberation movement: Where are all the Asian American women? In *Asian American women,* edited by Judy Yung and Diane Yen-Mei Wong. San Francisco: Asian American Women United.

Christiansen-Ruffman, Linda. 1982. Women's political culture and feminist political culture. Paper presented at the Tenth World Congress of the International Sociological Association, August 16-22, Mexico City.

Dill, Bonnie Thornton. 1983. Race, class, and gender: Prospects for an inclusive sisterhood. *Feminist Studies* 9:131-150.

Dong, Arthur. 1982. *Sewing women.* San Francisco: Deep Focus.

Elway, Rita Fujiki. 1979. Strategies for political participation of Asian-Pacific women. In *Civil rights issues of Asian and Pacific Americans: Myths and realities.* Washington, DC: U.S. Commission on Civil Rights.

Fallis, Guadalupe Valdes. 1974. The liberated Chicana—A struggle against tradition. *Women: A Journal of Liberation* 3:20.

Fong, Katheryn M. 1978. Feminism is fine, but what's it done for Asian America? *Bridge* 6:21-22.

Fujitomi, Irene, and Dianne Wong. 1976. The new Asian-American women. In *Female psychology: The emerging self,* edited by Susan Cox. Chicago, IL: Science Research Association.

Gee, Emma. 1971. Issei: The first women. In *Asian Women,* edited by Editorial Staff. Berkeley, CA: University of California Press.

Glenn, Evelyn Nakano. 1983. Split household, small producer and dual wage earner: An analysis of Chinese-American family strategies. *Journal of Marriage and Family* 45:35-46.

Green, Pearl. 1979. The feminist consciousness. *Sociological Quarterly* 20:359-374.

Hepburn, Ruth Ann, Viola Gonzalez, and Cecilia Preciado de Burciaga. 1977. The Chicana as feminist. In *Beyond sex roles,* edited by Alice Sargent. St. Paul, MN: West.

hooks, bell. 1984. *Feminist theory: From margin to center.* Boston, MA: South End Press.

Houston, L. N. 1982. Black consciousness among female undergraduates at a predominantly white college: 1973 and 1979. *Journal of Social Psychology* 118:289-290.

Jung, Betty. 1971. Chinese immigrant women. In *Asian women,* edited by Editorial Staff. Berkeley, CA: University of California.

Kim, Bok-Lim. 1977. Asian wives of U.S. servicemen: Women in shadows. *Amerasia Journal* 4:91-115.

Kumagai, Gloria L. 1978. The Asian women in America. *Bridge* 6:16-20.

LaRue, Linda. 1976. The black movement and women's liberation. In *Female psychology: The emerging self,* edited by Susan Cox. Chicago, IL: Science Research Associates.

Lee, G. M. 1971. One in sisterhood. In *Asian women,* edited by Editorial Staff. Berkeley, CA: University of California.

Ling, Susie, and Sucheta Mazumdar. 1983. Editorial: Asian American feminism. *Cross-Currents* 6:3-5.

Loo, Chalsa, and Paul Ong. 1982. Slaying demons with a sewing needle: Feminist issues for Chinatown women. *Berkeley Journal of Sociology* 27:77-88.

Lott, Juanita, and Canta Pian. 1979. *Beyond stereotypes and statistics: Emergence of Asian and Pacific American women.* Washington, DC: Organization of Pan Asian American Women.

Louie, Gayle. 1971. Forgotten women. In *Asian women,* edited by Editorial Staff. Berkeley, CA: University of California Press.

Palmer, Phyllis Marynick. 1983. White women/black women: The dualism of female identity and experience in the United States. *Feminist Studies* 9:152-170.

Pian, Canta. 1980. Immigration of Asian women and the status of recent Asian Women immigrants. In *The Conference on the Educational and Occupational Needs of Asian Pacific American Women.* Washington, DC: National Institute of Education.

Terrelonge, Pauline. 1984. Feminist consciousness and black women. In *Women: A feminist perspective,* edited by Jo Freeman. 3rd ed. Palo Alto, CA: Mayfield.

U.S. Bureau of the Census. 1993. *Asian and Pacific Islanders in the United States.* 1990. CP-3-5. Washington, DC: Department of Commerce.

Weitz, Rose. 1982. Feminist consciousness raising, self-concept, and depression. *Sex Roles* 8:231-241.

Wong, Germain Q. 1980. Impediments to Asian-Pacific/American women organizing. In *The Conference on the Educational and Occupational Needs of Asian Pacific American Women.* Washington, DC: National Institute of Education.

Wong, Joyce Mende. 1978. Prostitution: San Francisco Chinatown, mid and late nineteenth century. *Bridge* 6:23-28.

Wong, Nellie, Merle Woo, and Mitsuye Yamada. 1979. *3 Asian American writers speak out on feminism.* San Francisco: SF Radical Women.

Woo, Margaret. 1971. Women + man = political unity. In *Asian women,* edited by Editorial Staff. Berkeley, CA: University of California Press.

Yamada, Mitsuye. 1981. Asian Pacific American women and feminism. In *This bridge called my back: Writings by radical women of color,* edited by C. Moraga and G. Anzaldua. Watertown, MA: Persephone.

Yung, Judy. 1986. *Chinese women of America: A pictorial history.* Seattle: University of Washington Press.

14 Invisible Southern Black Women Leaders in the Civil Rights Movement: The Triple Constraints of Gender, Race, and Class

BERNICE McNAIR BARNETT

> Even in pre-civil war days, black [sic] women stood in the vanguard for equal rights; [sic] for freedom from slavery, for recognition of women as citizens and co-partners with men in all of life's endeavors. . . . However, because of the nature of American history, and particularly because of the institutions of slavery and segregation, the names and lives of black women leaders are all but unknown in American society—black as well as white.
>
> —Margaret Walker (in Sterling 1979, xvi)

Even while suffering the daily indignities heaped on them by their location in the structure of society, many southern Black women were much more than *followers* in the modern civil rights movement; many were also *leaders* who performed a variety of roles comparable to those of Black male leaders. Although seldom recognized as leaders, these women were often the ones who initiated protest, formulated strategies and tactics, and mobilized other resources (especially money, person-

AUTHOR'S NOTE: I gratefully acknowledge the assistance and generosity of civil rights activists who granted me an interview, gave me access to their personal papers, and in many other ways assisted me in this ongoing research. I also am grateful to *Gender & Society* reviewers for helpful comments on previous drafts of this chapter and to Margaret Andersen for invaluable editorial advice.

nel, and communication networks) necessary for successful collective action.

The diversity of their experiences is matched only by the diversity of their backgrounds. Sisters in struggle—sharecroppers, domestic and service workers, schoolteachers, college professors, housewives, beauticians, students, and office secretaries—all shed blood, sweat, and tears in the movement. In their homes, churches, voluntary associations, political organizations, women's clubs, college campus organizations, neighborhoods, and work groups, southern Black women of differing backgrounds shared a common desire for freedom from oppression. They courageously engaged in civil rights struggles in the South, a region historically characterized by a dangerous climate of legalized bigotry, labor exploitation, sexual assault and insult, and institutionalized violence and intimidation (Barnett 1994; Bartley 1969; Clark 1962, 1986; Dollard 1937; Nichols 1976; Raines 1977; Woodward 1955; Zinn 1964).

Although embedded within a structural context of three interlocking systems of oppression—racism, sexism, and classism—modern Black women activists in communities throughout the South nevertheless performed roles that by any standard would merit their being considered "heroes" and "leaders" of the movement. However, until recently, most of these women have remained anonymous, a category of invisible, unsung heroes of one of the most revolutionary periods of modern American history. During the period of more than thirty years of scholarship since the heyday of the civil rights movement, their experiences and their leadership roles have been neglected, virtually forgotten, or considered inconsequential or of secondary importance relative to those of men.[1]

The invisibility of modern Black women leaders and activists is in part a result of gender, race, and class biases prevalent in both the social movement literature and feminist scholarship. Social movement scholarship has focused almost exclusively on great men and elites as movement leaders (Jenkins and Perrow 1977; Oberschall 1981; Rose and Grenya 1984). Most of the leadership recognition and pioneering research covering the civil rights movement of the 1950s and early 1960s, in particular, has concentrated on the leading roles and charisma of elite male professionals within the Black community, such as ministers (McAdam 1982; Morris 1984; Piven and Cloward 1979; White 1990) or on the resource-providing role of elite supporters outside the Black community (Jenkins and Eckert 1986; McAdam 1982; Oberschall 1981; Zald and McCarthy 1979). Of those leaders within the Black community, Martin Luther King, Jr., has occupied the majority of that focus (Barnett 1990a; Branch 1988; Garrow 1986; White 1987, 1990). To a lesser but still significant degree, focus has been on three groups of Black men who can be categorized as the *Organization Heads-Positional leaders,*[2] the *Young Turks-Shock Troops,*[3] and the *Revolutionaries-Separatists.*[4] Thus, although the movement scholarship of sociologists typically has been critical of the "great man" theory of leadership (most forcefully promoted by Thomas Carlyle), it has nevertheless implicitly used this perspective in leadership analysis because it primarily has reported the activities and charismatic traits of male leaders.

Feminist scholarship, until recently, has focused almost exclusively on the activism of White women. Although White women performed crucial roles in the civil rights movement (Blumberg 1980a, 1980b; Evans 1979; Goldstein 1978; Rothschild 1979), Black women in communities and organizations throughout the South and other regions were struggling during a time that some feminist scholars initially labeled the "cessation" phase and "doldrums" for women's activism (Ferree and Hess 1985; Rupp and Taylor 1987). Black women and other women of color have been assumed to be uninvolved in feminist organizations or unconcerned about women's rights. However, challenging feminist accounts of modern women's organizing, my research (Barnett 1994) shows that in the 1940s and 1950s, southern Black women founded and led *collectivist feminist* movement organizations, the origins and patterns of which have been viewed as distinctive characteristics of White feminist organizing in the 1970s and 1980s. Lerner (1979, 81-82) has pointed out that women's liberation means different things to different women:

> There is much to be learned concerning the relationship between the ideology of woman's place and the reality of woman's place by examining the history of Black women. . . . Women, as all oppressed groups, perceive their status *relatively,* in comparison with their own groups, with previously known conditions, with their own expectations. White society has long decreed that while "woman's place is in the home," Black woman's place is in the White woman's kitchen. No wonder that many Black women define their own "liberation" as being free to take care of their own homes and their own children, supported by a man with a job. (emphasis in original)

Indeed, the critics of the prevailing research on Black women have pointed out three major biases: (1) a negative problem-oriented image that stereotypically connects Black women with various "pathologies" within the family, such as female-headedness, illegitimacy, teen pregnancy, poverty, and welfarism (Barnett, Robinson, and Bailey 1984; Hill Collins 1989; Higginbotham 1982; Scott 1982); (2) a middle-class orientation that excludes, ignores, or makes inconsequential the experiences of poor and working-class women, a large percentage of whom are Black (Bookman and Morgen 1988; Higginbotham 1982); and (3) an apolitical-nonleadership image of Black and poor women as political passivists or as followers and organizers, rarely as movement leaders (Barnett 1989, 1990b, 1994).[5] Thus the majority of existing research on modern social movement leadership has neglected the crucial roles of Black women and presented the erroneous image that "all of the women are White, all of the Blacks are men" (Hull, Scott, and Smith 1982).[6]

Yet emerging scholarship and recent recollections are beginning to illustrate that, far from being apolitical or inconsequential, Black women were crucial to the civil rights movement, that their personal experiences were unique as well as political, and that Black women's activism should be central to social movement scholarship (Barnett 1989, 1990b, 1994; Blumberg 1990; Crawford, Rouse, and Woods 1990; Robinson 1987). Giddings (1984, 5-6) points out that

> Black women had *a history of their own,* one which reflects their distinct
> concerns, values and the role they have played as both Afro-Americans and
> women. And their unique status has had an impact on both racial and
> feminist values. (emphasis added)

This chapter represents an ongoing effort to broaden the narrow traditional notion of leadership and to reconstruct American history to include the leadership roles of contemporary southern Black women in the modern civil rights movement in the United States. Specifically, the purpose of this essay is threefold. First, it explores the multiple dimensions of leadership and the particular leadership roles of southern Black women and men in the civil rights struggle. Second, it describes the experiences of selected Black women activists primarily from their own standpoint.[7] Third, it offers explanations for the lack of recognition and *non*inclusion of southern Black women in the recognized leadership cadre of the civil rights movement, within which the interlocking systems of gender, race, and class structured Black women's participation.

METHODS

This chapter is based on data analyzing leadership roles performed by Black men and women during the civil rights movement from 1955 to 1968. I systematically analyzed previously published oral histories and archival data, including published works on the civil rights movement, newspapers (e.g., the *New York Times*), and the personal papers of movement participants. Beginning in 1986, papers and other movement documents were examined at the King Center in Atlanta, Georgia; the E. D. Nixon Library in Montgomery, Alabama; the Southern Christian Leadership Conference in Atlanta; the Carter G. Woodson Institute for the Study of Civil Rights in Charlottesville, Virginia; the Schlesinger Library of Radcliffe College in Cambridge, Massachusetts; and the residences of civil rights activists.

In addition, I conducted personal interviews with leaders and activists involved in the civil rights movement, primarily in the South during the 1950s and 1960s. Based on the archival analysis, I developed a list of activists to interview and later modified the list because of the death or the unavailability of respondents. With the aid of many respondents from the original list, I also used a modified snowball sampling technique that was invaluable in obtaining information from less well-known activists. Thirty-four detailed, semistructured formal interviews plus ten informal interviews were conducted in 1987.[8] Three additional informal interviews were conducted in 1988. The length of interviews averaged one hour but some lasted three to eight hours. Interviews were conducted in homes, congressional and municipal offices, churches, law offices, a courthouse lobby following a city council meeting, and other places of work and special gatherings. This paper is based on a subsample of thirty-six activists interviewed (13 women and 23 men).

Initially, women as a category of activists were not my primary focus; however, as I became enmeshed in the research, I was amazed to stumble on new information about the role of a particular Black woman or to hear about the significance of certain women from the movement leaders and activists themselves. I realized that prior accounts of the civil rights movement had left these Black women leaders invisible. As I learned more about and from these women, I found it incredible that the experiences of these modern foremothers had been so long unrecognized, not only by academia and the general public, but also by most Black Americans.

TABLE 14.1   Rank Order of Most Important Leadership Roles
as Perceived by Civil Rights Leaders and Activists
Interviewed

Rank	Leadership Role	Total Weighted Score
1	Articulate/express concern and needs of followers	52
2	Define/set goals	25
3	Provide an ideology justifying action	23
4	Formulate tactics and strategies	14
5	Initiate action	13
6	Mobilize/persuade followers	10
7	Raise money	9
7	Serve as an example to followers and leaders	9
8	Organize/coordinate action	7
9	Control group interactions (e.g., conflict)	6
10	Teach/educate/train followers and leaders	5
11	Ability to not alienate colleagues and followers	3
12	Lead or direct action	2
13	Generate publicity	1
13	Obtain public sympathy and support	1

BLACK WOMEN ACTIVISTS
AND THEIR LEADERSHIP ROLES

Leadership is multidimensional and embedded within a structural context (see Barnett 1994). Thus the best approach to studying leadership in the civil rights movement is to analyze the specific roles that individuals or categories of individuals performed. For this study, I selected roles on the basis of three criteria: (1) their relevance to research on leadership; (2) their theoretical relevance, representativeness, and appropriateness to the study of leadership in a social movement; and (3) their theoretical significance and appropriateness to the study of leadership in the civil rights movement. On the basis of these criteria, I developed a list of thirteen leadership roles (see Table 14.1) and attempted to determine through archival and interview data the significance of these roles as performed by Black women.

Each civil rights activist was asked to review the list of roles that I had prepared and to add any other leadership roles that she or he considered important. Respondents added two roles (teach, educate, train followers and other leaders, and the ability to not alienate colleagues and followers) to the list. Almost all respondents indicated that they felt my list was "very good," "excellent," or "thorough." In addition, five respondents asked to have a copy of the list to use in their lectures on the movement. Hence, although I do not contend that the list is exhaustive, I feel that it is indicative of the multiple roles that leaders (both women and men) performed in the civil rights movement.

To determine the relative importance of these roles, respondents were asked to rank what they considered to be the first, second, and third most important leadership roles. Roles rated as first, second, and third were given weighted scores of 3, 2, and 1, respectively. Weighted scores for each role were summed, providing a total weighted score and measure of the sample's overall ranking and perception of the relative importance of the roles. As indicated in Table 14.1, articulating and expressing the needs and concerns of followers was ranked the most important role of leaders—far more important than other leadership items. In order of importance, the other leadership components ranked by respondents were defining and setting goals, providing an ideology, formulating strategies and tactics, initiating action, mobilizing followers, raising money, and serving as an example. That generating publicity and public sympathy were the least significant supports Morris's (1984) contention that the success of the civil rights movement was due more to forces indigenous to the Black community than to external support.

Within the community and local, state, and national organizations, Black women performed some of the most important of these roles. These women were diverse in terms of age, education, and socioeconomic background. For instance, although it propelled Martin Luther King, Jr., into a position of national recognition as the leader of the "new" movement, the Montgomery Bus Boycott was nevertheless an event that was initiated and sustained by Black women active in the community (Barnett 1989; Blumberg 1990; Crawford, Rouse, and Woods 1990; Garrow 1986; Robinson 1987). JoAnn Robinson, an English professor at Alabama State University, and other mostly educated women of the Women's Political Council (WPC), planned and organized the boycott. They also mobilized others by disseminating information about the boycott—mimeographing and distributing 35,000 leaflets following the arrest of Rosa Parks. With as much vigor and initiative as the middle-class women of the WPC, Georgia Gilmore, a cook and domestic worker, performed another of the most important ranked roles. To raise money to support the boycott, Gilmore single-handedly organized the Club From Nowhere, which she ingeniously named to avoid compromising White as well as Black patrons. In an interview with one of the women respondents who led the Montgomery boycott, I was told of the Club From Nowhere:

> The Club From Nowhere was truly something Mrs. Georgia Gilmore should be proud of. She headed this club and even lost her job working in a cafe when she started it. The club went door to door asking for donations and selling dinner plates and baked goods. . . . [They] made weekly reports on all the money collected from all kinds of people—Blacks and Whites. Some of these people didn't want it known that they had given money to the movement, so they wouldn't give Mrs. Gilmore and the other ladies checks that could be traced, only cash. And Mrs. Gilmore made sure they didn't tell anybody who had made the donations. That's why it was called the Club From Nowhere, so that none of the people giving the money could be in the least bit accused of supporting the movement.

During another interview, a respondent who was a high school teacher and one of the women leaders in the Albany Movement in South Georgia said of the roles of women educators as organizers among public school students:

> Many of us [Black women] were active in organizing young people—teen-agers—to attend meetings and demonstrations, almost anything that had to do with organized action. . . . We also helped organize voter registration in Albany. Although we worked closely with Dr. King, most of us were doing this long before he and SCLC came into town.

Ella Baker, one who advocated participatory democracy, was not only the quintessential organizer but also a great inspiration to those young college student leaders she advised and trained. While Baker, Daisy Bates, and Modjeska Monteith Simkins were training and organizing younger people, Septima Clark, Bernice Robinson, Dorothy Cotton, and other Black women educators were busy teaching and training older people. Had it not been for Clark and her mastery at teaching illiterate adult Blacks how to read and write, the 1965 Voting Rights Act would have been meaningless because Southern states had successfully disenfranchised the majority of the Black population by establishing gerrymandered districts, the grandfather's clause, all-White primaries, and high poll taxes and by requiring Blacks to pass literacy and citizenship tests before they were allowed to register to vote. Blackwell (1991, 332) emphasizes the difficulty of literacy tests because they "demanded that potential voters be able to read and recite from memory previously unspecified sections of either a state or federal constitution." Many respondents recalled Septima Clark with fondness, with respect, and with praise for her role as a teacher and organizer of adult "citizenship schools" throughout the South. One prominent male respondent, who himself was a "trainer" of civil rights field workers in the South, commented:

> Ah! What a human being. . . . There simply was no one like Septima Clark. Martin [King] knew and we all knew how courageous and how gifted this lady was. . . . She could talk on several intellectual levels. . . . As brilliant as she was, she could always get down on your level to make you understand and to make you comfortable. . . . Her role was essential . . . she taught citizenship.

Two follow-up questions were used to determine how these significant roles might relate to specific leaders. The first follow-up question asked of leaders and activists was, "Whom do you consider to be the ten most important individual leaders of the civil rights movement from 1955 to 1968?" [9] The responses to this question yielded three interesting, although not entirely unexpected, results. First, without a doubt, Martin Luther King, Jr., was considered by the sample to have been the most important individual leader of the movement. Second, the highest ranked leaders tended to be those who were ministers or heads and officers of the five major national rights organizations—the National Association for the Advancement of Colored People (NAACP), the Southern Christian Leadership Conference (SCLC), the Congress of Racial Equality (CORE), the Student Nonviolent Coordinating Committee (SNCC), and the Urban League—and therefore men. This was not surprising given that Evans (1979) and McAdam (1988) found sexism tended to relegate Black and White women to nonexecutive positions within the organizational structure of the civil rights and student movements. Although they have traditionally performed crucial roles and have been considered the "backbone" of the church, Black women historically have not been allowed the opportunity to become ministers, deacons, or trustees—the "heads" and top decision makers in the male-dominated hierarchy of the Black Baptist church (Cone 1989; Cone and Wilmore 1979; Grant 1990; Lincoln 1974). Indeed, in her longitudinal studies of Black women in the church, Grant (1990, 190) has observed Black women's continued subordination and has questioned ostensibly positive connotations assumed by the backbone analogy:

> On the surface this may appear to be a compliment, especially when one considers the function of the backbone in the human anatomy . . . [but] the telling portion of the word backbone is "back." It has become apparent to me that most of the ministers who use the term have reference to location rather than function. What they really mean is that women are in the "background" and should be kept there. They are really support workers. This is borne out by my observations that in many churches women are consistently given responsibilities in the kitchen, while men are elected or appointed to the important boards and leadership positions. While decisions and policies may be discussed in the kitchen, they are certainly not made there. . . . It is by considering the distinction between prescribed support positions and the policymaking, leadership positions that the oppression of Black women in the Black church can be seen more clearly.

Third, men were named and cited much more often than women. Of the eighty-one individuals who were named by respondents, twenty-two (27.2%) were women compared to fifty-nine (72.8%) men. Of those women named, nineteen were Black and three were White. Table 14.2 presents the names of the women cited, rank ordered by number of citations. Cutting across lines of race, ethnicity, and class, these women reflect a variety of backgrounds—teachers, college professors, cooks and domestics, secretaries, seamstresses, housewives, college students, journalists, lawyers, and sharecroppers.

The second follow-up question asked respondents to name the individual who *most effectively* performed the leadership role that she or he had considered first, second, and third most important. An effectiveness score for each leader was derived by summing the products of the frequency at which the leader was mentioned in association with each of the three leadership roles selected as most important by respondents and the weight assigned to the role based on its overall ranking (see Table 14.1). Roles ranked as first, second, third, . . . thirteenth in the overall respondent rankings were given weights of 13, 12, 11, . . . 1.5, respectively. Two roles having the same rank were given weights falling at the midpoint of the upper and lower weights. In instances when two leaders were named as most effectively performing a single role, the frequency was counted as 0.5 for each leader. In the two instances when a respondent named three leaders for most effective performance of a single role, the frequency was counted as 1 for the three-person group.

TABLE 14.2   Women Named Among the Most Important Leaders
of the Civil Rights Movement in the United States,
1955-1968, Rank Ordered by Number of Respondent
Citations[a]

Rank	Cited Leader	Number of Citations
7	Rosa Parks[b]	6
8	JoAnn Robinson	5
9	Ella Baker	4
10	Mary Francis Burks	3
10	Septima Poinsette Clark	3
10	Georgia Gilmore	3
11	Daisy Bates	2
11	Dorothy Cotton	2
11	Erna Dungee	2
11	Virginia Durr[c]	2
11	Dorothy Height	2
11	Diane Nash	2
11	Inez Ricks	2
12	Ann Braden	1
12	Johnnie Carr	1
12	Marie Foster	1
12	Thelma Glass	1
12	Hazel Gregory	1
12	Fannie Lou Hamer	1
12	Viola Liuzo	1
12	Constance Baker Motley	1
12	Idessa Redding	1

a. Because six respondents did not answer this question, these results are based on a sample size of 30 respondents, some of whom named fewer than ten persons. The list represents only the women who were named and does not contain the names of the many (59) men who were named.

b. Parks, Gilmore, Ricks, Hamer, and perhaps a few other women on the list would be considered working-class, if not poor, women. Gilmore, Ricks, and Carr are three of the most invisible of the many unsung heroines of the movement. Yet these invisible Black women struggled against injustices just as the middle-class, more privileged, and educated Black women, such as Clark, Robinson, and Bates did.

c. Although most Black women activists faced the triple constraints of race, gender, and class, it is important to point out that civil rights activism cut across lines of class, race, and gender. For example, Braden, Durr, and Liuzo were White women whose roles were considered significant, as evidenced by their being named by this sample of Black leaders interviewed.

Based on frequency of association with performance of ranked roles, total leader scores were obtained and resulted in the leader rankings presented in Table 14.3.[10] With a combined score of 739, Martin Luther King, Jr., and other male leaders overwhelmingly were ranked higher

TABLE 14.3   Leaders Rank Ordered by Frequency of Respondent
Association With Most Effective Performance of Roles
Considered Most Important

Rank	Leader	Total Score
1	Martin Luther King, Jr.	473.0
2	Ralph David Abernathy	88.0
3	Charles Sherrod	49.0
4	Local leaders	37.5
5	President of organizations	25.0
6	Women	23.0
7	E. J. Grant	21.0
8	E. D. Nixon	20.0
9	Joseph Lowery	19.5
10	Martin Luther King, Sr.	13.0
11	Hosea Williams	12.0
11	James Bevel	12.0
12	Vernon Johns	10.0
12	SNCC workers	10.0
12	NAACP lawyers	10.0
13	James Lawson	9.0
14	Georgia Gilmore	7.5
14	JoAnn Robinson/Mary Fair Burks/Sadie Brooks	7.5
14	Charles Jones/Slater King/Cordell Reagon	7.5
15	Rufus Lewis	5.0

than women, whose combined score was only 38. The two roles that
were associated with most effective performance by women cited as a
group and as individuals were mobilizing or persuading followers and
raising money. Interestingly, although fund-raising was Georgia Gilmore's
primary role, JoAnn Robinson and other Women's Political Council
members who were Montgomery Bus Boycott's key planners, strate-
gists, and organizers were cited only for their fund-raising role in the
movement. Perhaps respondents also considered these specific individual women when they cited "local leaders," "presidents of organizations," "SNCC workers," and "NAACP lawyers."

These findings support my contention that leadership is multidimensional; however, they also indicate that those role dimensions are
differentially valued or recognized and that those differences are *gender*
linked. For instance, the leadership role ranked the most important
(articulating and expressing concerns of followers) was de facto a *male*

role in both Black and White communities in the South. In terms of opportunities to perform this role, King and most other male leaders had a double advantage of being a Black minister who headed a church as well as a major civil rights organization. Typically, positional leaders and spokespersons were, in fact, males and may have been more highly respected not only by Black and White supporters but also by White opposition. Indeed, in the Southern social structure of the 1950s, women were expected to adhere to the adage that they should be seen, not heard, and in Southern Baptist churches women's place was "in the pew" and "out of the pulpit" (Grant 1990).[11] However, this does not explain why Black women activists who were also respected organizational heads, such as Robinson and Bates, were not recognized as were their male counterparts (Barnett, 1994). Hence, although they were extremely active in their professions and organizations and were indispensable to the movement, Black women's experiences were unique, unlike those of White women activists or Black men, because they were structured by triple constraints of gender, race, and class.

CONSTRAINTS OF GENDER, RACE, AND CLASS

Respondents were asked to elaborate on their response to this question: "Do you think the leadership roles performed by female leaders of the movement are as widely known or recognized as those of male leaders?" Every respondent interviewed, including the men, replied no. Respondent comments, as well as the archival data, illustrate how gender, race, and class are inextricably linked and make Black women's experiences in social movement participation and leadership comprise "a history of their own."

Economic and Family Constraints

Some respondents cited family responsibilities and economic concerns as two interconnected constraints on Black women's leadership. One respondent said:

> Many male leaders were really free to make contacts and relay information. Female leaders, many of whom were public school teachers, were constrained by family roles and more so by their jobs and the school superintendent. If he found out we were involved in any way, the superintendent could fire any of us any time he wanted to.

Not only were Black women in the South constrained by their jobs as public school teachers, but they were constrained as well by their jobs as domestics in White homes and public buildings. The Southern Black male minister, perhaps the traditional counterpart to the Black female schoolteacher, generally did not have the same constraints on him. He was not as economically vulnerable as his male counterpart or a domestic worker, such as Georgia Gilmore. He generally had to answer only to his Black congregation, not to the White school superintendent or the White mistress or master of the house. As Morris (1984) illustrated, the minister had relative job security.

One respondent involved in the Montgomery Bus Boycott recalled JoAnn Robinson's role in spite of her job vulnerability:

> JoAnn could have been fired from her job at the college [Alabama State University]. . . . Most of us [professors] had families to support and had to be careful about being openly involved. . . . JoAnn was something else . . . so determined . . . didn't even seem to be afraid if they [Black as well as White administrators] found out. . . . Hah! She used the mimeograph machines in the college to run off leaflets about the boycott!

Robinson and most other Black women professors involved in the boycott eventually were forced to resign from their positions at the university.

Economic vulnerability cut across socioeconomic class lines. When Georgia Gilmore's employer learned of her activism, she was fired from her job as a cook and blacklisted from other jobs in Montgomery. However, Gilmore was undaunted and continued her fund-raising activities by cooking and baking goods in her home, selling the items door-to-door, and then turning over all monies to the Montgomery Improvement Association, the boycott's male-dominated organizing unit. McCree Harris, a public school teacher, organized voter registration marches and Black high school and college students in Albany, Georgia. Harris, Bernice Reagon, and Shirley Sherrod took the initiative in the day-to-day fight for civil rights in the heart of Dixie. Harris and Sherrod risked losing their jobs just as Reagon, Diane Nash, and other college student activists placed their future livelihoods in jeopardy when they were jailed or suspended from college for leading protest campaigns.

In spite of economic retaliations, however, Black women continued their activism. When I asked one veteran leader why she refused to give up her membership in the NAACP and risk losing her more than thirty years' teaching retirement benefits, she described how she felt the day she met with the White male school superintendent who had summoned her to his office:

> I looked him straight in the eye and asked him: "Did any body tell you what color suit to wear when you got up this morning?" He said "No" in astonishment at my question. . . . So I told him I was not going to allow him or anyone else to tell me I could not be a member of the NAACP. . . . If I allowed them to do that, then I was giving them the right to tell me where to eat, what I should eat, what to wear.

Patriarchy in Black and White

Patriarchy was particularly prevalent in the South and structured White women's experiences as well as those of Black women. For instance, one respondent who led voter registration drives and whose husband was one of the most highly recognized SNCC leaders in the community, indicated that traditional gender stratification within Black society was a possible explanation for the neglect of women's roles:

> When you're dealing with Black men and women and the fragile position of Black males, you can expect that Black women, even though they might do all the work, will not be recognized as doing the work or leading anything. . . . In the South, women still look to men as leaders when women are actually doing the work. . . . A lot of this comes from traditions of the church and the male minister as the leader, the person whom you're supposed to obey. The movement was no different than anything else. Women obeyed and supported their husbands, looked up to them as leaders, and didn't take any credit even if it was offered. . . . Black women especially had to work hard, but *never ever* threaten the fragile position of their Black men. They still have to do this. (emphasis in original)

Another veteran civil rights leader interviewed suggested an explanation beyond traditional gender-role differences and expectations within the Black community and within the South. She pointed to the general problem of patriarchy that historically has constrained all women in American society:

> When Europeans came to America, women had to take a back seat to males. . . . Men didn't do the work that women did and yet they got all the praises. This European patriarchal influence is evident not just among

Blacks but also among Whites. . . . Women don't get credit and praised for
the work they do because that's how the White European tradition sets
things up.

One woman who was interviewed mentioned that Black women
activists encountered sexism when they tried to get funding from businesses, banks, and local governments. She indicated that many of the
community-based self-help projects that she organized and directed
were often not funded because she was a woman; those from whom she
solicited funds told her so in both overt and subtle ways. Although Daisy
Bates and Ella Baker both held key positions in established civil rights
organizations, each received little recognition as the "movement leaders" within the Black community, and both paid an economic price for
their leadership roles. Bates, head of Little Rock's NAACP, lost the
newspaper owned by her and her husband (Bates 1962). Because of
sexism within the movement, Baker was never given a permanent
position in SCLC or a salary comparable to the man who replaced her.
Yet one well-known male respondent, who held key leadership positions in both CORE and SCLC, recalled during our interview:

> You take women like Ella Baker, they were indispensable. . . . Besides Dr.
> King, she was one of my heroes. She had a way with us [young Black
> students]. . . . We knew she cared and she understood that we didn't want
> any compromises.

Baker, as Payne (1989) has pointed out, had a different style and
conception of leadership, one that contrasted sharply with that of the
Black Baptist ministers and other male organizations' heads. Advocating decentralized leadership and believing in participatory democracy,
Baker and perhaps many other Black women who desired or felt compelled to work behind the scenes did not want to be leaders in the
traditional sense of public spokesperson or central figure (Barnett,
1994). Baker once said of her style (in Cantarow and O'Malley 1980,
69-72):

> You didn't see me on television, you didn't see news stories about me. The
> kind of role that I tried to play was to pick up the pieces or put together
> pieces out of which I hoped organization would come. . . . I had no
> ambition to be in the leadership. I was only interested in seeing that a
> leadership had the chance to develop.

In fact, King and other heads of the top organizations resented Baker's insistence that the college students whom she organized to form SNCC remain autonomous from the established organizations and have no elitist leadership structure (Garrow 1986; Morris 1984). Fundamental differences in conceptions of leadership are also reflected in scholarship. In his study of women in the Mississippi Delta, for instance, Payne (1990) argues that "men led, but women organized" (p. 158). In response, I contend that we need to rethink the traditional notion of leadership, for organizing is one important leadership role, as the data here and elsewhere (Barnett 1994) have illustrated. The organizing activities of Baker and other Black women, especially working-class women at the grass-roots level, should be considered as valid leadership roles. Baker's loss of her SCLC job after so much hard work may have been a consequence of the gender- and class-linked differences in role valuation and recognition.

Baker's replacement also may have been a consequence of the tendency for women to be the initiators and to assume leadership roles in the early phase of revolutionary protest (which is "unstructured," "emergent," and "dangerous") and for men to take over and assume positions of leadership during the later phase of the protest. According to Blumberg (1990), in revolutionary conditions, there is a shortage of men and less competition for leadership roles, making it "possible and even necessary for women to act in ways usually closed to them, to take the initiative, or to manipulate their traditional gender definitions to fool the enemy" (p. 135). Certainly, the 1955 Montgomery Bus Boycott and the 1957 Little Rock school integration cases support this.

CONCLUSIONS

Black women in their homes, churches, social clubs, organizations, and communities throughout the South performed valuable leadership roles during the modern civil rights movement in the United States. Although race, gender, and class constraints generally prohibited their being the recognized articulators, spokespersons, and media favorites, these women did perform a multiplicity of significant leadership roles, such as the initiation and organization of action, the formulation of tactics, and the provision of crucial resources (e.g., money, communication channels, personnel) necessary to sustain the movement. Sisters in struggle, they were empowered through their activism.

The women briefly mentioned in this chapter are only a few examples of the Black women who were politically active in their communities and struggled for civil rights. In countless ways, Black women who lived and worked in the South in the 1950s and 1960s led the way in the fight against oppression, in spite of and because of their race, gender, and class. The blood, sweat, and tears that they shed generated protest and activism by other disadvantaged groups—women, farm workers, gays and lesbians, the handicapped, welfare rights activists—all of whom have been in profound ways the beneficiaries of the civil rights movement. The roles that they performed, whether at the grass-roots level or behind the scenes, represent profiles in courage and suggest that they were *leaders* in their communities, *leaders* in the day-to-day fight against various forms of oppression, and *leaders* in the modern civil rights movement.

However, further systematic research is needed to answer several questions: How did the personal-political experiences of women leaders differ from those of male leaders in the civil rights movement? What gender, race, and class differences existed in opportunities for as well as constraints on the performance of leadership roles? What were the significant roles of working-class Black women (such as Johnnie Carr, Inez Ricks, and Georgia Gilmore)? What were the neglected roles of Black women professionals, especially lawyers (such as Constance Baker Motley, Marian Wright Edleman, Eleanor Holmes Norton, and Gloria Richardson) and educators (such as Septima Clark, Dorothy Cotton, Modjeska Monteith Simkins, and Bernice Robinson)? How was the activism of Black women lawyers and educators facilitated or constrained by their professions and what impact did their activism have on their careers? Answering these questions will be a step toward broadening the patricentric and Eurocentric notions of leadership and making Black women central to movement scholarship and a way of ensuring that they will not remain invisible, unsung leaders in the civil rights movement.

NOTES

1. To be sure, the roles of a few antebellum and early Black women activists, such as Sojourner Truth, Harriet Tubman, Mary Church Terrell, Ida Wells, and Mary McLeod Bethune, are generally known; however, with the exception of Rosa Parks and perhaps Fannie Lou Hamer, the names and roles of most contemporary Black women who initiated, organized, and sustained the modern civil rights movement in the South during

the 1950s and 1960s are not. The recent Crawford, Rouse, and Woods (1990) edited volume is an exception to the prevailing neglect of these invisible women.

2. *Organization Heads-Positional leaders* included King as well as Roy Wilkins, Whitney Young, James Farmer, James Forman, Ralph Abernathy, Hosea Williams, Joseph Lowery, and other "establishment"-oriented leaders. These positional leaders were typically ministers who headed Black churches or the chief executive officers in the largest civil rights organizations, such as the NAACP, CORE, SCLC, the National Urban League, and SNCC. However, nothing approaching a comparable amount of attention has been given to the Black women activists who served as the backbone of the churches and who often held key positions in major organizations, such as Daisy Bates, who headed Little Rock's NAACP chapter and led the Little Rock Nine school integration in 1957; or Ella Baker, who was executive director of SCLC and who almost single-handedly organized SCLC's Atlanta office as well as SNCC in 1960; or Ruby Doris Robinson, who was executive secretary of SNCC in the 1960s.

3. *Young Turks-Shock Troops* were primarily idealistic, educated, highly motivated, and often impatient college students, such as John Lewis, Julian Bond, Bob Moses, James Bevel, and Stokely Carmichael. They were typically members of campus fraternities and student government associations as well as youth divisions of the NAACP, SNCC, and CORE (McAdam 1982; Morris 1984; Zinn 1965). However, relatively little recognition has been given to the women student leaders, such as Diane Nash, who led the Nashville sit-ins and was elected head of the central committee of the Nashville Student Movement, and Bernice Johnson Reagon, whose songs lifted the spirits of those involved in the Albany Movement in Georgia (Barnett 1989, 1990b).

4. *Revolutionaries-Separatists* included heads and members of organizations such as the Black Panther party and Black Muslims as well as CORE and SNCC after the mid-1960s, which advocated revolution, racial separatism, or armed self-defense. Although much has been written by and about H. Rap Brown, Eldridge Cleaver, Huey Newton, and Malcolm X, relatively little attention has been focused on the roles and experiences of women revolutionaries, such as Kathleen Cleaver, who was an officer in the Black Panther party, or Angela Davis, whose significance has been obscured, denigrated, or minimized by sensationalized media portrayals of her involvement in a "love relationship" that resulted in a courtroom shootout.

5. Franklin and Meier (1982) include only three women (Bethune, Wells, and Staupers) in their analysis of fifteen "Black leaders of the twentieth century." White does not include any woman in his 1987 studies of Black leadership in America from 1895 to 1968 or in his 1990 studies of Black leadership in America from Booker T. Washington to Jesse Jackson. Reflecting a narrow and masculinized conception of leadership and neglecting the multidimensionality of leadership, Payne (1990) argues in an otherwise insightful essay that Black "men led, but women organized" in the Mississippi civil rights struggle.

6. My research has found that Black women's movement organizations developed in large part as a result of both the race-based exclusionary practices of White feminist organizations, such as the League of Women Voters, and the gender-based hierarchies of male-dominated Black organizations, such as Black churches and the NAACP (Barnett 1994).

7. Hine (1986) and Collins (1989) demonstrate the value of understanding the historical experiences of Black women through their own voices and ways of knowing.

8. The names of respondents are not used in this chapter because they were promised anonymity.

9. Caution should be exercised in interpreting the results of responses to this question. Several respondents indicated that naming individuals would be "impossible" for them to do without leaving out someone, that it was an "academic question" that they did not care to try to answer, and that it would be an "injustice" to name just ten individuals because there were so many. Although one respondent proceeded to name individuals, he prefaced his list by indicating that the most important leaders of the movement really were "not individuals but groups of individuals," such as the staffs of organizations like SNCC, SCLC, and the NAACP. In answer to another question, one respondent indicated that "women" performed what he considered to have been the most important leadership roles. In addition, some of the respondents who did answer this question named fewer than ten individuals.

10. Although most respondents answering this question named specific individuals, some also cited groups, such as "local leaders" and "women."

11. Grant (1990, 192) vividly recalls how her research efforts were constrained in a Chicago Baptist church at the 1971 Annual Convocation of the National Conference of Black Churchmen by a "no women allowed in the pulpit" rule that she encountered when she attempted to approach the pulpit and place her cassette tape recorder near the speaker as Walter Fauntroy and other men had done.

REFERENCES

Barnett, Bernice McNair. 1989. Southern Black women of the civil rights movement: The unsung heroes and leaders. Paper presented at the annual meeting of Sociologists for Women in Society, San Francisco.

———. 1990a. Leadership and social change in the U.S. civil rights movement. Paper presented at the 12th World Congress of Sociology, International Sociological Association, Madrid.

———. 1990b. Sharecroppers, domestics, and the Club From Nowhere: Poor and working class women organizing for indigenous collective action. Paper presented at the annual meeting of the Southern Sociological Society, Louisville.

———. 1994. Black women's collectivist movement organizations: Their struggles during "the doldrums." In *Feminist organizations: Harvest of the new women's movement,* edited by Myra Marx Ferree and Patricia Yancey Martin. Philadelphia: Temple University Press.

Barnett, Bernice McNair, Ira Robinson, and Wilfrid Bailey. 1984. The status of husband/father as perceived by the wife/mother in the intact lower class urban Black family. *Sociological Spectrum* 4:421-41.

Bartley, Norman V. 1969. *The rise of massive resistance: Race and politics in the south during the 1950's.* Baton Rouge: Louisiana State University Press.

Bates, Daisy. 1962. *The long shadow of Little Rock: Memoir.* New York: David McKay.

Blackwell, James E. 1991. *The Black community: Diversity and unity.* New York: Harper-Collins.

Blumberg, Rhoda Lois. 1980a. Careers of women civil rights activists. *Journal of Sociology and Social Welfare* 7:708-29.

————. 1980b. White mothers in the American civil rights movement. In *Research in the interweave of social roles: Women and men*. Vol. 1, edited by Helen Z. Lopata. Greenwich, CT: JAI.

————. 1990. Women in the civil rights movement: Reform or revolution? *Dialectical Anthropology* 15:133-39.

Bookman, Ann, and Sandra Morgen, eds. 1988. *Women and the politics of empowerment*. Philadelphia: Temple University Press.

Branch, Taylor. 1988. *Parting the waters: America in the King years, 1954-1963*. New York: Simon & Schuster.

Cantarow, Ellen, and Susan O'Malley. 1980. *Moving the mountain: Women working for social change*. Old Westbury, NY: Feminist Press.

Clark, Septima P. 1962. *Echo in my soul*. New York: E. P. Dutton.

————. 1986. *Ready from within: Septima Clark and the civil rights movement*. Navarro, CA: Wild Tree Press.

Collins, Patricia Hill. 1989. The social construction of Black feminist thought. *Signs: Journal of Women in Culture and Society* 14:745-73.

Cone, James. 1989. Black theology, Black churches, and Black women. In *Black male-female relationships*, edited by Delores P. Aldridge. Dubuque, IA: Kendall/Hunt.

Cone, James, and Gayraud S. Wilmore, eds. 1979. *Black theology: A documentary history, 1966-1979*. Maryknoll, NY: Orbis.

Crawford, Vickie, Jacqueline Rouse, and Barbara Woods, eds. 1990. *Women in the civil rights movement: Trailblazers and torchbearers*. New York: Carlson.

Dollard, John. 1937. *Caste and class in a southern town*. New Haven, CT: Yale University Press.

Evans, Sara. 1979. *Personal politics*. New York: Random House.

Ferree, Myra Marx, and Beth B. Hess. 1985. *Controversy and coalition: The new feminist movement*. Boston: Twayne.

Franklin, John Hope, and August Meier, eds. 1982. *Black leaders of the twentieth century*. Chicago: University of Chicago Press.

Garrow, David J. 1986. *Bearing the cross: Martin Luther King Jr. and the Southern Christian Leadership Conference*. New York: William Morrow.

Giddings, Paula. 1984. *When and where I enter*. New York: Harper & Row.

Goldstein, Rhoda Lois. 1978. Wife-husband companionship in a social movement. *International Journal of Sociology of the Family* 8:101-10.

Grant, Jacquelyn. 1990. Black theology and the Black woman. In *Black male-female relationships*, edited by Delores P. Aldridge. Dubuque, IA: Kendall/Hunt.

Higginbotham, Elizabeth. 1982. Two representative issues in contemporary sociological work on Black women. In *All the women are white, all the Blacks are men, but some of us are brave: Black women's studies*, edited by Gloria T. Hull, Patricia Bell Scott, and Barbara Smith. Old Westbury, NY: Feminist Press.

Hine, Darlene Clark. 1986. Lifting the veil, shattering the silence: Black women's history in slavery and freedom. In *The state of Afro-American history*, edited by Darlene Clark Hine. Baton Rouge: Louisiana State University Press.

Hull, Gloria, Patricia Bell Scott, and Barbara Smith, eds. 1982. *All of the women are white, all of the Blacks are men, but some of us are brave: Black women's studies*. Old Westbury, NY: Feminist Press.

Jenkins, J. Craig, and Craig M. Eckert. 1986. Channelling Black insurgency: Elite patronage and professional social movements organizations in the development of the Black movement. *American Sociological Review* 51:812-29.

Jenkins, J. Craig, and Charles Perrow. 1977. Insurgency of the powerless: Farm workers movements, 1946-1972. *American Sociological Review* 42:248-68.

Lerner, Guida. 1979. *The majority finds its past: Placing women in history.* New York: Oxford University Press.

Lincoln, C. Eric. 1974. *The Black church since Frazier.* New York: Schocken.

McAdam, Doug. 1982. *Political process and the development of Black insurgency, 1930-1970.* Chicago: University of Chicago Press.

————. 1988. *Freedom summer.* New York: Oxford University Press.

Morris, Aldon. 1984. *Origins of the civil rights movement.* New York: Free Press.

Nichols, Patricia. 1976. Black women in the rural south: Conservative and innovative. In *The sociology of the languages of American women: Papers in southwest English.* Vol. 4, edited by Betty Lou Dubois and Isabel Crouch. San Antonio, TX: Trinity University.

Oberschall, Anthony. 1981. *Social conflict and social movements.* Englewood Cliffs, NJ: Prentice Hall.

Payne, Charles. 1989. Ella Baker and models of social change. *Signs: Journal of Women in Culture and Society* 14:885-89.

————. 1990. Men led, but women organized. In *Women in the civil rights movement: Trailblazers and torchbearers,* edited by Vickie Crawford, Jacqueline Rouse, and Barbara Woods. New York: Carlson.

Piven, Frances Fox, and Richard Cloward. 1979. *Poor people's movements: Why they succeed, how they fail.* New York: Vintage.

Raines, Howell. 1977. *My soul is rested: Movement days in the deep South remembered.* New York: G. P. Putnam.

Robinson, JoAnn Gibson. 1987. *The Montgomery Bus Boycott and the women who started it.* Knoxville: University of Tennessee Press.

Rose, Thomas, and John Grenya. 1984. *Black leaders: Then and now.* Garrett Park, MD: Garrett Park Press.

Rothschild, Mary Aikin. 1979. White women volunteers in the Freedom Summers: Their life and work in a movement of social change. *Feminist Studies* 5:466-95.

Rupp, Leila, and Verta Taylor. 1987. *Survival in the doldrums: The American women's rights movement, 1945 to the 1960's.* New York: Oxford University Press.

Scott, Patricia Bell. 1982. Debunking Sapphire: Toward a non-racist and non-sexist social science. In *All the women are white, all the men are Black but some of us are brave: Black women's studies,* edited by Gloria T. Hull, Patricia Bell Scott, and Barbara Smith. Old Westbury, NY: Feminist Press.

Sterling, Dorothy. 1979. *Black foremothers: Three lives.* Old Westbury, NY: Feminist Press.

White, John. 1987. *Black leadership in America, 1895-1968.* New York: Longman.

————. 1990. *Black leadership in America, from Booker T. Washington to Jesse Jackson.* New York: Longman.

Woodward, C. Vann. 1955. *The strange career of Jim Crow.* New York: Oxford University Press.

Zald, Mayer N., and John B. McCarthy, eds. 1979. *The dynamics of social movements.* Cambridge, MA: Winthrop.

Zinn, Howard. 1964. *The southern mystique.* New York: Alfred A. Knopf.
———. 1965. *SNCC: The new abolitionists.* 2d ed. Boston: Beacon.

PAPER COLLECTIONS

Papers of Septima Clark, Charleston, SC.
Martin Luther King, Jr., Papers, King Center, Atlanta, GA.
E. D. Nixon Papers, E. D. Nixon Library, Montgomery, AL.
Papers of the Southern Christian Leadership Conference, Atlanta, GA.
Papers of the Women's History Collection and of the Black Women's Oral History Project of the Schlesinger Library, Radcliffe College, Cambridge, MA.
Papers of the Carter G. Woodson Institute for the Study of Civil Rights, Charlottesville, VA.

15 Gender, Race, and Class Politics and the Inclusion of Women in Title VII of the 1964 Civil Rights Act

CYNTHIA DEITCH

> On page 68, line 23, after the word "religion," insert the word "sex."
> (*Congressional Record,* February 8, 1964, 2577)[1]

The reading of the preceding amendment in Congress was met by laughter. Although it was introduced as a joke and a tactic to defeat or weaken civil rights legislation, the inclusion of the word *sex* in Title VII of the 1964 Civil Rights Act became the legal basis for most gender discrimination policy in the United States (Brauer 1983; Hoff-Wilson 1987; Robinson 1979). This chapter analyzes the interaction of the political dynamics of race, class, and gender in the making of landmark gender discrimination policy. By *political dynamics,* I mean oppositional movements, policy conflicts within the state, and the construction of patterns of meaning in the dominant and oppositional discourse. The discussion proceeds on two levels. The first analyzes the historical context and political actions that produced the policy outcome. The second considers the conflict at the level of discourse through a textual analysis of the actual debate.

A dichotomy between equality versus difference and an analogy between race and gender have long dominated the discourse on women's rights in the United States. King (1988) suggests that the race-gender analogy historically has helped White women mobilize for their rights but it has also made Black women invisible. We shall see that this

288

applies to the conditions surrounding the inclusion of gender in Title VII. An equality-versus-difference debate has characterized conflicting feminist strategies.[2] The equality-versus-difference dichotomy equates equality with sameness and thereby defines the demand for equality as incompatible with the recognition of difference (MacKinnon 1989; Scott 1988). Both the dichotomy and the analogy are relevant for the analysis of gender politics in Title VII.

To understand state action on gender in the case of Title VII, a conceptualization of a gendered, racial, capitalist state is needed. Several recent theoretical perspectives on the state offer pieces of a useful framework but none is sufficient to stand alone. Feminist theories that conceptualize the state as both patriarchal and capitalist (e.g., Connell 1990; Eisenstein 1984; MacKinnon 1989) have not adequately addressed the racial character of the U.S. state. Theories that account for the race and class character of the state (e.g., Greenberg 1980; Omi and Winant 1986) are silent on gender. State autonomy theories (e.g., Orloff and Skocpol 1984; Skocpol 1985) explain the importance of political interests and conflicts in shaping policy in the absence of social demand, but these analyses often tend, implicitly, to treat the capitalist state as race and gender neutral.[3] Despite individual shortcomings, taken together these theories all contribute to an understanding of how the state actively intervenes in race, gender, and class conflicts, but not always in a unified way. The state itself is increasingly the site of these conflicts. State policy making helps shape gender, race, and class relations and the state itself is structured by those relations. When gender policy is made, it is made in the context of the race and class as well as gender dynamics of the moment. At a juncture when racial conflicts are at a point of rupture, as in 1964, gender policy is marked by that conflict.

THE GENDER DISCRIMINATION
AMENDMENT TO TITLE VII

In contrast to the broader civil rights bill of which it was a part, the specific enactment of the gender discrimination provision of Title VII was *not* a response to growing popular demand (Burstein 1985; Robinson 1979). Congresswoman Edith Green noted that

there was not one word of testimony in regard to this amendment given before the Committee on the Judiciary of the House, or on the Committee on Education and Labor of the House, where this bill was considered. . . .

There was not one organization in the entire United States that petitioned either one of these committees to add this amendment to the bill. (*Congressional Record* 1964, 2582)

A small group of feminists, some associated with the National Woman's Party (NWP), did lobby behind the scenes and did keep a careful watch throughout the legislative process. A handful of congresswomen advocated for the gender amendment to Title VII.[4] These relatively few women played a crucial role and the amendment would not have been included without the women's effort (Bird 1968; Brauer 1983; Freeman 1975; Harrison 1988; Robinson 1979; Rupp and Taylor 1987). Most analysts concur, however, that this small group lacked the clout, visibility, popular support, organization, or numbers to have successfully lobbied for such legislation under other circumstances. To understand why Congress acted as it did on women's rights, in the relative absence of significant external pressure or popular demand, it is necessary to examine the political stakes involved for those in power.

There was an overwhelming sense of national urgency for federal action on civil rights in 1964. Domestic and international media attention exposing police violence against the civil rights movement and the southern Black population was a major source of embarrassment to the U.S. government. This potentially threatened the legitimacy of the incumbent regime in a presidential election year. Failure to act and failure to deliver promised legislation could reflect very badly on the incumbent president (Johnson) in his bid for reelection that year. Failure to pass promised civil rights legislation could hurt the Democratic party's chances of remaining the party in power at the national level. Senators and representatives up for reelection in 1964 were aware that public opinion had moved in favor of federal action to prohibit race discrimination in employment and that their action on this issue could influence voters (Burstein 1985).

The battle for civil rights legislation in Congress in 1964 also reflected regional power struggles within the Democratic Party that had been building for several decades (Piven and Cloward 1979, 180-85). Southern Democrats led the opposition to civil rights within Congress, while northern and liberal Democrats organized the support. Given the intransigent opposition of southern Democrats, the formation and maintenance of a bipartisan coalition within Congress in support of civil rights was crucial to the passage of the bill. This meant that some of the pro-business Republicans were allied with pro-labor Democrats. Title

VII, as the only section of the bill to deal with employment practices, had the potential of dividing the coalition.

The southern strategy for opposing the entire civil rights bill was to attempt to splinter the bipartisan coalition supporting the bill, delay the vote by prolonged debate, and weaken the bill with extraneous amendments that would make enforcement difficult (Congressional Quarterly Staff 1968; Robinson 1979). Title VII was the last major section of the bill debated before the House voted on the bill as a whole. The gender discrimination amendment to Title VII fit the southern strategy: It was potentially divisive, it could sidetrack debate, and it promised to complicate matters for the enforcement agency (the Equal Employment Opportunity Commission, or EEOC) created by Title VII. When Representative Howard Smith of Virginia, a conservative southern Democrat and a leader of the opposition to the bill, proposed the insertion of the word "sex" at several points in the text of Title VII, he played the amendment as a joke. Laughter ensued and jokes were made by men of both parties and on both sides of the civil rights issue (Bird 1968; *Congressional Record* 1964; Freeman 1975; Robinson 1979; Whalen and Whalen 1985). When the civil rights bill passed the House, two days after the debate over the gender amendment, all but one of the men who had voted for the amendment voted against the whole bill (Freeman 1991).

Freeman (1991) suggests that it was not simply a case of Smith or the southern Democrats using the gender amendment in an effort to defeat the bill. The idea for the amendment was initiated by the NWP, and women advocates strategically asked Smith to introduce the amendment because they believed that would increase the number of votes (Freeman 1991). Nonetheless, it was the lack of primacy and lack of seriousness accorded women's rights by those in power and the inability to imagine that women would mobilize to use their rights that facilitated state action on gender equality.

Class politics also played a role in the inclusion of gender in the Civil Rights Act, interwoven with those of race and gender in a somewhat complex pattern. Equal employment opportunity (EEO) legislation, prohibiting employment discrimination based on race, religion, and national origin—but not gender—had been pending in Congress for several decades (Burstein 1985). Historically, business opposed EEO and labor supported it. Title VII of the 1964 civil rights bill represented the most recent and best chance to pass EEO legislation.

Organized business interests were noticeably absent during the many months of intense lobbying on the 1964 civil rights bill (Congressional Quarterly Staff 1968). Southern business elites were divided on civil rights issues. Newer ascending urban and industrial sectors of southern capital had little stake in maintaining the old racial order, whereas traditional southern business interests resisted change (Bloom 1987; Greenberg 1980). At the national level, organized labor supported civil rights legislation. Union members in the South, however, were almost exclusively White, and some union locals had, at times, threatened to leave the AFL-CIO if it continued to support civil rights legislation (Greenberg 1980).

The gender amendment added a new twist to the class dynamics just described. Some supporters and some opponents of the gender amendment viewed it as a possible alternate route in the direction of an Equal Rights Amendment (ERA). The ERA had been introduced in Congress (but not passed) repeatedly since 1923. Business interests tended to support the ERA and labor opposed it in that period. Both sides believed that the ERA could be used to strike down state-level protective labor legislation for women. Organized labor, social welfare advocates, and many traditional women's organizations opposed the ERA because they feared that it would take away needed protection for women, especially for the most economically vulnerable women. Republicans and business interests historically supported the ERA because they believed it would invalidate state laws restricting business prerogatives through protective legislation for women. Although there was not a roll call vote on the gender amendment to Title VII, Freeman (1991) presents evidence to suggest that it was the Republicans who provided the critical margin of votes to pass the amendment.

To explain policy innovation in the absence of popular demand, Orloff and Skocpol (1984) suggest that elected and appointed officials may take new policy initiatives ahead of social demands if doing so may further their own organizational or career interests, if existing state capacities are readily adapted for the new initiatives, and if they expect their action may advantage them in struggles with political competitors. These conditions apply to the behavior of Congress on the gender amendment. Gender policy, and to an extent race policy, was used by state actors to further their own political agendas in the electoral arena and in interparty as well intraparty power struggles. Class interests were also involved but were less salient than questions of race.

Omi and Winant (1986) also analyze conflicts within the state to explain policy change. Under "normal" conditions of what Omi and Winant (1986) term "unstable equilibrium," state institutions routinize the enforcement and organization of the prevailing racial order. When the unstable equilibrium is disrupted, as with the emergence of a mass-based racial movement in the 1960s, competition and conflict within the state are heightened. Some groupings within the state move to accommodate the challenging forces, whereas others resist change. In part because of instability and divisions within the state, the civil rights movement of the 1960s resulted in a series of reforms. The reforms only partially met movement demands but in the process restored relative unity within the state and an unstable equilibrium in the racial order. The movement and the reforms also changed the rules of the game, opening up a new political terrain for a variety of new social movements in the 1960s and 1970s.

The women activists who wanted gender discrimination included in Title VII were able to take advantage of the disrupted equilibrium and consequent heightened conflict over race within the state. Under the race-gender analogy, the rules of the game were rewritten to promise to cover gender as well as racial conflict; that change provided the women's movement, when it mobilized, an important new legal terrain.

MacKinnon (1989) observes that the state is patriarchal in that it operates from the standpoint of men; it sees women as men do; it makes law and constructs meaning consistent with men's experiences. Given this standpoint, MacKinnon suggests, when the state makes policy that supposedly benefits women or expands women's rights, it does so within a framework that also reinforces women's subordination. Women, however, may still gain from such laws, according to MacKinnon, and the contradictory character of gender policy-making may provide political openings for feminism. In the case of the gender amendment to Title VII, the processes that MacKinnon describes are evident in the examination of the text of the debate that follows. This analysis also reveals the standpoint of the state as race and class specific as well as patriarchal.

TEXTUAL ANALYSIS OF THE CONGRESSIONAL DEBATE

Several aspects of a postmodernist approach are useful for a textual analysis of the debate. Using this framework, texts (not necessarily written) are analyzed for specific historical and contextual meanings and for what they reveal about how meanings change and how power operates. Discourse is a historically, socially, and institutionally specific structure of statements, terms, categories, and beliefs (Scott 1988, 34). A focus on difference is employed to reveal the underlying unity or interdependence of what appears to be a fixed binary opposition (Scott 1988, 37). In this approach, it is not necessary to figure out what the author of a text, or a speaker, "really meant." Rather, the point is to see how meanings are constructed and constituted within and through texts and in relation to other texts (Lemert 1990). Examination of the structure of an argument, the categories constructed, the meanings invoked, and the historical context in which the text was produced often demonstrates that the text conveys a political position or viewpoint not evident in more traditional analyses of the overt content.

In the case of the gender amendment to Title VII, the debate itself, at one level, is about the insertion of a word into a text and how this will affect the meaning of other related texts. Whereas historians have speculated about the "real" motives and intentions of Representatives Howard Smith and Martha Griffiths (Brauer 1983; Freeman 1991; Robinson 1979), I am more interested in analyzing the discursive strategies they used. My reading of the debate reveals that the two groups of men who appear to speak in opposition to each other—they espouse opposite positions on the civil rights issue and on the gender amendment —are acting in consort to make a joke of women's rights and to reinforce women's subordination. In the debate, the race-gender analogy operates to deny the discrimination in employment faced by African American women and to construct the category *women* to include only White women. It was not just conservative men who did this, but also liberal men and feminist women.

Men Supporting the Amendment

The men who spoke in favor of the amendment were all southern Democrats. They employed three discursive strategies. These were to show that they were joking, to show that they were chivalrous and protective toward the weaker or "minority sex," and to protest that, without the amendment, White Christian women would be treated unfairly.

The amendment was introduced by Howard Smith. His attempt to use the gender amendment to make a joke worked well. His statement was interrupted several times by laughter and according to some reports the proceedings almost ground to a halt because of the laughter (Bird 1968). In his opening remarks, as supposed evidence of the just grievances of the "female minority," Smith read from a letter he reportedly received from a woman who complained that the numerical "imbalance of the sexes" denied spinster women their "right to a nice husband and family" (*Congressional Record* 1964, 2577). In the letter, she asked that Congress act to protect that right and remedy the imbalance. Reading this letter clearly demonstrated that Smith's intention was to make a joke, even while he stated how serious he was about his "little amendment." The letter suggests that women's legitimate rights and concerns are satisfied in marriage. Smith's use of the letter also might be interpreted as a commentary on the foolishness, as he perceived it, of people thinking that Congress should remedy imbalances produced by nature through legislation.

By making the gender discrimination amendment a joke, Smith accomplished several things. He rendered the idea of equality for women laughable, thus reinforcing women's subordination in the very act of extending women's legal rights. Proposing that gender discrimination was equivalent in some sense to discrimination based on race or religion was apparently comical or ludicrous to many of the men present. That everyone was aware of his purposes also marked the proposal as a joke. The subordination of women was commonly understood as a taken-for-granted part of both nature and culture. Equality for women was thus contrary to biology and tradition. Many men viewed women this way, whether they were for or against equality for Blacks. For Smith and other opponents of civil rights legislation, the attempt to legislate racial equality also went against nature and culture.

This reading is consistent with Brauer (1983, 48), who suggests that Smith's comments were aimed at satirizing the logic behind the civil rights bill as a whole, which in the view of many conservatives was attempting to defy human nature. In this sense the race-gender analogy was used to ridicule the civil rights bill as a whole. If the idea of equality for women was not viewed as at least somewhat incongruous, the joke would not have worked and the gender discrimination amendment would not have been an effective way to belittle the race discrimination legislation. Furthermore, mention of the three-letter word *s-e-x* could be counted on to elicit jokes and innuendos, which it regularly did, in public discussion of Title VII, even for several years after the bill was passed (Bird 1968).

Smith's support of the amendment was not inconsistent with his previous stands on related issues. Although Smith had not supported the Equal Pay Act a year earlier, he had spoken in support of a women's rights amendment to previously proposed EEO legislation eight years earlier, and he had sponsored the ERA as early as 1943. As Rupp and Taylor (1987) explain, it was not unusual at that time for someone like Smith to oppose civil rights legislation but support the ERA.

Presenting the amendment as a gesture of chivalry was another discursive strategy of the southern men, as reflected by Congressman Tuten of Georgia,

> Some men in some areas of the country might support legislation which would discriminate against women, but never let it be said that a southern gentleman would vote for such legislation. (*Congressional Record* 1964, 2583)

The combination of the joke and the chivalry was used to reinforce patriarchal attitudes toward women in the process of ostensibly promoting women's rights.

An appeal to race and ethnicity was linked to the appeal to chivalry in regard to White women, as, historically, it often had been in the White discourse on race in the South. The implied meaning was to justify efforts to keep African Americans in their place in the name of protecting White womanhood. The effect was also to appropriate part of the language and logic of civil rights legislation to satirize the legislation and to reinforce ideas of race and gender inequality. The following are remarks by three different southern Democratic men:

> Unless this amendment is adopted, the white women of this country would be drastically discriminated against in favor of a Negro woman. (*Congressional Record* 1964, 2583)

> It is incredible to me that the authors of this monstrosity—whomever they are—would deprive the white woman of mostly Anglo-Saxon or Christian heritage equal opportunity before the employer. I know this Congress will not be party to such an evil. (*Congressional Record* 1964, 2583)

> There can be no plausible reason that a white woman should be deprived of an equal opportunity to get a job simply because of her sex and a colored woman obtain that position because of her preferential rights as contained in this bill. (*Congressional Record* 1964, 2584)

Men Opposing the Amendment

Whereas the first group of men used the discourse of chivalry to argue in favor of the amendment, other men used it to argue against the amendment. Congressman Thompson of New Jersey, for example, stated:

We do not want to go so fast and so far that the old rule of abandoning ship will be changed and the woman will have to take her place in line rather than to go first. (*Congressional Record* 1964, 2582)

Men who supported the civil rights bill joined in the joking as they objected to the amendment. Leading the opposition, Emanual Celler of New York quipped, "You know, the French have a phrase for it . . . *vive la difference,*" and "Lives there a man with hide so tough / Who says two sexes are not enough?" Addressing the 80-year-old Smith, 75-year-old Celler remarked, "It is rather anomalous that two men of our age should be on the opposite sides of this question." Smith rejoined, "I am sure we are not" (*Congressional Record* 1964, 2577-78).

On a more serious note, Celler warned against a revolution in gender roles:

Imagine the upheaval that would result from adoption of blanket language requiring total equality. . . . What would become of traditional family relationships? . . . You know the biological differences between the sexes. In many States we have laws favorable to women. Are you going to strike those laws down? This is the entering wedge. . . . The list of foreseeable consequences, I will say to the committee, is unlimited. (*Congressional Record* 1964, 2578)

Other men speaking in opposition to the amendment made much more moderate claims, generally arguing that the amendment was ill conceived and inappropriate for one or more of the following reasons (*Congressional Record* 1964, 2577-84): (1) this was not the appropriate time or place to introduce legislation on discrimination against women; (2) civil rights legislation was the priority of the day—the amendment would weaken the bill and harm its chances of passage; (3) the existing language of this bill and other laws were sufficient to protect women; (4) discrimination against women is not analogous to race discrimination, either because women are not really discriminated against or because women need special protective legislation because of biological difference; (5) a number of respected women and women's organizations, which supported women's rights in principle, opposed such an amendment; and (6) the amendment was a back door effort on behalf of the ERA and, like the ERA, would lead to the invalidation of state-level protective legislation covering women's employment. These objections reflect a mix of gender ideologies and political agendas.

Women Supporting the Amendment

Women speaking in support of the amendment made a point of rejecting gestures of chivalry or protection from men. In doing so, they rejected the words of men who supported the amendment as a gesture of protection for the "weaker sex," and they rejected the words of men who opposed the amendment on the grounds that women needed protective legislation. For example, after making many of the classic arguments against protective legislation, pointing out that such policies "prevent women from going into higher salary brackets," (*Congressional Record* 1964, 2581) Katherine St. George (Republican, New York) declared:

> We do not want special privileges. We do not need special privileges. We outlast you—we outlive you—we nag you to death. So why should we want special privileges? (*Congressional Record* 1964, 2581)

Martha Griffiths (Democrat, Michigan) presented the longest and most detailed argument for the amendment. Rejecting the joke, she asserted, "I presume that if there had been any necessity to have pointed out that women were a second-class sex, the laughter would have proved it" (*Congressional Record* 1964, 2578). She proceeded with her remarks as follows:

> I rise in support of the amendment primarily because I feel as a white woman when this bill has passed this House and the Senate and has been signed by the President that white women will be last at the hiring gate. (*Congressional Record* 1964, 2578)

She noted that "in his great work *The American Dilemma,* the Swedish sociologist pointed out 20 years ago that White women and Negroes occupied relatively the same positions in American society" (*Congressional Record* 1964, 2578). The author in question, Gunnar Myrdal (1944), drew a parallel between the treatment of women—not just

White women—and Blacks in American society. Griffiths seems to reconstruct the category *woman* to include only White women. For Griffiths, the analogy between race and gender is an analogy between the position of White women, on one hand, and Black men and Black women, on the other. The analogy also represents, in Griffiths's arguments, a competition between Black and White women.

Griffiths asked Celler, the chair of the Judiciary Committee, "Is it your judgment that this bill will protect colored men and colored women at the hiring gate equally?" Celler responded that it would. Brauer (1983) notes that Celler could have countered Griffiths's line of argument rather easily but did not do so. There was not, however, any basis for assuming that the bill would protect Black women against gender discrimination.

Griffiths's line of argument developed as follows: Does the bill cover Black women and Black men equally? If so, does it cover all Black men and all Black women? If so, is there anything in it that says Black women are protected only if applying for a job historically held by White woman? If not, then if a restaurant hires only White men as dishwashers, an experienced, qualified Black woman could invoke the provisions of the act but an equally experienced and qualified White woman could not. Griffiths then gave the example of a university that had never hired a woman to teach political science. A Black woman political scientist denied employment could invoke the act but a White woman would have no recourse, according to Griffiths. Summing up her points, Griffiths proclaimed,

> And if you do not add sex to this bill, I really do not believe there is a reasonable person sitting here who does not by now understand perfectly that you are going to have white men in one bracket, you are going to try to take colored men and colored women and give them equal employment rights, and down at the bottom of the list is going to be a white woman with no rights at all. (*Congressional Record* 1964, 2579)

To Griffiths's credit, it should be noted that, in all of her hypothetical examples, she always made the case that the Black woman is qualified. She never suggests that White women will lose out to less-qualified Black women. That was not her point. But neither was she merely dramatizing inconsistencies in the logic of the bill, as some have suggested (e.g., Robinson 1979). Griffiths very clearly and explicitly appealed to White racism and the tradition of race and gender chauvinism in protection of White women.

It would be incredible to me that white men would be willing to place white
women at such a disadvantage except that white men have done this before
... your great grandfathers were willing as prisoners of their own prejudice
to permit ex-slaves to vote, but not their own white wives. (*Congressional
Record* 1964, 2580)

Griffiths concluded that "a vote against this amendment today by a
White man is a vote against his wife, or his widow or his daughter, or
his sister" (*Congressional Record* 1964, 2580).

Congresswoman May (Republican, Washington) also invoked the
racial argument when she spoke in favor of the amendment. She spoke,
she stated, "on behalf of the various women's organizations in this
country that have for many years been asking for action from the
Congress in this field" (*Congressional Record* 1964, 2582). The organizations she cited were the League of Women Voters, some Federated
Women's Clubs, and the National Federation of Business and Professional Women, all working in conjunction with the NWP. May noted
the efforts on behalf of the ERA since 1923 and the more recent strategy
of these women's organizations of "consistently asking" that "sex
discrimination" be included in any laws or executive orders that forbid
discrimination on account of race, color, religion, or national origin.
She read from a letter sent to House members by the NWP:

We are alarmed over the interpretation that may be given to the words
discrimination on the account of race, color, ... used in the bill. ... We
are informed that in the past some government officials have interpreted
"race, color, religion, and national origin" in a way that has discriminated
against the White, native-born American woman of Christian religion.
(*Congressional Record* 1964, 2582)

Griffiths's and May's public appeals on the floor of Congress to racial
sentiments in the service of women's rights were quite typical of the
women's rights discourse, centered around the NWP in the 1940s
through the mid-1960s (Rupp and Taylor 1987, 154-78). Such appeals
have roots in the nineteenth- and earlier twentieth-century U.S. wom-
en's movement. They make use of the race-gender analogy to piggyback
the demand for women's rights on the gains of the movement for racial
equality, expressing solidarity with Black women in one breath and
appealing to White racism (sometimes along with anti-Semitism and
xenophobia) in the next. As Rupp and Taylor note, throughout its history
race has been central to the women's rights movement in the United

States, emerging out of the abolitionist movement. At the same time, the movement always defined its priorities in relation to White middle- or upper-class women (Rupp and Taylor 1987, 154). The women's suffrage movement appealed to racist arguments that giving women the vote would dilute the immigrant vote in the North and maintain White supremacy in the South (Aptheker 1982; Davis 1981; DuBois 1978).

As the Black civil rights movement gained momentum in the 1940s and 1950s, the NWP both sought alliances with activist Black women and their organizations and protested that Black men and women were gaining rights denied to White women. Appeals to racial interests similar to Griffiths's were not uncommon in NWP politics. Rupp and Taylor (1987) suggest that the frustration of feminists in the 1940s and 1950s "sometimes led even those who were committed to racial equality to adopt positions that set Black and Jewish women and men in competition with white Christian women" (p. 159).

Griffiths had been a member of the NWP since 1955, although perhaps only on paper (Rupp and Taylor 1987). She was not closely associated with the party and had described it as ineffectual (Brauer 1983; Rupp and Taylor 1987). It is important to remember, however, that there was not a broader feminist movement to draw upon at that time. The main alternative available was to choose the "difference" argument of the women's groups who opposed the ERA. It appears that Griffiths used the available feminist discourse of the National Woman's Party to make her argument.

One Woman Opposed to the Amendment

Edith Green, a veteran Democratic congresswoman from Oregon, is described in several accounts as the one woman who "broke rank" and spoke in opposition to the amendment. She herself noted that she might be called an "Uncle Tom" or "Aunt Jane" for her position. Brauer (1983) reports that Green had considered introducing a gender amendment of her own but had been effectively persuaded by the president and the democratic leadership neither to do so nor to support Smith's amendment. Green's statement stands out as significantly different from that of the pro-civil rights men in that she unequivocally presented herself as an advocate for women's rights and as one who recognized the widespread existence of discrimination against women. She stated that she feared the amendment would clutter up the bill and might be used to destroy Title VII "by the very people who today support it."

Green also added to the debate some observations on the gender politics of the proceedings. She noted that more women than usual were speaking out that afternoon and the debate might go down as the "women's afternoon," but ultimately it was men who had the balance of power to decide and all the women knew this. She observed that the men who were supporting the amendment that day were the very same men who had opposed including women in the Equal Pay Act just a few months earlier. She offered that she welcomed their sudden conversion and hoped it would last.

Green was the only speaker the afternoon of the debate to present a double-jeopardy analysis of the position of Black women. She stated:

> May I also say I am not in complete agreement with everything that has been said by my women colleagues. I think that I, as a white woman, have been discriminated against, yes—but for every discrimination that I have suffered, I firmly believe that the Negro Woman has suffered 10 times that amount of discrimination. She has a double discrimination. She was born as a woman and she was born as a Negro. (*Congressional Record* 1964, 2581-82)

Green concluded, however, that because Black women have suffered so much more, she, as a White woman, was willing to wait a few years to end discrimination against women, if there was an opportunity to end race discrimination. She described race discrimination and racial prejudice, compared to discrimination against women, as ten times worse and "a way of life." Despite her double jeopardy statement, Green, like others present, seemed to accept the idea that Black women would be adequately protected by the race provision and that gender discrimination law would be for White women.

During the debate, no one made the argument that the double jeopardy of Black women necessitated protection against both race and gender discrimination. African American women's organizations had presented such an analysis to White women's rights activists on previous occasions (Rupp and Taylor 1987). Pauli Murray, an African American woman activist, professor of law, and advocate of women's rights, made that point about Title VII subsequently, while the 1964 civil rights bill was pending a Senate vote (Harrison 1988). During the debate, however, the race-gender analogy was used in a way that ignored the discrimination faced by African American women.

Thus the inclusion of gender in Title VII was not a result of a politics of inclusion, coalition, or common cause. Quite the contrary, the race-gender analogy was used to play off the just demands of women's rights activists against those of the civil rights movement. The analogy was invoked to contrast the interests of White "non-ethnic" women with those of women of color and other ethnic minority women, implying that gender discrimination affected only White women and that Black women could face discrimination only on the basis of their race. The construction of these oppositional categories was not only the work of racist southern White men, as many accounts of the debate would suggest; it was shared by White liberal men and White feminist women.

SHIFTING CONFIGURATIONS

The gender amendment to Title VII contributed to shifts in the configuration of gender, race, and class politics in the period after the 1964 Civil Rights Act was passed. The mobilization of women, just two years after the Civil Rights Act passed, to demand implementation of the gender discrimination provision of Title VII led directly to the founding of the National Organization for Women (Freeman 1975). This is one of the events often cited as marking the emergence of the second wave of American feminism (Freeman 1975; Robinson 1979; Rupp and Taylor 1987). Title VII became one of the movement's most important vehicles for expanding women's rights under the law. Subsequent gains in employment policy, such as laws covering pregnancy leave and sexual harassment, for example, were won as extensions to Title VII. Following the precedent of Title VII, including gender along with race in antidiscrimination policy became an established practice. Feminists were not an active part of the coalition that pushed for EEO legislation prior to 1964. The inclusion of gender in Title VII changed that situation and paved the way for increased interdependence between civil rights and women's rights efforts in subsequent decades.

Title VII also has had a significant impact on the intersection of class and gender politics. It removed a historic barrier to certain labor-feminist coalitions. This barrier was the issue of protective legislation mentioned earlier. In the early 1970s, the courts used Title VII to strike down state-level protective legislation for women and to extend such state laws to protect both women and men. These actions cleared the way for the liberal and labor opponents of the ERA to move to the pro-ERA camp (Mansbridge 1986, 10). Republicans, conservatives, and business interests had less reason to support the ERA and eventually shifted to the opposition.

Prior to the court decisions in the 1970s mentioned earlier, the equality-versus-difference debate played a significant role in structuring the interaction of class-based and gender-based politics. Women activists more allied with labor or more involved with the concerns of poor and working-class women tended to support protective legislation and favor the difference strategy. Women's rights advocates who were more probusiness or less involved in class-based politics were more likely to favor the equality strategy and the ERA. The gender amendment to Title VII ultimately led to a restructuring of those gender-class interactions, alliances, and divisions; but it did so by legitimating equality versus difference as a dichotomous choice, with equality as the accepted strategy.

One consequence of the equality strategy is that discrimination law, as MacKinnon (1989) explains, does not consider situated social inequalities, such as poverty or lack of power, that women may suffer because they are women. It only promises equal treatment to those women already most like men in relation to employment. For this reason, antidiscrimination policy often has been most successful in improving access to education and employment for the relatively most advantaged of their race (Wilson 1987) or gender (MacKinnon 1989). Furthermore, EEO policy in the United States, created under Title VII, has never been linked to any kind of full employment policy, nor is it linked to social welfare policy such as child care. Thus the "multiple jeopardies" (King 1988) that women experience because of the interconnections of race, class, and gender are not addressed under the framework of Title VII.

CONCLUSION

In conceptualizing race, class, and gender as interlocking systems, it is important to specify how they actually operate in a given historical context. The analysis of Title VII suggests several considerations for doing this. First, although race, class, and gender are all significant in shaping state action, they are not necessarily equally salient in determining any specific policy outcome. Second, interlocking does not always mean mutually reinforcing. Third, the way that race, class, and gender intersect in shaping state action or oppositional movement politics is not constant or static. Patterns of interaction between feminists and labor on the ERA and between women's rights and civil rights groups on employment issues shifted significantly as an indirect result of Title VII.

Certain dynamics specific to the case of the gender discrimination amendment to Title VII suggest several lessons for the study of gender policy. The size and strength of the women's movement and the level of popular support for the movement's goals do not necessarily determine the form and timing of policy on gender equality. Sometimes it is critical to pay close attention to political conflicts within the state. These conflicts may include interparty and intraparty struggles for power and position waged by politicians not particularly concerned with gender issues. In a state such as the United States that is structured by race as well as class and gender politics, a breakthrough in gender policy may become possible because of division within the state produced by a crisis in the racial (or class) order.

The interpretation of the text of the debate suggests an additional level of analysis. The way in which race, gender, and class categories are constructed in political discourse reinforces inequalities, obscures common interests, and denies the experience of many women (and men). When both the dominant and the oppositional discourse tend to construct *women, Blacks,* and *labor* as separate and distinct categories or constituencies, the underlying interconnections are distorted. Part of the task of a feminist analysis of interlocking systems is to deconstruct that discourse.

The political and legal success that women have had in using Title VII to challenge their employers and to make claims upon the state, combined with the lack of viable alternative legal models, legitimates the race-gender analogy and the equality-over-difference dichotomy at the expense of other, more inclusive, understandings of equality and difference. Title VII remains one of the most important legal vehicles for fighting discrimination in the workplace. The challenge for feminism is to continue to use Title VII as a vehicle for change while contesting the patterns of meaning, of gender, race, and class, that are part of its legacy.

NOTES

1. The text of the amendment continues in this mode to cover additional places in the bill where the word *sex* is to be inserted. All quotes from the debate are from pp. 2577-84 of the February 8, 1964, *Congressional Record.*

2. The *equality* strategy argues that gender differences should not be a consideration in schools, jobs, courts, and so on. The *difference* position argues for recognition (in law and policy, for example) of needs, interests, and characteristics common to women as a group and generally not shared by men (Scott 1988).

3. The use of state autonomy theory to explain expansion of women's rights in the absence of popular demand draws upon a comparative analysis of gender and the state developed in collaboration with Mounira Charrad (Charrad forthcoming; Charrad and Deitch 1986).

4. Previous efforts by southern Democrats to introduce gender discrimination to other sections of the bill had been easily defeated without much debate. They had not been supported by the pro-civil rights congresswomen because these women viewed them as simply tactics to derail the bill without much meaning for women's rights (Loevy 1990).

REFERENCES

Aptheker, Bettina. 1982. *Women's legacy.* Amherst: University of Massachusetts Press.

Bird, Caroline. 1968. *Born female: The high cost of keeping women down.* New York: David McKay.

Bloom, Jack M. 1987. *Race, class, and the civil rights movement.* Bloomington: Indiana University Press.

Brauer, Carl. 1983. Women activists, southern conservatives, and the prohibition of sex discrimination in Title VII of the 1964 Civil Rights Act. *Journal of Southern History* 49:37-56.

Burstein, Paul. 1985. *Discrimination, jobs, and politics.* Chicago: University of Chicago Press.

Charrad, Mounira. Forthcoming. *States and women's rights: A comparison of Tunisia, Algeria, and Morocco.* Berkeley: University of California Press.

Charrad, Mounira, and Cynthia Deitch. 1986. Gender and state power: A theoretical analysis. Paper presented at the annual meeting of the American Sociological Association, New York.

Congressional Quarterly Staff. 1968. *Revolution in civil rights.* Washington, DC: Congressional Quarterly.

Congressional record. 1964. Part 2. 8 February, 2577-2584.

Connell, R. W. 1990. The state, gender and sexual politics. *Theory and Society* 19:507-44.

Davis, Angela. 1981. *Women, race, and class.* New York: Random House.

DuBois, Ellen Carol. 1978. *Feminism and suffrage.* Ithaca, NY: Cornell University Press.

Eisenstein, Zillah. 1984. *Feminism and sexual equality.* New York: Monthly Review Press.

Freeman, J. 1975. *The politics of women's liberation.* New York: Longman.

———. 1991. How sex got into Title VII: Persistent opportunism as a maker of public policy. *Law and Inequality: A Journal of Theory and Practice* 9:163-186.

Greenberg, Stanley. 1980. *Race and state in capitalist development.* New Haven, CT: Yale University Press.

Harrison, Cynthia. 1988. *On account of sex: The politics of women's issues, 1945-1968.* Berkeley: University of California Press.

Hoff-Wilson, Joan. 1987. The unfinished revolution: Changing legal status of U.S. women. *Signs: Journal of Women in Culture and Society* 1:7-36.

King, Deborah. 1988. Multiple jeopardy, multiple consciousness: The context of Black feminist ideology. *Signs: Journal of Women in Culture and Society* 14:42-72.

Lemert, Charles C. 1990. The uses of French structuralism in sociology. In *Frontiers of social theory,* edited by George Ritzer. New York: Columbia University Press.

Loevy, Robert D. 1990. *To end all segregation.* Lanham, MD: University Press of America.

MacKinnon, Catharine. 1989. *Toward a feminist theory of the state.* Cambridge: Harvard University Press.

Mansbridge, Jane J. 1986. *Why we lost the ERA.* Chicago: University of Chicago Press.

Myrdal, Gunnar. 1944. *An American dilemma.* New York: Harper & Row.

Omi, Michael, and Howard Winant. 1986. *Racial formation in the United States.* New York: Routledge & Kegan Paul.

Orloff, Ann Shola, and Theda Skocpol. 1984. Why not equal protection? Explaining the politics of public social spending in Britain, 1900-1911 and the United States, 1880s-1920. *American Sociological Review* 48:726-50.

Piven, Frances Fox, and Richard A. Cloward. 1979. *Poor people's movements: Why they succeed, how they fail.* New York: Vintage.

Robinson, Donald A. 1979. Two movements in pursuit of equal employment opportunity. *Signs: Journal of Women in Culture and Society* 4:413-33.

Rupp, Leila, and Verta Taylor. 1987. *Survival in the doldrums.* New York: Oxford University Press.

Scott, Joan. 1988. Deconstructing equality-versus-difference: Or, the uses of poststructuralist theory for feminism. *Feminist Studies* 14:33-50.

Skocpol, Theda. 1985. Bringing the state back in: Strategies of analysis in current research. In *Bringing the state back in,* edited by P. Evans, D. Rueschemeyer, and T. Skocpol. New York: Cambridge University Press.

Whalen, Charles, and Barbara Whalen. 1985. *The longest debate: A legislative history of the 1964 Civil Rights Act.* Washington, DC: Seven Locks Press.

Wilson, William J. 1987. *The truly disadvantaged.* Chicago: University of Chicago Press.

16 Bringing Gender and Race In: U.S. Employment Discrimination Policy

KIM M. BLANKENSHIP

In 1963, Congress passed the Equal Pay Act (29 U.S.C. 206 [d])—the first comprehensive federal bill prohibiting employment discrimination. The act, which marked the culmination of over 20 years of struggle, prohibited sex discrimination in employment by mandating equal pay for equal work on jobs requiring equal skill, effort, and responsibility, performed under similar working conditions. One year later, the Civil Rights Act of 1964 became law. Title VII (42 U.S.C. 2000e) of the act signified the second federal statute prohibiting discrimination, declaring it unlawful to discriminate in hiring, firing, compensation, classification, promotion, and other conditions of employment on the basis of race, sex, color, religion, or national origin or to limit, segregate, or classify employees in any way that might deprive them of employment opportunities or otherwise adversely affect their status.

Although the bills passed within a year of each other and although each included prohibitions against sex discrimination, they continue a long history of separating the issues of race and gender inequality in public policy (see Boris and Honey 1988). Never in the nearly 20 years of debates on employment discrimination and the more than 25 congressional hearings devoted to it, was adding *race* to equal pay legislation considered. Nor was adding *sex* to civil rights legislation formally

AUTHOR'S NOTE: I am very grateful to Jill Quadagno for her support, guidance, and valuable comments. I would also like to thank Paul Burstein, Paul DiMaggio, Ray Elling, and David Plotke for their thoughtful comments on an earlier draft of this work. A version of this work was presented at the annual meeting of Sociologists for Women in Society, Cincinnati, OH, 1991.

considered. Instead, the prohibition against sex discrimination was introduced in floor debate over the bill as a last-minute effort to thwart its passage (Burstein 1985; Robinson 1979). These two pieces of legislation, then, set in place two different views of discrimination and two distinct enforcement structures—one aimed at sex and the other at race discrimination. One bill attributed discrimination to wage-setting practices in the jobs in which women worked alongside men. The other attributed it to barriers that excluded people of color from jobs altogether. "Equal pay" became the language of sex discrimination initiatives; "equal opportunity," the language of race discrimination bills. Furthermore, Title VII created the Equal Employment Opportunity Commission (EEOC) to administer the act, whereas the Equal Pay Act, an amendment to the Fair Labor Standards Act of 1938, was enforced by the Department of Labor.[1] Thus, these two pieces of legislation laid the foundations for two distinct approaches to inequality in the labor market.

Even Title VII, which includes prohibitions against both race and sex discrimination, distinguishes between them in several important ways. First, it permits employment decisions based on sex when sex is a "bona fide occupational qualification" (BFOQ) reasonably necessary to the operation of a business. In essence, the legislation allows that under certain conditions sex discrimination is legal. Race, however, can never be a BFOQ. Second, Title VII's Bennett Amendment restricts the claims of women, but not of people of color, to wage equity. The amendment allows an employer to differentiate on the basis of sex in determining wages if such differentiation is permitted by the Equal Pay Act. For many years, both the EEOC and the federal courts held that the amendment restricted Title VII's scope to the equal pay for equal work standard when it came to the question of sex-based wage discrimination.[2] No such statutory restriction existed for race-based wage discrimination claims under Title VII. The legislative history of Title VII also suggests that women of color as *women* of color were not its intended beneficiaries. Most of the debate and discussion of the bill centered on the needs of Black men and, to a lesser extent, other men of color. And since the passage of the act, the courts have tended to separate issues of race and sex when deciding the Title VII claims of women of color (Crenshaw 1989; Smith 1990).

An explanation for why this bifurcated approach to employment discrimination developed requires analysis not only of social class but of gender and race relations as well. Both race and sex discrimination initiatives were consistent with some of the needs of postwar capital-ism. At the same time, however, a bifurcated approach to discrimination maintained women's dependence on men in families by preserving the family wage, albeit in a modified form. Yet this, too, is only part of the story. The family wage ideology that both justified and perpetuated White men's privilege had little relevance for African Americans; few African American men earned a family wage and few African American women were dependent on men in families. Indeed, employment dis-crimination policy sought to affect African American men's position in families.

Thus an analysis of the development of a bifurcated approach to employment discrimination reveals the limitations of social class theo-ries of the state, which ignore gender and race, and of feminist theory's emphasis on the family wage, which disregards race. In what follows, I analyze the development of employment discrimination policy in terms of gender, race, and class. I begin with a brief discussion of the implications of feminist theory for analyses of the state. I then show how employment discrimination policy was shaped by business con-cerns in post-World War II America, the family wage ideology, and the position of African American men in families. I conclude by consider-ing the theoretical implications of this analysis and suggesting further areas for research.

SOCIAL CLASS, FEMINIST THEORY, AND THE STATE

Central to class-based theories of the state is the relationship between state activity and the class relations that constitute the capitalist econ-omy. Although there are important differences among theorists in this tradition, they generally agree that state structures and actions promote capitalist economic relations and the interests of the owning classes in particular (see Quadagno 1984; Skocpol 1980). In contrast, feminist theory emphasizes the need to include gender in analyses of the state, suggesting that policies can perpetuate gender privilege by preserving women's dependence on men, even though under certain conditions they may also liberate women (Hernes 1987).

Although feminists debate how gender inequality is structured, main-tained, and transformed, they agree that gender is a central organizing feature of society (Jaggar 1983). Rarely, however, have the implications of these insights for understanding U.S. social policy reform been a part of debates within mainstream political sociology (but see Quadagno 1990).[3]

What does feminist theory imply about the state and social policy reform? It suggests that class-based theories cannot recognize or account for the gendered nature of state structures and activities. As Burstyn (1983) notes:

> As each stage of capitalism has developed and been negotiated, the state has taken on the crucial role of mediation and regulation to advance capitalism's needs for a given form of labor power and surplus extraction in such a way as to retain masculine privilege and control—masculine dominance—in society as a whole. (p. 60)

From a feminist perspective, the state is patriarchal and gender creates, if not a single social cleavage, a fundamental one. State structures and actions promote gender inequality and gender interests, although socialist feminist theory implies that capitalist structures and interests also are important. For some feminists, the state is racist as well.

More concerned with labor and immigration policy, class-based theorists have ignored reproductive rights, divorce and family law, and child care (Calavita 1983; Quadagno 1984). They also do not recognize the systematic way in which policies can neglect women or confine them to a secondary status. For example, theorists in this tradition have recognized the extent to which the capitalist state operates to protect private property rights and, in so doing, to preserve class privilege. But property laws have protected male privilege as well (Basch 1986). Similarly, class theorists convincingly demonstrate the extent to which the expanding welfare state has served capitalist interests (e.g., Piven and Cloward 1971; Quadagno 1984). But feminists have documented how they also have supported women's dependence on men in the family, defined women as caregivers, and controlled their productive and reproductive labor (Eisenstein 1984; Pascal 1986; Wilson 1977).

A growing number of feminists, particularly women of color, urge that the diversity among women be incorporated into theories about them (e.g., Davis 1981; hooks 1984; Lorde 1984). For example, these women note that feminist theory's emphasis on family as the site of women's oppression has less relevance for the lives of women of color, who have often found in family a common ground from which to fight racism. More generally, they criticize the feminist focus on "men as the

enemy" and on gaining equality with men and seek, instead, to understand the interconnectedness of sex, race, and class oppression (hooks
1984). Although these theoretical insights have rarely been applied to
explain social policy reforms (except see Mink 1990), they imply that
the state may approach the same problems differently, depending on
race.

EMPLOYMENT DISCRIMINATION POLICY
AND POST-WORLD WAR II CAPITALISM

Neither equal employment opportunity (EEO) nor equal pay bills
have been major subjects of social class analyses of the state. Yet some
aspects of the history of these initiatives are consistent with class-based
theories. Postwar capitalism in the U.S. was characterized by an industrial structure and labor market segmented into monopoly and competitive sectors and by an increasingly bureaucratized structure of control
at the workplace, particularly in the monopoly sector (Castells 1980;
Edwards 1979). As class-based theories would predict, this context
affected the development of employment discrimination policy by shaping business interests regarding equal pay and EEO initiatives.

Business leaders consistently opposed equal pay bills. Yet they acknowledged that, under certain circumstances, sex discrimination worked
against management interests. Both the National Association of Manufacturers (NAM), as early as 1942, and the U.S. Chamber of Commerce,
in 1948, officially adopted a policy of equal pay for equal work. According to the NAM, this principle coincided with industry "policy that
the only sound and fair basis for payment of wages [was] the rate for
the job, without regard to the sex of the worker" (NAM 1962, 162).
Speaking on behalf of the NAM, George Kohn (1948) explained that
unequal pay for equal work reflected arbitrary wage-setting practices and
prompted considerable conflict at the workplace. Good employee relations, he insisted, required the elimination of such practices (p. 252).
Like the NAM, the U.S. Chamber of Commerce explained that a policy
of equal pay for equal work underlay the job classification and job
evaluation systems used by a growing proportion of its own members
and American industry more generally. Indeed, by 1960, nearly two-
thirds of employees were covered by job evaluation plans (Hester 1963,
100-101). According to business leaders from a variety of industries,
these plans rationalized and legitimized internal wage relationships.

The testimony of business leaders, then, indicates that sex discrimination was inconsistent with the progress of postwar capitalism, in which the highly bureaucratized firm was increasingly common. To be sure, formalization was more typical in the primary than in the secondary sector. Small firms in the periphery remained paternalistic and informal, and hiring, firing, payment, and promotion policies remained arbitrary. Here, it was common for the pay of two employees working at the same job to differ (Edwards 1979, 35). But for large, monopoly-sector firms, such policies were more difficult to tolerate.

If an equal pay standard coincided with bureaucratization and the prevalence of job evaluation, however, business still opposed equal pay legislation for several important reasons. First, almost every equal pay proposal advanced between 1944 and 1963 called for equal pay in jobs involving comparable work. Business complained that the comparability standard did not recognize many legitimate reasons for sex-based wage differentials. Interestingly, the particular way that businesses articulated their opposition to the standard reflects the segmented structure of capitalism. Representatives from primary-sector firms and organizations speaking for monopoly capitalist interests struggled for language that would exempt sex-based differentials arising out of job classification systems. Representatives of secondary-sector enterprises focused on piece-rate systems and on what they claimed were the higher costs of employing women. A spokesperson for the Council of State Chambers of Commerce criticized a 1963 equal pay initiative in these terms:

> By S. 910 limiting its exceptions to established seniority and merit systems, it discriminates against a substantial portion of American industry which still operates on a personal random method of wage adjustments. Further, these personal and random rate structures are not necessarily unsound or discriminatory. Varying situations within a plant justify personalized wage differentials. (Gross 1963, 132)

Business also opposed equal pay initiatives on the grounds that they would subject far too many employers to direct government intervention into wage setting. Most proposals covered all employers of 25 or more workers. Early bills proposed the establishment of industry committees, consisting of representatives from labor, management, and the public sector to set industrywide classification and wage-setting standards. Nearly all proposals gave significant powers of enforcement, including the right to issue cease and desist orders, to the secretary of labor.

The version of equal pay legislation enacted into law represented some important concessions to business interests. The language of comparability was replaced with the language of equal pay for equal work, as business desired. Equal work was further defined as work requiring equal skills, effort, responsibility, and similar working conditions so as to be consistent with job evaluation systems (see testimony of Congressman Frelinghuysen 1963, 10).

The Equal Pay Act also excepted wage differentials based on seniority, merit, and piece-rate systems and any factor other than sex. In floor debate over the bill, congressional leaders made it clear that this last exemption could refer to costs associated with employing women (e.g., *Congressional Record* 1963, 8705-6).

In prohibiting sex discrimination by amending the Fair Labor Standards Act (FLSA), congressional leaders sought to appease business concerns as well. Indeed, a representative from the Electronic Industries Council first suggested the strategy at 1962 hearings. Congressional leaders recognized that this significantly reduced the bill's coverage, because a large number of industries in which women were employed were exempted from the FLSA (e.g., *Congressional Record* 1963, 8681-85).

The struggle over equal opportunity reveals another way in which discrimination may have impeded capitalist development in postwar America. During this period, labor market segmentation gave rise to a tight market for skilled monopoly-sector labor (Castells 1980, 93-94). Discrimination only enhanced this problem. EEO initiatives, insofar as they allowed new groups to enter jobs from which they were previously excluded, could increase the supply of monopoly-sector labor. Also, because some of the barriers to entry in this sector reflected the power of more privileged workers, the challenge to those barriers contained in EEO bills might undermine worker power. Some support for this interpretation can be found in congressional hearings regarding EEO initiatives.

Representatives from the business community were infrequent participants in these hearings. Indeed, neither the NAM nor the U.S. Chamber of Commerce testified on EEO bills. When individual business and industry representatives did testify, most spoke in favor of proposed EEO legislation. In explaining why EEO promoted business interests, business leaders emphasized the impact of discrimination on the availability of labor. Denis Driscoll (1945) testifying on behalf of Associated Gas & Electric Company and in favor of EEO legislation, clearly articulated this view at 1945 hearings:

> The trustees are convinced that discrimination in employment is unprofitable to business . . . because ultimately it raises the cost of production. This effect is caused by narrowing the number from whom a choice must be made.
>
> It is clearly in the interest of the business which hires, the community which trains, and the purchaser who consumes that the abilities and skills of the members of the labor force be used where they are needed and not shut off by arbitrary barriers. We see no reason why business should object to this principle being incorporated in legislation. (p. 96)

Frank Folsom (1954), president of RCA, echoed these views at hearings before the Senate. Mr. Folsom indicated that RCA's commitment to EEO included vigorous recruitment efforts at "Negro" colleges and universities for engineers and other high-level professional workers (1954, 11-19). Both gentlemen were also concerned with the impact of discrimination on purchasing power and the business and social climate.

In hearings throughout the 1960s, representatives from business spoke on behalf of EEO proposals invoking similar concerns, although their definitions of discrimination varied in ways associated with sectoral location. RCA and some other primary sector firms supporting EEO initiatives had been commended by the Urban League for their vigorous efforts to recruit, train, and promote skilled workers of color. As a result of such efforts, more than a token number of Blacks held highly skilled and professional positions in the firms. But, many of the other business leaders testifying on behalf of EEO initiatives were accused of discrimination by civil rights groups, because they employed few workers of color in either executive positions or the more prestigious of the lower-level jobs. When asked to reconcile their commitment to EEO with such figures, they explained that they did not discriminate when faced with two equally qualified candidates for a job, but that few Blacks applied for the better jobs (e.g., Genet 1962, 440-45).

The few business leaders who outwardly opposed EEO legislation generally represented smaller, secondary-sector firms, frequently located in the South. Like equal pay initiatives, EEO bills fit with segmentation and the shift from smaller, more paternalistic business organizations typified by random and arbitrary employment practices, to larger and more formalized enterprises with systematic and standardized employment policies. EEO initiatives also addressed a concern on the part of monopoly capitalists with the shortage of skilled labor. And at least some business leaders worried about the impact of discrimination on purchasing power and the business climate as well.

This discussion suggests that race and sex discrimination may have impeded capitalist development. Ultimately, Congress fashioned both an EEO bill and an equal pay bill that were consistent with business interests in some important ways. But the structure of postwar capitalism and the subsequent configuration of business interests alone cannot explain why a bifurcated discrimination policy developed. Both women and men of color were excluded from the primary sector and both were paid less than White men for the same work. Yet women were the sole focus of equal pay initiatives and men of color the primary focus of EEO. To explain the bifurcated structure of employment discrimination policy, it is important to consider the interaction between changing workplace and family structures during the postwar years. Employment discrimination threatened not just expanding capitalism but men's power in the family as well; employment discrimination policy represented an effort to reinstate this power. As we will see, this took a different form, depending on race.

EMPLOYMENT DISCRIMINATION POLICY
AND THE FAMILY WAGE

Feminist analyses of employment discrimination policy have focused on equal pay and comparable worth initiatives, rather than on EEO or the bifurcated approach to discrimination more generally (Milkman 1981; Steinberg 1982). In keeping with feminist theory, these analyses suggest that equal pay legislation was spawned more by working-class men's concern for the impact of sex discrimination on men's dominance over women than for its effects on women. There is much in the history of this legislation to support such an interpretation.

As feminist accounts emphasize, World War II brought a substantial number of women workers into the labor force, many of whom entered the predominantly male jobs left vacant when men went overseas. Many labor advocates of a sex discrimination bill feared that, at the war's end, these cheaper women would permanently replace men. In addition, they feared that the existence of a cheap female labor force would hasten the development of the secondary sector. According to one representative from the AFL-CIO at 1963 Senate hearings: "Unless there is equal pay legislation, the age of automation could bring with it a low-wage economy geared to the rising female labor supply" (Carey 1963, 82). Many labor proponents viewed an equal pay bill as protection against this.

This concern with protecting men's jobs also is revealed in patterns of participation at congressional hearings on the sex discrimination bill. At these hearings, representatives from labor groups constituted two-thirds to three-fourths of those testifying on behalf of equal pay initiatives. Three unions were particularly vocal: the Communication Workers of America (CWA) (mostly representing telephone company workers), the International Union of Electrical Workers (IUE) (representing electrical workers), and the United Auto Workers (UAW) (representing auto workers). These were not necessarily the industries with the highest proportions of women in their work forces. Nor were they the industries employing the greatest proportion of women in the labor market. These were, however, industries in which women had made significant inroads during the war or whose female work forces had expanded rapidly after the war. In short, they were among those industries in which men and women were most likely to compete for jobs. To be sure, representatives of workers in the retail, hotel, textile, apparel, food, and tobacco industries, which had much higher proportions of women in their work forces, sent statements (often brief) in support of equal pay. But if participation at congressional hearings is any indication, they were far less active than the CWA, IUE, or the UAW.

Unlike business, labor groups pushed for an equal pay for comparable work standard. However, their demand for comparable worth did not encompass predominantly female jobs as it does today. Instead, labor leaders sought this language to keep employers from circumventing an equal pay law. Witnesses from states with such laws described how employers would slightly change the work done in a particular job and thereby reclassify it into two jobs, a lower-paid woman's job and a higher-paid man's job. Labor also saw the language of comparable worth as a means of protecting men's unskilled jobs. They argued that this language would require employers to pay the same starting rates to unskilled entry-level positions, regardless of the particular type of work done. The demand for comparable worth, then, did not express a concern with the practice of paying low wages to predominantly female jobs as it does today. Instead, this was a demand for broad protection against the potential threat of cheap women workers to men's jobs.

To explain why women's labor is cheap, feminists frequently invoke the concept of the "family wage." They argue that the "family wage"—a

wage rate adequate to support a male worker and his family—has justified women's low wages and preserved male dominance and women's
dependence in the family. It is also the primary mechanism through
which state policies preserve men's power. In keeping with feminist
theory, the struggle for equal pay legislation was, in part, a struggle over
the family wage.

Throughout most of the twentieth century, two wage rates for a job
were common: a higher men's rate and a lower women's rate. Although
some argue that this practice originated in working-class unity and was
opposed by capitalists, by the turn of the twentieth century, the "family
wage became a cross-class ideology" (May 1985, 15). Employers supported it because, in the short term, it increased profitability by ensuring
women as a cheap source of labor. And it helped divide the working
class. But the family wage also operated in the interests of male workers
by preserving gender privilege at work and in the home. It helped
counter wage rates that fell steadily between 1929 and 1933 and ensure
job security for men (May 1985, 13). At home, it translated into greater
power for men and greater dependence for women. In the postwar
period, however, it became clear to working-class men that the family
wage ideology and the sex-based wage differential to which it gave rise
no longer worked to their advantage. Joseph Bierne, president of CWA,
expressed this clearly in 1948 congressional hearings. Describing how
employers began to hire women operators in what was once a male job,
he testified:

> As they were breaking in they [the women] were working right beside us
> getting less money. . . . We as males should have risen up in revolt and said,
> "You can't do that to us." But we didn't. We like to be the big fellow who
> says, "I am the head of the house, the head of the family," and all that. "The
> woman should get less than us." By doing that we cut our own throats. We
> get lower standards by permitting these lower standards to be injected right
> in the telephone industry where they got rid of men. (Bierne 1948, 229-30)

On the one hand, sex discrimination policy was meant to challenge
the family wage ideology, as indicated in debate on the Senate floor:

> There perhaps was a time in the country's history when a man, because of
> his commanding position as the head of the family and breadwinner, was
> entitled to more compensation than the single woman.

But in modern day America, woman's role as a provider, for not only herself but her family, has become an essential role. These considerations, documented as they are by the evidence that is before this body, must lead to the support of S. 1409 [equal pay bill]. (*Congressional Record* 1963, 8413)

The Equal Pay Act guaranteed that at least some women would have access to a man's (family) wage. The equal pay for equal work standard eliminated that form of promoting the family wage that most immediately threatened men's earning power and job security by helping to guarantee that, where men and women worked alongside each other or where men and women competed for jobs, employers would not replace men's with women's cheaper labor. And it provided better wages to these women, many of whom contributed significantly to family income.

On the other hand, the act's guarantee was limited in at least two ways, so that it continued to preserve a form of the family wage. First, many women were not covered by the law. Exempted were employers in agriculture, hotels, motels, restaurants, and laundries, as well as professional, managerial, and administrative personnel, outside sales-workers, and private household workers.[4] Data regarding occupational distribution by gender (U.S. Department of Labor 1974, Table 19) suggest that women, especially women of color, were concentrated in precisely these jobs. Indeed, between two-thirds and three-fourths of employed women of color and about one-third of White women were exempted from the act. All told, nearly 45 percent of all employed women appear to have been exempt from the Equal Pay Act: employers were not obliged to pay them a family wage. The same was true for sex-segregated or sex-typed jobs, in which women and men rarely competed for employment. The Equal Pay Act also was limited because it did nothing to promote women's access to jobs, and thereby perpetuated the sex-segregated workplace. Interestingly, labor proponents of equal pay initiatives clearly recognized this limitation. Representing IUE, Ruth Roemer (1948) echoed the words of her counterparts in other unions:

This legislation is no panacea. It does not begin to touch the big problem of job opportunities for women or the less favorable job security for women workers. It does not take into account that women have less opportunity to advance. (p. 197)

Yet labor representatives typically argued that the solution to this problem "probably c[ould not] be legislated" (Bierne 1948, 215), even though Congress was holding hearings on race discrimination legislation addressing precisely this issue during this same period. Similarly, congressional leaders, aware of women's limited opportunities for advancement, did not consider including sex discrimination in EEO legislation.

Equal pay bills, then, by their impact on the family wage, preserved men's dominance and women's dependence in the labor market and at home. In a political-economic context in which men and women began to compete for jobs, the family wage, once a rationale for and source of male privilege, hurt men by maintaining women as a cheap source of labor. Equal pay initiatives helped to eliminate this threat. Ironically, by providing for some women's access to a family wage in this way, equal pay legislation restricted most women's access to a family wage in the long run. For, once employers were required to pay women the same as men, they had less incentive to hire them. And, of course, equal pay proposals did not challenge the barriers that kept women out of higher-paying men's jobs.

EMPLOYMENT DISCRIMINATION, AFRICAN AMERICAN MEN AND FAMILY

If employment discrimination policy represented an effort to assert men's power over women at work and in the family, as feminist theory would suggest, equal pay legislation alone could not accomplish this. As much as the explanation of employment discrimination policy is advanced by analyzing it in terms of the family wage, it remains limited by a failure to account adequately for racism in American society and its relation to the state. The family wage may underlie *White* men's dominance over women, but it has little relevance for men of color, many of whom, like White women, do not receive a family wage, and many of whom do not live with women in families or, if they do, are unemployed while women work. Furthermore, the feminist emphasis on World War II as a pivotal point in the history of sex discrimination policy has more relevance to the history of White women than to some women of color, particularly African American women.

During the first half of the twentieth century, changes in the agricultural industry affected the employment patterns of African Americans more than World War II did. Although the labor force participation rates of European American women increased by nearly 20 percent between 1940 and 1950, those of African American women actually declined slightly during that period (Amott and Matthaei 1991, Table C-1). And, in both years, the participation rates of African American women were significantly higher than those of European American women. The war, then, did not suddenly draw these women of color into the labor force. But changes in the agricultural industry did push African Americans *out* of the labor force.

The expanding and increasingly productive monopoly sector could not generate enough jobs to absorb these workers (Castells 1980, 160). Racial prejudice exacerbated the situation. African American women's employment opportunities were severely restricted: almost one-half of all Black women worked in private household employment (Jones 1986, 262). Rates of unemployment among African American men soared during the postwar years. Employed African Americans also earned substantially less than their White counterparts. In the first decade after the war ended, Black men earned less than one-half of White men's earnings. Although women as a group earned less than two-thirds of men's earnings, Black women earned even less—under one-half of White women's earnings (Jones 1986, 261). African American men rarely earned enough to support their families. As a consequence, poverty rates among African American families greatly exceeded poverty rates among White families (U.S. Department of Commerce 1980, Table 9/24). Furthermore, a growing proportion of African American families were headed by single women. In 1959, such families constituted nearly one-fourth of all Black families (U.S. Department of Commerce 1960).

Race discrimination legislation was a way to challenge the low wages and high unemployment and poverty rates among people of color, particularly African Americans. Instead of focusing on wages, however, it focused on increasing employee access to jobs, albeit in a limited way. In so doing, it had the potential not only to ease the tight market for primary-sector labor, as social class theories of the state would suggest, but also to promote men of color, especially African Americans, as heads of families.

Policymakers were concerned about the impact of discrimination on African American men's earning power and their subsequent ability to support families. This is less frequently stated by public officials in testimony and in debate than is assumed. Thus nearly every advocate of EEO in both the House and the Senate described race discrimination as economically unsound. In elaborating on this concern, many focused on the low-income family, whose presence dealt an "inexcusably serious blow to the economic, social, and spiritual welfare of the Nation" (Roosevelt 1954, 139). Yet in documenting the plight of low-income families, public officials contrasted rates of unemployment among White and African American *men,* median income of White and African American *men,* and the occupational distribution of White and African American *men.* Clearly, they were concerned with the impact of discrimination on men of color.

Sometimes, policymakers explicitly connected discrimination and African American men's positions in families with poverty, social unrest, or the state of the economy in explaining the need for a race discrimination policy. In floor debate over a proposed amendment to eliminate Title VII from the Civil Rights Act, for example, Congressman Celler, a well-known civil rights advocate and cosponsor of civil rights legislation, called employment discrimination the most harmful and widespread form of discrimination faced by Blacks (*Congressional Record* 1964a, 2600-2602). When describing the "gravity of the problem" of discrimination, he referred to the unemployment rates of *"male family breadwinners"* (my emphasis). And, in arguing that eliminating employment discrimination would go far in eliminating poverty, he described poverty in these terms:

> I know of no greater agony or more degrading experience to mortal man than the deprivations of poverty as mirrored in the eyes of hungry children; the helpless look of the mother; and the voiceless protest of the jobless father. (*Congressional Record* 1964a, 2601)

When Congressman Cellar thought of the population made poor by discrimination, he thought of jobless men who could not support their wives and children. Yet in 1959, poverty rates for Black households headed by women (64 percent) were half again as high as for other Black households (42 percent) (U.S. Department of Commerce 1980, Chart 9/24a). And in 1963 the comparable rates were 60 percent and 32 percent, respectively. Senator Clark, also a vocal civil rights advocate, connected African American men's position in families with poverty and social unrest during a Senate filibuster on the civil rights bill:

> Nothing produces alienation from society and a lack of motivation among negroes more than not being able to get a job in keeping with their training

and ability. Nothing produces school dropouts more than that. If the lad in high school *sees his father,* who is a high school graduate, pushing a broom in town, then what motivation is there for him to go ahead and finish high school? (my emphasis, *Congressional Record* 1964b, 7205)

Only one year after Title VII passed, and as policymakers worked to implement the bill, the connection between a race discrimination bill and the position of African American men in families was made explicit in the Moynihan Report. Moynihan (1965) worried that many Black women were forced into the labor market because Black fathers were not present, unemployed, or received less than a family wage. But his concern was not with the conditions these women faced. Nor was it with the impact of unemployment and low earnings on Black men per se. Instead, Moynihan argued that Black men's unemployment caused the breakup of the Black family. And Black men's low earnings produced a dependence on the mother's income that "undermine[d] the position of the father and deprive[d] the children" (p. 25). Moynihan argued that a national effort to reduce race discrimination "must be directed towards the question of family structure. The object should be to strengthen the Negro family so as to enable it to raise and support its members as do other families" (p. 48). A clearer expression of the belief that race discrimination undermined African American men's position in the family would be harder to find.

Equal opportunity legislation, then, was more than a policy to address monopoly capital's labor supply problems. It, like equal pay initiatives, sought to promote male dominance and women's dependence in the labor market and at home. Both sought to accomplish this by giving people who had not before had it, access to the family wage. But each accomplished this differently, one focusing on women, the other on people of color. Furthermore, women of color, although covered by both, were not the primary concern of either. The Equal Pay Act exempted most of the jobs in which women of color worked. It is clear from discussion of Title VII that EEO was viewed as a way to give men, not women, of color access to jobs.

GENDER, RACE, CLASS, AND THE STATE

In 1964, Congress passed Title VII, civil rights legislation that would become the basis for challenging many forms of sex-based inequality at the workplace. Yet Title VII was conceived to address race, not sex, discrimination. Various analysts have debated why the prohibition against sex discrimination was added to the bill. Generally, they agree that, in the most immediate sense, it was introduced by a congressman unfriendly to the Civil Rights Act to bring about the act's demise. But it is probably also true that, if Congress had not spent the previous 20 years debating sex discrimination bills, this strategy might have succeeded.

At least as interesting, then, as the question of why was "sex" added to Title VII, is the question why, given this 20-year history of efforts to eliminate sex discrimination, was it not added sooner. Was it simply that congressional leaders sought to eliminate sex discrimination one step at a time—first with a narrowly conceived bill aimed directly at wages and then with a broader one aimed at other employment practices? I think not, for several reasons. Nothing in the legislative history of Title VII suggests that it was meant to address sex discrimination. Nor is there anything to suggest that Congress, cognizant of barriers to women's employment opportunities but not wanting to further complicate civil rights proposals, intended to initiate legislation promoting EEO for women once a civil rights bill was passed. Furthermore, when the sex amendment was added to the bill, congressional leaders did not see it as an opportunity to overcome some of the limitations of the Equal Pay Act so much as they worried about it conflicting with the act. Hence they passed the Bennett Amendment. Finally, in its early years, the EEOC was far from enthusiastic about enforcing the prohibitions against sex discrimination (Bird 1966). This probably would not have happened were Title VII intended as a second step in the fight against sex discrimination.

Instead of viewing the Equal Pay Act and Title VII as successive steps toward ending sex discrimination in employment, I have suggested here that they be viewed as two distinct efforts to deal with the problem of employment discrimination. In much the same way that social insurance and social assistance programs in the United States constitute a dual welfare system (Pearce 1986)—with means-tested assistance programs supporting mostly women and entitlement programs supporting mostly men—the Equal Pay Act and Title VII constitute a bifurcated employment discrimination policy. This bifurcated approach emerged out of a struggle over women's expanding and shifting labor force participation in post-World War II America. That gender interests were operating helps explain why initiatives aimed at discrimination against women focused on wages and not access to jobs: Sex discrimination legislation developed that would *save men's jobs* from women, not give women greater access to these jobs.

Still, gender interests alone do not explain the form this legislation took. Employment discrimination policy also reflected class interests in the context of a segmented labor market and industrial structure. Both equal pay and EEO bills gave state support to and may even have hastened the development of the bureaucratized monopoly-sector firm. For each was formulated in a way that fit with formalized employment practices. At the same time, each recognized some sectoral differences among businesses.

Racial divisions, too, shaped employment discrimination policy. For one thing, they produced a sex discrimination law that, whatever its limitations, had more potential to address discrimination against White women than discrimination against women of color. The double impact of race and sex segregation meant that women of color were less able than White women to take advantage of the equal pay for equal work challenge to wage discrimination. Furthermore, women of color were more likely than White women to work in exempted jobs or industries. More generally, the bifurcated approach to employment discrimination reflected an effort to preserve male dominance in a race- and sex-divided society. In this context, a policy to protect White men's interests and power in the family was of little help to men of color, many of whom did not work or worked in low-paying jobs. For this, policymakers formulated a policy that would break down the barriers that kept men of color, especially African American men, out of better-paying jobs.

Much more work needs to be done to demonstrate the links among gender, race, class, and the state; employment discrimination policy offers an extremely fruitful focus for such an analysis. Here I have emphasized the structures of gender, race, and class privilege as they shaped the development of employment discrimination policy. At the same time, it is important to recognize that this policy emerged from clashing interests and struggles.

Although the sex discrimination bill that passed accommodated many of the concerns of business leaders, had business truly had its way, no equal pay bill would have passed. Business groups insisted that, however consistent the equal pay principle was with their policies, federal legislation was unnecessary. The passing of the Equal Pay Act represented, in part, a victory of gender over class interests.

Class and gender interests came closer to converging in the struggle for a race discrimination bill. Capitalists benefited from EEO initiatives insofar as they challenged arbitrary barriers to employment that reduced the supply of skilled labor. Similarly, men of color benefited from a bill that, by giving them jobs, might increase their power in the family. These interests prevailed over deeply rooted racist beliefs and practices, particularly among Southerners. Indeed, the Southern Industrial Council represented one of the few business groups to oppose EEO legislation even though it represented some large-scale enterprises. Executives from other southern firms expressed bitter racism in their testimony against EEO proposals (see Spence 1947, 600-601).

Civil rights and women's groups also participated in the struggle for discrimination policy. Middle-class women's organizations fought hard for equal pay initiatives. Civil rights groups constituted the majority of those testifying on behalf of EEO. Among other things, they insisted that nondiscrimination meant more than substituting individual qualification for skin color in making employment decisions. Indeed, they convinced many members of Congress that race discrimination was structurally rooted and that its elimination would require fundamental changes in employment practices.

Women also worked to pass Title VII. Organizations representing professional women, church women, and African American women supported EEO initiatives throughout the 20 years of hearings, although they did so almost entirely on behalf of men of color. When the sex amendment was added to Title VII on the House floor, some women's groups worked hard to ensure that it would be included in the Senate's version (Bird 1966; Robinson 1979). But others, such as the YWCA, the AAUW, the National Council of Negro Women, and the National Consumers League, were concerned with the impact that the amendment would have on protective labor legislation and so opposed it (Keyserling 1965, 25-29).

Clearly, to further our understanding of the relationships among race, class, gender, and the state, research must give more systematic attention to these struggles. Such research can suggest the conditions under which these interests will clash or coincide. It may also indicate whether social policy typically represents the victory of one set of interests over others or a compromise among various competing and converging interests.

NOTES

1. President Carter's Reorganization Plan in 1979 made the EEOC responsible for enforcing the Equal Pay Act.

2. In 1972, the commission issued a new set of guidelines regarding the Bennett Amendment, holding that it was intended to permit employers to defend themselves against a Title VII charge of sex discrimination in wages by invoking one of the Equal Pay Act's four affirmative defenses. Specifically, an employer could refute a claim of discrimination by demonstrating that wages were not based on sex but on a seniority system, a merit system, a piece-rate system, or a system based on any factor other than sex. The courts, however, did not adopt this interpretation until 1981 (see *County of Washington* v. *Gunther,* 101 S.Ct. 2242 [1981]).

3. This is not to argue that analyses of the relationship between women and the state do not exist. For some examples of such work that focus on social policy in developed, Western societies, see Baldcock and Cass (1989), Pascal (1986), Petchesky (1984), and Wilson (1977). In addition, there is an expanding body of literature examining the relationship among women, development, and both industrial and agrarian policies in the Third World, including Acosta-Belen and Bose (1990), Deere and Leon (1987), Musisi (1991), and Schmidt (1991). Little of this work gets published in mainstream social science journals.

4. In 1972, amendments to the Fair Labor Standards Act brought professionals, managerial, administrative, and outside sales workers under the Equal Pay Act.

REFERENCES

Acosta-Belen, Edna, and Christine E. Bose. 1990. From structural subordination to empowerment: Women and development in Third World contexts. *Gender & Society* 4:299-320.

Amott, Teresa L., and Julie A. Matthaei. 1991. *Race, gender, and work: A multicultural economic history of women in the United States.* Boston: South End Press.

Baldcock, C. V., and B. Cass, eds. 1989. *Women, social welfare, and the state in Australia.* Sydney, Australia: Allen & Unwin.

Basch, Norma. 1986. The emerging legal history of women in the U.S.: Property, divorce, and constitution. *Signs: Journal of Women in Culture and Society* 12:97-117.

Bierne, Joseph A. 1948. Statement of Joseph A. Bierne, president, Communication Workers of America. *Equal Pay for Equal Work for Women: Hearings before Subcommittee no. 4 of the Committee on Education and Labor,* U.S. House of Representatives. Washington, DC: GPO.

Bird, Caroline. 1966. Civil rights for women now. Paper presented at Eleanor Roosevelt Memorial Award Ceremony, Poughkeepsie, NY.

Boris, Eileen, and Michael Honey. 1988. Gender, race, and the policies of the Labor Department. *Monthly Labor Review* 111:26-36.

Burstein, Paul. 1985. *Discrimination, jobs, and politics: The struggle for equal employment opportunity in the United States since the New Deal.* Chicago: University of Chicago Press.

Burstyn, Varda. 1983. Masculine dominance and the state. *Socialist Register* 1983:45-89.

Calavita, Kitty. 1983. California's "employer sanctions" legislation: Now you see it, now you don't. *Politics & Society* 2:205-30.

Carey, James B. 1963. Statement of James B. Carey, secretary-treasurer, Industrial Union Department, AFL-CIO, president, IUE, AFL-CIO. *Equal Pay Act of 1963: Hearings before the Subcommittee on Labor of the Committee on Labor and Public Welfare,* U.S. Senate. Washington, DC: GPO.

Castells, Manuel. 1980. *The economic crisis and American society.* Princeton, NJ: Princeton University Press.

Congressional record. 1963. 88th Cong., 1st sess. Vol. 109, pt. 7.

———. 1964a. 88th Cong. 2d sess. Vol. 110, pt. 2.

———. 1964b. 88th Cong. 2d sess. Vol. 110, pt. 6.

Crenshaw, Kimberlee. 1989. Demarginalizing the intersection of race and sex: A Black feminist critique of antidiscrimination doctrine, feminist theory and antiracist politics. *University of Chicago Legal Forum* 1989:139-67.

Davis, Angela. 1981. *Women, race, and class.* New York: Random House.

Deere, Carmen Diana, and Magdalena Leon, eds. 1987. *Rural women and state policy: Feminist perspectives on Latin American agricultural development.* Boulder, CO: Westview.

Driscoll, Denis J. 1945. Statement of Denis J. Driscoll, St. Mary's, PA., trustee of Associated Gas & Electric Corporation, in Reorganization. *Fair Employment Practice Act: Hearing before a Subcommittee of the Committee on Education and Labor,* U.S. Senate. Washington, DC: GPO.

Edwards, Richard C. 1979. *Contested terrain: The transformation of the workplace in the twentieth century.* New York: Basic Books.

Eisenstein, Zillah R. 1984. *Feminism and sexual equality: Crisis in liberal America.* New York: Monthly Review Press.

Folsom, Frank M. 1954. Statement of Frank M. Folsom, president, Radio Corporation of America. *Antidiscrimination in employment: Hearings before the Subcommittee on Civil Rights of the Committee on Labor and Public Welfare,* U.S. Senate. Washington, DC: GPO.

Frelinghuysen. 1963. Explanation of H.R. 6060, Mr. Frelinghuysen. *Legislative history of the Equal Pay Act of 1963,* U.S. House of Representatives. Washington, DC: GPO.

Genet, Milton. 1962. Statement of Milton Genet, executive director, Los Angeles Restaurant Hotel Employers Council. *Equal employment opportunity: Hearings before the Special Subcommittee on Labor of the Committee on Education and Labor,* U.S. House of Representatives. Washington, DC: GPO.

Gross, Geraldine L. 1963. Statement of Geraldine L. Gross on behalf of the Council of State Chambers of Commerce. *Equal Pay Act of 1963: Hearings before the Subcommittee on Labor of the Committee on Labor and Public Welfare,* U.S. Senate. Washington, DC: GPO.

Hernes, Helga. 1987. *Welfare state and women power.* Oslo: Norwegian University Press.

Hester, Ezra. 1963. Statement of Ezra Hester, director, Industrial Relations and Research, Corning Glass Co., New York. *Equal Pay Act of 1963: Hearings before the Subcommittee on Labor of the Committee on Labor and Public Welfare,* U.S. Senate. Washington, DC: GPO.

hooks, bell. 1984. *Feminist theory: From margin to center.* Boston: South End Press.

Jaggar, Alison M. 1983. *Feminist politics and human nature.* Totowa, NJ: Rowman & Allanheld.

Jones, Jacqueline. 1986. *Labor of love, labor of sorrow: Black women, work and the family, from slavery to the present.* New York: Vintage.

Keyserling, Mary D. 1965. Statement of Mary D. Keyserling, director, Women's Bureau, U.S. Department of Labor. *The White House Conference on Equal Employment Opportunity: Panel 3, Discrimination because of Sex.* Washington, DC: Ward & Paul, Official Reporters.

Kohn, George F. 1948. Statement of George F. Kohn, president, Precision Grinding Wheel Co., Inc., Philadelphia, PA, member, Industrial Relations Committee, National Association of Manufacturers. *Equal pay for equal work for women: Hearings before Subcommittee no. 4 of the Committee on Education and Labor,* U.S. House of Representatives. Washington, DC: GPO.

Lorde, Audre. 1984. *Sister outsider.* Trumansberg, NY: Crossing Press.

May, Martha. 1985. Bread before roses: American workingmen, labor unions, and the family wage. In *Women, work, and protest: A century of U.S. women's labor history,* edited by Ruth Milkman. Boston: Routledge & Kegan Paul.

Milkman, Ruth. 1981. Female factory labor and industrial structure: Control and conflict over "woman's place" in auto and electrical manufacturing. *Politics & Society* 12:159-203.

Mink, Gwendolyn. 1990. The lady and the tramp: Gender, race, and the origins of the American welfare state. In *Women, the state, and welfare,* edited by Linda Gordon. Madison: University of Wisconsin Press.

Moynihan, Daniel Patrick. 1965. *The Negro family: The case for national action.* Washington, DC: U.S. Department of Labor, Office of Policy Planning and Research.

Musisi, Nakanyike B. 1991. Women, "elite polygyny," and Buganda state formation. *Signs: Journal of Women in Culture and Society* 16:757-86.

National Association of Manufacturers. 1962. Statement of National Association of Manufacturers. *Equal pay for equal work: Hearings before the Subcommittee on Labor of the Committee on Education and Labor,* U.S. House of Representatives. Washington, DC: GPO.

Pascal, Gillian. 1986. *Social policy: A feminist analysis.* London: Tavistock.

Pearce, Diana M. 1986. Toil and trouble: Women workers and unemployment compensation. In *Women and poverty,* edited by Barbara C. Gelpi, Nancy C. M. Hartsock, Clare C. Novak, and Myra H. Strober. Chicago: University of Chicago Press.

Petchesky, Rosalind Pollack. 1984. *Abortion and woman's choice: The state, sexuality, and reproductive freedom.* Boston: Northeastern University Press.

Piven, Frances Fox, and Richard Cloward. 1971. *Regulating the poor: The functions of public welfare.* New York: Random House.

Quadagno, Jill S. 1984. Welfare capitalism and the Social Security Act of 1935. *American Sociological Review* 49:632-47.

———. 1990. Race, class, and gender in the U.S. welfare state: Nixon's failed family assistance plan. *American Sociological Review* 55:11-28.

Robinson, Donald A. 1979. Two movements in pursuit of equal employment opportunity. *Signs: Journal of Women in Culture and Society* 4:413-33.

Roemer, Ruth. 1948. Statement of Ruth Roemer, legislative representative, United Electrical, Radio, and Machine Workers of America, CIO. *Equal pay for equal work for women: Hearings before Subcommittee no. 4 of the Committee on Education and Labor,* U.S. House of Representatives. Washington, DC: GPO.

Roosevelt, Franklin D., Jr. 1954. Statement of Hon. Franklin D. Roosevelt, Jr., a representative in Congress from the State of New York. *Antidiscrimination in employment: Hearings before the Subcommittee on Civil Rights of the Committee on Labor and Public Welfare,* United States Senate. Washington, DC: GPO.

Schmidt, Elizabeth. 1991. Patriarchy, capitalism, and the colonial state in Zimbabwe. *Signs: Journal of Women in Culture and Society* 16:732-86.

Skocpol, Theda. 1980. Political response to capitalist crisis: Neo-Marxist theories of the state and the case of the New Deal. *Politics & Society* 10:155-201.

Smith, Peggie R. 1990. Justice denied: Black women and the search for equality under Title VII. Master's thesis, Yale University, New Haven, CT.

Spence, Paulsen. 1947. Statement of Paulsen Spence, president, Spence Engineering Co., Walden, NY. *Antidiscrimination in employment: Hearings before a Subcommittee of the Committee on Labor and Public Welfare,* U.S. Senate. Washington, DC: GPO.

Steinberg, Ronnie. 1982. *Wages and hours: Labor and reform in twentieth century America.* New Brunswick, NJ: Rutgers University Press.

U.S. Department of Commerce, Bureau of the Census. 1960. Population characteristics, household and family characteristics: March, 1960. *Current population reports,* ser. P-20, no. 106. Washington, DC: GPO.

———. 1980. *Social indicators. III, Selected data on social conditions and trends in the United States.* Washington, DC: GPO.

U.S. Department of Labor. 1974. *Handbook of labor statistics, 1974.* Washington, DC: GPO.

Wilson, Elizabeth. 1977. *Women and the welfare state.* London: Tavistock.

Part V

Thinking Race, Class, and Gender:
Theory and Method

For more than a decade, feminist critiques, primarily by women of color and other concerned scholars, have provided an impetus for shifting the center of mainstream knowledge and reconstructing it into an inclusive scholarship. As Margaret Andersen and Patricia Hill Collins (1995, 3) put it: "Thinking more inclusively opens up the way the world is viewed, making the experience of previously excluded groups more visible and central in the construction of knowledge." The call to add "race, class, and gender" to analyses is a firm step toward the transformation of feminist scholarship. The main question is: How do we do thinking and rethinking about race, class, and gender? Theorizing about race, class, and gender and some methodological issues in feminist epistemology are explored in this section.

Challenging conventional assumptions and paradigms, Brenner and Laslett in Chapter 17 and West and Fenstermaker in Chapter 18 address the limited capacities in the conventional social sciences and even in feminist scholarship for uncovering how women's and men's experiences are interconnected within race- and class-specific boundaries. Brenner and Laslett suggest a "single system" rather than the "dual system" model of Marxist feminism for doing historical analysis of women's self-organization, and West and Fenstermaker explore the theoretical potential of reconceptualizing the simultaneity of race, class, and gender through use of an ethnomethodological model. Part V ends with a critical discussion by Gorelick, who challenges us to rethink a standpoint-based methodology, informed by researchers and participants from diverse race, class, gender, and other oppressed categories to refocus and re-vision feminist knowledge based on theory, action, and experience.

Emphasizing the historical agency of women, Brenner and Laslett theorize that women act with resources and under constraints set by gender and class relations structured by social reproduction and the gendered division of labor, constraints that affect women's political self-organization in the larger society. They consider production and social reproduction to be two domains of an integrated process of species reproduction and the gendered division of labor to be central to the organization of social reproduction, which both limits and provides resources for women's collective politics. Explaining why White middle-class women were major political actors in the U.S. from the late nineteenth century through World War I, Brenner and Laslett point out the great irony of this period; the same gendered division of labor that marginalized White middle-class women in paid labor and mandated their economic dependence on men simultaneously provided them with an institutional base from which to organize politically. The differences in the politics of self-organized African American and White middle-class women reflected the different demands and possibilities for social reproduction as constrained by race and class. The organization of social reproduction and the gendered division of labor also diminished working-class women's capacities for self-organization and limited their ability to challenge either the working-class men or middle-class women who dominated political movements.

In Chapter 18, "Doing Difference," West and Fenstermaker take on the challenging task of theorizing about race, class, and gender. Offering an ethnomethodological model, they reconceptualize relationships among gender, race, and class through "doing differences" as ongoing interactional and institutional accomplishments that result in multiple forms of domination. Although race, class, and gender can be seen as different axes of social structure, these authors conceive of each axis as "the whole of experience" that individuals undergo simultaneously. In everyday life, people categorize themselves and each other on the basis of sex, race, and class membership and behave accordingly in interactional and institutional processes. Once institutionalized, these processes become the mechanism that creates and recreates the differences themselves. The accomplishment of gender, race, and class presents the social arrangements based on these categories as normal and natural, legitimizing ways of organizing social life and maintaining gender, racial, and class order.

The provocative thesis offered by West and Fenstermaker supports an understanding of the accomplishment of race, gender, and class as constituted by the differential "doings" of "others," inspiring intellectual excitement among feminist scholars. A collection of five responses to "Doing Difference" published in the August issue of *Gender & Society* in 1995 assessed the theoretical formulation offered by West and Fenstermaker and challenged further thinking and rethinking about race, class, and gender.

Finally, the book ends with Gorelick's thoughtful discussion in Chapter 19, "Contradictions of Feminist Methodology." Questioning the dogmas of positivism, she insists that feminist research is more than just gathering descriptive statistics or experiential data about women. To her, feminist research must be part of the process by which women's oppression is not only described but challenged.

Gorelick is critical of the women's standpoint approach and the symbolic interactionist and ethnomethodological perspectives. Merely incorporating the standpoint of women to study "their everyday world as problematic" as Smith (1976) suggested, and "giving voice," is not enough. Gorelick maintains that women's internalization of oppression and false consciousness, as well as the hidden structure of oppression external to individuals, often prevent them from having an adequate understanding of their conditions. Hence, "doing difference" based on race, class, and gender categories may not be sufficient for understanding the organization of social life in the larger society.

Recognizing that feminist theory lacks a broad analysis that can encompass the wide variety of women's experience, Gorelick suggests that White feminist scholarship must be revised by views from below, or from "the margin," and that the perspectives of women of color must move to the center of feminist theory and the feminist movement. Researchers need to reconstruct women's experience in ways that account for both the active voice of the subject and the researchers' own dialectical analysis. In other words, the social milieus of the women studied have to be considered from the viewpoint and personal narrative of the subject as well as from the standpoint of the researcher-interpreter within a particular cultural and social system. Contradictions are not limited to the lives of those being studied, as Gorelick cautions us. Relationships between the researchers and the researched are a set of contradictions involving elitism and hierarchy. Attention must be paid to investigators' race, class, and gender and to their location in the social structure when interpreting their work.

To move beyond the rhetoric of "race, class, and gender," one of the main missions of this book is to encourage those who are interested in

COMMON BONDS, DIFFERENT VOICES

this substantive topic to think and rethink about the interconnections among these structural bases of inequality. Transforming feminist knowledge to be inclusive necessitates the thorough exploration and examination of the experiences of marginalized groups as well as of those in the dominant society. By reconceptualizing race, class, and gender as a set of stratifying forces and processes, the combined outcome is a stimulus for innovative approaches to theory, research, and practice that will lay foundations for evolving paradigms.

17 Gender, Social Reproduction, and Women's Self-Organization: Considering the U.S. Welfare State

JOHANNA BRENNER
BARBARA LASLETT

The end of the 1970s brought formal recognition that things were not well between Marxism and feminism; there was, to use Heidi Hartmann's phrase, an "unhappy marriage" between them. Women's oppression and feminist struggles, she argued, had consistently been subordinated to class oppression and class struggle. Women's issues were seen "at best [as] less important than class conflict and at worst divisive of the working class" (Hartmann 1979, 1). To resolve the dilemma, Hartmann proposed that patriarchy and capitalism be seen as separate systems of domination, each of which has to accommodate the other (Hartmann 1979). In this chapter, we take issue with this "dual-systems" approach as it has been used to account for the gendered character of the welfare state.

Within the dual-systems—or capitalist-patriarchy—framework, socialist-feminists have argued that the state mediates between the conflicting interests of male capitalists and workers, on the one hand, and their common interests as white men on the other. They point out that state policy with regard to both services (education, welfare, health

AUTHORS' NOTE: We would like to thank the American Sociological Association Committee on Problems of the Discipline for supporting the conference at which this work was discussed and the conference participants for their responses and suggestions. We would also like to thank Chris Bose and Barrie Thorne for their helpful readings.

care, etc.) and regulation (labor legislation, public health and housing laws, etc.) reflects and perpetuates women's marginalization in paid labor and their assignment to unpaid labor in the home. From this perspective, state provision for women and children is understood as a "negotiated settlement" among contending groups of men. The development of the welfare state, rather than providing women access to income and services as an alternative to their dependence on men for support, established a "public patriarchy" that reinforced women's dependence on the male-breadwinner family and on a male-controlled state (Abramovitz 1988; Boris and Bardaglio 1983, 1987). This analysis, however, ignores the impact and existence of women's political agency and misses the possibility that state programs provide women with resources as well as constraints.

A second interpretation of the gendered character of the welfare state does recognize women's agency. Skocpol (1992) argues that women were architects of the welfare state in late nineteenth- and early twentieth-century America, especially through state-level political activities. Indeed, she argues that in the Progressive Era, white middle-class women were more effective than working-class men in implementing reforms. And Nelson (1990) points out that from its beginning social welfare in the United States has been a gendered, two-track system. Protective legislation was implemented for women but not men. Contributory, non-means-tested programs such as pensions and workmen's compensation, considered to be entitlements, have been directed toward men as workers. Noncontributory, means-tested programs such as mothers'/widows' pensions and maternal and child health care, understood as public charity, have been directed toward women, primarily as mothers. This two-track system of social benefits, and its legitimating ideology, was embedded in state structures during the Progressive Era. Since that time, Nelson observes, it has been expanded and elaborated but not substantially changed. Also working within a state-centered approach, Orloff (1991), while agreeing with Nelson that programs were gendered, argues that in the Progressive Era "social contribution" was the basis of entitlement for both men and women. She contends that the emergence of differential legitimation connected to contributory programs for men versus noncontributory programs for women did not emerge until the 1930s (Orloff 1993).

While incorporating women's historical agency, this approach, which focuses more than does the capitalist-patriarchy framework on political institutions and processes, also has problems. First, it does not theorize why middle-class women were organized and effective as political actors in the Progressive Era. Nor does it explain why they organized for programs that substantially institutionalized a male-breadwinner family model. Second, the emphasis on the timing and institutionalization of particular policies draws attention away from the possibility of continued contestation over them. It neglects variation in women's capacities for political organization or changes in what women organized to achieve.

In this chapter we present an alternative to both the capitalist-patriarchy and state-centered frameworks that builds upon them but attempts to transcend the shortcomings we have identified. Our approach draws on Marxist and feminist theory, but we are part of that strand within the socialist-feminist project that seeks to develop a "single-system" rather than a "dual-systems" model (Maroney and Luxton 1987; Smith 1989). In line with state-centered approaches, we recognize the importance of political structure and political activity. State policy outcomes cannot be "read off" the interests of social groups —of men as men or as workers and employers. But in line with the capitalist-patriarchy analysis and in contrast with the state-centered approach, we argue that women act with resources and under constraints set by gender and class relations. For this reason, Marxist analysis that concentrates on the ways in which the dynamic of the capitalist mode of production sets limits on and opens opportunities for political action has to be expanded to include the structures of social reproduction—the socially organized labor necessary to renew life. In analyzing the development of state policy, then, we focus on how the organization of social reproduction and, in particular, the gender division of labor within it, affected women's political self-organization: why women organized, with what goals in mind, within what range of alternatives, and with what capacities to affect outcomes. We begin with the observation that not only in the Progressive period but also in the 1960s and 1970s, women were engaged in political action on their own behalf, while in the other major period of contestation over state policy, the 1930s, women's political self-organization was substantially absent.

By political self-organization we mean any collective action in which women as activists and leaders define goals and construct strategies, not only self-consciously feminist organizing. Thus the "woman movement" at the turn of the century that helped establish models of social welfare and industrial regulation based on the assignment of women to unpaid labor in the family is an example of women's political self-organization. So, too, is the organization of a new generation of women activists in the 1960s and 1970s who saw their interests quite differently and challenged those very models that Progressive Era women had worked to institutionalize. In both eras "women's needs and rights" entered the political discourse concerning the obligations of the state. In the New Deal, by contrast, the debate over state policy focused overwhelmingly on men, particularly men as workers and family providers.

This variation in women's self-organization has to be accounted for. We do so by asking about the ways in which women's responsibilities as mothers and wives provided resources for, but also imposed constraints on, their capacity for collective action. Changes in the organization of social reproduction in the twentieth century, we believe, account for differences in women's political self-organization across the three periods.

In the late nineteenth century and through the Progressive Era, the conditions under which white middle-class women carried out their responsibilities for social reproduction provided organizational resources and legitimation for their collective action. Their political reform activities were based in voluntary associations and institutions built in their separate "female world" and were justified in terms of their special responsibilities as mothers. African American middle-class women, usually denied entrance to white women's groups, formed their own organizations that operated under a similar charge, although their concerns and ideologies were broader and less likely to be on behalf of women and children only (Brown 1989; Mink 1990).

A reorganization of social reproduction, substantially completed by the 1920s, opened up new possibilities for women as individual actors in the modern world but undermined the women-centered institutions and maternalist ideology on which their previous self-organization had been based. In the post-World War II decades, another reorganization of women's responsibilities for social reproduction—including the increased access of young middle-class women to higher education and the increased entry of married middle-class women into paid labor as an extension of their responsibilities to their families—laid the groundwork for women's political self-organization but on a very different institutional basis and with a correspondingly different set of legitimations. Most centrally, it became possible for women to challenge the gender division of labor itself.

GENDER AND SOCIAL REPRODUCTION

Relations of gender and generation are fundamental properties of how social reproduction is organized. Often naturalized around age and sex differences, all known systems of social reproduction have been based on a gender division of labor. Although this pattern appears to be mandated by the relationship between procreation, sexuality, and the needs of infants, the distribution of the work of social reproduction between families, markets, communities, and states—and between women and men—has varied historically. Systems of social reproduction are the historical outcomes of class, race, and gender struggles— struggles that are often about sexuality and emotional relations, as well as political power and economic resources. (For further discussion of social reproduction and gender division of labor, see Brenner and Glazer 1993; Glenn 1992; Laslett 1986; Laslett and Brenner 1989.)

Changes in the organization of social reproduction and the social construction of gender in the early twentieth century substantially altered the lives of middle-class women who had been the backbone of women's political self-organization in the Progressive Era. Increasing participation in education and wage work, especially for unmarried women, encouraged a greater emphasis on middle-class women's sexual and personal autonomy. Women's low wages, however, put economic autonomy out of reach even for many single women and certainly for mothers. Despite declining fertility for all occupational groups in the first part of the twentieth century, the continuing demands on women for domestic labor and child care, along with the rising standards of household maintenance and child rearing, made it extremely difficult for most women to combine paid and unpaid work (Grabill, Kiser, and Whelpton 1958). Thus women, especially with children, continued to have few alternatives outside dependence on a male breadwinner (Breckinridge 1933; Wandersee 1981). This discrepancy between middle-class women's possibilities as single women and their limitations as mothers/wives (Fine 1990; Laslett 1990b; Norwood 1990; Tyack and Hansot 1990) helps to explain why women participated in a new emphasis on sexuality and companionship in marriage. But this participation affected women's identities and sense of themselves— steering them in the direction of heterosexual rather than homosocial interests and ties.

In contrast to nineteenth-century beliefs about women's sexual passionlessness (Cott 1978), the early twentieth century celebrated sexuality as a source of pleasure, personal fulfillment, and personality development (D'Emilio and Freedman 1988). Lesbianism, now labeled perverse and selfish, was used to denounce the political reform activities that had been central to women activists in the Progressive Era (Smith-Rosenberg 1985). The new emphasis on women's heterosexual relationships bestowed a sacred aura on relations between husbands and wives in the name of "normalcy" and "adjustment," a sharp contrast to the moral authority that relations among women had in the nineteenth century. Women's links to their own husbands and children—to their nuclear families—were reinforced; women's responsibility for morality within the society as a whole was marginalized.

For the modern housewife of the 1920s, consumerism was connected to a new definition of domestic work, to new ways for middle-class women to guard the health and well-being of their families, and to the new material standards for middle-class family life (Cowan 1983). The continuing supply of an exploitable pool of women workers, particularly immigrant and black women, to help carry the burden of attaining the higher standards for domestic health and comfort, encouraged most middle-class women to accept rather than challenge the work involved in maintaining the modern household (Palmer 1989). Shaped by changing economic conditions that affected the intergenerational transmission of social status—particularly the greater importance of education for occupational placement—new, class-specific definitions of maternal adequacy and inadequacy developed (Wrigley 1990). For example, this shift was reflected in the parent education movement. To the PTA in the Progressive Era, parent education was a means for changing society by organizing mothers of the nation in common cause. By the 1920s, parent education "referred by and large to the instruction of middle-class women in ways they could rear their own children in accordance with new behavioral science dictums" (Schlossman 1976, 456; Schlossman 1981).

This increasing focus on nuclear family affairs was not simply forced upon middle-class white women by human services professionals— often other women who had begun to establish themselves as experts in professions such as social work, child development, home economics, education—or by the sellers and advertisers of consumer goods. The increasingly professionalized activities of service workers such as teachers, social workers, and nurses not only provided some middle-class women with occupations but also made it possible for other middle-class women, the very women who had been the backbone of reform politics in the Progressive Era, to affiliate themselves with the culture of modernity that was developing around them. Given the limited range of their alternatives, it is, perhaps, not too surprising that middle-class women followed this course.

In contrast to the maternalist ideology that had existed earlier, the new culture with which middle-class women were now identifying and helping to construct was legitimated by rationalist values of modern science rather than moral values of a more communitarian culture. And this new culture was male, not female, dominated. Although women like Lucy Sprague Mitchell were important figures in developing this culture, particularly in fields such as child development (Antler 1987), and women were unusually prominent in constructing the new psychiatry of family relationships (Chodorow 1989), developments in the social sciences meant that scientific educators such as Lawrence K. Frank and scientific sociologists like William F. Ogburn were the experts whose voices dominated the new discussions of sexuality, education, and family relationships (Laslett 1990a; Ross 1979). As a consequence, the culture of expertise in family affairs developed, in the first instance, as primarily male professions and most of the women involved in them affiliated and identified themselves with men's worlds and practices. Each of these developments underscored women's dependence on men —on the male wage, on male culture, and on the nuclear family. It is this economic and psychocultural dependence, we believe, and the decline in women's political self-organization associated with it, that helps explain the absence of women's voices in the Great Depression.

During the 1930s, married women came under pervasive attack for wage work outside the home despite their increased participation in the labor force. The Depression undercut any rationale for women's employment except family economic need and reinforced the traditional division of labor in which men were breadwinners and women were wage spenders and household workers on behalf of their families (Scharf 1980; but see Kessler-Harris 1990, chap. 3). While it is important to remember that not all U.S. families experienced extreme loss of income during the Depression, Elder (1974) concludes that the economic hardship experienced during the 1930s contributed to the increased value of the family and children for both women and men. Indeed, the experience of U.S. families during the Depression seems to have strengthened norms about the gender division of labor within the family, regardless of how behavior may have contradicted them. Whatever incipient critique of gender inequalities the ideal of companionship in middle-class marriage or the reality of married women's increased labor force activity may have presented in the 1920s, norms about the gender division of labor that would become central to feminist challenge in the 1970s were firmly rerooted in the family and gender culture of the 1930s.

The organization of social reproduction for middle-class white families in post-World War I America was inherently unstable. Gender relations and identities based in companionate marriage and full-time motherhood as career raised women's aspirations and modern capacities and then denied them the possibility for achievement. But these contradictions only exploded in the 1950s and 1960s.

Of particular importance were the changing demographics of family formation and fertility (Glick 1977) and the rising standards for family comfort begun in the 1920s (Wandersee 1981). Lowered fertility, earlier ages at marriage, and lower age at the birth of the last child from the 1950s onward meant that women were freed from full-time mothering at a relatively young age (Glick 1977). Married women were now able to consider interests outside the family at younger ages, and such interests were particularly legitimate if they were pursued in the name of family well-being. Oppenheimer's analysis of the demand for female labor in the postwar period (1970) and her analyses of the family "life-cycle squeeze" in 1960 (1974) demonstrates the economic and demographic components of these dynamics. She shows that for all occupational groups, although more strongly among lower- than higher-status ones, women's participation in the paid labor force corresponded to the period of the family life cycle when family expenses were highest—that is, when there were adolescent children in the home—and the husband's earnings had not risen to meet them. In order to maintain the same standard of living, married women entered, or reentered, the labor force. Smaller families and the availability of household appliances and consumer goods and services meant that it was now possible for women to do a double day, combining domestic and child-rearing responsibilities with paid work.

The rising demand for women's paid labor, especially in clerical work and the service professions (Oppenheimer 1970) was thus met with an increasing supply of educated women looking for employment. The resulting massive reentry of women into the labor force was inherently explosive around issues of gender inequality. Although women could work outside the home without fundamentally challenging the reigning gender ideology, nonetheless, once women were working, they had access to new experiences and resources that could support their political organization. Both the increasing number of married women in the paid labor force and the increasing number of their daughters attending college created the structural conditions for a mass base to a new women's movement. The political movements of the 1960s and 1970s—in the United States, the civil rights and antiwar movement—were its catalyst (Evans 1979).

WOMEN'S POLITICAL SELF-ORGANIZATION

From the late nineteenth century through World War I in the United States, white middle-class women were major political actors in formulating and winning reforms that, however limited in scope and funding, did expand state responsibility for social reproduction. In analyzing the relationship between women's self-organization and state policy, we focus particularly on white middle-class women. First, although African American middle-class women were organized and played crucial political roles in their own communities in this period, they were excluded from the organizations and activities of the "woman movement." Second, while working-class women appear to have supported many of the goals of the women reformers at the turn of the century, it was more difficult for them, especially once married and mothers, to participate in the organization building through which middle-class women exercised influence within the male-dominated political system (Jones 1985; Tilly 1981). Even when working-class women participated in reform organizations and campaigns, these tended to be dominated by middle-class women who set the reform agenda in ways that both represented and denied the needs of their working-class allies (Tax 1980).

Middle-class white women's political influence was accomplished through organized educational, research, and lobbying activities based in the women's club movement, settlement house movement, and child welfare and mother's groups—all organizations whose mandate for action was grounded in the nineteenth-century doctrine of separate spheres. The great irony of this period is that the same gender division of labor that marginalized white middle-class women from paid labor and mandated their economic dependence on men also provided them an institutional base from which to organize politically. For it was through voluntary associations that grew out of their responsibilities for social reproduction (for managing homes and raising children) that white middle-class women developed the political resources necessary for collective action. This collective action had two dimensions—the demand for political equality and the demand for social protection and support for motherhood. Its apparently contradictory elements were integrated in the claim that women's responsibilities as mothers justified, indeed demanded, their access to political power.

The maternalist politics so central to middle-class women's political activism in the Progressive Era reflected the social position and experience of the women who put it forward. Campaigns for state intervention had allowed some middle-class women to carve out alternatives to marriage and motherhood by taking up work as providers of social services in the new "female" professions—school teaching, home economics, social work (Glazer and Slater 1987); public health (Morantz-Sanchez 1985, 282-315); and nursing (Reverby 1987, 109-110). Many of these women, and the single-sex institutions they built, provided leadership and organizational resources to the movement (Freedman 1979). But in calling for the state to increase the resources available to women, including working-class and immigrant women, to fulfill their maternal role, the vast majority of middle-class activist women were reflecting their own life experience and goals as married mothers dependent on a male breadwinner.

Whatever the limits of the Progressive Era women's movement (including its class and race biases and the powerful political opposition it faced), advocates for women had an impact on law and public policy outcomes. In the 1930s by contrast, and despite African American and white women's continuing involvement in voluntary and political organizations (Cott 1990; Higginbotham 1990), feminism was fundamentally marginalized in political organization and political discourse. There was, as a consequence, no challenge to the institutionalization of the gender division of labor in relief programs, education and job training, social security legislation, unemployment insurance, labor relations law, and, of course, Aid to Families with Dependent Children (Abramovitz 1988; Faue 1990; Ware 1982).

Several explanations have been put forward for why the broad-based "women's rights" movement declined in the 1920s. Splits in the movement between "equal rights feminists" and "social-feminists" (Cott 1987), the increasingly single-issue focus on suffrage and the consequent emphasis on electoral politics (Mueller 1988) that left the movement without political influence once a women's voting block failed to materialize, the postwar repression of the Left and the increasingly

conservative political climate (Jensen 1983)—all contributed to undermining feminist organization. We would agree that the conservative
political climate and sectarian divisions of the 1920s would have discouraged political activism and made it more difficult to recruit new
members during that decade. But, all else being equal, we would also
expect a resurgence of activity and organization as the political climate
changed in the 1930s. Certainly, this was the case for the African
American movement, which recovered from the decline suffered during
the late 1920s and early 1930s as a result of political repression and the
impoverishment of the African American community (Sitkoff 1978).
Indeed, during this decade, migration northward and to the cities increased African American capacity for organization and mobilization
(Clark-Lewis 1987). In contrast, we would argue, the changing organization of social reproduction had undermined the development of gender solidarity among white, middle-class women and their potential for
self-organization.

Unlike their white counterparts, African American middle-class
women could not hope to advance the careers of sons and husbands
through an exclusively private strategy. Traditions of women's political
self-organization remained strong, and their organizations played leadership roles in the political defense of the African American community
(Giddings 1984; Terborg-Penn 1983). White middle-class women's
rights activists and organizations also continued into the 1930s, and
women who saw themselves as advocates for women gained influence
in the Democratic party and the New Deal administration (Cott 1987;
Ware 1987). Although this elite of professional and activist women was
better positioned than ever before within political institutions, they had
lost their access to a mass base. The changing material conditions of
married white middle-class women's lives undermined the information
networks, social solidarities, and self-definitions that had facilitated
their political mobilization. Without that potential mass support, advocates for women within the New Deal administration and the Democratic party, no matter how well placed, could not turn their personal
influence and expertise into legislative and policy victories. A different
set of circumstances constrained the activities of working-class women.

During the 1930s, working-class communities waged historic struggles and women played important roles in both community and labor
movements. Yet their activism rarely took the form of women's self-
organization, either within these movements (as in the case of women
in the African American movement) or outside them (as in the cross-

class alliances of women in the Progressive Era). It might be argued that in the face of the economic hardships of the Depression, working-class women would be concerned more with survival than "equality"; or that the need for class solidarity demanded by the community and labor struggles of the decade prevented alliances with the middle-class women and organizations who continued to advocate for women in the 1930s. Yet the experience of the African American movement demonstrates that it was possible to participate in working-class protest and organize for equality at the same time. Indeed, the activity of a cross-class movement based in race solidarity was critical to the inclusion of African American working people in the organizations of working-class struggle and political representation.

Of course, the movement for African American equality was hardly victorious in this period. Racist policies of segregation, exclusion from labor law protection, and discrimination in relief and social services persisted at both federal and local levels. But taking the period as a whole, the New Deal and World War II brought tremendous steps forward in consciousness and political organization for African Americans. For women, however, things were quite different. Reform demands and state policies in the 1930s revolved around the assumption that families were or should be supported by male breadwinners (Kessler-Harris 1990). Women's rights organizations and women trade-union activists protested bans on married women's employment, the exclusion of unemployed women from relief programs, underrepresentation of women in work programs, and the exclusion of women's jobs from Fair Labor Standards legislation (Scharf 1983).

To understand why organized women were so unsuccessful in winning support for these demands, we have to consider that, while women's labor force participation increased during the decade, the vast majority of married women did not work for wages. In 1940 only 15 percent of married women were in paid labor; even at the lowest levels of family income, only 25 percent worked for pay (Ware 1982). In addition, working-class women who did work for pay were doubly burdened by their domestic responsibilities. Women trade-union activists tended to be young and single or older women whose children were also older (Frankel 1984; Meyerowitz 1980). Domestic burdens did not keep women from participating in bursts of militant action—but they were a barrier to participation in day-to-day organization building. Yet without an organizational base, the women trade-union activists were limited in how successfully they could challenge male domination within the labor movement. In contrast to the issue of racism, feminist concerns remained marginal within the organizations leading the social movements of the 1930s: the Congress of Industrial Organizations (CIO) and the Communist party.

While increasing numbers of women entered paid labor in the 1930s, the majority of workers were still men—88 percent of employed workers nationally and 78 percent in manufacturing. African American workers were also a minority within the labor force. But whereas occupational gender segregation meant that organizing men usually did not require organizing women, organizing white men did require organizing African American men, especially in the mass-production industries that were the focus of the CIO.

The trade-union movement began to recognize that it had to identify itself with African American civil rights—not just the inclusion of blacks in unions but, more broadly, the struggle for equal opportunity in employment and against discrimination in education, housing, and the legal system. Pressure for this recognition came from two directions: from the importance of African American men in the mass-production industries and from the political self-organization of African Americans in the communities where the CIO was organizing. Some of the individuals leading the CIO had personal histories of support for African American equality. Communists in the unions were especially active in pushing for antiracist policies and the inclusion of African Americans in leadership positions. But their ability to win the point with the rank-and-file in the CIO rested in part on the reality of the conditions for organizing in the mass-production industries—the often pivotal role of African American men in the labor process and the employers' use of African American workers as scabs. White workers in the CIO were by no means immediately won over to support African American workers' rights, but although racism was persistent and pervasive throughout the 1930s and during the war, it was at least contested within the CIO, while sexism went substantially unchallenged.

In some times and places, the CIO unions became significant allies of the movement for civil rights (Sitkoff 1978, 184-85). For example, African American workers constituted 12 percent of Ford employees, concentrated at the strategic River Rouge plant in Detroit. The United Auto Workers (UAW) became the most vocal advocate in the labor movement of anti-lynching and anti-poll tax legislation, the most lavish contributor to Negro rights associations, and the most constant lobbyist in Congress for legislation favorable to African Americans. Civil rights spokesmen in return marched in UAW picket lines around the Rouge plant. This was crucial for the union, because up to this point, Ford's "welfarist" policies toward institutions in the African American community had recruited the black community leadership to his side. Ford capitulated in 1941, recognizing the UAW and agreeing to wage increases (Sitkoff 1978, 186).

As women's share of the labor force increased during the war and as women workers began to organize, they were able to force the CIO unions give greater recognition to their needs (Milkman 1987; Strom 1983). But even where working women were able to win over their local unions, they still were operating in a political and social climate in which the male-breadwinner ideology was hegemonic. Without a broader social movement that effectively challenged the gender division of labor and supported their rights to work, women workers found themselves politically isolated. In contrast, African American men could rely on movements, such as the NAACP, that had increased in membership and militancy (Foner 1979; Sitkoff 1978). Thus African American men workers and women workers fared very differently in the postwar industries that they had entered during the war (Milkman 1987).

The militancy and self-organization of African Americans not only affected the unions but also the revolutionary Left, which gave important, although not always consistent, support to their organizing efforts. Whereas the struggle against African American oppression was at the center of Communist party politics, the party's relationship to feminism remained ambivalent, if not hostile. Since the Communist party dominated the Left and its culture during the 1930s, the party's organization and politics constituted another barrier to the development of women's self-organization.

Although never dominant, socialist feminist politics had emerged in the Progressive Era. Many of the first generation of "new women," such as Jane Addams and Florence Kelly, identified with the socialist movement (Jensen 1983). And the "sex radicals" of the Bohemian world of Greenwich Village, Paris, and Berlin in the 1920s also provided an alternative vision of gender possibilities (Trimberger 1983). These traditions were suppressed within the Communist party. The hierarchical structure of the party made it extremely difficult to challenge official programs and policy. Without norms of free debate and discussion, women on the Left had little space to raise questions that were not on the leadership's agenda (Shaffer 1979; Trimberger 1979).

The Communists' emphasis on workplace organizing and on the historic center of trade unionism—male blue-collar workers—tended to marginalize issues of concern to women. Nevertheless, and despite the lack of interest from their party, Communist women spearheaded women's organization as workers and as members of working-class communities (Strom 1983). On the whole, however, this organizing focused primarily on public discrimination rather than on the gender division of labor and male power in the household. While defending women's rights to work and demanding help for women workers to negotiate a double day, the Communist party never questioned that home and family remained primarily a woman's responsibility.

While the political culture and structure of the Communist Party restricted women's opportunities for challenging the dominant view, many women members, like the majority of adult women outside the party, were also housewives dependent on men for economic support. For them, for much the same reasons as for other women, the notion that the key issue in the defense of the working class was the demand for employment, unionization, and higher wages for men would have been quite compelling. Thus neither the women nor the men within the Communist party could articulate a critique of the gender division of labor in both working-class and middle-class families.

Had there been a feminist movement in the 1930s as radical in its critique of domestic life as the Communist party was of capitalism, Communist women might well have organized on their own behalf and developed "communist-feminist" politics. In the 1930s, however, in the absence of feminist movements and organizations in the larger society, it was impossible for women on the Left to envision, let alone organize, a new way of accomplishing the work of social reproduction.

In the 1960s, the political ideas of the civil rights and student movements, challenging inferiority based on biological difference and demanding democratic and egalitarian forms of governance, provided a powerful intellectual framework that women could adopt to further their own ends. In comparison to Left culture of the 1930s, the 1960s counter-culture legitimated the search for individual self-expression as a political goal, opening up more space for women to question sexism in personal as well as political life (Trimberger 1979). While these differences are important in explaining the emergence of feminism in the 1960s, we would also emphasize the changing conditions of middle-class women's lives.

Whereas turn-of-the-century women's organization found a mass base in middle-class homemakers, second-wave feminism was based on social networks and institutional and economic resources that grew out of middle-class women's increasing participation in employment and higher education. While suburban housewives swelled the ranks of recruits, the mainstream movement developed from preexisting networks and organizational resources of women professionals, trade-union officials, and political party activists (Gabin 1990; Rossi 1982). With one in five women enrolled in higher education, the radical organizations of the second wave found a mass base, facilities, and institutional resources in and around colleges and universities (Ferree and Hess 1985).

Older married women may have reentered paid labor in fulfillment of their responsibilities to their families and younger women may have entered college expecting to follow their mothers' life courses, but within a short time of its emergence, second-wave feminism had begun to challenge the gender division of labor in social reproduction itself. This challenge originated in the young women of the movement, a generation for whom the contradictions of companionate marriage and phallocentric and compulsory heterosexuality were especially explosive (D'Emilio and Freedman 1988). Since that time, and partly through the articulation of the interests of working-class women and women of color in the welfare rights, civil rights, and trade-union movements (Balser 1987; West 1981), the gender division of labor and the role of the state in fostering or undermining women's social and sexual autonomy has come to be a political issue.

This challenge to the gender division of labor responds to the change in women's labor force participation over the last two decades—that now the vast majority of women do a "double day." However, the political response is accounted for not by the problem of the double day itself but by women's increased resources for self-organization. In part because of the previous gains of the women's movement and in part because of the continued demand for women's labor (their growing share of trade-union membership, their presence in the upper-level professions), women's self-organization has been institutionalized in professional associations, trade unions, and political organizations. While no longer a radical movement, feminism has maintained a political presence through a loose network of organizations advocating for women (Brenner 1993). No battles have been definitely won, and some may be temporarily lost, but men's responsibility for child care and domestic work, the privileging of heterosexual marriage in the provision of employee benefits and state services, and the legitimacy of women-headed families are now matters of political debate as well as personal conflict.

CONCLUSION

We have argued that the development of welfare state policy cannot be explained by its functions in protecting the interests of men as a group or capitalists as a class but has to be explained historically as the outcome of political conflict and political interventions, including the collective action of women. But drawing on Marxist and feminist theory, we emphasize the ways in which the political goals and resources of contesting groups are historically constrained, and we locate those constraints in structures of gender as well as class. We argue that the organization of social reproduction and the gender division of labor central to it not only have placed limits on but also, at times, have provided resources for women's self-organization.

Our approach is a historical materialist one, for we take as a starting point the socially necessary and socially organized labor through which humans reproduce themselves—not only the production of things but the work involved in using those things to renew life. In addition to what we consider a more comprehensive historical analysis, our approach also aims at developing a single-system theory, based on the recognition that production and social reproduction are two domains of an integrated process of species reproduction. Although a full account of the interrelationship has not been possible here, our analysis indicates the ways in which the changes in the organization of social reproduction that were so crucial to the presence and absence of women's self-organization in twentieth-century United States were related to qualitative changes in the capitalist economy (the rise of corporate capitalism, mass production, and the beginnings of mass consumption in the early twentieth century; the rise of multinational firms, the spread of mass education, and mass consumption and the consequent demand for women's labor after World War II).

The advantages of our framework are clear in its ability to cut through the counterpositions in feminist analysis of the welfare state between those that emphasize women's political agency (and, therefore, the ways in which the state conferred resources on women) and those that emphasize women's political powerlessness (and, therefore, the ways in which the welfare state has reinforced women's economic marginalization and dependence on the male-dominated nuclear family). We have tried to show that although the gender division of labor remained constant, its implications for women's political self-organization changed quite radically over the course of the twentieth century. Qualitative shifts in the organization of social reproduction, material and ideological, explain why middle-class women achieved self-organization during the Progressive Era and during the 1960s and 1970s but not in the 1930s. These changes also explain why white middle-class women organized around maternalist politics that helped to institutionalize the ideal of the male breadwinner family in state policy, while second-wave feminism has contested the gender division of labor in the state, the family, and the economy.

In considering the impact of the organization of social reproduction on women's collective action, we have also argued that the differences in the politics of self-organized African American and white middle-class women reflected the different demands and possibilities African American women faced in carrying out their responsibilities for social reproduction. In particular, African American middle-class women could not rely on the individualized strategies of upward mobility available to the white middle class. Further, we have argued that continuities in the organization of social reproduction, especially the substantial privatization of the burdens of caregiving that fall especially heavily on working-class women, also explain outcomes. The gender division of labor diminished working-class women's capacities for self-organization and limited their ability to challenge either the working-class men or middle-class women who dominated political movements and organizations purporting to represent them in the contest over state policy.

Our account is by no means a finished one that fully incorporates class, race, and gender into an explanation of the welfare state. But we hope we have demonstrated the potential of our conceptual framework and the value of pursuing a single-system socialist-feminist analysis.

REFERENCES

Abramovitz, M. 1988. *Regulating the lives of women: Social welfare policy from colonial times to the present.* Boston: South End Press.

Antler, J. 1987. *Lucy Sprague Mitchell: The making of a modern women.* New Haven, CT: Yale University Press.

Balser, D. 1987. *Sisterhood and solidarity: Feminism and labor in modern times.* Boston: South End Press.

Boris, E., and P. Bardaglio. 1983. The transformation of patriarchy: The historical role of the state. In *Family, politics, and public policy: A feminist dialogue on women and the state,* edited by I. Diamond. New York: Longman.

————. 1987. Gender, race and class: The impact of the state on the family and the economy, 1790-1945. In *Families and work,* edited by N. Gerstel and H. E. Gross. Philadelphia: Temple University Press.

Breckinridge, S. P. 1933. The activities of women outside the home. In *Recent social trends,* edited by President's Research Committee. Vol. 1. New York: McGraw-Hill.

Brenner, J. 1993. The best of times, the worst of times: U.S. feminism today. *New Left Review 200* (July/August): 101-160.

Brenner, J., and B. Laslett. 1986. Social reproduction and the family. In *Sociology from crisis to science? Vol. 2., The social production of organization and culture,* edited by U. Himmelstrand. London: Sage.

Brown, E. B. 1989. Womanist consciousness: Maggie Lena Walker and the independent order of Saint Luke. *Signs* 14:610-33.

Chodorow, N. 1989. Seventies questions for thirties women: Gender and generation in a study of early women psychoanalysts. In *Feminism and psychoanalytic theory,* edited by N. Chodorow. New Haven, CT: Yale University Press.

Clark-Lewis, E. 1987. This work had an end: African-American domestic workers in Washington, D.C., 1919-1940. In *"To toil the live long day": America's women at work, 1780-1980,* edited by C. Groneman and M. B. Norton. Ithaca, NY: Cornell University Press.

Cott, N. F. 1978. Passionlessness: An interpretation of Victorian sexual ideology, 1790-1850. *Signs* 4:219-36.

————. 1987. *The grounding of modern feminism.* New Haven, CT: Yale University Press.

————. 1990. Across the great divide: Women in politics before and after 1920. In *Women, politics and change,* edited by L. Tilly and P. Gurin. New York: Russell Sage.

Cowan, R. S. 1983. Two washes in the morning and a bridge party at night: The American housewife between the wars. In *Decades of discontent: The women's movement, 1920-1940,* edited by L. Scharf and J. M. Jensen. Westport, CT: Greenwood.

D'Emilio, J., and E. B. Freedman. 1988. *Intimate matters: A history of sexuality in America.* New York: Harper & Row.

Elder, G. H. 1984. *Children of the Great Depression: Social change in life experience.* Chicago: University of Chicago Press.

Evans, S. M. 1979. *Personal politics: The roots of women's liberation in the civil rights movement and the New Left.* New York: Knopf.

Faue, E. 1990. Women, family, and politics: Farmer-labor women and social policy in the Great Depression. In *Women, politics and change,* edited by L. Tilly and P. Gurin. New York: Russell Sage.

Ferree, M. M., and B. B. Hess. 1985. *Controversy and coalition: The new feminist movement.* Boston: Twayne.

Fine, L. M. 1990. *The souls of the skyscraper: Female clerical workers in Chicago, 1870-1930.* Philadelphia: Temple University Press.

Foner, P. S. 1979. *Women and the American labor movement.* New York: Free Press.

Frankel, L. 1984. Southern textile women: Generations of survival and struggle. In *My troubles are going to have trouble with me,* edited by K. Sacks and D. Remy. New Brunswick, NJ: Rutgers University Press.

Freedman, E. B. 1979. Separatism as strategy: Female institution building and American feminism, 1870-1930. *Feminist Studies* 5:512-20.

Gabin, N. F. 1990. *Feminism in the labor movement: Women and the United Auto Workers, 1935-1975.* Ithaca, NY: Cornell University Press.

Giddings, P. 1984. *Where and when I enter: The impact of Black women on race and sex in America.* New York: William Morrow.

Glazer, Nona. 1993. *Women's paid and unpaid labor: The work transfer in health care and retailing.* Philadelphia: Temple University Press.

Glazer, P. M., and M. Slater. 1987. *Unequal colleagues: The entrance of women into the professions, 1890-1940.* New Brunswick, NJ: Rutgers University Press.

Glenn, Evelyn Nakano. 1992. From servitude to service work: Historical continuities in the racial division of paid reproductive labor. *Signs* 18:1-43.

Glick, P. C. 1977. Updating the life cycle of the family. *Journal of Marriage and the Family* 39:5-14.

Grabill, W. H., C. V. Kiser, and P. K. Whelpton. 1958. *The fertility of American women.* New York: John Wiley.

Hartmann, H. 1979. The unhappy marriage of Marxism and feminism: Towards a more progressive union. *Capital and Class* 8:1-33.

Higginbotham, E. B. 1990. In politics to stay: Black women leaders and party politics in the 1920s. In *Women, politics, and change,* edited by L. Tilly and P. Gurin. New York: Russell Sage.

Jensen, J. M. 1983. All pink sisters: The war department and the feminist movement in the 1920s. In *Decades of discontent: The women's movement, 1920-1940,* edited by L. Scharf and J. M. Jensen. Westport, CT: Greenwood.

Jones, J. 1985. *Labor of love, labor of sorrow: Black women, work, and the family from slavery to the present.* New York: Basic Books.

Kessler-Harris, A. 1990. *A woman's wage: Historical meanings and social consequences.* Lexington: University Press of Kentucky.

Laslett, B. 1990a. Unfeeling knowledge: Emotion and objectivity in the history of sociology. *Sociological Forum* 5:413-34.

―――. 1990b. Women's work in Los Angeles, California: 1880-1900: Implications of class and gender. *Continuity and Change* 5:417-41.

Laslett, B., and J. Brenner. 1989. Gender and social reproduction: Historical perspectives. *Annual Review of Sociology* 15:381-404.

Maroney, H. J., and M. Luxton. 1987. From feminism and political economy to feminist political economy. In *Feminism and political economy: Women's work, women's struggles.* Toronto: Methuen.

Meyerowitz, R. 1980. Women unionists and World War II: New opportunities for leadership. A paper delivered at the meetings of the Organization for American Historians, San Francisco, April.

Milkman, R. 1987. *Gender at work.* Urbana: University of Illinois Press.

Mink, G. 1990. The lady and the tramp: Gender, race and the origins of the American welfare state. In *Women, the state and welfare,* edited by L. Gordon. Madison: University of Wisconsin Press.

Morantz-Sanchez, R. M. 1985. *Sympathy and science: Women physicians in American medicine.* New York: Oxford University Press.

Mueller, C. M. 1988. The empowerment of women: Polling and the women's voting block. In *The politics of the gender gap,* edited by C. M. Mueller. Newbury Park, CA: Sage.

Nelson, B. 1990. The gender, race and class origins of early welfare policy and the U.S. welfare state: A comparison of workmen's compensation and mothers' aid. In *Women, politics and change,* edited by L. Tilly and P. Gurin. New York: Russell Sage.

Norwood, S. H. 1990. *Labor's flaming youth: Telephone operators and worker militancy, 1878-1923.* Urbana: University of Illinois Press.

Oppenheimer, V. K. 1970. *The female labor force in the United States.* Population Monograph Series, no. 5. Berkeley: University of California Press.

———. 1974. The life-cycle squeeze: The interaction of men's occupational and family life cycles. *Demography* 11:227-45.

Orloff, A. 1991. Gender in early U.S. social policy. *Journal of Policy History* 3:249-281.

———. 1993. *The politics of pensions: A comparative analysis of the origins of pensions and old-age insurance in Canada, Great Britain and the United States, 1880-1940.* Madison: University of Wisconsin Press.

Palmer, P. 1989. *Domesticity and dirt: Housewives and domestic servants in the United States, 1920-1945.* Philadelphia: Temple University Press.

Reverby, S. M. 1987. *Ordered to care: The dilemma of American nursing, 1850-1945.* Cambridge, UK: Cambridge University Press.

Ross, D. 1979. The development of the social sciences. In *The organization of knowledge in modern America, 1860-1920,* edited by A. Oleson and J. Voss. Baltimore, MD: Johns Hopkins University Press.

Rossi, A. S. 1982. *Feminists in politics.* New York: Academic Press.

Scharf, L. 1980. *To work and to wed: Female employment, feminism, and the Great Depression.* Westport, CT: Greenwood.

———. 1983. The forgotten woman: Working women, the New Deal, and women's organizations. In *Decades of discontent: The women's movement, 1920-1940,* edited by L. Scharf and J. M. Jensen. Westport, CT: Greenwood.

Schlossman, S. L. 1976. Before Home Start: Notes toward a history of parent education in America, 1897-1929. *Harvard Educational Review* 46:436-67.

———. 1981. Philanthropy and the gospel of child development. *History of Education Quarterly* 21:275-99.

Shaffer, R. 1979. Women and the Communist party, USA, 1930-1940. *Socialist Review* 9(3):73-118.

Sitkoff, H. 1978. *A New Deal for Blacks.* New York: Oxford University Press.

Skocpol, T. 1992. *Protecting soldiers and mothers: The political origins of social policy in the United States.* Cambridge, MA: Harvard University Press.

Smith, D. E. 1989. Feminist reflections on political economy. *Studies in Political Economy* 30:37-59.

Smith-Rosenberg, C. 1985. *Disorderly conduct: Visions of gender in Victorian America.* New York: Oxford University Press.

Strom, S. H. 1983. Challenging "woman's place": Feminism, the new left, and industrial unionism. *Feminist Studies* 9:361-86.

Tax, M. 1980. *The rising of the women: Feminist solidarity and class conflict, 1880-1917.* New York: Monthly Review Press.

Terborg-Penn, R. 1983. Discontented Black feminists: Prelude and postscript to the passage of the nineteenth amendment. In *Decades of discontent: The women's movement, 1920-1940,* edited by L. Scharf and J. M. Jensen. Westport, CT: Greenwood.

Tilly, L. 1981. Paths of proletarianization: Organization of production, sexual division of labor, and women's collective action. *Signs* 7:400-417.

Trimberger, K. E. 1979. Women in the old and new left: The evolution of a politics of personal life. *Feminist Studies* 5:432-61.

———. 1983. Feminism, men and modern love: Greenwich Village, 1900-1925. In *Powers of desire,* edited by A. Snitow, C. Stansell, and S. Thompson. New York: Monthly Review Press.

Tyack, D., and E. Hansot. 1990. *Learning together: A history of coeducation in American schools.* New Haven, CT: Yale University Press.

Wandersee, W. D. 1981. *Women's work and family values, 1920-1940.* Cambridge, MA: Harvard University Press.

Ware, S. 1982. *Holding their own: American women in the 1930s.* Boston: Twayne.

———. 1987. *Partner and I: Molly Dewson, feminism and New Deal politics.* New Haven, CT: Yale University Press.

West, G. 1981. *The national welfare rights movement: The social protest of poor women.* New York: Praeger.

Wrigley, J. 1990. Children's caregivers and ideologies of parental inadequacy. In *Circles of care,* edited by E. Abel and M. K. Nelson. Albany: State University of New York Press.

18 Doing Difference

CANDACE WEST
SARAH FENSTERMAKER

Few persons think of math as a particularly feminine pursuit. Girls are not supposed to be good at it and women are not supposed to enjoy it. It is interesting, then, that we who do feminist scholarship have relied so heavily on mathematical metaphors to describe the relationships among gender, race, and class.[1] For example, some of us have drawn on basic arithmetic, adding, subtracting, and dividing what we know about race and class to what we already know about gender. Some have relied on multiplication, seeming to calculate the effects of the whole from the combination of different parts. And others have employed geometry, drawing on images of "interlocking" or "intersecting" planes and axes.

To be sure, the sophistication of our mathematical metaphors often varies with the apparent complexity of our own experiences. Those of us who, at one point, were able to "forget" race and class in our analyses of gender relations may be more likely to "add" these at a later point. By contrast, those of us who could never forget these dimensions of social life may be more likely to draw on complex geometrical imagery all along. Nonetheless, the existence of so many different approaches to the topic seems indicative of the difficulties all of us have experienced in coming to terms with it.

AUTHORS' NOTE: We gratefully acknowledge the critical comments and suggestions of John Brown Childs, Adele Clark, Evelyn Nakano Glenn, Herman Gray, Aída Hurtado, Valerie Jenness, Nancy Jurik, Patricia Merriwether, Pamela Roby, Dana Takagi, James R. West, Don H. Zimmerman, Maxine Baca Zinn, the graduate students of UCSB's Sociology 212P (Winter 1993), and especially Denise Segura. Thanks to Pattie Forgie for bibliographic assistance.

357

Not surprisingly, proliferation of these approaches has caused considerable confusion in the existing literature. In the same book or article, we may find references to gender, race, and class as "intersecting systems," as "interlocking categories," and as "multiple bases" for oppression. In the same anthology, we may find some chapters that conceive of gender, race, and class as distinct axes and others that conceive of them as concentric circles. The problem is that these alternative formulations have very distinctive yet unarticulated theoretical implications. For instance, if we think about gender, race, and class as additive categories, the whole will never be greater (or lesser) than the sum of its parts. By contrast, if we conceive of these as multiples, the result could be larger or smaller than their sum, depending on where we place the signs.[2] Geometric metaphors further complicate things, since we still need to know where those planes and axes go *after* they cross the point of intersection (and if they are *parallel* planes and axes, they will never intersect at all).

Our purpose in this chapter is not to advance yet another new math but to propose a new way of thinking about the workings of these relations. Elsewhere (Fenstermaker Berk 1985; Fenstermaker, West, and Zimmerman 1991; West and Fenstermaker 1993; West and Zimmerman 1987), we have offered an ethnomethodologically informed and hence distinctively sociological conceptualization of gender as a routine, methodical, and ongoing accomplishment. We argued that doing gender involves a complex of perceptual, interactional, and micropolitical activities that cast particular pursuits as expressions of manly and womanly "natures." Rather than conceiving of gender as an individual characteristic, we conceived of it as an emergent property of social situations: both an outcome of and a rationale for various social arrangements and a means of justifying one of the most fundamental divisions of society. We suggested that examining how gender is accomplished could reveal the mechanisms by which power is exercised and inequality is produced.

Our earlier formulation neglected race and class; thus, it is an incomplete framework for understanding social inequality. In this chapter, we extend our analysis to consider explicitly the relationships among gender, race, and class, and reconceptualize *difference* as an ongoing interactional accomplishment. We start by summarizing the prevailing critique of much feminist thought and next we consider how existing conceptualizations of gender have contributed to the problem, rendering mathematical metaphors the only alternatives. Then, calling on our earlier ethnomethodological conceptualization of gender, we develop the further implications of this perspective for our understanding of race and class. We assert that, while gender, race, and class—what people come to experience as organizing categories of social difference—exhibit vastly different descriptive characteristics and outcomes, they are nonetheless comparable as *mechanisms* for producing social inequality.

WHITE MIDDLE-CLASS BIAS IN FEMINIST THOUGHT

What is it about feminist thinking that makes race and class such difficult concepts to articulate within its own parameters? The most widely agreed upon and disturbing answer to this question is that feminist thought suffers from a white middle-class bias. The privileging of white and middle-class sensibilities in feminist thought results both from who did the theorizing and how they did it. White middle-class women's advantaged viewpoint in a racist and class-bound culture, coupled with the Western tendency to construct the self as distinct from "other," distorts their depictions of reality in predictable directions (Young 1990). The consequences of these distortions have been identified in a variety of places and analyses of them have enlivened every aspect of feminist scholarship (see, for example, Aptheker 1989; Baca Zinn 1990; Collins 1990; Davis 1981; Hurtado 1989).

Racism and classism can take a variety of forms. Adrienne Rich contends that, although white (middle-class) feminists may not consciously believe that their race is superior to any other, they are often plagued by a form of "white solipsism"—thinking, imagining, and speaking "as if whiteness described the world," resulting in "a tunnel-vision which simply does not see nonwhite experience or existence as precious or significant, unless in spasmodic, impotent guilt reflexes, which have little or no long-term, continuing usefulness" (1979, 306). Therefore, white middle-class feminists may offer conscientious expressions of concern over "racism-and-classism," believing that they have thereby taken into consideration profound differences in women's experience; simultaneously, they can fail to see those differences at all (Bhavani 1993).

There is nothing that prevents any of these dynamics from coexisting and working together. For example, Collins (1990) argues that the suppression of Black feminist thought stems both from white feminists' racist and classist concerns and from Black women intellectuals' consequent lack of participation in white feminist organizations. Similarly, Cherríe Moraga (1981) argues that the "denial of difference" in feminist organizations derives not only from white middle-class women's failure to "see" it but also from women of color's and working-class women's reluctance to challenge such blindness. Alone and in combination with one another, these sources of bias do much to explain why there has been a general failure to articulate race and class within the parameters of feminist scholarship; however, they do not explain the attraction of mathematical metaphors to right the balance. To understand this development, we must look further at the logic of feminist thought itself.

Mathematical Metaphors and Feminist Thought

Following the earlier suggestion of bell hooks (1981; see also Hull, Scott, and Smith 1982), Elizabeth Spelman contends that, in practice, the term *women* actually functions as a powerful false generic in white feminists' thinking:

> The "problem of difference" for feminist theory has never been a general one about how to weigh the importance of what we have in common against the importance of our differences. To put it that way hides two crucial facts: First, the description of what we have in common "as women" has almost always been a description of white middle-class women. Second, the "difference" of this group of women—that is, their being white and middle-class—has never had to be "brought into" feminist theory. To bring in "difference" is to bring in women who aren't white and middle class. (1988, 4)

She warns that thinking about privilege merely as a characteristic of individuals—rather than as a characteristic of modes of thought—may afford us an understanding of "what privilege feeds but not what sustains it" (1988, 4).

What are the implications of a feminist *mode of thought* that is so severely limited? The most important one, says Spelman, is the presumption that we can effectively and usefully isolate gender from race and class. To illustrate this point, she draws on many white feminists who develop their analyses of sexism by comparing and contrasting it with "other" forms of oppression. Herein she finds the basis for additive models of gender, race, and class, and "the ampersand problem":

de Beauvoir tends to talk about comparisons between sex and race, or between sex and class, or between sex and culture . . . comparisons between sexism and racism, between sexism and classism, between sexism and anti-Semitism. In the work of Chodorow and others influenced by her, we observe a readiness to look for links between sexism and other forms of oppression as distinct from sexism. (1988, 115)

Spelman notes that in both cases, attempts to *add* "other" elements of identity to gender, or "other" forms of oppression to sexism, disguise the race (white) and class (middle) identities of those seen as "women" in the first place. Rich's "white solipsism" comes into play again, and it is impossible to envision how women who are not white and middle class fit into the picture. Spelman's (1988) analysis highlights the following problem: If we conceive of gender as coherently isolatable from race and class, then there is every reason to assume that the effects of the three variables can be multiplied, with results dependent on the valence (positive or negative) of those multiplied variables; yet if we grant that gender *cannot* be coherently isolated from race and class in the way we conceptualize it, then multiplicative metaphors make little sense.

If the effects of "multiple oppression" are not merely additive nor simply multiplicative, what are they? Some scholars have described them as the products of "simultaneous and intersecting systems of relationship and meaning" (Andersen and Collins 1992, xiii; see also Almquist 1989; Collins 1990; Glenn 1985). This description is useful insofar as it offers an accurate characterization of persons who are simultaneously oppressed on the basis of gender, race, and class, in other words, those "at the intersection" of all three systems of domination; however, if we conceive of the basis of oppression as more than membership in a category, then the theoretical implications of this formulation are troubling. For instance, what conclusions shall we draw from potential comparisons between persons who experience oppression on the basis of their race and class (e.g., working-class men of color) and those who are oppressed on the basis of their gender and class (e.g., white working-class women)? Would the "intersection of two systems of meaning in each case be sufficient to predict common bonds among them"? (Jordan 1985, 46). Clearly not, says June Jordan: "When these factors of race, class and gender absolutely collapse is whenever you try to use them as automatic concepts of connection." She goes on to say that, while these concepts may work very well as indexes of "commonly felt conflict," their predictive value when they are used as "elements of connection" is "about as reliable as precipitation probability for the day after the night before the day" (1985, 46).

What conclusions shall we draw from comparisons between persons who are said to suffer oppression "at the intersection" of all three systems and those who suffer in the nexus of only two? Presumably, we will conclude that the latter are "less oppressed" than the former (assuming that each categorical identity set amasses a specific quantity of oppression). However, Moraga warns that "the danger lies in ranking the oppressions. *The danger lies in failing to acknowledge the specificity of the oppression*" (1981, 29).

Spelman (1988, 123-25) attempts to resolve this difficulty by characterizing sexism, racism, and classism as "interlocking" with one another. Along similar lines, Margaret Andersen and Patricia Hill Collins (1992, xii) describe gender, race, and class as "interlocking categories of experience." An image of interlocking rings (like a Venn diagram) comes to mind, with the rings linked in such a way that the motion of any one of them is constrained by the others. Certainly this image is more dynamic than those conveyed by additive, multiplicative, or geometric models: We can imagine where the rings would be joined (and where they would not), as well as how the movement of any one of them would be restricted by the others. But note that this image would still depict the rings as *separate parts*.

If we try to imagine situating particular persons within this image, the problem with it becomes clear. We can, of course, conceive of the whole as "oppressed people" and of the rings as "those oppressed by gender," "those oppressed by race," and "those oppressed by class." This would allow us to situate women and men of all races and classes within the areas covered by the circles, save for white middle- and upper-class men, who fall outside them. However, what if we conceive of the whole as "experience"[3] and of the rings as gender, race, and class?

Then, we would face an illuminating possibility and leave arithmetic behind: No person can experience gender *without simultaneously* experiencing race and class. As Andersen and Collins (1992, xxi) put it, "While race, class and gender can be seen as different axes of social structure, individual persons experience them simultaneously."[4] It is this simultaneity that has eluded our theoretical treatments and is so difficult to build into our empirical descriptions (for an admirable effort, see Segura 1992). How do forms of inequality, which we now see are more than the periodic collision of categories, operate *together?* How do we see that all social exchanges, regardless of the participants or the outcome, are simultaneously "gendered," "raced," and "classed"?

To address these questions, we first present some earlier attempts to conceptualize gender. Appreciation for the limitations of these efforts, we believe, affords us a way to the second task: reconceptualizing the dynamics of gender, race, and class as they figure simultaneously in human institutions and interaction.

TRADITIONAL CONCEPTUALIZATIONS OF GENDER

To begin, we turn to Arlie Russell Hochschild's "A Review of Sex Roles Research," published in 1973. At that time, there were at least four distinct ways of conceptualizing gender within the burgeoning literature on the topic: (1) as sex differences, (2) as sex roles, (3) in relation to the minority status of women, and (4) in relation to the caste/class status of women. Hochschild observed that each of these conceptualizations led to a different perspective on the behaviors of women and men:

> What is to type 1 a feminine trait such as passivity is to type 2 a role element, to type 3 is a minority characteristic, and to type 4 is a response to powerlessness. Social change might also look somewhat different to each perspective; differences disappear, deviance becomes normal, the minority group assimilates, or power is equalized. (1973, 1013)

Nona Glazer observed a further important difference between the types Hochschild identified, namely, where they located the primary source of inequality between women and men:

> The *sex difference* and [*sex*] *roles* approaches share an emphasis on understanding factors that characterize individuals. These factors may be inherent to each sex or acquired by individuals in the course of socialization. The *minority group* and *caste/class* approaches share an emphasis on factors that are external to individuals, a concern with the structure of social institutions, and with the impact of historical events. (1977, 103)

Feminist scholars have largely abandoned the effort to describe women "as a caste," "as a class," or "as a minority group" as a project in its own right (see, for example, Aptheker 1989; Hull, Scott, and Smith

1982). What we have been left with, however, are two prevailing conceptualizations: (1) the sex differences approach and (2) the sex roles approach. And note, while the minority group and caste/class approaches were concerned with factors external to the individual (e.g., the structure of social institutions and the impact of historical events), the approaches that remain emphasize factors that characterize the individual (Glazer 1977).

Arguably, some might call this picture oversimplified. Given the exciting new scholarship that focuses on gender as something that is socially constructed and something that converges with other inequalities to produce difference among women, have we not moved well beyond "sex differences" and "sex roles"? A close examination of this literature suggests that we have not. New conceptualizations of the bases of gender inequality still rest on old conceptualizations of gender (West and Fenstermaker 1993, 151). For example, those who rely on a sex differences approach conceive of gender as inhering in the individual, in other words, as the masculinity or femininity of *a person*. Elsewhere (Fenstermaker, West, and Zimmerman, 1991; West and Fenstermaker 1993; West and Zimmerman 1987), we note that this conceptualization obscures our understanding of how gender can structure distinctive domains of social experience (see also Stacey and Thorne 1985). "Sex differences" are treated as the explanation instead of the analytic point of departure.

Although many scholars who take this approach draw on socialization to account for the internalization of femininity and masculinity, they imply that by about five years of age these differences have become stable characteristics of individuals—much like sex (West and Zimmerman 1987, 126). The careful distinction between sex and gender is obliterated, as gender is reduced effectively to sex (Gerson 1985).[5] When the social meanings of sex are rerooted in biology, it becomes virtually impossible to explain variation in gender relations in the context of race and class. We must assume, for example, that the effects of inherent sex differences are either added to or subtracted from those of race and class. We are led to assume that sex differences are more fundamental than any other differences that might interest us (see Spelman 1988, 116-19, for a critical examination of this assumption)—unless we also assume that race differences and class differences are biologically based (for refutations of this assumption, see Gossett 1965; Montagu 1975; Omi and Winant 1986; Stephans 1982).

Those who take a sex roles approach are confounded by similar difficulties, although these may be less apparent at the outset. What is deceptive is role theory's emphasis on the specific social locations that result in particular expectations and actions (Komarovsky 1946, 1992; Linton 1936; Parsons 1951; Parsons and Bales 1955). In this view, the actual enactment of an individual's "sex role" (or, more recently, "gender role") is contingent on the individual's social structural position and the expectations associated with that position. The focus is on gender as a role or status, as it is learned and enacted. In earlier work (Fenstermaker, West, and Zimmerman 1991; West and Fenstermaker 1993; West and Zimmerman 1987), we have noted several problems with this approach, including its inability to specify actions appropriate to particular "sex roles" in advance of their occurrence and the fact that sex roles are not situated in any particular setting or organizational context (Lopata and Thorne 1978; Thorne 1980). The fact that "sex roles" often serve as "master statuses" (Hughes 1945) makes it hard to account for how variations in situations produce variations in their enactment. Given that gender is potentially omnirelevant to how we organize social life, almost any action could count as an instance of sex role enactment.

The most serious problem with this approach, however, is its inability to address issues of power and inequality (Connell 1985; Lopata and Thorne 1978; Thorne 1980). Conceiving of gender as composed of the "male role" and the "female role" implies a "separate but equal" relationship between the two, one characterized by complementary relations rather than conflict. Elsewhere (Fenstermaker, West, and Zimmerman 1991; West and Fenstermaker 1993; West and Zimmerman 1987), we illustrate this problem with Barrie Thorne and her colleagues' observation that social scientists have not made much use of role theory in their analyses of race and class relations. Concepts such as "race roles" and "class roles" have seemed patently inadequate to account for the dynamics of power and inequality operating in those contexts.

As many scholars have observed, empirical studies of the "female role" and "male role" have generally treated the experiences of white middle-class persons as prototypes, dismissing departures from the prototypical as instances of deviance. This is in large part what has contributed to the charges of white middle-class bias we discussed earlier. It is also what has rendered the "sex role" approach nearly useless in accounting for the diversity of gender relations across different groups.

Seeking a solution to these difficulties, Joan Acker has advanced the view that gender consists of something else altogether, namely, "patterned, socially produced distinctions between female and male, feminine and masculine . . . [that occur] in the course of participation in work organizations as well as in many other locations and relations" (Acker 1992b, 250). The object here is to document the "gendered processes" that sustain "the pervasive ordering of human activities, practices and social structures in terms of differentiations between women and men" (1992a, 567).

We agree fully with the object of this view and note its usefulness in capturing the persistence and ubiquity of gender inequality. Its emphasis on organizational practices restores the concern with "the structure of social institutions and with the impact of historical events" that characterized earlier class and caste approaches and facilitates the simultaneous documentation of gender, race, and class as basic principles of social organization. We suggest, however, that the popular distinction between "macro" and "micro" levels of analysis reflected in this view makes it possible to empirically describe and explain inequality without fully apprehending the common elements of its daily unfolding. For example, "processes of interaction" are conceptualized *apart* from the "production of gender divisions," that is, "the overt decisions and procedures that control, segregate, exclude, and construct hierarchies based on gender, and often race" (Acker 1992a, 568). The production of "images, symbols and ideologies that justify, explain, and give legitimacy to institutions" constitutes yet another "process," as do "the [mental] internal processes in which individuals engage as they construct personas that are appropriately gendered for the institutional setting" (Acker 1992a, 568). The analytic "missing link," as we see it, is the mechanism that ties these seemingly diverse processes together— one that could "take into account the constraining impact of entrenched ideas and practices on human agency, but [could] also acknowledge that the system is continually construed in everyday life and that, under certain conditions, individuals resist pressures to conform to the needs of the system" (Essed 1991, 38).

In sum, if we conceive of gender as a matter of biological differences or differential roles, we will be forced to think of it as standing apart from and outside other socially relevant, organizing experiences. This prevents us from understanding how gender, race, and class operate simultaneously with one another. It also prevents us from seeing how the particular salience of these experiences might vary across interactions. Most important, it gives us virtually no way of adequately addressing the mechanisms that produce power and inequality in social life. Instead, we propose a conceptual mechanism for perceiving the relations between individual and institutional practice and among forms of domination.

AN ETHNOMETHODOLOGICAL PERSPECTIVE

Don Zimmerman concisely describes ethnomethodological inquiry as proposing "that the properties of social life which seem objective, factual, and transsituational, are actually managed accomplishments or achievements of local processes" (1978, 11). In brief, the "objective" and "factual" properties of social life attain such status through the situated conduct of societal members. The aim of ethnomethodology is to analyze situated conduct in order to understand how "objective" properties of social life achieve their status as such.

The goal of this chapter is not to analyze situated conduct per se but to understand the workings of inequality. We should note that our interest here is not to separate gender, race, and class as social categories but to build a coherent argument for understanding how they work simultaneously. How might an ethnomethodological perspective help with this task? As Marilyn Frye observes,

> For efficient subordination, what's wanted is that the structure not appear to be a cultural artifact kept in place by human decision or custom, but that it appear natural—that it appear to be quite a direct consequence of facts about the beast which are beyond the scope of human manipulation. (1983, 34)

Gender

Within Western societies, we take for granted in everyday life that there are two and only two sexes (Garfinkel 1967, 122). We see this state of affairs as "only natural" insofar as we see persons as "essentially, originally and in the final analysis either 'male' or 'female' " (Garfinkel 1967, 122). When we interact with others, we take for granted that each of us has an "essential" manly or womanly nature—one that derives from our sex and one that can be detected from the "natural signs" we give off (Goffman 1976, 75).

These beliefs constitute the *normative conceptions* of our culture regarding the properties of normally sexed persons. Such beliefs support the seemingly "objective," "factual," and "transsituational" character of gender in social affairs, and in this sense, we experience them as exogenous (i.e., as outside of us and the particular situation we find ourselves in). Simultaneously, though, the meaning of these beliefs is dependent on the context in which they are invoked—rather than transsituational, as implied by the popular concept of "cognitive consensus" (Zimmerman 1978, 8-9). What is more, because these properties of normally sexed persons are regarded as "only natural," questioning them is tantamount to calling ourselves into question as competent members of society.

Consider how these beliefs operate in the process of sex assignment —the initial classification of persons as either female or male (West and Zimmerman 1987, 131-32). We generally regard this process as a biological determination requiring only a straightforward examination of the "facts of the matter" (cf. the description of sex as an "ascribed status" in many introductory sociology texts). Yet the criteria for sex assignment can vary across cases (e.g., chromosome type before birth or genitalia after birth). They sometimes do and sometimes do not agree with one another (e.g., hermaphrodites) and they show considerable variation across cultures (Kessler and McKenna 1978). It is our *moral conviction* that there are two and only two sexes (Garfinkel 1967, 116-18) that explains the comparative ease of achieving initial sex assignment. This conviction accords females and males the status of unequivocal and "natural" entities whose social and psychological tendencies can be predicted from their reproductive functions (West and Zimmerman 1987, 127-28). From an ethnomethodological viewpoint, *sex* is socially and culturally constructed rather than a straightforward statement of the biological "facts."

Now, consider the process of *sex categorization*—the ongoing identification of persons as girls or boys and women or men in everyday life (West and Zimmerman 1987, 132-34). Sex categorization involves no well-defined set of criteria that must be satisfied to identify someone; rather, it involves treating appearances (e.g., deportment, dress, and bearing) as if they were indicative of underlying states of affairs (e.g., anatomical, hormonal, and chromosomal arrangements). The point worth stressing here is that while sex category serves as an "indicator" of sex, it does not depend on it. Societal members will "see" a world populated by two and only two sexes, even in public situations that preclude inspection of the physiological "facts." From this perspective, it is important to distinguish sex category from sex assignment and to distinguish both from the "doing" of gender.

Gender, we argue, is a situated accomplishment of societal members, the local management of conduct in relation to normative conceptions of appropriate attitudes and activities for particular sex categories (West and Zimmerman 1987, 134-35). From this perspective, gender is not merely an individual attribute but something that is accomplished in interaction with others. Here, as in our earlier work, we rely on John Heritage's (1984, 136-37) formulation of accountability: the possibility of describing actions, circumstances, and even descriptions of themselves in both serious and consequential ways (e.g., as "unwomanly" or "unmanly"). Heritage points out that members of society routinely characterize activities in ways that take notice of those activities (e.g., naming, describing, blaming, excusing, or merely acknowledging them) and place them in a social framework (i.e., situating them in the context of other activities that are similar or different).

The fact that activities can be described in such ways is what leads to the possibility of conducting them with an eye to how they might be assessed (e.g., as "womanly" or "manly" behaviors). Three important but subtle points are worth emphasizing here. One is that the notion of accountability is relevant not only to activities that conform to prevailing normative conceptions (i.e., activities that are conducted "unremarkably," and, thus, do not warrant more than a passing glance) but also to those activities that deviate. The issue is not deviance or conformity; rather, it is the possible *evaluation* of action in relation to normative conceptions and the likely consequence of that evaluation for subsequent interaction. The second point worth emphasizing is that the process of rendering some action accountable is an interactional accomplishment. As Heritage explains, accountability permits persons to conduct their activities in relation to their circumstances—in ways that permit others to take those circumstances into account and see those activities for what they are. Hence "the intersubjectivity of actions ultimately rests on a symmetry between the *production* of those actions on the one hand and their *recognition* on the other" (1984, 179)—both in the context of their circumstances.[6] And the third point we must stress is that, while individuals are the ones who do gender, the process of rendering something accountable is both interactional and institutional in character: It is a feature of social relationships and its idiom derives from the institutional arena in which those relationships come to life.

In the United States, for example, when the behaviors of children or teenagers have become the focus of public concern, *The Family* and *Motherhood* (as well as individual mothers) have been held accountable to normative conceptions of "essential" femininity (including qualities like nurturance and caring). Gender is obviously much more than a role or an individual characteristic: It is a mechanism whereby situated social action contributes to the reproduction of social structure (West and Fenstermaker 1993, 158).

Thus, womanly and manly natures achieve the status of objective properties of social life (West and Zimmerman 1987). They are rendered natural, normal characteristics of individuals and, *at the same time,* furnish the tacit legitimation of the distinctive and unequal fates of women and men within the social order. If sex categories are potentially omnirelevant to social life, then persons engaged in virtually any activity may be held accountable for their performance of that activity *as women or as men,* and their category membership can be used to validate or discredit their other activities. This arrangement provides for countless situations in which persons in a particular sex category can "see" that they are out of place, and if they were not there, their current problems would not exist. It also allows for seeing various features of the existing social order as "natural" responses, for example, the division of labor (Fenstermaker Berk 1985), the development of gender identities (Cahill 1986), and the subordination of women by men (Fenstermaker, West, and Zimmerman 1991). These things "are the way they are" by virtue of the fact that men are men and women are women —a distinction seen as "natural," as rooted in biology, and as producing fundamental psychological, behavioral, and social consequences.

Through this formulation, we resituate gender, an attribute without clear social origin or referent, in social interaction. This makes it possible to study how gender takes on social import, how it varies in its salience and consequence, and how it operates to *produce and maintain* power and inequality in social life. Below, we extend this reformulation to race and then to class. Through this extension, we are not proposing an equivalence of oppressions. Race is not class and neither is gender; nevertheless, while race, class, and gender will likely take on different import and will often carry vastly different social consequences in any given social situation, *how they operate* may be productively compared. Here, our focus is on the *social mechanics* of gender, race, and class, for that is the way we may perceive their simultaneous workings in human affairs.

Race

Within the United States, virtually any social activity presents the possibility of categorizing the participants on the basis of race. Attempts to establish race as a scientific concept have met with little success (Gossett 1965; Montagu 1975; Omi and Winant 1986; Stephans 1982). There are, for example, no biological criteria (e.g., hormonal, chromosomal, or anatomical) that allow physicians to pronounce race assignment at birth, thereby sorting human beings into distinctive races.[7] Moreover, since racial categories and their meanings change over time and place, they are arbitrary.[8] In everyday life, nevertheless, people can and do sort out themselves and others on the basis of membership in racial categories.

Michael Omi and Howard Winant argue that the "seemingly obvious, 'natural' and 'common sense' qualities" of the existing racial order "themselves testify to the effectiveness of the racial formation process in constructing racial meanings and identities" (1986, 62). Take, for instance, the relatively recent emergence of the category *Asian American.* Any scientific theory of race would be hard pressed to explain this in the absence of a well-defined set of criteria for assigning individuals to the category. Furthermore, in relation to ethnicity, it makes no sense to aggregate in a single category the distinctive histories, geographic origins, and cultures of Cambodian, Chinese, Filipino, Japanese, Korean, Laotian, Thai, and Vietnamese Americans. But, Omi and Winant contend, despite important distinctions among these groups, "the majority of Americans cannot tell the difference" among their members (1986, 24). Thus, "Asian American," affords a means of *achieving* racial categorization in everyday life. Notions such as this one are not supported by any scientific criteria for reliably distinguishing members of different "racial" groups. What is more, even state-mandated criteria (e.g., the proportion of "mixed blood" necessary to legally classify someone as *Black*)[9] are distinctly different in other Western cultures and have little relevance to the way racial categorization occurs in everyday life. As in the case of sex categorization, appearances are treated *as if they were indicative* of some underlying state.

Beyond preconceived notions of what members of particular groups look like, Omi and Winant suggest that Americans share preconceived notions of what members of these groups *are like.* They note, for example, that we are likely to become disoriented "when people do not act 'Black,' 'Latino,' or indeed 'white' " (1986, 62). From our ethnomethodological perspective, what Omi and Winant are describing is the *accountability of persons to race category.* If we accept their contention that there are prevailing normative conceptions of appropriate attitudes and activities for particular race categories and if we grant Heritage's (1984, 179) claim that accountability allows persons to conduct their activities in relation to their circumstances (in ways that allow others to take those circumstances into account and see those activities for what they are), we can also see race as a *situated accomplishment of societal members.* From this perspective, race is not simply an individual characteristic or trait but something that is accomplished in interaction with others.

Now, to the extent that race category is omnirelevant (or even verges on this), it follows that a person involved in virtually *any* action may be held accountable for their performance of that action as a member of their race category. As in the case of sex category, race category can be used to justify or discredit other actions; accordingly, virtually any action can be assessed in relation to its race categorical nature. The accomplishment of race (like gender) does not necessarily mean "living up" to normative conceptions of attitudes and activities appropriate to a particular race category; rather, it means engaging in action *at the risk of* race assessment. Thus, even though individuals are the ones who accomplish race, "the enterprise is fundamentally interactional and institutional in character, for accountability is a feature of social relationships and its idiom is drawn from the institutional arena in which those relationships are enacted" (West and Zimmerman 1987, 137).

The accomplishment of race renders the social arrangements based on race as normal and natural, that is, legitimate ways of organizing social life. Although the distinction between "macro" and "micro" levels of analysis is popular in the race relations literature too (e.g., in distinguishing "institutional" from "individual" racism or "macro-level" analyses of racialized social structures from "micro-level" analyses of identity formation), we contend that it is ultimately a false distinction. Not only do these "levels" operate continually and reciprocally in "our lived experience, in politics, in culture [and] in economic life" (Omi and Winant 1986, 67), but distinguishing between them "places the individual outside the institutional, thereby severing rules, regulations and procedures from the people who make and enact them" (Essed 1991, 36). We contend that the accountability of persons to race categories is the key to understanding the maintenance of the existing racial order.

Note that there is nothing in this formulation to suggest that race is necessarily accomplished *in isolation* from gender. To the contrary, if we conceive of both race and gender as situated accomplishments, we can see how individual persons may experience them simultaneously. For instance, Spelman observes that

> insofar as she is oppressed by racism in a sexist context and sexism in a racist context, the Black woman's struggle cannot be compartmentalized into two struggles—one as a Black and one as a woman. Indeed, it is difficult to imagine why a Black woman would think of her struggles this way except in the face of demands by white women or by Black men that she do so. (1988, 124)

To the extent that an individual Black woman is held accountable in one situation to her race category, and in another, to her sex category, we can see these as "oppositional" demands for accountability. But note, it is a *Black woman* who is held accountable in both situations.

Despite many important differences in the histories, traditions, and varying impacts of racial and sexual oppression across particular situations, the mechanism underlying them is the same. To the extent that members of society know their actions are accountable, they will design their actions in relation to how they might be seen and described by others. And to the extent that race category (like sex category) is omnirelevant to social life, it provides others with an ever-available resource for interpreting those actions. In short, inasmuch as our society is divided by "essential" differences between members of different race categories and categorization by race is both relevant and mandated, the accomplishment of race is unavoidable (cf. West and Zimmerman 1987, 137).

In sum, the accomplishment of race consists of creating differences among members of different race categories—differences that are neither natural nor biological (cf. West and Zimmerman 1987, 137). Once created, these differences are used to maintain the "essential" distinctiveness of "racial identities" and the institutional arrangements that they support. From this perspective, racial identities are not invariant idealizations of our human natures that are uniformly distributed in society. Nor are normative conceptions of attitudes and activities for one's race category templates for "racial" behaviors. Rather, what is invariant is the notion that members of different "races" *have* essentially different natures, which explain their very unequal positions in our society.[10]

Class

This, too, we propose, is the case with class. Here, we know that even sympathetic readers are apt to balk: gender, yes, is "done," and race, too, is "accomplished," but class? How can we reduce a system that "differentially structures group access to material resources, including economic, political and social resources" (Andersen and Collins 1992, 50) to "a situated accomplishment"? Do we mean to deny the material realities of poverty and privilege? We do not. There is no denying the very different material realities imposed by differing relations under capital; however, we suggest that these realities have little to do with class categorization—and ultimately, with the accountability of persons to class categories—in everyday life.

For example, consider Shellee Colen's description of the significance of maids' uniforms to white middle-class women who employ West Indian immigrant women as child care workers and domestics in New York City. In the words of "Judith Thomas," one of the West Indian women Colen interviewed,

> She [the employer] wanted me to wear the uniform. She was really preju-
> diced. She just wanted that the maid must be identified. . . . She used to go
> to the beach every day with the children. So going to the beach in the sand
> and the sun and she would have the kids eat ice cream and all that sort of
> thing. . . . I tell you one day when I look at myself, I was so dirty . . . just
> like I came out from a garbage can. (1986, 57)

At the end of that day, says Colen, Thomas asked her employer's permission to wear jeans to the beach the next time they went and the employer gave her permission to do so. But when she did wear jeans and the employer's brother came to the beach for a visit, Thomas noted,

> I really believe they had a talk about it, because in the evening, driving
> back from the beach, she said "Well, Judith, I said you could wear some-
> thing else to the beach other than the uniform [but] I think you will have
> to wear the uniform because they're very informal on this beach and they
> don't know who is guests from who isn't guests." (1986, 57)

Of the women Colen interviewed (in 1985), not one was making more than $225 a week and Thomas was the only one whose employer was paying for medical insurance. All (including Thomas) were supporting at least two households: their own in New York and that of their kin back in the West Indies. By any objective social scientific criteria, then, all would be regarded as members of the working-class poor; yet in the eyes of Thomas's employer (and, apparently, the eyes of others at the beach), Thomas's low wages, long hours, and miserable conditions of employment were insufficient to establish her class category. Without a uniform, she could be mistaken for "one of the guests" and, hence, not be held accountable "as a maid."

There is more to this example, of course, than meets the eye. The employer's claim notwithstanding, it is unlikely that Thomas, tending to white middle-class children who were clearly not her own, would be mistaken for "one of the guests" at the beach. The blue jeans, however, might be seen as indicating her failure to comply with normative expectations of attitudes and behaviors appropriate to "a maid" and, worse yet, as belying the competence of her employer. Thomas displaying herself as a maid affirms the authority of her employer. As Evelyn Nakano Glenn notes in another context, "the higher standard of living of one woman is made possible by, and also helps to perpetuate, the other's lower standard of living" (1992, 34).

Admittedly, the normative conceptions that sustain the accountability of persons to class category are somewhat different from those that sustain accountability to sex category and race category. For example, despite earlier attempts to link pauperism with heredity and thereby justify the forced sterilization of poor women in the United States (Rafter 1992), scientists today do not conceive of class in relation to the biological characteristics of a person. Moreover, there is no scientific basis for popular notions of what persons in particular class categories "look like" or "act like." But even though the dominant ideology within the United States is no longer based explicitly on Social Darwinism (see, for example, Gossett 1965, 144-75) and even though we believe that, in theory, "anyone can make it," we *as a society* still hold certain truths to be self-evident. As Donna Langston observes:

> If hard work were the sole determinant of your ability to support yourself and your family, surely we'd have a different outcome for many in our society. We also, however, believe in luck and on closer examination, it certainly is quite a coincidence that the "unlucky" come from certain race, gender and class backgrounds. In order to perpetuate racist, sexist and classist outcomes, we also have to believe that the current economic distribution is unchangeable, has always existed, and probably exists in this form throughout the known universe, i.e., it's "natural." (1991, 146)

Langston pinpoints the underlying assumptions that sustain our notions about persons in relation to poverty and privilege—assumptions that compete with our contradictory declarations of a meritocratic society, with its readily invoked exemplar, Horatio Alger. For example, if someone is poor, we assume it is because of something *they* did or did not do: they lacked initiative, they were not industrious, they had no ambition, and so forth. If someone is rich, or merely "well-off," it must be by virtue of *their own* efforts, talents, and initiative. While these beliefs certainly *look* more mutable than our views of women's and men's "essential" natures or our deep-seated convictions regarding the characteristics of persons in particular race categories, they still rest on the assumption that a person's economic fortunes derive from *qualities of the person.* "Initiative" is thus treated as inherent among those who "have," and laziness is seen as inherent among those who "have not."[11] Given that "initiative" is a prerequisite for employment in jobs leading to upward mobility in this society, it is hardly surprising that "the rich get richer and the poor get poorer." As in the case of gender and race, profound historical effects of entrenched institutional practice result, but they unfold one accomplishment at a time.

As Benjamin DeMott (1990) observes, Americans operate on the basis of a most unusual assumption, namely, that we live in a classless society. On the one hand, our everyday discourse is replete with categorizations of persons by class. DeMott (1990, 1-27) offers numerous examples of television shows, newspaper articles, cartoons, and movies that illustrate how class "will tell" in the most mundane of social doings. On the other hand, we believe that we in the United States are truly unique "in escaping the hierarchies that burden the rest of the developed world" (DeMott 1990, 29). We cannot *see* the system of distribution that structures our unequal access to resources. Because we cannot see this, the *accomplishment of class* in everyday life rests on the presumption that everyone is endowed with equal opportunity and, therefore, that real differences in the outcomes we observe must result from individual differences in attributes like intelligence and character.

The *accomplishment of class* renders the unequal institutional arrangements based on class category accountable as normal and natural, that is, as legitimate ways of organizing social life (cf. West and Zimmerman 1987). Differences between members of particular class categories that are created by this process can then be depicted as fundamental and enduring dispositions.[12] In this light, the institutional arrangements of our society can be seen as responsive to the differences —the social order being merely an accommodation to the natural order.

In any given situation (whether or not that situation can be characterized as face-to-face interaction or as the more "macro" workings of institutions), the simultaneous accomplishments of class, gender, and race will differ in content and outcome. From situation to situation, the salience of the observables relevant to categorization (e.g., dress, interpersonal style, skin color) may seem to eclipse the interactional impact of the simultaneous accomplishment of all three; nevertheless, we maintain that just as the mechanism for accomplishment is shared, so too is their simultaneous accomplishment ensured.

CONCLUSION: THE PROBLEM OF DIFFERENCE

As we have indicated, mathematical metaphors describing the relations among gender, race, and class have led to considerable confusion in feminist scholarship. As we have also indicated, the conceptualizations of gender that support mathematical metaphors (sex differences and sex roles) have forced scholars to think of gender as something that stands apart from and outside of race and class in people's lives.

In putting forth this perspective, we hope to advance a new way of thinking about gender, race, and class, namely as ongoing, methodical, and situated accomplishments. We have tried to demonstrate the usefulness of this perspective for understanding how people experience gender, race, and class simultaneously. We have also tried to illustrate the implications of this perspective for reconceptualizing "the problem of difference" in feminist theory.

What are the implications of our ethnomethodological perspective for an understanding of relations among gender, race, and class? First, and perhaps most important, conceiving of these as ongoing accomplishments means that we cannot determine their relevance to social action apart from the context in which they are accomplished (Fenstermaker, West, and Zimmerman 1991; West and Fenstermaker 1993). While sex category, race category, and class category are potentially omnirelevant to social life, individuals inhabit many different identities, and these may be stressed or muted, depending on the situation.

A second implication of our perspective is that the accomplishment of race, class, and gender does not require categorical diversity among the participants. To paraphrase Erving Goffman, social situations "do not so much allow for the expression of natural differences as for the production of [those] difference[s themselves]" (1977, 302). Some of the most extreme displays of "essential" womanly and manly natures may occur in settings that are usually reserved for members of a single sex category, such as locker rooms or beauty salons (Gerson 1985). Some of the most dramatic expressions of "definitive" class characteristics may emerge in class-specific contexts (e.g., debutante balls). Situations that involve more than one sex category, race category, and class category may *highlight* categorical membership and make the accomplishment of gender, race, and class more salient, but they are not necessary to produce these accomplishments in the first place. This point is worth stressing, since existing formulations of relations among gender, race, and class might lead one to conclude that "difference" must be present for categorical membership and, thus, dominance to matter.

A third implication is that, depending on how race, gender, and class are accomplished, what looks to be the same activity may have different meanings for those engaged in it. Consider the long-standing debates among feminists (e.g., Collins 1990; Davis 1971; Dill 1988; Firestone 1970; Friedan 1963; hooks 1984; Hurtado 1989; Zavella 1987) over the significance of mothering and child care in women's lives. For white middle-class women, these activities have often been seen as *constitutive* of oppression in that they are taken as expressions of their "essential" womanly natures and used to discredit their participation in other activities (e.g., Friedan 1963). For many women of color (and white working-class women), mothering and child care have had (and continue to have) very different meanings. Angela Davis (1971, 7) points out that, in the context of slavery, African American women's efforts to tend to the needs of African American children (not necessarily their own) represented the only labor they performed that could not be directly appropriated by white slave owners. Moreover, bell hooks observes,

> Black women have identified work in the context of the family as humanizing labor, work that affirms their identity as women, as human beings showing love and care, the very gestures of humanity white supremacist ideology claimed black people were incapable of expressing. (1984, 133-34)

And looking specifically at American family life in the nineteenth century, Bonnie Thornton Dill (1988) suggests that *being* a poor or working-class African American woman, a Chinese American woman, or a Mexican American woman meant something very different from being a European American woman. Normative, class-bound conceptions of "woman's nature" at that time included tenderness, piety, and nurturance—qualities that legitimated the confinement of middle-class European American women to the domestic sphere and that promoted such confinement as the goal of working-class and poor immigrant European American families' efforts.

> For racial-ethnic women, however, the notion of separate spheres served to reinforce their subordinate status and became, in effect, another assault. As they increased their work outside the home, they were forced into a productive sphere that was organized for men and "desperate" women who were so unfortunate or immoral that they could not confine their work to the domestic sphere. In the productive sphere, however, they were denied the opportunity to embrace the dominant ideological definition of "good" wife and mother. (Dill 1988, 429)

Fourth and finally, our perspective affords an understanding of the accomplishment of race, gender, or class as constituted in the context of the differential "doings" of the others. Consider, for example, the very dramatic case of the U.S. Senate hearings on Clarence Thomas's nomination to the Supreme Court. Wherever we turned, whether to visual images on a television screen or to the justificatory discourse of print media, we were overwhelmed by the dynamics of gender, race, and class operating in concert with one another. It made a difference to us as viewers (and certainly to his testimony) that Clarence Thomas was a Black *man* and that he was a *Black* man. It also made a difference, particularly to the African American community, that he was a Black man who had been raised in *poverty* (Bikel 1992). Each categorical dimension played off the others and off the comparable but quite different categorizations of Anita Hill (a "self-made" Black woman law professor, who had grown up as one of thirteen children). Most white women who watched the hearings identified gender and men's dominance as the most salient aspects of them, whether in making sense of the Judiciary Committee's handling of witnesses or understanding the relationship between Hill and Thomas (Bikel 1992). By contrast, most

African American viewers saw racism as the most salient aspect of the hearings, including white men's prurient interest in Black sexuality and the exposure of troubling divisions between Black women and men (Bikel 1992; Morrison 1992). The point is that how we *label* such dynamics does not necessarily capture their complex quality. Foreground and background, context, salience, and center shift from interaction to interaction, but all operate interdependently.

Of course, this is only the beginning. Gender, race, and class are only three means (although certainly very powerful ones) of generating difference and dominance in social life.[13] Much more must be done to distinguish other forms of inequality and their workings. Empirical evidence must be brought to bear on the question of variation in the salience of categorical memberships, while still allowing for the simultaneous influence of these memberships on interaction. We suggest that the analysis of situated conduct affords the best prospect for understanding how these "objective" properties of social life achieve their ongoing status as such and, hence, how the most fundamental divisions of our society are legitimated and maintained.

NOTES

1. In this chapter, we use *race* rather than *ethnicity* to capture the commonsensical beliefs of members of our society. As we will show, these beliefs are predicated on the assumption that different "races" can be reliably distinguished from one another.

2. Compare, for example, the very different implications of "Double Jeopardy: To Be Black and Female" (Beale 1970) and "Positive Effects of the Multiple Negative: Explaining the Success of Black Professional Women" (Epstein 1973).

3. In this context, we define *experience* as participation in social systems in which gender, race, and class affect, determine, or otherwise influence behavior.

4. Here, it is important to distinguish an individual's *experience* of the dynamics of gender, race, and class as they order the daily course of social interaction from that individual's sense of *identity as a member* of gendered, raced, and classed categories. For example, in any given interaction, a woman who is Latina and a shopkeeper may experience the simultaneous effects of gender, race, and class yet identify her experience as only "about" race, only "about" gender, or only "about" class.

5. The ambivalence that dogs the logic of social constructionist positions should now be all too familiar to feminist sociologists. If we are true to our pronouncements that social inequalities and the categories they reference (e.g., gender, race, and class) are not rooted in biology, then we may at some point seem to flirt with the notion that they are, therefore, rooted in nothing. For us, biology is not only not destiny but also not the only reality. Gender, race, and class inequalities are firmly rooted in the ever-present realities of individual practice, cultural conventions, and social institutions. That's reality enough, when we ponder the pernicious and pervasive character of racism, sexism, and economic oppression.

6. That persons *may be* held accountable does not mean that they necessarily *will be* held accountable in every interaction. Particular interactional outcomes are not the point here; rather, it is the possibility of accountability in any interaction.

7. To maintain vital statistics on race, California, for instance, relies on mothers' and fathers' self-identifications on birth certificates.

8. Omi and Winant (1986, 64-75) provide numerous empirical illustrations, including the first appearance of *white* as a term of self-identification (circa 1680), California's decision to categorize Chinese people as *Indian* (in 1854), and the U.S. Census's creation of the category *Hispanic* (in 1980).

9. Consider Susie Guillory Phipps's unsuccessful suit against the Louisiana Bureau of Vital Records (Omi and Winant 1986, 57). Phipps was classified as "Black" on her birth certificate, in accord with a 1970 Louisiana law stipulating that anyone with at least one-thirty-second "Negro blood" was "Black." Her attorney contended that designating a race category on a person's birth certificate was unconstitutional and that, in any case, the one-thirty-second criterion was inaccurate. Ultimately, the court upheld Louisiana's state law quantifying "racial identity" and thereby affirmed the legal principle of assigning persons to specific "racial" groups.

10. As Spelman observes, "The existence of racism does not require that there are races; it requires the belief that there are races" (1988, 208, n. 24).

11. Here, a devil's advocate might argue that gender, race, and class are fundamentally different because they show different degrees of "mutability" or latitude in the violation of expectations in interaction. Although class mobility is possible, one might argue, race mobility is not; or, while "sex change" operations can be performed, "race change" operations cannot. In response, we would point out that the very notion that one cannot change one's race—but can change one's sex and manipulate displays of one's class—only throws us back to biology and its reassuring but only apparent immutability.

12. Thus, even though we as a society believe that some people may "pull themselves up by their bootstraps" and others may "fall from grace," we still cherish the notion that class will reveal itself in a person's fundamental social and psychological character. Hence, we commonly regard the "self-made man," "the welfare mother," and the "middle-class housewife" as *distinct categories of persons,* whose attitudes and activities can be predicted on categorical grounds.

13. We cannot stress this strongly enough. Gender, race, and class are obviously very salient social accomplishments in social life, because so many features of our cultural institutions and daily discourse are organized to perpetuate the categorical distinctions on which they are based. As Spelman observes, "the more a society has invested in its members' getting the categories right, the more occasions there will be for reinforcing them, and the fewer occasions there will be for questioning them" (1988, 152). On any given occasion of interaction, however, we may also be held accountable to other categorical memberships (e.g., ethnicity, nationality, sexual orientation, place of birth), and, thus, "difference" may then be differentially constituted.

REFERENCES

Acker, Joan. 1992a. Gendered institutions: From sex roles to gendered institutions. *Contemporary Sociology* 21:565-69.

——. 1992b. Gendering organizational theory. In *Gendering Organizational Theory,* edited by Albert J. Mills and Peta Tancred. London: Sage.

Almquist, Elizabeth. 1989. The experiences of minority women in the United States: Intersections of race, gender, and class. In *Women: A feminist perspective*, edited by Jo Freeman. 4th ed. Mountain View, CA: Mayfield.

Andersen, Margaret L., and Patricia Hill Collins. 1992. Preface to *Race, class and gender*, edited by Margaret L. Andersen and Patricia Hill Collins. Belmont, CA: Wadsworth.

Aptheker, Bettina. 1989. *Tapestries of life: Women's work, women's consciousness, and the meaning of daily experience.* Amherst: University of Massachusetts Press.

Baca Zinn, Maxine. 1990. Family, feminism and race in America. *Gender & Society* 4:68-82.

Beale, Frances. 1970. Double jeopardy: To be Black and female. In *The Black woman: An anthology*, edited by Toni Cade (Bambara). New York: Signet.

Bhavani, Kum-Kum. 1993. Talking racism and the editing of women's studies. In *Introducing women's studies*, edited by Diane Richardson and Victoria Robinson. London: Macmillan.

Bikel, Ofra. 1992. *Frontline*. PBS October 14, 1992.

Cahill, Spencer E. 1986. Childhood socialization as recruitment process: Some lessons from the study of gender development. In *Sociological studies of child development*, edited by Patricia Adler and Peter Adler. Greenwich, CT: JAI.

Colen, Shellee. 1986. "With respect and feelings": Voices of West Indian child care and domestic workers in New York City. In *All American women*, edited by Johnetta B. Cole. New York: Free Press.

Connell, R. W. 1985. Theorizing gender. *Sociology* 19:260-72.

Davis, Angela. 1971. The Black woman's role in the community of slaves. *Black Scholar* 3:3-15.

———. 1981. *Women, race and class.* New York: Random House.

DeMott, Benjamin. 1990. *The imperial middle: Why Americans can't think straight about class.* New Haven, CT: Yale University Press.

Dill, Bonnie Thornton. 1988. Our mothers' grief: Racial ethnic women and the maintenance of families. *Journal of Family History* 13:415-31.

Epstein, Cynthia Fuchs. 1973. Positive effects of the multiple negative: Explaining the success of Black professional women. In *Changing women in a changing society*, edited by Joan Huber. Chicago: University of Chicago Press.

Essed, Philomena. 1991. *Understanding everyday racism: An interdisciplinary theory.* Newbury Park, CA: Sage.

Fenstermaker Berk, Sarah. 1985. *The gender factory: The apportionment of work in American households.* New York: Plenum.

Fenstermaker, Sarah, Candace West, and Don H. Zimmerman. 1991. Gender inequality: New conceptual terrain. In *Gender, family and economy: The triple overlap*, edited by Rae Lesser Blumberg. Newbury Park, CA: Sage.

Firestone, Shulamith. 1970. *The dialectic of sex.* New York: William Morrow.

Friedan, Betty. 1963. *The feminine mystique.* New York: Dell.

Frye, Marilyn. 1983. *The politics of reality: Essays in feminist theory.* Trumansburg, NY: Crossing Press.

Garfinkel, Harold. 1967. *Studies in ethnomethodology.* Englewood Cliffs, NJ: Prentice Hall.

Gerson, Judith. 1985. *The variability and salience of gender: Issues of conceptualization and measurement.* Paper presented at the annual meeting of the American Sociological Association, Washington, DC, August.

Glazer, Nona. 1977. A sociological perspective: Introduction. In *Woman in a man-made world,* edited by Nona Glazer and Helen Youngelson Waehrer. Chicago: Rand McNally.

Glenn, Evelyn Nakano. 1985. Racial ethnic women's labor: The intersection of race, gender and class oppression. *Review of Radical Political Economics* 17:86-108.

———. 1992. From servitude to service work: Historical continuities in the racial division of paid reproductive labor. *Signs: Journal of Women in Culture and Society* 18:1-43.

Goffman, Erving. 1976. Gender display. *Studies in the Anthropology of Visual Communication* 3:69-77.

———. 1977. The arrangement between the sexes. *Theory and Society* 4:301-31.

Gossett, Thomas. 1965. *Race: The history of an idea in America.* New York: Schocken.

Heritage, John. 1984. *Garfinkel and ethnomethodology.* Cambridge, England: Polity.

Hill Collins, Patricia. 1990. *Black feminist thought.* New York: Routledge.

Hochschild, Arlie Russell. 1973. A review of sex roles research. *American Journal of Sociology* 78:1011-29.

hooks, bell. 1981. *Ain't I a woman: Black women and feminism.* Boston: South End Press.

———. 1984. *From margin to center.* Boston: South End Press.

Hughes, Everett C. 1945. Dilemmas and contradictions of status. *American Journal of Sociology* 50:353-59.

Hull, Gloria T., Patricia Bell Scott, and Barbara Smith, eds. 1982. *All the women are white, all the blacks are men, but some of us are brave.* Old Westbury, NY: Feminist Press.

Hurtado, Aída. 1989. Relating to privilege: Seduction and rejection in the subordination of white women and women of color. *Signs: Journal of Women in Culture and Society* 14:833-55.

Jordan, June. 1985. Report from the Bahamas. In *On call: Political essays.* Boston: South End Press.

Kessler, Suzanne J., and Wendy McKenna. 1978. *Gender: An ethnomethodological approach.* New York: John Wiley.

Komarovsky, Mirra. 1946. Cultural contradictions and sex roles. *American Journal of Sociology* 52:184-89.

———. 1992. The concept of social role revisited. *Gender & Society* 6:301-12.

Langston, Donna. 1991. Tired of playing monopoly? In *Changing our power: An introduction to women's studies,* 2d ed., edited by Jo Whitehorse Cochran, Donna Langston, and Carolyn Woodward. Dubuque, IA: Kendall-Hunt.

Linton, Ralph. 1936. *The study of man.* New York: Appleton-Century.

Lopata, Helena Z., and Barrie Thorne. 1978. On the term "sex roles." *Signs: Journal of Women in Culture and Society* 3:718-21.

Montagu, Ashley, ed. 1975. *Race & IQ.* London: Oxford University Press.

Moraga, Cherríe. 1981. La güera. In *This bridge called my back: Radical writing by women of color,* edited by Cherríe Moraga and Gloria Anzalduá. New York: Kitchen Table Press.

Morrison, Toni, ed. 1992. *Race-ing justice, engender-ing power: Essays on Anita Hill, Clarence Thomas, and the construction of social reality.* New York: Pantheon.

Omi, Michael, and Howard Winant. 1986. *Racial formation in the United States from the 1960s to the 1980s.* New York: Routledge & Kegan Paul.

Parsons, Talcott. 1951. *The social system.* New York: Free Press.

Parsons, Talcott, and Robert F. Bales. 1955. *Family, socialization and interaction process.* New York: Free Press.

Rafter, Nichole H. 1992. Claims-making and socio-cultural context in the first U.S. eugenics campaign. *Social Problems* 39:17-34.

Rich, Adrienne. 1979. Disloyal to civilization: Feminism, racism, gynephobia. In *On lies, secrets, and silence.* New York: Norton.

Segura, Denise A. 1992. Chicanas in white collar jobs: "You have to prove yourself more." *Sociological Perspectives* 35:163-82.

Spelman, Elizabeth V. 1988. *Inessential woman: Problems of exclusion in feminist thought.* Boston: Beacon.

Stacey, Judith, and Barrie Thorne. 1985. The missing feminist revolution in sociology. *Social Problems* 32:301-16.

Stephans, Nancy. 1982. *The idea of race in science.* Hamden, CT: Archon.

Thorne, Barrie. 1980. Gender . . . How is it best conceptualized? Unpublished manuscript, Department of Sociology, Michigan State University, East Lansing.

West, Candace, and Sarah Fenstermaker. 1993. Power, inequality and the accomplishment of gender: An ethnomethodological view. In *Theory on gender/feminism on theory,* edited by Paula England. New York: Aldine.

West, Candace, and Don H. Zimmerman. 1987. Doing gender. *Gender & Society* 1:125-51.

Young, Iris Marion. 1990. Impartiality and the civic public. In *Throwing like a girl and other essays in feminist philosophy.* Bloomington: Indiana University Press.

Zavella, Patricia. 1987. *Women's work and Chicano families: Cannery workers of the Santa Clara Valley.* Ithaca, NY: Cornell University Press.

Zimmerman, Don H. 1978. Ethnomethodology. *American Sociologist* 13:6-15.

19 Contradictions of Feminist Methodology

SHERRY GORELICK

Feminist methodology grows out of an important qualitative leap in the feminist critique of the social sciences: the leap from a critique of the invisibility of women, both as objects of study and as social scientists, to the critique of the method and purpose of social science itself. This is the leap from a sociology *about* women to a sociology *for* women, as Dorothy Smith (1974) put it. Smith argued that male-dominated science objectifies, but something very fundamental happens when both the knower and the known are women. When the pronoun applied to the knower is *she,* rather than the *seemingly* impersonal *he,* the knower is changed immediately from The Scientist to a person with a gender. And when this scientist with a female personal pronoun studies women, she is apt to feel a different relationship with her subjects, because she is subject to finding herself mirrored in them, a fact with revolutionary implications for the relationships among observer and observed, theory and experience, science, politics, race, and class. In the past two decades, however, we have learned that this mirroring process has its own limits, reflecting divisions based on race, class, and other forms of oppression, and requiring that we push the methodological revolution even further.

AUTHOR'S NOTE: This is an *abridged* version of the article that originally appeared in *Gender & Society 5*, No. 4 (December 1991). The article has been reprinted in its entirety, and with a reflective "Postscript" in *Feminism and Social Change: Bridging Theory and Practice*, Heidi Gottfried, ed., Urbana, University of Illinois Press, 1996.

EARLY FEMINIST METHODOLOGICAL MANIFESTOS

In 1978 Maria Mies set forth methodological guidelines for feminist research that proposed that the hypocritical "postulate of *value-free research,* of neutrality and indifference toward the research objects, has to be replaced by *conscious partiality*" toward the oppressed, engagement in their struggles for change, and the creation of a form of research that fosters *conscientization* of both the researcher and the researched (Mies 1983, 122-26, her emphasis). These guidelines set the dominant formula for research practice on its head. The dogmas of positivism—its hands-off approach, its clinical fastidiousness about mutual contamination, its insistence that research must precede change, that indeed change is the business of politicians and not scientists—were overturned. For feminist methodologists, as for the Marxist and interpretive sociologists on whose work they built, social science is much more profound than the mere collection of "facts." Said Mies:

> Most empirical research on women has concentrated so far on the study of superficial or surface phenomena such as women's attitudes toward housework, career, . . . etc. Such attitude or opinion surveys give very little information about women's true consciousness. Only when there is a rupture in the "normal" life of a woman, i.e. a crisis such as divorce, end of a relationship etc. is there a chance for her to become conscious of her true conditions. (1983, 125)

As Cook and Fonow put it much later,

> Feminism is a vision of freedom as future intention and this vision must indicate which facts from the present are necessary knowledge for liberation. Description without an eye for transformation is inherently conservative and portrays the subject as acted-upon rather than as an actor or potential actor. (1986, 12)

The implication is quite clear: Merely collecting descriptive statistics or experiential data about women does not constitute feminist research. Feminist research must be part of a process by which women's oppression is not only described but challenged.

Similarly, beginning in 1974, Dorothy Smith argued that sociology as currently practiced expressed unreflectively the distortions of a male ruling-class standpoint. She urged that instead research must be done

"from the standpoint of women," taking "the everyday world as problematic," and beginning from women's ordinary, everyday experience
(Smith 1974, 1979). Smith specifically cautioned against *confining* the
inquiry to the world of experience (Smith 1974, 12; Smith 1979, 174).
Some later feminist methodologists, however, have argued for a social
science that is "inductive rather than deductive" (Reinharz 1983, 172),
that "focuses on processes rather than structures" (p. 168), and is
"interested in generating concepts *in vivo,* in the field itself" rather than
using "predefined concepts" (p. 168). The role of the researcher is to
"give voice" to hitherto silenced groups and facilitate their own discov-
eries (Kasper 1986).

GIVING VOICE IS NOT ENOUGH: THE LIMITS OF FEMINIST EMPIRICISM

"Giving voice" was a progressive development in the history of
feminist theory. It went beyond criticism of the use of "mainstream"
social science as a tool of oppression and began the quest for a libera-
tory social science. But the more radically empiricist forms of the
feminist critique have their own limitations, which threaten to encap-
sulate feminist social science within each specific milieu being studied
and even preclude understanding the very milieu being examined. For
example, use of such techniques as interviews, participant observation,
and oral history helps to describe the world as perceived by the persons
studied, but it may remain confined within their perceptions and thus
not be able to provide them with much that they do not already know.

The agonizing and cumulative process of feminist discovery over the
years has revealed how much of sexism is deeply internalized and
therefore buried beneath the conscious level (MacKinnon 1987). Consciousness raising as a technique of research and political action may
enable women to give voice to knowledge that they did not know they
had. But this knowledge, too, is limited to what each group of women
is able to discover anew. Maria Mies's emphasis on the importance of
crises or ruptures in the pattern of normality, so that the pathology of
the normal may be perceived, is of crucial importance. Even so, giving
voice is not enough. Women know much and may learn more about their
own pain, but some of the underlying causes of that pain may be very
well hidden from them (cf. Maguire 1987, 37).

THE HIDDEN DETERMINANTS OF OPPRESSION

In *Capital,* Marx ([1867] 1967) showed that the most fundamental social relations occur "behind the backs" of the actors. That is, much of the underlying structure of oppression is hidden, not only by means of ideology but also by means of a contradictory daily life. Appearance contradicts reality: Workers feel dependent on capitalists for employment and wages, yet in reality they produce daily, in surplus value, the wages with which they are paid and the wealth that permits their continued subjugation. The "developing" world appears dependent on the "First World" for technology and investment, yet in reality the imperial world is dependent on the colonized world for raw materials, markets, and cheap labor. Wives appear to be dependent on husbands for support and protection, yet in reality it is husbands who are dependent on wives for their unpaid labor, emotion-management, and much else. Suniti Namjoshi's amusing but chilling fable, "The Monkey and the Crocodiles" (1981, 26), shows women's need for male physical protection to be little more than a protection racket. In reality each of these dependencies is substantially reversed, yet none of these realities is immediately apparent to those most oppressed by them.

In "A Sociology for Women," Smith (1979) described the dependence of professional and managerial men practicing "the abstracted conceptual mode of ruling" on the concrete invisible labor of women as computer specialists, secretaries, administrative assistants, wives, and so on. Their own social determinants are invisible to the men (Smith 1974, 10; Smith 1979, 168) yet the importance of their own role may be invisible to the women themselves, for two reasons. First, the dominant ideology obscures their role: "Ideas and social forms of consciousness may originate outside experience, coming from an external source and becoming a forced set of categories into which we must stuff the awkward and resistant actualities of our worlds" (Smith 1979, 141). Second, women's vision of their own oppression is masked by the development of corporate capitalism, in which local events are determined by social forces far from the site (1979, 161). In short, although oppression can *only* be understood from the standpoint and experience of the oppressed, the very organization of the everyday world of oppression in modern capitalism obscures the structure of oppression. "The everyday world is not fully understandable within its own scope. It is organized by social relations not fully apparent in it nor contained in it" (Smith 1979, 176).

In contrast to the reified conceptualizations of social structure produced by functionalist (and radical functionalist) social scientists (Gorelick 1977), the feminist concept of social relations does not connote a rigid and reified social structure impervious to human action. Rather, social relations are relatively enduring relationships among people, relationships that embody contradiction and change (Acker, Barry, and Esseveld 1983, 425, 425n). Some of the methodological implications of the structure of social relations were developed in Hartsock's pivotal "The Feminist Standpoint: Developing the Ground for a Specifically Feminist Historical Materialism" (1985). According to Hartsock, "If material life is structured in fundamentally opposing ways for two different groups . . . the vision of each will represent an inversion of the other, and in systems of domination the vision available to the rulers will be both partial and perverse" (p. 232). It is perverse because it enforces and justifies oppression, even including murder. Both the partiality and perversity of this view undermine the claims of objectivity made by those who practice establishment science.

Yet although the standpoint of the ruling group is perverse and self-serving, it cannot be dismissed as simply false, because "the vision of the ruling class (or gender) structures the material relations in which all parties are forced to participate" (Hartsock 1985, 232). If the White male Anglo-Saxon Protestant ruling class and gender has the power to structure ideology, reality, and perception, then everyday material reality will obscure the causes of oppression. "In consequence, the vision available to the oppressed group must be struggled for and represents an achievement which requires both science to see beneath the surface of the social relations in which all are forced to participate, and the education which can only grow from struggle to change those relations" (Hartsock 1985, 232).

To some extent these hidden relationships can be discovered (and are discovered) by the oppressed themselves as they begin to interact, collectivize their experience (for example, through consciousness raising), and start to change their situation. For the very act of trying to change the structure tends to bring the nature of the system of oppression into bolder relief (Mies 1983). To some extent, the hidden structure of oppression must be discovered anew by each group of women because of the great educative power of direct experience and because each concrete situation of oppression has its own historical specificity, its own specific lessons.

Direct experience has its limitations, however. Besides the lack of cumulative knowledge, there are some hidden aspects of oppression that no amount of direct struggle will reveal. In view of these limitations, the researcher may play a role that is quite different from that of the participants. For example, in their study of industrial homework in Mexico City, Benería and Roldán (1987) not only interviewed homeworkers, they traced the subcontracting links from those homeworkers on up through major corporations. Decisions of managers to employ women rather than men, and to employ them directly in factories or to subcontract out the work, had a major impact on the lives of the women who were assembling parts, polishing plastics, sorting pieces, and finishing textiles in their homes. Yet the women themselves would never have been privy to these decisions if Benería and Roldán had not had the institutional resources giving them access to these managers and the theory leading them to seek that access. Because the structure of oppression is often hidden, a feminist standpoint "is achieved rather than obvious, a mediated rather than immediate understanding" (Hartsock 1985, 234).

FALSE CONSCIOUSNESS AND
THE SOCIAL RELATIONS OF RESEARCH

The notion of hidden determinants—the determination of women's oppression by factors beyond their immediate experience—raises the issue of false consciousness, an idea that exposes some of the contradictions in Marxism. If social relations occur "behind the backs of the actors," how can the researcher know them, unless she claims a source of knowledge or understanding beyond that of her respondents? If she makes that claim, doesn't she run the risk of elitism? But if she does *not* attempt to uncover social relations and structures of oppression that may be hidden from her respondents' view, is she not limiting her contribution to them and to feminist science and political practice? If we reject the solipsism of feminist empiricism, from what standpoint does the scientist know the "reality" masked by appearances? If structural conflict produces opposing worldviews, then the social biography of Marxist theorists becomes problematic. In conceptualizing the false consciousness of a group, their imperfect comprehension of their own interests, what is the theorist's relation to the multifaceted structures of oppression?

In her excellent study of *Life and Health in Three Palestinian Villages,* Rita Giacaman describes how her team of health scientists discovered their own class and urban bias and the limitations of their attempt to apply an unalloyed Marxist-feminist analysis:

> The women interviewed had their own agendas, and we were incessantly grilled with such questions as "How many children do you have?" "Why aren't you married?" "Where are your parents?" As we were being interviewed we would try to slip in a question or two in the midst of the confusion. The experience slowly led us away from the stereotyped images we had of "poor, weak and obedient" peasant women. . . . We had begun by looking at the women condescendingly: We were there to help them, to "raise their consciousness." But these women did not necessarily need their consciousness raised. They knew what was going on and . . . how to solve their problems. What they needed was the power and authority to change their lives. (1988, 37)

The concept of false consciousness has been passionately criticized by many feminists, most notably, Stanley and Wise (1983b):

> We reject the idea that scientists, or feminists, can become experts in other people's lives. . . . [F]eminism's present renaissance has come about precisely because many women have rejected other people's (men's) interpretations of our lives. Feminism insists that women should define and interpret our own experiences. . . . [F]eminists must attempt to reject the scientist/person dichotomy and, in doing so, must endeavor to dismantle the power relationship which exists between researcher and researched. (pp. 194-95)

Stanley and Wise took pains to state that they were "in no way opposed to theorizing as such": Instead they espoused symbolic interactionism, because it "adopts a non-deterministic attitude towards social life and interaction, . . . [and] insists that structures are to be found *within* [the] processes [of interaction]" (1983, 201-2). They also embraced ethnomethodology because it "accords well with the egalitarian ethos of feminism" (p. 204).

The Struggle for Egalitarian Feminist Methodologies

If it is true that women's oppression is created entirely within the process of social interaction, then they can come to understand their oppression themselves, through ethnomethodological and symbolic interactionist techniques. The researcher's role would be limited to facilitating that process of discovery "from the ground up." In *Street Corner Society,* one of the original, paradigm-founding exemplars of symbolic interactionism, William Foote Whyte (1943) showed that the "corner boys" in a Boston slum created, through their patterns of interaction, the social and symbolic hierarchies in their gangs, their religion, and their politics. The structure he analyzed could have been made visible by the "members," since to a great extent, it was already known by them. But why were thirty-year-old men hanging out like "boys" on street corners? Because it was the Great Depression and they were unemployed. The depression was certainly not a result of their patterns of interaction. Looking at their own patterns of interaction, they would only have been able to blame themselves, each other, and the people they knew.

If women make their own history, they can uncover the roots of their oppression in the patterns of their own making. But if women "make their own history, but not under conditions of their own choosing" (Marx [1851] 1963;[1] Personal Narratives Group 1989, 13), then women must be able to examine those conditions as well as their own patterns of interaction and understanding. While it may be more egalitarian to reject the notion of outside determination, that does not stop the president of Ingersoll Rand from making decisions in his New Jersey office that affect the work lives, choices, and susceptibility to cancer of women in Singapore (Fuentes and Ehrenreich 1984). Nor does it prevent those decisions from being influenced by the investment climate in Brazil. Understanding the implications for Singapore women of those international investment patterns and capital flows and understanding the location of Mexican homeworkers in the labor process (Benería and Roldán 1987) require theories that generalize from realities outside the immediate experiential frame of the Singapore and Mexican women, theories more derived from Marxist-feminism than from ethnomethodology.

The difficulty with the concept of false consciousness is not, in my view, that it asserts that people may have an imperfect understanding of their own conditions. Nor does the solution lie in asserting that their understanding is perfectly valid, as if the nature of the world were merely a matter of opinion (cf. Acker, Barry, and Esseveld 1983; Fisher 1984, on relativism). The difficulty with the concept of false consciousness lies in the implication that (a) there is a true consciousness that is known and complete, and (b) the researcher-activist knows it, and the participant does not.

Beginning their research on women going out to work at midlife with a commitment to egalitarian relations, Acker, Barry, and Esseveld (1983) discovered that their respondents demanded a more complex understanding of their respective roles:

> What they wanted, they said, was more of our own sociological analysis. They wanted us, the researchers, to interpret their experience to them. . . . If we were to fulfill the emancipatory aim for the people we were studying, we had to go beyond the faithful representation of their experience, beyond "letting them talk for themselves" and put those experiences into the theoretical framework with which we started the study, a framework that links women's oppression to the structure of Western capitalist society. (pp. 429-30)

Exploring the "incompatibilities between various components of our feminist approach to social research," they conclude with a commitment to "reconstructing women's experience in a way that accounts for both their and our explanations of that experience and the relation between the two . . . " (p. 430). This reconstruction must include both the active voice of the subject and the researchers' own dialectical analysis (p. 431). Similarly, the Personal Narratives Group (1989) concluded that the social context of the women they studied "had to be considered from the standpoint of the subject of the personal narrative, as well as from the standpoint of the interpreter's analysis of a particular cultural and social system" (p. 12).

Paradoxically, the ideology of complete equality between researcher and researched reintroduced the notion of value-free science in new guise, because it obscured the differences of their roles and the power complexities of their relationship (Personal Narratives Group 1989, 13; Stacey 1988). The researcher is not a mere vessel of consciousness raising or social action, any more than a psychotherapist is a merely neutral facilitator of personal growth. The newer notion of research as a sort of dialogue or contrapuntal duet, while recognizing that the viewpoints of researcher and participants are not necessarily compatible (Personal Narratives Group 1989, 264), remains somewhat problematic, however, as long as the vast majority of researchers (or "interpreters") remains predominantly White and privileged (Riessman 1987).

To her interaction with the participants, the researcher brings her social location, culture, motivations, limitations, ignorances, skills, education, resources, familiarity with theory and methodology, the trained incapacities of socialization in dominant institutions, and an outside perspective that may be useful as well as troublesome (Acker, Barry, and Esseveld 1983; Gorelick 1989; Riessman 1987; Stanley and Wise 1983a). The researcher is transformed in the process of research—influenced and taught by her respondent-participants as she influences them. Theory and practice emerge from their interaction. The researcher is ultimately responsible for the final version, however. She cannot avoid this responsibility (Acker, Barry, and Esseveld 1983, 428-29; Benería and Roldán 1987, 27-28; Gorelick 1989, 352; Mbilinyi 1989, 224-25; Sacks 1989; Stacey 1988).

Stanley and Wise's critique of the researcher-respondent relationship was similar to the critiques many of us made, during the 1960s and 1970s, of the elitism involved in teacher-student, psychologist-patient relationships. In no way do I wish to associate myself with the reactionary arrogance, the suffocating smugness, with which social pundits of the 1980s look back (and down) on the radical and creative spirit of the 1960s and 1970s. We have learned from our experience of living and struggling in a backlash era, however, that these relationships are a set of contradictory interactions, and our successes and limitations in resolving them are historically determined. Teachers cannot *alone* undermine their own oppressive power over students, nor can researchers in relation to respondents. Even the possibility of their working together to overcome these oppressive relations is shaped by outside forces (Sacks 1989).

Even in the worst of times, however, we must not simply succumb to the institutional forces recreating hierarch. We must always push at the margins, push at the limits, push at ourselves. In the worst of times, we must be most on guard against the hierarchy within ourselves. But we must, collectively, try to understand the times and how they frame our possibilities of transcendence.

THE HIDDEN RELATIONS OF OPPRESSION

A purely inductive research project such as that advocated by the feminist empiricists can generate only those progressive understandings available to the women studied. If the participants are White, heterosexual, middle-class, or North American, they are likely to generate a standpoint that is on the wrong side of racial, sexual, class, and imperial oppression. If they are Christian, they may not be able to find within their milieu the basis for understanding their own anti-Semitism. Hartsock's observation regarding the ruling class and gender applies here: "There are some perspectives on society from which, however well-intentioned one may be, the real relations of humans with each other and with the natural world are not visible" (1985, 232). If generalizations are not to be made from one field situation to another, none of these groups of women can learn from each other and all must remain mired in the ignorance of their various privileges.

Combining interviews, participant observation, and an extensive historical analysis of domestic work, Judith Rollins found that maids and their employers had very different views of themselves, each other, domestic work, wages, and their relationship:

> Domestics were able to describe in precise detail the personalities, habits, moods, and tastes of the women they had worked for. (The descriptions employers gave were, by comparison, less complex and insightful—not, it seemed to me, because employers were any less capable of analyzing personalities but rather because they had less need to study the nuances of their domestics). . . . The domestics I interviewed knew the importance of knowledge of the powerful to those without power. (1985, 213, 216)

Rollins, a Black sociologist doing participant observation as a domestic, was able to reveal contradictions her White respondents could not see:

> The middle-class women I interviewed were not demanding that their husbands play a greater role in housekeeping; they accepted the fact that responsibility for domestic maintenance was theirs, and they solved the problem of their dual responsibilities by hiring other women to assist. (p. 104)

Her work reveals the White employer as caught in a contradictory location: oppressed as a woman, oppressing another woman as her employee, under the particular conditions of race, gender, and political economy in the late twentieth century (cf. Fisher 1988, 223-24). It is for this reason that a methodology based purely on induction and on the conclusions that the participants are able to generate for themselves cannot even help them to understand their own milieu completely. As Stanley and Wise (1990) put it, discussing Frye (1983),

"Maleness, heterosexuality and whiteness all 'work' . . . by being states of *unawareness* in which the key privilege of the privileged group is not to notice that they are such" (1990, 33). "Feelings are useless without facts," said Rich, "[and] all privilege is ignorant at the core" (1986, 226).

To understand both the domestics and their employers, therefore, and for them to understand themselves, Rollins needed both perspectives, but they were not equal. The maids' perspective had primacy. Consistent with the insights of all of the feminist methodologists, *theirs* is the view from below. This idea goes beyond "different perspectives" and "difference" to the nature of oppression as a multifaceted structure of unequal social relations.

In this sense, *Interpreting Women's Lives* (Personal Narratives Group 1989) is a way station along the road "from feminist empiricism to feminist standpoint epistemologies" (Harding 1986). Its authors recognize the necessity and inevitability of interpretation and theory and the likelihood that the perspectives and motivations of "narrator" and "interpreter" may differ (Personal Narratives Group 1989, 4-6). Yet the Personal Narratives Group does not adequately analyze the consequences of the interpreter's social biography (her race, class, nationality, sexuality) for her interpretation. Although the authors are excruciatingly, fascinatingly honest about their difficulties, ideological commitments, errors, and contradictions, they generally do not mention their own social characteristics, even when exploring race and class differences among their narrators. As Acker, Barry, and Esseveld (1983, 431) pointed out, "The interpretation must locate the researcher in the social structure and also provide a reconstruction of the social relations that produce the research itself" (also see Riessman 1987).

The Personal Narrative Group's solution to the problem of different perspectives (between narrator and interpreter, and among women of different race, class, and nationality) is limited to invoking the necessity of substituting "truths" for "Truth," and urging "a reconstruction of knowledge that admits the fact and value of difference into its definition" (1989, 263). Understanding the necessity and problematics of interpretation, they have moved from "giving voice" to hearing voices. That is, they dissolve the structure of inequality into a cognitive pluralism supplanting standpoint (cf. Stanley 1986). To solve the problem of different conditions of oppression by focusing on different "truths," however, is to equalize what is not equal, to spread a patina of equivalence over brutal realities and their inverse insights.

STANDPOINT AND MOVEMENT:
A COMPLEX OF MANY DETERMINATIONS

In *Feminism and Methodology,* Sandra Harding (1987) considers whether the critiques of science by both the "postmodernists" and by women of color mean that no unitary science is possible:

> For instance, Bell Hooks [sic] insists that what makes feminism possible is not that women share certain kinds of experiences, for women's experiences of patriarchal oppression differ by race, class, and culture. Instead, feminism names the fact that women can federate around their common resistance to all the different forms of male domination. Thus there could not be "a" feminist standpoint as the generator of true stories about social life. There could, presumably, only be feminist oppositions, and criticisms of false stories. (p. 188; she is referring to hooks 1984)

I believe that this is a misreading of hooks and of the implications of the works by women of color for the creation of a feminist standpoint (in contrast see Fisher 1989; Hartsock 1987; Smith 1987, 121-22, 134). hooks did not call her book *Another Country* or *A Different Voice.* She called it *Feminist Theory: From Margin to Center.* She argued that as a result of the dominance of feminism by relatively privileged women, "feminist theory lacks wholeness, lacks the broad analysis that could encompass a wide variety of human experiences" (1984, end of preface). To create such an analysis, the perspectives of women of color must move to the center of feminist theory and the feminist movement. White feminists' definitions of feminism must be overturned by the view from below, or from "the margin."

The notion that there must be "many stories," that is, a fragmentary science, is similar to men's assumptions that the study of gender is only about women's worlds. On the contrary, difference of condition does not mean absence of relationship. Black women's experiences are relevant not only to other Black women but to understanding the situation of White women and indeed of Black and White *men.* It is only because Black women empty bedpans that White men can run hospitals. It is only because Native American women are poor that ruling class men and women are rich. It is only because Guatemalan peasant women are oppressed that North American businessmen have power. And it is not only lesbians, but all women, who are oppressed by the compulsory heterosexuality that lies at the heart of sexism (Rich 1980).

Theory making, therefore, cannot be ghettoized, because reality does not come in separate boxes. We must uncover not only the different experiences of diverse groups of women but the processes creating these differences. We must trace how these processes—of racism, imperialism, class, and national, religious and sexual oppression—are connected to each other and determine, in very different patterns, the lives of all and each of us.

Within a feminist approach, we need an analysis of racism from the standpoint of women of color, national oppression from the standpoint of oppressed minorities, Christian chauvinism from the standpoint of Jews and other ethnoreligious minorities, class from the standpoint of working-class women, and heterosexism from the standpoint of lesbians. All of these systems (or axes) of oppression intersect and implicate virtually everyone (at least in U.S. society), since everyone stands on one or the other side of these axes of oppression and privilege. Therefore, every piece of research must include an analysis of the specific social location of the women involved in the study with respect to these various systems of oppression.

Such an analysis requires that someone be able to step back and do that analysis, or facilitate its emergence among the participants, raising again the questions of the segregation of milieus, the social biography of researchers, the researcher-participant relationship, and so on. Ultimately, what we can build toward is an understanding of the "complex of many determinations" as a set of dynamic interrelations (Marx [1859] 1970, 206).

The notion of a "complex of many determinations" goes beyond "academic feminist pluralism" (Stanley and Wise 1990, 47) and beyond both the notion of a fragmentary science and of a simple hierarchy of standpoints (Harding 1986; Stanley and Wise 1990, 28). Rather, a methodology based on a "complex of many determinations" implies a cumulative social science that is not merely additive. The visions of each subgroup of women must refocus and re-vision the knowledge of all. The field is continually decomposed and reconceptualized at deeper and more complex levels of understanding (Smith 1987, 215-16, 222-23), always giving primacy to the vision of the oppressed.

Such a science may imply an amazing goodwill, transcending opposing interests, for example, between White employers and "their" maids. That is, the idea of such a cumulative social science may seem to ignore conflict. The conflicts are real, however. The problem of creating a women's social science encompassing the consciousness and diverse conditions of different women is similar to and related to the problem of creating a nonoppressive women's movement. Are there any material supports for unity? Are there at least creative contradictions to counter the differences in material interests? Can we begin to analyze our present situation as a complex of many contradictions? And will "we" all want to do so?

We have learned this much: The old top-down methods of politics and science will no longer do. To end the oppression of women we need a political movement and a social science that gives voice to women. But because of the multifaceted structure of oppression, giving voice is not enough. To understand the different milieus in which women experience their oppression and to trace their connections with each other, we need a social science produced by women of various social conditions (race, class, sexual preference, nationality, or ethnicity), a social science that reveals the commonalities and structured conflicts of the hidden structures of oppression, both as they are felt and as they are obscured. The quest for such a science confronts and comprises a dynamic tension among the researcher and the researched, struggle and science, action, experience, method, and theory.

NOTE

1. Of course, Marx and Engels said, "*Men* make their own history, but . . . they do not make it under circumstances chosen by themselves" ([1851] 1963, 15, emphasis added).

REFERENCES

Acker, Joan, Kate Barry, and Joke Esseveld. 1983. Objectivity and truth: Problems in doing feminist research. *Women's Studies International Forum* 6:423-35.

Benería, Lourdes, and Martha Roldán. 1987. *The crossroads of class and gender.* Chicago: University of Chicago Press.

Cook, Judith A., and Mary Margaret Fonow. 1986. Knowledge and women's interests: Issues of epistemology and methodology in feminist sociological research. *Sociological Inquiry* 56:2-29.

Fisher, Berenice. 1984. What is feminist method? *Feminist Review (New Women's Times),* May/June.

———. 1988. Wandering in the wilderness: The search for women role models. *Signs* 13:211-33.

———. 1989. Feminist academics at mid-life crisis. Unpublished paper.

Frye, Marilyn. 1983. *The politics of reality: Essays in feminist theory.* New York: Crossing Press.

Fuentes, Annette, and Barbara Ehrenreich. 1984. *Women in the global factory.* Boston: South End Press.

Giacaman, Rita. 1988. *Life and health in three Palestinian villages.* London: Ithaca.

Gorelick, Sherry. 1977. Undermining hierarchy: Problems of schooling in capitalist America. *Monthly Review* 29:20-36.

———. 1989. The changer and the changed: Methodological reflections on studying Jewish feminists. In *Gender/body/knowledge: Feminist reconstructions of being and knowing,* edited by Alison M. Jaggar and Susan R. Bordo. New Brunswick, NJ: Rutgers University Press.

Harding, Sandra. 1986. *The science question in feminism: From feminist empiricism to feminist standpoint epistemologies.* Ithaca, NY: Cornell University Press.

———, ed. 1987. *Feminism and methodology.* Bloomington: Indiana University Press.

Hartsock, Nancy C. M. 1985. *Money, sex, and power: Toward a feminist historical materialism.* New York: Longman.

———. 1987. Rethinking modernism: Minority vs. majority theories. *Cultural Critique* 7:187-206.

hooks, bell. 1984. *Feminist theory: From margin to center.* Boston: South End Press.

Kasper, Anne. 1986. Consciousness re-evaluated: Interpretive theory and feminist scholarship. *Sociological Inquiry* 56:30-49.

MacKinnon, Catharine. 1987. Feminism, Marxism, method, and the state: Towards feminist jurisprudence. In *Feminism and methodology,* edited by Sandra Harding. Bloomington: Indiana University Press.

Maguire, Pat. 1987. Doing participatory research: Feminist approach. *Perspectives* 5 (3): 35-37.

Marx, Karl. [1851] 1963. *The 18th Brumaire of Louis Bonaparte.* New York: International Publishers.

———. [1867] 1967. *Capital.* Vol 1. New York: International Publishers.

———. [1859] 1970. Introduction. In *A contribution to the critique of political economy.* Moscow: Progress Publishers.

Mbilinyi, Marjorie. 1989. "I'd have been a man": Politics and the labor process in producing personal narratives. In *Interpreting women's lives: Feminist theory and personal narratives,* edited by the Personal Narratives Group. Bloomington: Indiana University Press.

Mies, Maria. 1983. Towards a methodology for feminist research. In *Theories of women's studies,* edited by Gloria Bowles and Renate Duelli Klein. London: Routledge & Kegan Paul.

Namjoshi, Suniti. 1981. *Feminist fables.* London: Sheba Feminist Publishers.

Personal Narratives Group, ed. 1989. *Interpreting women's lives: Feminist theory and personal narratives.* Bloomington: Indiana University Press.

Reinharz, Shulamith. 1983. Experiential analysis: A contribution to feminist research. In *Theories of women's studies,* edited by Gloria Bowles and Renate Duelli Klein. London: Routledge & Kegan Paul.

Rich, Adrienne. 1980. Compulsory heterosexuality and lesbian existence. Reprinted in *Blood, bread and poetry: Selected prose, 1979-1985.* New York: Norton.

———. 1986. *Blood, bread and poetry: Selected prose, 1979-1985.* New York: Norton.

Riessman, Catherine Kohler. 1987. When gender is not enough: Women interviewing women. *Gender & Society* 1:172-207.

Rollins, Judith. 1985. *Between women: Domestics and their employers.* Philadelphia: Temple University Press.

Sacks, Karen Brodkin. 1989. What's a life story got to do with it? In *Interpreting women's lives: Feminist theory and personal narratives,* edited by the Personal Narratives Group. Bloomington: Indiana University Press.

Smith, Dorothy E. 1974. Women's perspective as a radical critique of sociology. *Sociological Inquiry* 44:7-13.

———. 1979. A sociology for women. In *The prism of sex: Essays in the sociology of knowledge,* edited by Julia A. Sherman and Evelyn Torton. Madison: University of Wisconsin Press.

———. 1987. *The everyday world as problematic: A feminist sociology.* Boston: Northeastern University Press.

Stacey, Judith. 1988. Can there be a feminist ethnography? *Women's Studies International Forum* 11 (1): 21-27.

Stanley, Liz. 1986. Biography as microscope or kaleidoscope? *Studies in Sexual Politics* 13-14:28-46.

Stanley, Liz, and Sue Wise. 1983a. "Back into the personal" or: Our attempt to construct "feminist research." In *Theories of women's studies,* edited by Gloria Bowles and Renate Duelli Klein. London: Routledge & Kegan Paul.

———. 1983b. *Breaking out: Feminist consciousness and feminist research.* London: Routledge & Kegan Paul.

———. 1990. Method, methodology, and epistemology in feminist research processes. In *Feminist praxis: Research, theory and epistemology in feminist sociology,* edited by Liz Stanley. London: Routledge & Kegan Paul.

Whyte, William Foote. 1943. *Street corner society.* Chicago: University of Chicago Press.

About the Contributors

Karen S. Adler received a joint M.A. in social welfare policy and women's studies from the Florence Heller Graduate School for Advanced Studies in Social Welfare, Brandeis University. Her research has examined how race, class, and gender informed the social welfare activism of select White and Black women in U.S. history.

Maxine Baca Zinn is Professor of Sociology at Michigan State University, where she is also Research Associate at the Julian Samora Research Institute. In 1990, she was the Cheryl Miller Lecturer for Sociologists for Women in Society. She is the coeditor of *Women of Color in U.S. Society* (with Bonnie Thornton Dill) and the coauthor of *Diversity in Families, Social Problems, and In Conflict and Order: Understanding Society* (with D. Stanley Eitzen).

Bernice McNair Barnett is Assistant Professor in the Department of Educational Policy Studies and Sociology at the University of Illinois, Urbana-Champaign. She authored a chapter on "Black Women's Collectivist Movement Organizations: Their Struggles During 'the Doldrums.' " Her forthcoming book, *Sisters in Struggle: Black Women Civil Rights Movement Leaders, 1945-1975,* challenges patricentric conceptions of leadership and Eurocentric conceptions of feminism that marginalize Black women's roles in modern social movements.

Kim M. Blankenship is Assistant Professor of Sociology at Yale University. Her research and writing has focused on gender, race, and class as they intersect 3with politics and public policy. In addition, she is currently researching how these factors shape the response to HIV/AIDS both in New Haven and nationally.

Johanna Brenner is Coordinator of Women's Studies and Professor of Women's Studies/Sociology at Portland State University. She writes on issues of feminist politics and theory.

Esther Ngan-ling Chow is Professor of Sociology at the American University in Washington, D.C. She is a feminist scholar and community activist. She has published extensively on the social construction of gender, work and family, race and immigration, women and development, state and social policy, leadership, and organizational studies. She also coauthored and coedited *Women, the Family, and Policy: A Global Perspective* (with Catherine White Berheide, 1994).

Cynthia Deitch received a Ph.D. in Sociology from the University of Massachusetts at Amherst. She teaches in the Women's Studies Program at George Washington University and works as an independent research consultant. She has published articles and continues research on women's employment and on gender and public policy.

Karen Dugger is Associate Professor of Sociology and founding director of the Race/Gender Resource Center at Bucknell University. Her articles on race and gender include, "Race Difference in Determinations of Support for Legalized Abortion" and "Changing the Subject: Race and Gender in Feminist Discourse."

Sarah Fenstermaker is Professor of Sociology and Women's Studies at the University of California, Santa Barbara. Her book, *The Gender Factory,* (1985) explored gendered determinants of the household division of labor. Her current work further articulates the relationship between work and inequality. Her chapter in the present volume is the third published with Candace West to explore the accomplishments of race, class, and gender.

Sherry Gorelick is Associate Professor of Sociology at Rutgers University, teaching race, ethnicity, gender, and feminist methodology. The author of *City College and the Jewish Poor,* she is writing a book on Jewish feminists and the Israeli/Palestinian conflict, studying how women deal with the intersection of privilege and oppression, and is interested in the implications of the "complex of many determinations" for identity politics and coalition work.

Elizabeth Higginbotham grew up in a working-class family in New York City. She is the Associate Director of the Center for Research on Women and Professor in the Department of Sociology and Social Work at the University of Memphis. She has published widely on issues of race, class, and gender and is completing a manuscript on college-educated Black women.

Pierrette Hondagneu-Sotelo is Assistant Professor at the University of Southern California. She is the author of *Gendered Transitions: Mexican Experiences of Immigration* (1994) and is currently conducting research and engaged in activism with paid domestic workers in Los Angeles.

Nazli Kibria is Assistant Professor of Sociology at Boston University. She is currently writing a book on race, ethnic, and gender identities among second-generation Chinese and Korean Americans. Her publications include *Family Tightrope: The Changing Lives of Vietnamese Americans* (1993).

Barbara Laslett is Professor of Sociology at the University of Minnesota. She has published extensively on the historical sociology of gender and the family. She was editor of *Signs: A Journal of Women in Culture and Society* from 1991 to 1995.

Ann Leffler is Professor of Sociology at Utah State University and also directs a general educational program. Once active in the U.S. women's liberation movement, she now teaches the sociology of gender. With colleagues, she is writing a book, *Passionate Avocations,* about stratification in leisure life with a focus on dog hobbies.

Michael A. Messner is Associate Professor in the Department of Sociology and the Program for the Study of Women and Men in Society at the University of Southern California. He is the coeditor of *Men's Lives* (1995) and *Sport, Men, and the Gender Order: Critical Feminist Perspectives* (1990). He has authored *Power at Play: Sports and the Problem of Masculinity* (1992), and he coauthored *Sex, Violence, and Power in Sports: Rethinking Masculinity* (1994).

Nancy A. Naples is Assistant Professor of Sociology and Women's Studies at the University of California, Irvine. She was drawn to explore the community based work of low-income women by her experiences as a social worker in New York City during the 1970s. She is writing a book, *Grassroots Warriors: Activist Mothers and Community Work in the War on Poverty*, and editing a collection on the diversity of women's community-based activism.

Chuck W. Peek is completing his graduate studies in sociology at the University of Michigan, after which he will be a postdoctoral fellow at the Institute for Health Policy Research at the University of Florida. His research interests include occupational sex segregation, the sociology of work, demography, and quantitative methodologies.

Denise A. Segura is Associate Professor of Sociology and Acting Director of the Center for Chicano Studies at the University of California, Santa Barbara. She has published numerous articles on Chicanas and Mexican immigrant women in the labor force; Chicana/o family structure, gender personality and motherhood; Chicana feminism; and Chicana political consciousness. Currently she is doing research on the social context of Latina/o immigrant settlement.

Becky W. Thompson is Visiting Assistant Professor of African American Studies and American Studies at Wesleyan University. She is the author of *A Hunger So Wide and So Deep: American Women Speak Out on Eating Problems* (1994) and coeditor (with Sangeeta Tyagi) of *Beyond a Dream Deferred: Multicultural Education and the Politics of Excellence* (1993) and *Names We Call Home: Autobiography on Racial Identity* (1995).

Lynn Weber grew up in a working-class family. She is Director of the Center for Research on Women and Professor in the Department of Sociology and Social Work at the University of Memphis. She coauthored *The American Perception of Class* (with Reeve Vanneman). She has published widely on social class, race, and gender issues. Currently she is working with Tina Hancock on *Race, Class, and Gender in Everyday Life*, a volume for undergraduate students.

Candace West is Professor of Sociology at the University of California, Santa Cruz. Her recent articles "Reconceptualizing Gender in Physician-Patient Relationships," "Power, Inequality and the Accomplishment of Gender" (with Sarah Fenstermaker), and "Rethinking Sex Differences in Conversational Topics" focus on different aspects of the problem she addressed in the present volume: the interactional scaffolding of social structure.

Doris Wilkinson is Professor of Sociology and Director of the African American Studies and Research Program at the University of Kentucky. Her areas of intellectual interest include social theory and social criticism. She has published extensively in the areas of race and ethnic relations, gender, and health. In addition to six books, her articles include "Revitalizing the American University" (1989), "The Segmented Labor Market and African American Women from 1890-1960" (1991), "Transforming the Social Order: The Role of the University in Social Change" (1994), and "Gender and Social Inequality" (1995).

Wu Xu recalls that her first lesson on gender was realizing that having an uninspired name ("Number 5") instead of a meaningful one typically given by Chinese, like her four older siblings, was due to her being an "unwanted girl." Her perspective on gender/ethnicity intersection developed as a graduate student at Utah State University. Her dissertation was about the effects of gender, ethnicity, physicians' recommendations and, work site fitness programs on physical activity.

Barbara A. Zsembik is Assistant Professor of Sociology at the University of Florida, where she teaches race and ethnic relations, population studies, and research methods. Her current research interests are Latinas' work and family lives, Puerto Rican women's migration, and gender differences in ethnic identity.